Walter Riddell Carre

Border Memories

Sketches of Prominent Men and Women of the Border

Walter Riddell Carre

Border Memories
Sketches of Prominent Men and Women of the Border

ISBN/EAN: 9783337336554

Printed in Europe, USA, Canada, Australia, Japan

Cover: Foto ©Thomas Meinert / pixelio.de

More available books at **www.hansebooks.com**

BORDER MEMORIES;

OR,

SKETCHES OF PROMINENT MEN AND WOMEN OF THE BORDER.

BY THE LATE

WALTER RIDDELL CARRE, Esq.

OF CAVERS CARRE.

EDITED BY JAMES TAIT,

OF THE "KELSO CHRONICLE."

EDINBURGH: JAMES THIN, SOUTH BRIDGE.
LONDON: SIMPKIN, MARSHALL & CO.
1876.

PREFACE.

PREVIOUS to his decease in 1874, the late Mr Walter Riddell Carre had acquired a high reputation for his knowledge of Border men and women who had any claim to historical notice. During a succession of winters his lectures were heard with interest and appreciation in many Border towns and villages, as well as occasionally in Edinburgh. In the newspapers, instead of the brief paragraph usually accorded to popular lectures, the productions of Mr Riddell Carre were always reported more or less fully, and the reports were perused with pleasure by a wide circle of readers. His speeches delivered at meetings of the Edinburgh Border Counties Association were always carefully prepared, and in them, as well as in communications to newspapers, he was often bringing to light some new information regarding Border celebrities of a past generation.

With him it was a labour of love to collect from scattered sources, and place in a compact form before a popular audience, whatever was most characteristic of old Border worthies; and in these pleasant avocations he was engaged when suddenly the strong frame was prostrated with disease, and death ensued after a very short and painful illness.

A desire was very generally expressed to have the lectures of Mr Riddell Carre, or the substance of them, in a permanent form; and, as they were, in general, fully written, it was easy to gratify the wishes of his many friends. In preparing the lectures for the press, considerable changes have been made, while the general style and structure of the composition has, as far as possible, been retained. Colloquial expressions have been partly expunged, but it was considered desirable to retain in some measure the lecture form, and not altogether to exclude the free-and-easy mode of expression which is more adapted to spoken than to written discourse. Alterations in style have been made occasionally where it could be done with obvious advantage, but these changes have been made only to a limited extent, as it was thought desirable to present the author's works as nearly as possible in the form given them by himself.

Though it has been a general rule to interfere as little as possible with the text, it has in some parts been condensed, and in others expanded. The portion regarding Wat of Harden, and the Mertoun Scotts has been considerably extended, and other parts have been re-written; but generally, what additional matter was considered desirable, has been put in the form of foot-notes. When one person has been noticed in different lectures, only one of the references has been retained, but supplemented from the others where that seemed to be needful. When one individual has been sketched under more than one heading, the different portions have generally been conjoined, as that seemed to give the subject greater unity.

PREFACE.

The field traversed is extensive, and the notices are consequently brief in each individual instance; but there will be found a great amount of information collected from many different sources, and relating to families who have long held a prominent position in the Border land.

HIGHRIDGE HALL, KELSO,
  September 1876.

CONTENTS.

THE DOUGLAS FAMILY, ... Page 1

Its ancient ancestry—Chalmers' opinion of its origin—Theobald its founder—Hume of Godscroft's theory as to the lineage—Sholto the Douglas—His services rewarded by King Solvatius of the Scots—Sholto's descendants—William of Douglas and Sir William Wallace—William succeeds his brother Hugh, and becomes the ancestor of the Douglases of Dalkeith, Maines, and Lochleven—Uncertainty as to the correct theory of the lineage—Sir James, the founder of the family's greatness—Edward I. deprives him of his estate—Douglas recovers his property while in the service of King Robert the Bruce—Sir James' capture of Roxburgh and Berwick—The Douglas Tragedy—Bruce's commission to Douglas—The latter's journey with the casquet and the heart—Douglas' death—The armorial bearings of the Douglas—The grave of the Douglas—The story of Castle Dangerous—The succession of Hugh and Archibald—Death of Archibald, Regent of Scotland—Sir William, the Flower of Chivalry—His imprisonment in England—His release and subsequent success in defeating the English, recovering Teviotdale, and recapturing Edinburgh Castle—Sir William's barbarous treatment of Sir Alexander Ramsay—The Black Douglas (Sir William) natural son of Archibald, Lord of Galloway—The Earls of Douglas—Archibald, son of the second Earl, ancestor of the Douglases of Cavers—The Douglases of Springwood Park—The Douglases of Adderston, descendants of Cavers—William, founder of the House of Queensberry—Archibald, the Grim, son of William the third Earl—Murder of the prospective sixth Earl by his brother David—The eighth Earl and his brother raised to the peerage—Archibald made Earl Murray, Hugh Earl Ormond, and John Lord Balveny—The forfeiture of the Douglas estates—Grants of the forfeited estates to the Earl of Angus, to Sir Walter Scott of Buccleuch, and to his son David.—THE EARLS OF ANGUS—The succession from George, son of the first Earl—The Marquises of Douglas—The assumption of the title of Douglas by Mr Stewart in 1771—The ancestors of the present Countess of Home—The four Baron Douglases.—THE QUEENSBERRY BRANCH—William the founder of this branch—James the second Earl and first Duke of Queensberry—His second son created Earl of March—The lineage—Marquisate of Queensberry—THE MORTON BRANCH—Sir James Douglas of London, originator of this branch—The first Earl of Morton created in 1457, also Lord of Dalkeith—The Morton succession—Divines of note among the Douglases—Noted Douglas Ladies.

THE SCOTT FAMILY, ... Page 46

Uchtred Filius Scoti, founder of the House of Scott—Supposed origin of the Scott of Balwearie branch—Sir Michael Scott and his succession—Richard, lineal descendant of Uchtred, called Richard Scott of Murdeston—The Scotts of Murdeston, Rankleburn, and Kirkurd—Sir Walter Scott of Buccleuch—David successor to Sir Walter Scott—His descendants—Sir Walter of Branxholm and Buccleuch—The Betons—Sir Walter Scott afterwards Lord Scott of Buccleuch—Mary Countess of Buccleuch, wife of Lord Tarras (Walter Scott of High Chesters)—Countess Anne, wife of the Duke of Monmouth, who was created Duke of Buccleuch, Earl of Dalkeith, and Lord Scott—Lady Isabella Scott—Lord Dalkeith (James)—Henry Scott, Earl of Deloraine and Viscount Hermitage—Francis II., Duke of Buccleuch—Succeeding Dukes.—OTHER BRANCHES OF THE SCOTT FAMILY- Marjory Scott—General Scott, M.P. — THE HARDEN SCOTTS—William Scott, first of Harden—" Auld Wat "—Walter Scott—Sir Walter Scott of Harden and Mertoun—Hugh of Deuchar—Admiral Sir George Scott—The descendants of the second Earl of Tarras—The succession to the Barony of Polwarth—Hugh Scott, eighth Lord Polwarth—Henry Francis—Sir William Scott and his descendants—Gideon Scott of High Chesters—Walter Scott, first of Raeburn, ancestor of Sir Walter Scott the novelist—"Beardie Scott"—Robert Scott—The Scotts of Synton—Scotts of the House of Woll—Scots of Howpasley—Gamescleugh and Thirlestane—The Scotts of Tushelaw—Scotts of Hassendean—The Wauchop branch—Scotts of Whitchaugh, &c.—Dr John Scott—Dr William Henry Scott—Other noted Scotch Scotts—English Scotts.

THE KER FAMILY, ... Page 95

The origin of the Ker Family—Its Anglo-Norman lineage—John, ancestor of the Kers of Cessford—Ralph, ancestor of the Kers of Fernieherst.— THE KERS OF CESSFORD—The succession—Andrew, the fifth—Walter, the sixth, the first possessor of Roxburgh Castle—Robert and Mark Ker, sons of Walter—Habbie Ker—Sir Andrew Ker—George Ker of Fawdonside, and Sir Andrew his son—The descendants of Sir Andrew—William Ker—Sir Robert Ker, first Earl of Roxburgh—Hon. William Drummond assumed the name of Ker and became second Earl—John, fifth Earl and first Duke of Roxburgh—Robert, second Duke—John, third Duke—William, fourth Duke—James, fifth Duke.—THE KERS OF FERNIEHERST Ralph, first laird, and his descendants to the sixth laird—The Kers of Yair—Andrew and Thomas, the seventh and eighth lairds—Ralph Carre, first of Cavers—Change in the orthography of the name—The Barons of Fernieherst and Oxnam—James of Crailing—Thomas of Oxnam—Robert, the favourite of James VI., and created Earl of Somerset—Robert, third Lord Jedburgh—Kers of Ancrum.—THE HOUSE OF LOTHIAN—Mark, second son of Sir Andrew Ker of Cessford—His succession in the Earldom of Lothian—The Countess of Lothian—Lords John and Mark Kerr —The Marquises of Lothian.

THE ELLIOT FAMILY, ... Page 132

Opinions regarding the ancestry of the Elliot Family—Sir John Eliot, author of the "Monarchy of Man"—John Eliot, the missionary—Eliot's Bible —Thomas Elyot, diplomatist in the Court of Henry VIII.—His literary works—Other English Elliots—The Elliots of Liddesdale—William Elliot of Stobbs—Robert of Redheugh, the first known Border Elliot ancestor —His descendants.—THE ELLIOTS OF STOBBS, representatives of the Border clan—The Elliots of Midlem Hill, the ancestors of the FAMILY OF MINTO—Gilbert, founder of the House of Minto, created Lord Minto in 1705—The Minto succession down to Sir Gilbert Elliott, the first Earl, who died in 1814—The lineage from that date.—OTHER BRANCHES OF THE ELLIOT FAMILIES—The Selkirk Elliots—Individual members of the Elliot family—Conclusion, and tables showing the pedigree of the families of Redheugh and Lauriston.

THE HOUSE OF RIDDELL, ... Page 181

Monsieur Ridel, founder of the Family, and companion of William the Conqueror—Property in England bestowed on Ridel by the King—Celebrated descendants of Ridel—Gervasius appointed High Sheriff of Roxburgh by David I. in 1116—Sir Auskittel Ridel—Subsequent knights and baronets—Riddells of Glenriddell and Granton—Some cadets of the old Riddell stock—The Muselee branch—Imprisonment of the Rev. Archibald Riddell in Jedburgh, Edinburgh, and on the Bass Rock as a Covenanter, and his subsequent imprisonment in France as a captive of war—His release, and departure to America—His return from that country, and appointment to the pastorate of Trinity Church, Edinburgh—Rev. James Riddell of Baliol College, representative of the Granton Riddells—Other celebrated members of the House of Riddell.

EMINENT ROXBURGH MEN, . . Page 206

LEGAL CELEBRITIES.—The Constitution of the Court of Session—Richard Bothwell, a judge appointed in 1532—William Durie—Mark Ker and his son, commendators of Newbattle—David Macgill, appointed Lord Advocate in 1582—Sir Walter Pringle of Newhall—John Pringle (Lord Hanning)—Robert Pringle of Edgefield, a Lord of Session—Andrew Pringle (Lord Alemore)—Sir Patrick Scott of Ancrum—Walter Pringle of Graycrook, W.S.—Lord Chancellor Campbell, remarkable for his legal knowledge; made Lord Chancellor of Ireland and Lord Chief Justice of the Queen's Bench, and raised to the Woolsack in 1859.— DIVINES—Gavin Douglas—John Rutherford—William Fowler—Thomas Forrester, third Protestant minister of Melrose—David Calderwood, famous for his vigorous opposition to the Parliamentary jurisdiction of bishops, and the other Episcopal elements introduced into the government of the Reformed Church by James VI. in 1603, and subsequent years—George Johnson—Samuel Rutherford, author of the book entitled "Lex Rex"—John Livingstone—Gabriel Semple—Archibald Riddell—Alexander Orrock, minister of Hawick—William Crawford, author of "Dying Thoughts and Sermons"—Adam Milne—William Hunter—James Ramsay, minister of Kelso, remarkable for his great natural gifts, his shrewdness, and humour—Robert Riccalton, minister of Hobbkeith, author of several sermons, essays, and poems, and the friend of James Thomson, author of "The Seasons"—George Redpath—John Home—Joseph Leek—David Clerk—Stephen Oliver—Dr James Macknight, author of "The Harmony of the Gospels"—Dr Thomas Somerville—Thomas Elliot—Thomas Dyce—Dr Samuel Charters—William Campbell—John Scade, minister of St Boswells—Dr Thomson, minister of Sprouston—Dr Chalmers, minister of Cavers—Robert Story.—DIVINES AMONG THE DISSENTERS—John Hunter—James Scott, son-in-law of the Rev. Ebenezer Erskine — Thomas Boston of Ettrick, and minister at Jedburgh—Alexander Shanks—Dr John Young—Dr Alexander Waugh —Robert Hall of Kelso, author of "The State of the Heathen World Disclosed"—John Pitcairn—Dr Alexander Pringle.—MEDICAL MEN— Dr Scott of Thirlstane—Dr Thomas Wilson—Sir John Pringle, Professor of Moral Philosophy at Edinburgh—Dr John Armstrong—Dr William Buchan, author of "Domestic Medicine"—Dr Richard Hall—Dr John Leyden, the poet—Dr Thomas Trotter—Dr William Turner, a distinguished naval surgeon.— NAVAL AND MILITARY MEN—Sir Thomas Mac. Dougall Brisbane of Makerston—Sir Adam Fergusson, an army captain —Sir James Douglas of Springwood Park, a naval hero—Admiral James Douglas—Admiral William Dickson of Sydenham—Admiral Archibald Dickson—Admiral Archibald Collingwood Dickson—Admiral Sir William George Fairfax—Admiral Robert Elliot of the Harwood family—Admiral Lord Mark Robert Kerr—Admiral John Macpherson Ferguson—Admiral Robert Riddell Carre of Cavers—Captain Robert Campbell.—POETS—

James Thomson, author of "The Seasons"—Sir Walter Scott—Thomas Pringle of Blakelaw—William Knox, noted for his songs and anecdotes—Robert Davidson of Morebattle—William Laidlaw—Miss Jane Elliot, authoress of "The Flowers of the Forest"—Elizabeth Rutherfurd of Capehope—Andrew Scott, the self-taught bard of Bowden—George Scott—John Younger of St Boswells—Alexander Hume, a native of Kelso—William B. C. Riddell, author of "The Lament of Wallace"—Robert Bower—James Telfer, author of "Tales and Sketches"—Jean Gordon (Meg Merilees)—Andrew Gemmell.

EMINENT SELKIRKSHIRE MEN, . . . Page 283

The Warriors of the Forest—Colonel William Russell—General Sir James Russell.—THE NAPIER FAMILY—John Napier of Merchiston, the inventor of Logarithms—His descendants—Lord Napier—Sir Charles Napier, distinguished military officer—General Sir George Thomas Napier—General Sir William Francis Patrick Napier.—NAVAL HEROES—John Boston—Sir George Scott—Sir Charles Napier—James Pringle of Torwoodlee—William John, Lord Napier.—DIVINES—John Welch, minister of Selkirk—Interesting history of Mr Welch—Thomas Boston, author of "The Fourfold State," "The Crook in the Lot," and other works—Henry Davidson of Galashiels—Dr Robert Douglas—Dr Robert Russell of Yarrow—Thomas Robertson, minister of Selkirk—John Campbell—Dr John Lee, Professor of Church History at St Andrews, and of Moral Philosophy at Aberdeen—Andrew Moir—George Lawson.—LEGAL CELEBRITIES—Sir Gideon Murray of Elibank, a Lord of Session—Sir Archibald Napier, a Lord of Session—Sir Alexander Napier—James Murray—John Murray (Lord Bowhill)—The Pringle family—John Pringle (Lord Haining)—Andrew Pringle (Lord Alemoor)—Andrew Plummer—Sir Walter Scott.—MEDICAL CELEBRITIES—Dr John Rutherford—Dr Andrew Plummer—Mungo Park, the African traveller—Dr Daniel Rutherford, famous for his chemical knowledge—Dr Ebenezer Clarkson of Selkirk—Dr John Scott of Singlee—William Henry Scott.—POETS—Mrs Alison Cockburn—James Hogg, the Ettrick Shepherd—William Laidlaw.—HISTORIANS—Alexander Cunningham—William Russell, author of the "History of Modern Europe," &c.—Sketch of the life and travels of Mungo Park.—MISCELLANEOUS NOTABLES—John Riddell of Haining, Sheriff-Principal and M.P. for the County—Sir Gilbert Elliot—John Murray of Philiphaugh, John Pringle of Clifton, and Sir John B. Riddell, Parliamentary representatives of the burgh of Selkirk—The Murrays of Deuchar—Mr Inglis—Jock Gray of Gillmanscleugh.

MISCELLANEOUS CELEBRITIES, . . . Page 349

David Robertson—Rev. Henry Francis Lyte, author of several hymns, among them " Abide with Me "—James Wilson of Hawick—John, third Duke of Roxburghe, a great patron of literature—James Gray, the erudite Rector —James Sibbald—James Hooper Dawson, editor of the *Kelso Chronicle*, author of several works, including "The Legitimate Consequences of Reform"—Agricultural Improvers, Henry Duke of Buccleuch, Lord Somerville, Sir John Riddell, Dr Rutherford of Melrose, Dr Mercer of Selkirk, Mr Dawson of Frogdean, and others—Merchants, and tradesmen, and mechanics belonging to the Borders—Wits and humorous characters.

PECULIAR CELEBRITIES, . . . Page 366

Archie Armstrong—John of Gilnockie—Kinmont Willie — "Jock o' the Syde"—Christie's Will—Jock Gray of Gilmanscleugh.

BIOGRAPHICAL SKETCH.

WALTER RIDDELL CARRE was born at Edinburgh on the 4th August 1807. He was the second son of Thomas Riddell of Camieston, and belonged to the old family of Riddell of Riddell, in the county of Roxburgh, which Scott has immortalised in the "Lay of the Last Minstrel," as connected with "Ancient Riddell's fair domains." At the High School he acquired the painstaking and industrious habits which made him in after-years always a worker. Deprived of his father, he had his way to make in the world betimes. Unlike his brothers, who embraced the Naval and Military professions, his turn was for sedentary pursuits, and in 1825 he entered the house of Messrs Fletcher, Alexander & Co., one of the most eminent mercantile establishments of the time. The temptations which beset a young man thrown in early years (his own master) on a great city like London, had no dangers for him. His habit of mind was serious and thoughtful, and he was strongly imbued with religious principles; none was more frequent than he as a listener to the sermons of the Rev. Henry Melville, then the most famous preacher of the day. Later on he took a warm interest in benevolent and religious societies, acting as secretary to local associations, advocating their cause on the platform, and lending his methodical and business-like capacities to their financial management.

During the twenty years he was in London he married a lady distantly connected with himself, his beloved companion, counsellor, and comfort, for thirty-nine years of married life.

In 1848 changes in the firm with which he was connected, led to Mr Riddell's retiring from business life, and taking up his residence in Hertfordshire. In his retirement he was much in want of an object to employ his time and exercise his abilities, and this was at length attained when, on removing to Scotland, he succeeded to the estate of Cavers Carre, the remains of what had once been a large and wealthy property. He had been selected by his uncle, the late respected Admiral Robert Riddell Carre, to inherit this estate, from his confidence and belief that he would, like his predecessor, promote the good of those among whom Providence had placed him. This hope was not disappointed. He now assumed the additional surname and arms of Carre. Part of the bequest consisted in a well furnished library of ancient and modern authors, especially rich in books of a historical and antiquarian character. Amongst these Mr Carre found himself quite at home, and he had an ample field opened to him for the pursuit he so dearly loved, research into family and county records, and the biography of Scottish worthies, more especially those connected with the Border land. To these studies he quickly devoted himself, and caring little for politics or local business, he had full leisure to gratify his favourite tastes. The opportunity to utilize his stores and materials for the benefit of others now offered itself by the establishment of popular lectures. These lectures were in full force when Mr Carre came to reside in Roxburghshire. He was requested to give a lecture in his own parish, the subject chosen being "Border Worthies." This theme was quite congenial to him, and the result of his carefully compiled sketch was completely successful. The lecture was called for in other places round, and fresh demands were made on him for similar efforts in successive winters.

Although the range of his studies was wide, and he might have ventured on "fresh fields and pastures new" in the choice of his subject, his predilections kept him chiefly to themes connected with the Borders, that romantic land, the home of his forefathers, ground trodden in old time by the moss-troopers and the freebooters, associated with many a wild foray and daring mêlée, in days when men carried out

> "The good old rule, the simple plan,
> That they should take who had the power,
> And they should keep who can."

A land, too, haunted by legends of fairies and wizards, vocal with minstrelsy and song, and above all made classical by the harp of the greatest of Border minstrels. Researches into family history always occupied much of Mr Carre's time. Naturally proud of the ancient lineage from which he sprang, both as a "Carre" and a "Riddele," he had made himself thoroughly acquainted with the genealogical trees of these families in all their branches; as well as the Elliots, the Scotts, the Douglas and others. To the local and other newspapers he was a frequent contributor, as well as to the useful and popular English periodical, "Notes and Queries."

Mr Carre was a great favourite with those of humble rank. He liked to chat with them on the road, and drop into their cottages and enquire kindly after their welfare.

Mr Carre may be said to have died at his post. It was, humanly speaking, owing to a cold caught in going to lecture at Coldstream that his death illness seized him. God has called him away in his own good time. He will be missed by many, by friends, neighbours, and acquaintances, in the homes of the poor who loved him, and at the winter gatherings for edification and improvement. But he has not lived in vain. He has left behind him the well-earned respect and esteem due to one who "did what he could," and used the particular talent given him, and the resources at his command for the benefit of his poorer neighbours, an example and encouragement to those similarly situated to "go and do likewise," not to hoard selfishly their stores of knowledge, but cheerfully and kindly to devote them to the pleasure and improvement of their fellow men.

The following particulars are taken from the "Kelso Chronicle," of December 4, 1874:—

"On the evening of Tuesday last Walter Riddell Carre, Esq. of Cavers Carre, was to have lectured in the Town Hall, Kelso, but on that very day he ceased to be an inhabitant of the earth. A fortnight previously he was in Kelso on his way to Coldstream, where he lectured in public for the last time. He was then suffering from a severe cold, and on the way home, when he again remained in the town for a short time, he had become worse. Serious symptoms set in soon after he reached home, and an intimation from his son, Captain Riddell Carre, was read after the lecture last week, to the effect that his father was suffering from a severe rheumatic attack, and would not be able to fulfil his engagement. On his arrival from Coldstream he complained of rheumatism; next day he was almost unable to move, and gradually he became quite helpless. The remedies applied gave him some relief, but the poisoned blood found its way to the head. Dr Begbie arrived from Edinburgh, and reported almost hopefully, but the same night the patient grew worse, and became very incoherent in his speech. Afterwards he became more feverish, and latterly quite unconscious. It was thought he did not suffer much, but his laborious breathing was very distressing to his loving relatives, by whom every want was most assiduously supplied. He got gradually worse, and on Tuesday evening, 1st December, breathed his last.

"He was twice married—first in 1830, to Elizabeth Maclauchlan, daughter of Lieutenant-Colonel Maclauchlan of the 10th Regiment, by whom he has one son, Captain Thomas Alexander, who now succeeds to the estate; and second in 1871, to Mary Falconer Currie, daughter of the late William Currie of Linthill, who survives him.

"Mr Carre was a Justice of the Peace and Commissioner of Supply for the county of Roxburgh. In politics he was a moderate conservative, but he disliked the turmoil of political strife, and preferred the quiet paths of literature.

"The decease of Mr Riddell Carre leaves a blank in the Border counties which will not easily be supplied. His acquaintance with the genealogical histories of the Border families was very extensive and accurate; and his delight was to impart his knowledge through the press and in the form of lectures, and in social conversation. It is believed that he has left a great store of valuable information in manuscript at Cavers Carre, which it is to be hoped may some day be published. He was an excellent lecturer, entering into his subject with much enthusiasm, and his elocution was characterised by grace and animation. In various Border societies he took a very lively interest. Of the Border Counties Association he was a steady supporter, and at most of their meetings he took a prominent part. His speeches on these occasions were always well prepared, and were so full of erudite and accurate information that they were listened to with interest and the reports read with pleasure. The mention of a Border name in any newspaper often called forth a note from Mr Riddell Carre, giving out of his abundant treasures some additional and valuable information. He was a gentleman of large and genial sympathies, and nothing seemed to afford him greater pleasure than to be doing good in whatever form it presented itself. Though advanced in years, and latterly not robust, his frame was so vigorous that a life prolonged for many years might have been reasonably expected. But he was always prepared for the great change, which came, alas, too soon; and amid his many engrossing pursuits, he was never neglectful of the great concerns of the future, on which he has entered. The universal testimony will be that he was a *good* man. He was good in every sense of the word. He had a cultured mind, a genial and kindly heart, and he was, we have every reason to believe, a genuine Christian."

The mortal remains of Mr Riddell Carre were interred at Bowden on Monday the 7th of December 1874.

THE DOUGLAS FAMILY.

THERE can be little doubt that the family of Douglas is one of the most ancient and illustrious in the history of Scotland. George Chalmers says, that the ancestor of that noble House came from the Netherlands * about the middle of the twelfth century, and obtained from the Abbacy of Kelso a grant of land called Douglas. He was named Theobald, but his son and successor William, assumed the surname of Douglas from the property so acquired, as was very frequently done in those early times. On the other hand, Hume of Godscroft—no mean authority—reports that the family of Douglas existed as far back as the eighth century, when Sholto the Douglas appeared, and came to the assistance of Solvatius, King of the Scots, against Donald Bane, who had pressed His Majesty sorely, and with the help of Douglas, the king obtained at length a most complete victory.† Solvatius, it is further stated by Godscroft, rewarded his service and merits by the grant of land in Lanarkshire, called Douglas. This Sholto had a son and other descendants, one being William, who, about the middle of the eleventh century, was made a Baron of the Parliament at Forfar, as we learn from Godscroft. He left at least two sons, Sir John, of Douglas Burn, Ettrick Forest, and Sir William, of Glendinning, Dumfriesshire, the latter being the supposed ancestor of the Douglases, of Pumpherston, of Pitten-

* Others assert that the name is of Spanish origin, and that the noble family of Douglas is still lineally represented among the "blue blood" of Spain.

† The alleged origin of this name is as follows:—When King Solvatius asked to whom this unexpected assistance was due, the attendants pointing to the stranger, said in Gaelic, "Sholto Dhu Glas,"—See that dark man.

dreigh, and other branches. Not long after him came another William, who assisted Sir William Wallace in some of his warlike exploits, and left a son, Hugh, whose marriage with a noble house, strengthened their connection with Galloway. Hugh, whom his foes never found sleeping, left no family, and was succeeded by his brother William, the gallant defender and governor of Berwick, surnamed the Hardy, from whom descend the Douglases of Dalkeith, Maines and Lochleven.

Though I am unable to say which account is correct, or that either story is free of fable, still it can be with truth asserted that the family is one of great antiquity, and connected with the best blood in Britain, and even in France, and that its members have generally been distinguished by the courage, stalwart frame, and swarthy complexion of their alleged progenitor, Sholto Dhu Glas.

Sir James Douglas was the first eminent member of the family, and undoubtedly laid the foundation of its greatness. He was a person of the most polished education, and of the highest accomplishments, considering the time in which he lived. He was educated at Paris, as Blind Harry the minstrel states, and no doubt spoke Latin as well as French with facility.

> Their speech they do govern and do as well rule,
> As they'd been taught at Julius Cæsar's school.

His father's opposition to Edward I., made that king inexorable, and he declined to restore to Sir James his patrimonial estates which had been seized and bestowed on Lord Clifford. But entering the service of King Robert Bruce, opportunities for the display of his valour and patriotism were soon afforded him, and it may be truly said that he established the fame of his family, and at the same time he recovered the property. It was in his time that the Douglas slogan—"A Douglas"—was adopted.

Douglas commanded one wing of the army at Bannockburn, and he was, on that occasion, made a Knight Banneret under the royal standard, a very high honour, and one immortalised by Shakespeare, who speaks of "a soldier by the honour-giving hand of Cœur-de-Lion knighted on the field."

Sir James took a prominent part in all the struggles of that period in our border lands. He captured Roxburgh and Berwick, of which latter place his father is stated to have been governor. Ettrick Forest and adjacent country was also captured from the English by Douglas, who obtained a grant of the same from King Robert Bruce, which the family held till the forfeiture of their estates in 1453. But Douglas Burn property had previously been in their possession, according to Godscroft, and the solitary glen there, was the retreat of Sir James when recruiting for his sovereign and friend. In this wild tract of country, too, tradition has placed the scene of the "Douglas Tragedy," and seven large stones in the neighbourhood are shown, as marking the spot where the seven brethren were killed.*

Sir James Douglas was one of the representatives of the king, at the nuptials of Prince David (afterwards David II.), and Joan, sister of Edward II., which were celebrated at Berwick in 1328. The Princess was called Make-Peace, and carried with her the Ragman Roll, and all records which had been seized by her grandfather, Edward I., to be again deposited

* The Douglas Tragedy. The farm of Blackhouse in Selkirkshire, is said to have been the scene of this melancholy event. There are the remains of a very ancient tower, adjacent to the farm-house, in a wild and solitary glen, through which flows the torrent called Douglas Burn, a tributary of the Yarrow. It is now part of the Traquair estate, but anciently was the seat of the family of Douglas. From this tower, Lady Margaret was carried under cloud of night by her lover; but they were speedily pursued by Lord Douglas and his seven sons. The lovers lighted down from their steed, and while Lord William faced the whole eight pursuers,

"She held his steed in her milk-white hand,
And never shed ane tear,
Until that she saw her seven brethren fa',
And her father hard fighting, who loved her so dear."

The father was left wounded, and the lovers rode away, but Lord William also had been wounded, and died before morning, Lady Margaret committing suicide. They were buried side by side at St Mary's Church, and out of their graves grew a rose and a briar which intertwined, till the Black Douglas plucked up the briar and threw it into St Mary's Loch.

in Scotland. Robert the Bruce at the time of his son's marriage in 1328, was infirm, and drawing near his end. His death taking place soon after, and before the young king had reached his majority, the Regency was assumed by Randolph, Earl of Moray; but the young king was crowned at Scone in 1331. King Robert, before his death, sent for Douglas, whom he commissioned to proceed with his heart to Palestine, for the purpose of depositing it in the Holy Sepulchre. He accordingly lost no time after the king's death, in starting on his mission with the precious relic, but unfortunately lost his life on his journey, having halted in Spain, and joined the Christian forces against the Moors in a battle, the seventieth he had been in, and of these he had gained fifty-seven. His last fight took place on the 25th August 1330, and after signalising himself with his usual gallantry, he fell, but ere he breathed his last, he had the happiness of knowing the Christians were victorious. When surrounded by the enemies of the cross, he took the casquet containing his sovereign's heart, and threw it before him, exclaiming, "Now pass onward gallant heart as thou wert wont, and Douglas will follow thee, or die." These were the last words of the great and good Douglas, and after his death the precious relic was taken care of by his friend, Sir Simon Locard, who brought it back to Scotland, and it was deposited in Melrose Abbey, which had been restored and enriched with many donations by Bruce. The king's body had been buried at Dunfermline, where it was discovered in 1818, when workmen were digging for the foundation of the parish church. The family of Sir James Douglas received as an addition to their armorial bearings, a heart ensigned with an imperial crown, which continues their special cognisance; and Sir Simon Locard, the bearer of Bruce's heart from Spain, assumed the name of Lock*hart*, and got an addition to his arms of a heart within a fetter lock, with the motto *Corda serrata pando,* "I lay open locked hearts." It is this family who possess the "Lee penny," upon which is founded the romance of the

"Talisman," by Sir Walter Scott. The body of Sir James was brought home, and buried in the aisle of St Bride's Church, Douglas.*

Sir James Douglas never having married, so far as I have been able to trace, was immediately succeeded by his brother HUGH, a man of no great repute, who became Lord of Douglas, but who soon demitted in favour of his younger brother, ARCHIBALD, Regent of Scotland, and brother-in-law of John Balliol, the king, and afterwards in favour of Archibald's son, Sir WILLIAM DOUGLAS, nephew of the Good Sir James.

Archibald, the Regent, who was Lord of Galloway, fell at

* Douglas Castle was three times taken by the English, but as often retaken by Douglas, who had made a vow that he would be revenged on any one who should dare take possession of it, and so terrified had the English become, that the fortress came to be known as Castle Dangerous, and hardly any Englishman would undertake to keep it in possession. In these circumstances, a rich and beautiful young lady who had many suitors, said she would give her hand only to a knight who should manifest his courage and valour by holding the perilous Castle of Douglas for a year and a day. This was undertaken by Sir John Wilton, who held the fortress for a while, but at length it was taken by stratagem, and he was slain. A letter from the lady was found in his pocket, a discovery which so affected Douglas, that he spared all the prisoners, and for this act he obtained an appellation of "The Good Sir James." The name of Douglas, however, had become so formidable, that it was used by women to frighten their children ; and the following rhyme seems to be well authenticated :—

> "Hush ye, hush ye, little pettie,
> Hush ye, hush ye, do not fret ye,
> And the Black Douglas shall not get ye."

Of the Good Sir James, the following portrait is given by Barbour :—

> "In visage he was some deal gray,
> And had black hair, as I heard say ;
> But, then, of limbs he was well made,
> With bones great, and shoulders braid ;
> His body well made and lenzie,
> As they that saw him said to me.
> When he was blyth he was lovely,
> And meik and sweet in company ;
> But who in battle might him see,
> Another countenance had he ;
> And in his speech he lisp't some deal,
> But that set him right wonder well."

Halidon Hill, near Berwick, on the 22d of July 1333. In this battle the English archers did terrific execution, for it has been said the "Arrows flew thick as motes in the sunbeam," and that "the Scots fell to the ground by thousands."

Two other members of the race who lived at the same period were men of renown,—Sir WILLIAM DOUGLAS, knight, the Lord of Liddesdale, popularly called the Flower of Chivalry, and Sir WILLIAM DOUGLAS, the Lord of Nithsdale, whose soubriquet was "the Black." Sir William Douglas, called the Flower of Chivalry, supposed to have been a natural son of the Good Sir James, possessed the lands of Liddesdale, including Hermitage Castle and other extensive domains. He was a man of great valour, saw much service, and took a prominent part in the expulsion of Edward Balliol, who disputed possession of the Scottish throne with David II., after the battle of Halidon Hill. He was, however, taken prisoner after being defeated at Lochmaben, and kept in confinement for two years in England. After being released, he returned to Scotland, and uniting himself to his fellow-countrymen, who were striving to maintain their rights in our border land, succeeded in defeating the English and recovering from them Teviotdale and other districts, besides recapturing the Castle of Edinburgh. The Flower of Chivalry, however, tarnished his fame by the barbarous manner in which he treated Sir Alexander Ramsay, who for taking Roxburgh Castle, which he did gallantly by escalade, was made Sheriff of Teviotdale, instead of Douglas. In 1342, Douglas dragged him from the seat of justice* at Hawick, and confined him in

---

* Sir Alexander Ramsay had succeeded in taking the Castle of Roxburgh from the English on the 20th March 1342, an enterprize in which Douglas had failed. On the 20th of June following, Ramsay was holding a court in the Church at Hawick, when Douglas appeared, and the sheriff was so unsuspecting as to ask his former companion-in-arms to take a seat on the bench beside him. But the purpose of Douglas was speedily disclosed, and the gallant knight was overpowered, carried over the hills to Hermitage, and let down into the dungeon, which may still be seen in the ruined pile of the Castle. There was probably no intention to prolong Ramsay's life by allowing the corn to trickle down; but such is traditionally said to have been the fact.

Hermitage Castle, where he allowed him to die of famine in an aggravated form, for it is said that above the dungeon there was a supply of corn, some particles of which found their way through the floor, which enabled Ramsay to sustain a miserable existence for seventeen days. About sixty years ago a bridle bit and some bones were found in the dungeon.

The dungeon as now visible is about twelve feet deep, in the solid wall of the castle, and with no aperture except one about two feet square at the top. Escape was hardly possible even had the entrance not been closed; but with any heavy lid covering the opening, it was one of the most horribly hopeless dungeons that the human mind could imagine. The Castle of Hermitage, now owned by the Duke of Buccleuch, stands in the centre of a desolate expanse close to the Hermitage Water, four miles from its confluence with the Liddel, and to this day it has the eerie look of a place which might still be haunted by evil spirits. It is believed to have been built by Lord William Soulis, grandson of Nicolas de Soulis, who claimed the crown of Scotland in right of his grandmother, daughter of Alexander II.; and who, could his legitimacy have been ascertained, must have excluded all other competitors. Lord William possessed the whole of Liddesdale, with Westerkirk and Kirkandrews in Dumfriesshire, and the rich baronies of Nisbet, Longnewton, Caverton, Maxton, and Mertoun in Roxburghshire. In 1320 the estates of Lord William Soulis were all forfeited, and he himself confined in the Castle of Dumbarton, because he with others had conspired against King Robert Bruce, with the object, according to Barbour, of elevating Lord Soulis to the Scottish throne. Subsequent to that date the family makes no figure in our annals. Such seem to be the historical facts about a chief whose name has been handed down by district tradition to popular execration. The traditional Lord Soulis is represented as uniting every quality which would render strength formidable, and cruelty detestable. Combining prodigious bodily strength with cruelty, avarice, dissimulation, and treachery, he was regarded as under the control and guidance of a demon, by whose help he practised the arts of sorcery, and was proof against the ordinary means of taking his life. Like the Flower of Chivalry, his successor in Hermitage, Lord Soulis could brook no rival near his throne, and by treachery he murdered Armstrong, laird of Mangerton, and the chief of Keildar, to the former of whom Lord Soulis himself had formerly owed his life. To obtain materials to fortify Hermitage Castle he compelled his vassals to work like beasts of burden. Tradition says that the King of Scotland, irritated by the repeated complaints against him, peevishly exclaimed, "Boil him if you please, but let me hear no more of him." Accordingly he was wrapped in a sheet of lead, carried to the Nine Stane Rig, a mile from the castle, and at a spot still marked by a small circle of upright stones, he was boiled to death. The cauldron is said to have been long preserved at Skelfhill in upper Teviotdale, but is not now in existence.

where it is supposed Ramsay was buried, and the former having been given to Sir Walter Scott, that illustrious man handed it to George Ramsay, ninth Earl of Dalhousie, the descendant of the chivalric but unfortunate knight. But frightful though the crime of Douglas was, King David restored him to the Sheriffship and his lands, conferring indeed upon him further distinction, and he is afterwards found at the battle of Durham, fighting with his sovereign. Both were then taken prisoners, when the Scotch army sustained a great defeat, and a heavy loss—amounting to about 15,000.

Sir William Douglas, the Flower of Chivalry, was induced, as an author states, "to purchase his liberty at the expense of his honour, by entering into a secret treaty with the English king."

After the return of Douglas to Scotland he was waylaid and killed while hunting in Ettrick forest at William's Hope, called so from his name, by his kinsman William Earl of Douglas, who may have wished to avenge his act of treason, although I suspect it is more likely to have been caused by domestic jealousy, for according to an old song :—

> "The Countess of Douglas, out of her bowere she came,
> And loudly there that she did call ;
> It is for the Lord of Liddesdale
> That I let all these teares downe fall."

Thus terminated, about seven or eight years after the battle of Durham, the life of the Flower of Chivalry, who, it is said, only left one daughter. His remains were deposited in Melrose Abbey.

The other Sir WILLIAM DOUGLAS, the Black, was the natural son of Archibald, Lord of Galloway. Sir William was an honour to his race, notwithstanding the circumstance of his birth. He was a man of graceful person and high valour,* and what is better, he possessed a noble heart. His good

---

* Tytler says, "This young knight appears to have been the Scottish Paladin of those days of Chivalry. His form and strength were almost gigantic, and what gave a peculiar charm to his warlike prowess was the extreme gentleness of his manners; sweet, brave, and generous, he was as faithful to his friends as he was terrible to his enemies."

qualities attracted the notice of royalty, and he won the affections and gained the hand of Egidia Bruce, youngest daughter of Robert II., by his first wife Elizabeth Mure—whom the King of France wished to wed, His Majesty having fallen in love with her from a picture which he had sent an artist to paint, on hearing of her loveliness. Douglas, however, forestalled the king—and acquired with his royal wife the lordship of Nithsdale.

This Douglas well maintained the martial character of the family, and performed many heroic exploits against the English. He also punished most severely a band of Irish pirates who did much mischief in Galloway, by proceeding against them in their own country. This he did with signal vengeance, for he ravaged and demolished the town of Carlingford, to which the pirates belonged, and actually loaded fifteen vessels with his spoils. On his way back to Galloway he visited the Isle of Man, and brought away more booty from thence, so that on his return to Lochryan he found himself a much richer man than when he departed. His knowledge of naval tactics must have been considerable, for he was afterwards appointed Admiral of the Fleet. He is next found at Dantzic, whither he went to aid in subduing the Infidels, and was created Prince of Dantzic and Duke of Spruce for his gallantry, as is shown by a monument to his daughter Giles, who married Henry Sinclair, second Earl of Orkney. Lord Clifford challenged Douglas to combat, but fearing to meet him when the time came, hired assassins, who took the life of Douglas, in the year 1390, on the bridge of Dantzic, where there was a gate on which his coat of arms was cut, as a memorial of his melancholy end.

THE EARLS OF DOUGLAS.

I now return to the main stem of the Douglas tree, and to its representative at this period, viz., WILLIAM DE DOUGLAS, created the FIRST EARL of DOUGLAS by King David II., in

1357. Our hero was the nephew of Good Sir James, the first of the Douglas name who acquired possessions in our border land. These he obtained partly from his friend and sovereign Robert Bruce, though a portion had been captured by himself, and therefore dearly earned. The Earl did good service in these districts by again getting rid of the English troops, who after the battle of Durham re-invaded the Border districts of Scotland. He also recovered his own territory of Douglasdale. But the chief scene of his prowess was Poictiers. Being at the time Ambassador for Scotland at the French Court, he fought on the side of France against the English, under the Black Prince, and, as usual, displayed the valour of his race. France, however, lost this battle, and the French King—John II.—was taken prisoner, while Douglas had a narrow escape. The first Earl of Douglas died in 1384, and was interred in Melrose Abbey, according to Wynton, the monk and historian.

JAMES, the SECOND EARL DOUGLAS, who succeeded his father in 1384, was the Scottish hero of Otterburn or Chevy Chase, fought between the English under Sir Henry Percy, the renowned Hotspur, and the Scots under Douglas. The battle took place on the 10th August 1388, only four years after Douglas had succeeded to his honors. Previous to the engagement he made an excursion to the Tyne, where he encountered and overthrew in single combat his gallant foe Hotspur, who, however, pursued Douglas on his way back to Scotland, giving him battle at Otterburn, where Douglas was killed and Hotspur and his brother were both taken prisoners. It was one of the hardest fought battles of the time, and though the Scots were at one period very hard pressed, their dauntless leader rallied them with his slogan of "Douglas," and though he fell he had turned the fight in favour of his country, which led to the capture of the Percys. When Douglas fell his priest Lundie protected him from further torture by his battle-axe, and on being asked how he felt, the dying hero exclaimed, "Indifferently, but blessed be God my ancestors have died in fields of battle, not on down beds. I sink fast, but let them still raise my war-cry, and conceal my death from my followers. There was a tradition in our family that a dead Douglas should win a field, and I trust it will be this day accomplished." The followers of Douglas attended to their leader's dying orders, and did great execution among the English, none of note escaping death or captivity, giving truth to the lines respecting the name of Douglas,

> " Hosts have been known at that dread sound to yield,
> And Douglas dead, his name hath won the field."

When dying, he desired his banner to be raised,* which was done by ARCHIBALD DOUGLAS, his son, not recognised as legitimate. He was the ancestor of the Douglases of Cavers, a family well known and highly respected, and among their archives there are still preserved a banner of Douglas and Percy's pennon. The Cavers-Douglas race, now represented by the amiable and earnest-minded James Douglas, the twentieth in descent from the hero of Otterburn, exhibit a pedigree highly honourable and extremely well allied. They have intermarried with the Kers of Cessford and Fernieherst, the

---

* A graphic account of the battle is given by the historian Froissart, and it has been made the subject of three ballads, of one of which Sir Philip Sidney said, he "never could hear the song of Douglas and Percy without having his heart stirred as with the sound of a trumpet." It is impossible not to agree with Froissart, that there never was a more chivalrous battle fought than that of Otterburn; the singular circumstances under which it was fought, in a fine moonlight autumn night after a very hot day: the heroic death of Douglas, the name of Hotspur, and the cause of the battle, to regain Percy's pennon, which Douglas had said he would plant on his castle at Dalkeith, all these circumstances give the battle an air of singularly romantic chivalry. But it was a battle of chivalry and nothing more, with no great principle at stake, as in the battles of Stirling and Bannockburn. The Douglas banner displayed at Otterburn is still preserved at Cavers House, and measures thirteen feet in length. The Percy relics, commonly called "Percy's pennon" by historians, are also at Cavers House, but instead of a pennon they consist of a pair of gauntlets bearing the white lion of the Percys embroidered in pearls and fringed with filigree-work of silver. These gauntlets, obviously the work of a lady, were attached to the handle of Percy's lance, and with it were captured by Douglas, in single combat, under the walls of Newcastle. No wonder that Hotspur was bent on recovering the trophy which had been the pledge of his lady's love.

Rigs of Airdrie, and latterly with the noble houses of Moray and Southesk. Katherine Rig, the wife of Sir William Douglas, eleventh of Cavers, was an eminent lady of the Covenant, and her life and sufferings are patent to all who are acquainted with church history. From the CAVERS family,—who were hereditary Sheriffs of Roxburghshire till 1745, when the office was abolished,—descend the Douglases of Springwood Park, represented by Sir George Douglas, whose first ancestor from the parent tree was Andrew Douglas of Friarshaw, Lilliesleaf, from whom have sprung several distingushed men, both sailors and soldiers, who have done honour to the name—the family baronetcy having been granted for eminent naval achievements. The Douglases of Adderston also descend from Cavers, the last of whom was the well known and once popular Archibald Douglas, who married Miss Pringle, the heiress of entail of the beautiful estate of Haining, the life-rent of which is now enjoyed by her daughter Mrs Pattison.

The hero of Otterburn had another son, born under similar circumstances, WILLIAM, who was the founder of the noble house of Queensberry. By his wife, who was a daughter of Robert II., he had no family, and was succeeded in his title by ARCHIBALD THE GRIM, supposed by some to have been a son of the first Earl by his second wife, while others have considered him a son of Good Sir James, who had succeeded by some special entail. At all events he became THIRD EARL, and was one of the most powerful men in the kingdom, being noted for his valour and sagacity. He was, like the first Earl, Ambassador in France, in which position he acquitted himself with honour and success. He added greatly to his possessions by marrying the heiress of Bothwell, which brought the said lordship to the illustrious house of Douglas. He defended Edinburgh Castle against Henry IV., in 1400, and died soon after, in 1401, being succeeded by his son

ARCHIBALD, the FOURTH EARL, who, like his forefathers, was a great warrior, though less fortunate than some of them. He suffered a defeat at Homildon Hill in a battle fought on Holyrood Day (14th September) 1402, with Hotspur, who was victorious—Douglas having been taken prisoner after being wounded, and with the loss of an eye. This battle, the design being to avenge a victory gained by the English under the Earl March at Nisbet muir, was provoked by Douglas, who had invaded England and done great mischief, having carried off a large amount of spoil. Hotspur pursued Douglas on his return, gave him battle, and gained the day, chiefly owing to the bad ground the Scots took up, which highly favoured the English, whose arrows again did fearful execution. Sir John Swinton, a valiant knight, disappointed with the arrangements made by Douglas, determined not to stand on the hillside to be shot " like a stag," rushed down with his men and made great havoc among the enemy, but they were overpowered and cut to pieces. The loss sustained by the Scotch was immense, and the battle must have been sanguinary, as the field on which it was fought is called "Redriggs." Douglas was taken prisoner, but was soon liberated by Hotspur, who persuaded him to join him against Henry IV. at the battle of Shrewsbury. It was the earnest desire of Douglas to overthrow King Henry, and at this battle he tried hard to pick him out; but His Majesty being well surrounded, he found it a most difficult matter to accomplish his deadly design. In his endeavour he slew three of the king's champions, dressed like royalty, one after another, and when he encountered Henry himself, Douglas called out, " Where the devil do all these kings come from?" Falling upon him with great fury, he overthrew the royal banner, despatched a gallant aide-de-camp who bore it, and was about to slay the king, when several valiant knights, and especially Henry Prince of Wales (afterwards Henry V.), the renowned hero of Agincourt, came to the sovereign's relief, and saved his life. At this point Hotspur was killed, which decided the battle in favour of King Henry; and on Douglas retreating, he was wounded and captured. On being released he returned to his native country, but ill-fortune accompanied him, for he was so unsuccessful in an attempt to besiege Roxburgh Castle, that it was called the "Foul Raid," or disgraceful expedition.* But better fortune attended him at Poictiers, whither he went to assist the French, then in danger of being conquered by Henry V. Fortunately for Douglas and his fellow Scots, the French, commanded by the Dauphin, were victorious, and the English sustained a heavy loss. The Duke of Clarence, their commander, was slain, having been unhorsed by Sir John Swinton's lance, and finally killed by the Earl of Buchan. This Sir John Swinton was the son of the gallant knight killed at Homildon. The battle of Baugé was the first battle that turned the tide of success against the English.

Douglas, for his gallantry, received many honours from Charles VII., including the Dukedom of Tourin and the Marshalship of France; and in the next battle, viz., that of Verneuil in 1421, he had a high command. The English, however, recovered in that action the prestige they lost at Baugé, but it was no fault of Earl Douglas that they were victorious, for he was overruled by the French General, whose policy lost the battle, and enabled the English archers to do such fearful execution. As Sir Walter Scott has said: "Douglas and Buchan stood their ground, fought desperately, and died nobly." The body of Douglas was recovered and buried at Tours. As Pinkerton says, "He was honourably interred in the capital of his short-lived duchy." Thus terminated the life of one who, though it was true "that no man was less fortunate, it is no less true that no man was more valorous." The noble Swinton, with the flower of Scottish chivalry then serving as auxiliaries in France, together with two thousand common soldiers, fell in this battle, the hero of

* This designation was not applied to the raid of Douglas alone, but to an enterprise undertaken against England by the Earl in conjunction with the Governor of Scotland, who besieged Berwick while Douglas made an effort against Roxburgh. Both enterprises failed, and the Scots, who had always been accustomed in one way or another to profit by expeditions into England, called them in ridicule "The Dirtin' Raid."

which was John Duke of Bedford, nicknamed by Douglas "John with the leaden sword."

Douglas married Margaret, second daughter of Robert III., and by her had two sons and two daughters.

The eldest son,

ARCHIBALD, the FIFTH EARL, was a man of great accomplishments. He was sent to France to treat for the redemption of James I. of Scotland, the first king of that name, and the only one of the Jameses that possessed endowments, which had been highly cultivated by the excellent education he received from Henry IV. James I. was the younger brother of the Duke of Rothesay (married to Marjory Douglas), who was starved to death.

This Earl of Douglas was at the battle of Verneuil, where he performed many valorous deeds, and returning soon after, died at Restalrig of fever, and was buried at Douglas, being the first Earl interred there. He left two sons and a daughter, the latter being called the Fair Maid of Galloway, to be referred to hereafter. The Earl's widow married the first Lord Hamilton, whose house became in later times the chief of the Douglases by the marriage of Anne, Duchess of Hamilton, with Lord William Douglas.

WILLIAM, the eldest son of Archibald, became SIXTH EARL of Douglas. He was very young when he inherited his vast domains, and resided quietly at his castle, acting, however, with all the magnificence of a prince. Crichton, the chancellor in the reigns of James I. and II., was jealous of the power of Douglas, and desirous of crushing it. He and his associate Livingston, the guardian of James II., divided the sway during that sovereign's minority; and the young Earl Douglas took no part in their alternate contests and reconciliations. They were determined, however, to bring this powerful nobleman to pay a willing submission to royal authority, or to humble his pride. The latter course was their chief aim, and under the pretence of not being able to conduct the public business without the presence and assistance of the representative of such an illustrious house, they invited him to attend the Parliament they had summoned to meet at Edinburgh, which Douglas agreed to do. Accordingly he set out for the city with his brother David and his faithful friend M. Fleming of Cumbernauld, attended by a princely retinue; and on Crichton being informed of his approach, he went some miles to meet the cavalcade, and to invite Douglas to visit Crichton Castle on his way to Edinburgh. The wily Crichton's invitation having been accepted, and his pretended kindness not having been suspected, the whole party, after a visit of two days, proceeded to Edinburgh, professedly to attend the Parliament; but that was only a ruse, for when they arrived there, Douglas was immediately invited to the Castle, along with his brother and Malcolm Fleming, their companion, to attend a royal feast. The invitation was unhesitatingly accepted by the young Earl for the three, though reminded that his father never wished his sons to place themselves in any jeopardy *together*. From the apparent hospitality and kindness, no plot was suspected, but it was soon unfolded by the production at the banquet of a Bull's head (the certain token in those times of an approaching slaughter), which was placed before Douglas. Becoming now conscious of their danger, they both started up and tried to escape, but armed men rushing in upon them, when they were entirely defenceless, their own retinue not having been admitted to the castle, they were secured and carried out to almost instant execution, Fleming sharing the same fate. This barbarous proceeding, says Sir Walter Scott, was as unwise as it was unjust. It did not reduce the power of the illustrious race, but only raised general detestation against those who managed the affairs of James II., who interceded in vain with Chancellor Crichton to save the lives of the two brothers. The following old lines give expression to the popular indignation at the deed:—

" Edinburgh Castle toun and tower,
God grant you sink for sin;
And that even for the black dinnour
Earl Douglas got therein."

An easy peaceable man, very unlike some of his race, succeeded the young Earl, viz., his grand-uncle. He married a daughter of the Earl of Orkney, by whom he had six sons, who all died without posterity, two of them being the eighth and ninth Earls of Douglas. He was, after a short incumbency, succeeded by his son WILLIAM as EIGHTH EARL, perhaps the most wealthy, powerful, and imperious of all the Douglas race,—wielding at times, as Lieutenant-General of the kingdom, an uncontrolled influence over the king, and at other times openly scorning the royal authority.

He succeeded in getting three of his brothers raised to the Peerage. Archibald was made Earl Murray, Hugh, Earl Ormond, and John, Lord Balveny.

Bishop Kennedy, a kinsman of James II., and one of his most faithful friends and advisers, tried to control Douglas, but was not very successful, and the king, fearful of the tremendous power he had acquired, deemed it prudent to deprive him of his military office of Lieutenant-Governor, though he permitted him to retain the wardenship of the middle and western marches.

The Earl's turbulence was no doubt increased by his desire to revenge the murder of his kinsmen, the sixth Earl and his brother, and being fired with the martial spirit of his race, as well as animated with the belief that he was a greater, or at any rate as great, a man as his Sovereign, committed all manner of daring exploits, thinking no one had a right to challenge or control him. He committed either personally or by his vassals some cold-blooded murders, the first being that of Sir R. Colville of Ochiltree, who had in some way injured Sir John Auchinleck, one of Douglas' supporters. Colville's castle was immediately stormed, and the whole garrison, with the knight himself, massacred. He attempted the life of Chancellor Crichton, who was concerned in the sixth earl's murder, but he failed in the attempt. Sir John Herries of Terreagles did not come off so well, for he, as also Sir John Sandilands of Calder (kinsman of the first earl), and M'Lellan, ancestor of Lord Kirkcudbright, were put to death; the murder of the latter being a most cruel affair. Douglas was so enraged at M'Lellan's refusing to join him against the king, and to acknowledge his pre-eminence over the barons and gentlemen of Galloway, that he at once seized and beheaded him at his Castle of Thrieve, the scene of many a foul deed. James II. interceded through Sir Patrick Gray, M'Lellan's uncle, but Douglas foreseeing the Sovereign's application, previously murdered his prisoner, and on Sir Patrick Gray remonstrating with the earl, he nearly shared the same fate for his interference, though done with the sanction and at the instance of his royal master.

In addition to these frightful deeds Douglas showed most plainly in other ways his contempt for all authority, and how determined he was to continue his hostility to the king. He joined Earl Crawford, whose soubriquet was Lord Beardie or the Tiger Earl, and Lord Ross, the Ocean Prince, with that view, but the king feeling that Douglas' ambition and insubordination passed all bounds, now determined at all risks to get rid of him. Accordingly he invited him to a conference at Stirling, which the earl agreed to attend, but not without first receiving from James a deed of protection under his hand and seal. Notwithstanding this promise, the king, after a short altercation with Douglas, deliberately stabbed him, and being assisted by Sir Patrick Gray, M'Lellan's uncle, and others, no less than twenty-six wounds were inflicted on the earl's body, which was ignominiously ejected from the castle. Ages afterwards a skeleton was found buried near the spot, which was supposed to be the remains of Douglas. This assassination was a great blot upon the character of King James, who was a man of strong passions. Though handsome he had a red spot on his face, which gained him the name of "James with the fiery face." Sir Walter Scott says they might have called him James with the fiery temper, for with very good qualities he had a hot and impetuous disposition.

William, the earl now under review, married in 1440 his cousin Margaret, the fair maid of Galloway, the only sister of William the sixth Earl, and his brother, and heir of their properties, which were alienated at their death, but which this marriage brought back, and centred in the Earldom though only to be again lost, for this turbulent and ambitious earl contributed largely to the downfall of this once powerful family, which his brother and successor

JAMES, THE NINTH AND LAST EARL, consummated. No doubt he took up arms and tried to revenge his brother's assassination, and at one time alarmed James so much, that it was a question whether he should fly and leave the throne to Douglas. The King was in a sad state of despondency as to the probable result of the crime he had committed, for the Douglas clan rose *en masse*, and, headed by the present Earl, treated most contemptuously the King's deed of protection, which they dragged through the public streets of Stirling tied to the tail of an old horse. James, in his extremity, threw himself upon his old and tried counsellor, Bishop Kennedy, and by degrees succeeded, by the administration of bribes, in wining over many of the late Earl's friends. Amongst them were Beardie, Earl Crawford, who in a humiliating manner, appearing in poor attire, bareheaded and barefooted, supplicated forgiveness; Sir John Douglas of Dalkeith; Earl Angus, also a Douglas, and representative of the younger branch of that house. Huntly also seceded from the Douglas party, but not without punishment, for the Earl of Murray, the murdered Earl's brother, attacked him; and it was jeeringly said of Huntly—

"Where did you leave your men,
Thou Gordon so gay?
In the bog of Dunkinty
Mowing the hay."

Douglas, notwithstanding these defections, did not lose heart, but, keeping together the friends that remained, he made some desperate efforts to maintain his position, though the royal army were meanwhile engaged destroying the estates of Douglas and Hamilton, and also besieging Abercorn. His prospects were very gloomy, and a further secession taking place, damped his ardour for a time. Hamilton, his kinsman, at last deserted him, having been persuaded by Bishop Kennedy, who in this case was guilty of gross intrigue; for he told Hamilton if he renounced his support of Douglas, and went over to the royal side, the King would pardon his rebellion and show him favour, which he did by giving him large grants of land, and his elder daughter Mary in marriage. Hamilton pretended that Douglas was not sincere in his policy, or courageous enough in following it up; but Douglas told him "that if he was afraid to stay, he was welcome to go home."

After this, and some further defections, Douglas's army encountered the Borderers at Arkinholme on the 1st May 1455, with diminished numbers, which caused him to be defeated. He there lost one brother—Archibald, Earl Murray —who was killed, his head being cut off and sent to James, who received it with thanks. Hugh, Earl Ormond, was in the battle also, but was only wounded, though, being taken prisoner, he was afterwards executed. The third brother, John, Lord Balveny, escaped and fled to England to join the Earl, who had already gone thither. Douglas, however, soon returned, and uniting with Lord Ross, the Lord of the Isles, made an attempt to subdue the western coast, including some of the islands, wreaking their vengeance upon Lauder, Bishop of Lismore, for supporting the King. These rebellious chiefs were, however, frustrated in their proceedings, and obliged to fly, Douglas finding again an asylum in England, where he was welcomed by the Duke of York, the Regent, and granted a pension of £500, "to be continued to him until he should be restored to his possessions, or to the greater part of them, by the person who then called himself the King of the Scots," to whom the Yorkist party had the greatest antipathy.

James received this information with indignation, and complained that the English nation encouraged the convicted traitor Douglas, a step which was calculated to disturb the relations of the two States, which it did, for there was a speedy renewal of hostilities.

Douglas having been in England for some time, determined once more to make an effort to conquer James, and sallying north, was joined by the Earl of Northumberland, when with a considerable army they crossed the borders and invaded the Merse in 1459, but they were encountered by the Earl of Angus and completely routed. Angus was rewarded with large grants of the forfeited Douglas estates, which, however, proved the beginning of fresh troubles, as it raised Angus, the Red Douglas, to immense power and wealth, and made him nearly as formidable as the Black. Douglas again retreated to England, where he remained for some years. In the meantime James II. died, his death having been caused by the bursting of an old overcharged Flemish gun at Roxburgh Castle which he wished to rescue from the English, who had held it since the battle of Durham in 1490. The same gun wounded the Earl of Angus very severely.

Among the recipients of the Douglas estates forfeited in 1455 was Sir Walter Scott of Buccleuch and Kirkurd, and his son David, who obtained part of Branxholm, to be held blench for the payment of a red rose, for their brave and faithful exertions in favour of the King against the house of Douglas. They likewise got part of the barony of Langholm. This Sir Walter first established the principal residence of the Buccleuch family at Branxholm, where he probably died not many years after his sovereign, who made the grants.

Douglas emerged from his last banishment in England some twenty-four years after the death of James, and, not contented with his many defeats, joined Albany, son of James II., regent to his nephew the young king, in his treasonable proceedings. They gave battle at Lochmaben, where, after a severe conflict, the rebels were defeated and Douglas taken prisoner by Kirkpatrick of Kirkmichael, one of his old vassals. Kirkpatrick, out of love for his old chief, offered to fly with him to England, instead of surrendering him; but Douglas declined going again into exile, and James III., taking compassion on him on account of his age and infirmities, ordered him to be sent to the monastery of Lindores, which he much preferred, saying, "He that cannot do better must be a monk." He died on the 15th April 1488, the very year James III. was murdered.

The last Earl Douglas married, under dispensation from the Pope, Margaret, the widow of his brother the eighth earl, who was murdered at Stirling, and sister of the sixth earl murdered at Edinburgh, but many years before his death, and during one of the periods of his exile, she petitioned the Scottish Court for mercy, complaining of the wretchedness she had suffered from her unnatural and forced marriage with the brother of her first husband. James II., struck with her beauty, and moved by her misfortunes, gladly welcomed, and sympathised with her, offering her for a husband his half-brother, Sir John Stewart, the son of Sir James Stewart, called the Black Knight of Lorn, by Jane his wife, the granddaughter of John o' Gaunt, the father of Henry IV. of England, and widow of James I. Sir John Stewart was created Earl of Athol, and distinguished himself highly by his valour and patriotism. He had one daughter by Margaret Douglas, the fair maid of Galloway.*

* The title of Earl of Douglas existed for ninety-eight years, giving an average of eleven years to each possessor. During that period, the House of Douglas rose to a degree of power scarcely inferior to that of the king, and it became a saying that "nae man was safe in the country, unless he were either a Douglas or a Douglas man." The earls kept a kind of court, and had a retinue of two thousand men, and created knights. Eleven times during its history did the House of Douglas measure its forces with the Royalty of Scotland, and once, under the Angus Branch, with that of England. The Angus Branch assisted so greatly to overthrow the parent house, that it became a proverb, in allusion to the complexion of the two houses, that "the Red Douglas had put down the Black."

THE EARLS OF ANGUS.

The Angus branch, known as the Red Douglas, though not so great a family as the elder race whom they followed and represented, nevertheless were noted for loyalty and military achievements, and for extensive possessions.

GEORGE DOUGLAS, son of the first Earl of Douglas, by his third wife Margaret Stewart, daughter and heir of Thomas Stewart, was created the first Earl Angus of the Douglas race, upon his mother's resignation of the honour in 1389. He married in 1397, Mary Stewart, elder daughter of King Robert III., by whom he had two sons and one daughter, who married an ancestor of the Marquis of Tweeddale. The sons William and George became in turn the second and the fourth Earls of Angus. The first earl no doubt possessed the military ardour of the family, though little has come down respecting him, except that he was at the battle of Homildon, where he was taken prisoner along with his kinsman, Archibald, Earl of Douglas. It is uncertain when the Earl of Angus died, but he is said to have died in England of the plague in 1402. At all events it must have been when he was in the prime of life, as there is evidence of his son being early called to the earldom, and besides his widow married thrice afterwards, viz.—

First, Sir James Kennedy, by whom she had James Kennedy, Bishop of St Andrews, the adviser of James II., and

Secondly, Sir William Graham, by whom she had a son Patrick, who also became Bishop of St Andrews, and

Thirdly, Sir William Edmonstone of Duntreath, by whom she had issue.

WILLIAM the SECOND EARL of ANGUS, maintained the character of his race for valour. Rymer reports that he was sent to England in 1423, as one of the negotiators for the ransom of James I., his uncle, at whose coronation he was knighted. Some time afterwards, he was made warden of the Middle Marches, and had special grants of a considerable portion of the property, which had been possessed by his ancestors. In September 1435, he was sent against Henry Percy the second Earl of Northumberland, whom he defeated at Piperden below the Cheviot Range. Angus married a daughter of an ancestor of the Marquis of Tweeddale, according to a dispensation granted by the Bishop of Glasgow in 1425, and, like his father, died in his prime, leaving at any rate, one son who succeeded in 1437, the year of his father's death.

JAMES, THIRD EARL ANGUS. Rymer mentions that this earl was a Conservator of the Peace with England in the second year of the reign of James II., which commenced in 1437, and that a truce between the two kingdoms was then concluded. He married Joanna or Jane, third daughter of James I., but died in early life without issue. The third Earl Angus, who was succeeded by his uncle George as fourth earl, is described in a bond as Lord of Liddesdale and Jedwood Forest, including Hermitage Castle.

GEORGE, FOURTH EARL ANGUS, was warden of the Eastern and Middle Marches, and commanded the Royal forces during the Douglas rebellion of 1455, and upon the attainder of the Earl, he got a charter to the Lordship of Douglas in 1455. There appears, says Sir Walter Scott, "some doubt whether in this division, the Earl of Angus received more than his natural right. If Archibald the Grim intruded into the earldom of Douglas, without being a legitimate son of that family, it follows that the House of Angus were kept out of their just rights for more than a century, being only restored to them after the battle of Arkinholme. Perhaps this may help to account for the eager interest taken by the Earl of Angus against his kinsman."

This earl did honour to the name of Douglas, and was much esteemed for his wisdom, loyalty, and valour. He took the side of the Lancaster party in England, during the reign of Henry VI., while his kinsman the ninth Earl of Douglas, took the side of the Yorkists.

On the return of Angus to Scotland, he, when on the way, boldly relieved and carried off a French garrison then shut up in Alnwick Castle, in the sight of the English army commanded by Edward IV., who, on the departure of Henry VI., became king, and Angus brought the French troops to Scotland in safety. This took place in 1462, and he died on the 14th November, the same year, well advanced in life, and was buried among his ancestors at Abernethy, in the beautiful vale of Strathearn. His wife was Elizabeth Sibbald, of Fifeshire, and by her he had one son, Archibald, his successor. He had a son George, supposed to be illegitimate, who acquired Bonjedward, and his descendants held that property for a very long period.

ARCHIBALD, FIFTH (commonly known as the great) EARL OF ANGUS, the next in order, made a figure in the reigns of James III. and IV. He took an active part with the rebels against the former monarch, and had a chief command at Sauchie, where the third James was killed, or rather assassinated after the battle, by a man representing himself to be a priest, though it has been said he was pursued by Lord Grey and Stirling of Keir, as well as the priest, by one of whom it is supposed he was killed. Sir Walter Scott states that it was not known how the king's body was disposed of, but antiquarians have discovered that it was interred in Cambuskenneth Abbey, near Sauchie, and the Board of Works lately erected a tomb, commemorative of James and his queen, Margaret of Denmark. Angus felt the king lowered himself by taking inferior persons into his counsels, excluding his nobles, and he was one of the chief actors in the siezure of Cochran and other minions of the king at Lauder, where some of them were hung, as a ditty says, " on Lauder's dreary flat." *

In James IV.'s time, Angus was placed in high position,

* I mean that Douglas, fifth of yore,
  Who coronet of Angus bore,
  And when his blood and heart were high
  Did the third James in court defy,
  And all his minions led to die
  In Lauder's dreary flat.
It was on this occasion Angus got the soubriquet of Bell the Cat.

and finally made Lord High Chancellor, but he was removed from that office to make way for Huntly, and resented the unfairness with which he was treated, by retiring to England. There he was suspected of collusion with Henry VII., father-in-law of James IV.; and on his return, was shut up in his own Castle of Tantallon, where he had again to submit to a diminution of his importance. The energy of James had a favourable influence upon him, and made him much more pacific in his views. He took great pains to divert the king from his mad project of invading England, an expedition which ended in the battle of Flodden, where the king lost his life, and the lives of two of the earl's sons, and some two hundred of the name of Douglas were also sacrificed. The king was so enraged at Angus' remonstrance, that "he told him he might go home, if he was afraid," and bursting into tears, the earl immediately left the camp, soon finding his fears as to the result of the battle more than realised.

He was a man of Herculean strength, and being offended with one of James's favourites, who spoke disparagingly of him, he challenged him to single combat, and at one blow cut asunder his adversary's thigh bone, " as woodknife lops the sapling sprig." He did not long survive the fatal battle of Flodden,

> " Where shivered was fair Scotland's spear,
> And broken was her shield."

He died at Whithorn Priory, Galloway, where he lived in seclusion, passing his time in acts of devotion and charity, and on his death, which happened in 1514, his body was opened and his heart removed and buried at Douglas, while the rest of his remains were interred in the Conventual Church at Whithorn. He had three sons by his first wife, two of whom, George Master of Angus, and William of Glenbervie, were killed at Flodden, and Gavin, the celebrated Bishop of Dunkeld, previously Rector of Hawick. By his second wife he had a son, Archibald, father of Sir Archibald of Kilspindie, a favourite of James V., who called him his Grey Steil. He was also his treasurer, but was afterwards attainted and went into exile. The king behaved very harshly to his old favourite, so much so that even the tyrannical Henry VIII. commented on it, and said that a king's face should give grace. His son and heir, Archibald Douglas of Kilspindie, to whom the estates were restored, was twice Lord Provost of Edinburgh, and it was in his provostship the town was first lighted with lanterns.

The Master of Angus, killed at Flodden with his brother Sir William of Glenbervie, left two sons, the eldest succeeding his grandfather as sixth Earl of Angus, while the second, Sir George, of Pittendreich, killed at Pinkie, left two sons, one becoming, as we shall see, seventh Earl, and the other fourth Earl of Morton. ARCHIBALD succeeded his grandfather as SIXTH EARL of ANGUS in 1514. He was handsome and highly accomplished, but the lust of power, the failing of the family, was strongly implanted in him. He travelled a great deal, and was well received everywhere, particularly by Henry II. of France, who conferred the honour of knighthood upon him. He returned home soon after James IV.'s death, when he proposed to the King's widow, Margaret, daughter of Henry VII. though, as he had just lost his first wife, a grand-daughter of the first Earl of Bothwell, it was considered too precipitate if not indecent. They however were married, and though Angus expected the Regency in consequence, he did not get it, much to his disgust, and not making a good husband to the Queen, they were divorced. They had one daughter, Margaret, who married the Earl of Lennox, father of Lord Darnley, and grandfather of James VI. of Scotland and first of England. He had a third wife and a son, and it is said he had illegitimate children besides, which no doubt caused the bad feeling which existed between himself and the Queen, his second wife, though she was capricious and given to flirtation also. After the divorce took place, the royal lady married Henry Stewart, Lord Methven, quite a youth.

Angus retired to England for a time, but on his return he renewed his former course, and having obtained the Chancellorship, he exercised great power, which seemed to threaten the independence of the crown and the liberties of the people. At length James V. succeeded in releasing himself from the grasp of the Douglas some little time after the battle of Melrose, which, however, went in favour of Angus, though he lost his heroic friend and supporter, Andrew Ker of Cessford, who was killed, it has been said, by an Elliot, one of the followers of Buccleuch.

It is recorded the King of England had promised Evers and Latoun a feudal grant of Teviotdale, which so roused Angus's blood that he is said to have sworn to write the deed of investiture upon their skins with sharp pens and bloody ink, in resentment for their having defaced the tombs of his ancestors at Melrose. On the King hearing that Evers was killed, he vowed vengeance against Angus, whose answer however, was worthy of a Douglas. "Is our brother-in-law offended that I, as a good Scotchman, have avenged my ravaged country and the defaced tombs of my ancestry upon Evers? They were better men than he, and I was bound to do no less; and will he take my life for that? Little knows King Henry that in the skirts of Cairntable I can keep myself against all his English host." An amazonian Scottish woman was said to have fought at Ancrum Moor, and to have distinguished herself in the same manner as Squire Witherington, who fought, like her, without his legs. Angus concluded his remaining years very quietly at Tantallon, where he died in 1556.

DAVID, nephew of the preceding Earl, being son of Sir George Douglas, killed at Pinkie, by his kinswoman Elizabeth Douglas, the heiress of Pittendreich, succeeded as SEVENTH EARL of ANGUS. He was unlike most of his race, being inactive in his habits and of a delicate constitution, and did not live long, for it is recorded he enjoyed the honours and estates barely two years. His wife was a daughter of Sir John Hamilton of Clydesdale, and by her he left a son, Archibald, and two daughters, one of whom married Sir Walter Scott of Buccleuch, the faithful adherent of Mary Queen of Scots and grandson of the first and great Sir Walter, who was celebrated for his deeds of valour during the minority of James V. This ARCHIBALD succeeded as EIGHTH EARL of ANGUS, when an infant. The Angus earldom having vested in Margaret Douglas, the mother of Darnley, as the only child and heir of the sixth Earl, she now renounced her claim in favour of Earl Archibald, the heir-male, which renunciation was confirmed by Parliament, who now restricted the succession to the male line. As a youth he lived in obscurity, and lurked about under the soubriquet of "James the Grieve," but his education and morals must have been carefully attended to, for he was surnamed the "Good Earl." He was appointed a Warden of the Marches and afterwards Lieutenant of the Borders. He executed his duties with great reputation. On the fall of his uncle, the Earl of Morton, who made a memorable figure in the annals of Scottish history, in connection with the murder of Darnley, he succeeded, by virtue of an entail, to that peerage. Believing the proceedings against Morton arose from an enmity between the Stuarts and his family, and that a conspiracy existed to destroy the whole race of Douglas, he resented the indignity heaped upon Morton. This obliged him to retire, and he went to England for a time, returning, however, in 1582, when he took part in the Raid of Ruthven. Subsequently he was attainted for opposing Arran, one of the King's favourites, but he afterwards obtained a revocation of his forfeiture, and died not long after, his death being attributed to sorcery. This Earl left behind him a character for sincere and unaffected piety, as well as a good reputation for learning, and the Latin epitaph on his tomb at Abernethy, where he was buried—the Angus family's last resting place—is highly honourable to him. It has been translated as follows :—

> "Angus, by cruel death lies here,
> The good man's hope, the wicked's fear,
> The praise and sorrow of the most
> Religious, who, as having lost
> A father, mourn; most men are known
> To find a woe if they have none.

> Envy, accustomed to wrong
> His guiltless life, employs her tongue,
> Now a loud trumpet of his fame,
> And weeps, if not for grief, for shame,
> Enforc'd to give herself the lie,
> O power of truth ! O victory !
> By which more honour is obtain'd,
> Than is in greatest triumphs gain'd."

Though thrice married, he left one daughter only by his third wife, but she died unmarried, Angus being succeeded by his cousin and heir-male

WILLIAM AS NINTH EARL OF ANGUS.—James the Sixth of Scotland, and First of England, however, claimed the earldom as heir of line, but after contesting it at law was non-suited, and William of Glenbervie was confirmed in the title. All the ancient privileges of the Douglases—viz., the first vote in Council or Parliament, the appointment of the King's hereditary lieutenant, and the leading of the van of the army in the day of battle, were also confirmed to him.

The first of the Glenbervie family was killed at Flodden, together with his brother the Master of Angus. He had married the heiress of Sir John Auchinleck of Auchinleck. The ninth Earl espoused in early life the interests of Queen Mary, and was a partisan of hers at the battle of Corrichie, but he afterwards became a Protestant, and supported James VI. He married at eighteen Miss Graham of Morphie, with whom he lived happily forty years, and by whom he had eight children, and when he died he was barely sixty. His eldest son, WILLIAM, succeeded as TENTH EARL OF ANGUS; while his second, Robert, got Glenbervie. His descendants, one of whom was the celebrated author of the "Peerage and Baronetage of Scotland," are still in possession of the property, though in the female line.

The tenth Earl of Angus was a literary man, and well up in antiquities and history, especially that branch relating to the origin of families. He wrote a Chronicle of the Douglases. He became a Romanist, and getting into disfavour in consequence of attempting to destroy the Protestant religion, he suffered imprisonment, but was finally allowed to retire to France, where he remained till his death in 1616. He was succeeded by his eldest son, William; his second son, James, being created by Charles I., with whom he was a favourite, Baron Mordington, a title now extinct.

WILLIAM, ELEVENTH EARL ANGUS, was created Marquis of Douglas on 17th June 1633. The Marquis was noted for the splendour of his hospitality at Douglas Castle, and died at an advanced age for a Douglas, having completed his seventieth year. He was married twice, and had twelve children. His eldest son, Archibald, Lord Angus, died before him, leaving two sons—viz., James, who succeeded his grandfather as second Marquis Douglas; and Archibald, who was Earl Forfar, a title now extinct. But the Marquis had other sons besides Lords Angus and Forfar, one being William, created Earl Selkirk, who married Anne, Duchess of Hamilton, and was created Duke, resigning the Earldom of Selkirk, which was conferred on his two younger sons primogenitarily. With the exception of the late Earl, who tried to form a settlement in Prince Edward's Island, which was not successful, none of the family have left any footprints behind them. The present Duke of Hamilton descends from this marriage, being through it the male heir of the great house of Douglas. A younger son was created Earl Dumbarton, and became a famous soldier, but that title is extinct; while a daughter married the first Duke of Queensberry.

JAMES, SECOND MARQUIS OF DOUGLAS, was a Privy Councillor to three kings, whom he served thirty years in all. He was rather loose in his habits, and got entangled with the daughter of one Widow Jack who kept a tavern, but afterwards married Lady Barbara Erskine, though the marriage proved an unfortunate one. They were separated after the birth of an only son, the gallant Angus, who raised when a youth in one day 1800 men composing the "Cameronians," still one of our crack regiments; and being appointed colonel, he led them with great bravery, and fell at Steinkirk, aged only twenty-one. The sorrows of his mother were described in a ballad of the day, some lines of which I quote :—

> " O wherefore should I busk my head,
>   Or wherefore should I kame my hair?
> Twice my true love has me forsook,
>   And says he'd never love me mair.
> Now Arthur's Seat shall be my bed,
>   The sheets shall ne'er be pressed by me;
> St Anton's well shall be my drink
>   Since my true love's forsaken me.
> O Martinmas wind, when wilt thou blaw,
>   And shake the green leaf off the tree?
> O gentle death, when wilt thou come
>   And take a life that wearies me?"

Having mentioned that Lady Barbara Erskine's son Angus raised the Cameronians, or 26th Foot, it may be interesting to notice that her brother, the tenth Earl Mar, raised the Scots Fusileers, the 21st Regiment.

The Marquis Douglas married, secondly, Lady Mary Kerr, of the house of Lothian, by whom he had two children—Archibald, who became the heir; and Lady Jane, who married Sir John Stewart of Grandtully at the age of forty-eight, and had twins at fifty-one, which many thought were surreptitious.

Archibald succeeded as third Marquis in 1700, aged only six, and in consideration of his illustrious descent was created by Queen Anne, when he was but nine, Duke of Douglas, with limitation to the heirs of his body.

Personally he had no claim to ducal honours, for he was almost a nonentity, being celebrated for no particular acquirement but that of fencing, which produced in him a taste for duelling. He used to practise fencing with Captain John Kerr, a natural son of his brother-in-law who visited at Douglas. Kerr was a first-rate fencer, being able to remove a button from his adversary's coat without cutting the garment. The Duke was jealous of his friend's superior fencing; but besides this, seeing his Grace's taste for inferior company, he took the liberty of cautioning him against it. This no doubt increased his feeling against Kerr, and when he suspected the young man of making up to his sister, Lady Jane, the Duke's displeasure knew no bounds, and he determined on shooting him, which he did when Kerr was asleep in his bed. The Duke of course fled, but the matter was soon hushed up, and his Grace returned. Human life was not so much thought of at that time, and human law not so justly dealt out as now.

The Duke afterwards married, at the age of sixty-two, a lady of the same name—Miss Douglas of Maines—who was well advanced in years also, or at anyrate in the meridian of life. There was no issue, and though the Duke had previously made a settlement in favour of the house of Hamilton, excluding his sister, to whom he behaved very ill, he was induced, probably under the influence of the Duchess, who must have felt for the treatment Lady Jane had received from her husband, though she was dead before the marriage, to alter his arrangements, and to substitute his nephew, Lady Jane's son, whom he appointed his heir. This no doubt displeased the Hamiltons, and caused the litigation which did not finally succeed,—though the Scotch Courts decided in their favour; for the House of Lords reversed the decision, determining in favour of Mr Stewart in 1771, several years after the Duke's death, the law-suit costing an immense sum of money. Mr Stewart accordingly assumed the name of Douglas, and took possession of the estates, said to be worth £60,000 a year, and some time after was created Lord Douglas. After enjoying the title and property many years, and marrying daughters of the Dukes of Montrose and Buccleuch in succession, he died at the advanced age of seventy-nine, leaving several sons and daughters. Three sons inherited in turn, but none of them left issue, and at length the property passed to the child of a sister of the last Lord Douglas, the present Countess of Home.

The four Baron Douglases were quiet, good men, leaving no particular marks behind them. The first used to entertain, and, like David Hume, preferred port, which he placed before his guests after dinner. A story is told of Lord Justice-Clerk

M'Queen, an excellent judge, though an eccentric man, one day dining with his friend Lord Douglas, who only produced port, which was not the judge's favourite wine. He accordingly asked the noble Lord if there was no claret in the cellar, the host said there was, but his butler told him it was not good. The judge, however, wished to sit in judgment on the claret, and said in his Scotch dialect, "Let's pree it." On its being produced it was pronounced excellent; so that the butler and his Lordship, who probably did not wish to part with it, were in a fix. The judge appealed to the parish minister, who was of the party at dinner, to absolve the *fama clamosa* against the claret, but the reverend divine, who no doubt liked it as well as the judge, said he could not do that according to ecclesiastical law till after three several appearances, which secured to the lovers of claret at least two additional bottles.

The Duchess of Douglas deserves further notice before closing the account of the old race. She enjoyed, according to Dr Carlyle, a traditional reputation for much freedom of speech and action. She, Carlyle, and others, were on one occasion in company at Hamilton, when they were joined by Mr Thomas Clelland, a clergyman of the neighbourhood, whom the Duchess, then Miss Peggy Douglas, rated on being an old fusty bachelor. After bearing patiently all the effects of her wit, Mr Clelland said to her, " Margaret, you know that I am master of the parish register where your age is recorded, and that I know when you must justly be called an old maid, in spite of your juvenile airs." " What care I now," said she, " for I have for some time renounced your worthless sex. I have sworn to be Duchess of Douglas, or never to mount a marriage-bed." This took place in 1745, when the lady was about thirty, but still beautiful and witty; and though she made good her prediction, it was about thirteen years after before she succeeded in securing the Duke, who only lived three or four years after the marriage. She visited Paris in 1762, and was advised to take the privilege of the tabouret at Court, but she declined, as one of her friends said, on account of the disproportioned size of the seat for the co-relative part of her figure.

The great Dr Johnson met her Grace some time after she became a widow, at Boswell's, I believe; but the Doctor, who, as we know, was not over complimentary, said she talked broad Scotch with a paralytic voice, and was scarcely intelligible. The Duchess might have received a little more favour from Johnson, as he had himself married an old lady, whose fortune enabled him to make his first start in life.

THE QUEENSBERRY BRANCH.

This branch sprang from an illegitimate son of the hero of Otterburn, William, who got a grant of the Baronies of Drumlanrig and Hawick from James I. when a captive in England, and it has been said the charter was written on vellum, holograph of the king, dated at Croyden 1412. Several of his early descendants well maintained the fame of their martial ancestors, and Sir James, the seventh baron, assisted Buccleuch in his attempt to rescue James V. from the grasp of Angus, and was afterwards actively engaged on the king's side in other battles, dying in 1578, after having been prisoner for some time in Edinburgh Castle. His son also assisted the king at the battle of Langside,* while his

* The eighth Baron of Drumlanrig was in possession on the perpetration of that fiendish act of revenge by those strong-minded women, Lady Howpaslot and her friend Jean Scott of Satchells, which is recorded in various places. Drumlanrig, who was a zealous magistrate for the suppression of Border disturbances, somehow or other became possessed of Howpaslot, probably by legal diligence, but which he did not hold long. The idea of a Douglas encroaching on the domains of her ancestors roused the Scott blood in Lady Howpaslot's veins to such a degree that she summoned a council of war in Hawick, the very town in which Drumlanrig was superior, which was presided over by Dame Satchells, and attended by all the bullies of the clan, the result being that Drumlanrig's sheep put upon the lands were cruelly and barbarously killed. Drumlanrig died soon after, but his son brought the miscreants to trial, and three at any rate of the band—all Scots—were ordered to be hanged and their goods to be escheated.

grandson or successor was most active in putting down the rebellious borderers. The feudal baronship gave place to a Peerage in 1628, when William Douglas was created Viscount Drumlanrig, and in 1633 Earl of Queensberry. His Lordship married a daughter of the first Earl Lothian, and granddaughter of Sir Andrew Ker of Cessford, by whom he had two sons,—James his heir, and

Sir William Douglas of Kilhead created a baronet, whose descendant Sir Charles became fifth Marquis of Queensberry.

JAMES THE SECOND EARL was a great royalist, and an intense sufferer in the cause, having been heavily fined; but his son and successor, William, was abundantly rewarded for all his father's losses, having been appointed to high offices of state, and received no end of additional honours, a dukedom into the bargain. His second son was made Earl March, from whom the fourth Duke, old Q., derived. The first Duke would not assist in relieving the Roman Catholics of their disability, and got his congé from James II. when he retired to Dumfriesshire, and raised the magnificent Castle of Drumlanrig. His son

JAMES THE SECOND DUKE had a further Peerage distinction conferred upon him, having been created Duke of Dover. He was a staunch supporter of the Union, having like his father previously concurred in the revolution of 1688. He got the Dukedom of Queensberry extended to heirs female as well as male, while the Marquisate remained untouched.

It has been said His Grace's defence of the Union was conducted with the most consummate ability. His third son Charles became the Third Duke, while his daughter Jean married the second Duke of Buccleuch whose grandson became fifth Duke of Queensberry. He married Lady Katherine Hyde, and had two sons. The elder was accidentally killed by one of his own pistols; while the second died unmarried, having while at Lisbon during the well-known earthquake with difficulty escaped. His wife was a person of great beauty and wit, and was commemorated by the leading poets of the day. She was a great admirer of Gay, and she and the Duke erected a monument to him in Poet's Corner; Pope writing the epitaph. Prior called the Duchess :—

> "Kitty beautiful and young,
> And wild as colt untamed."

In 1772 at the Princess Dowager of Wales' funeral she walked as one of the mourners to Westminster Abbey, when her Royal Highness was buried, on which occasion these lines were penned by H. Walpole :—

> " To many a Kitty Love his ear
> Would for a day engage;
> But Prior's Kitty, ever fair,
> Obtain'd it for an age."

The Duke and Duchess died within a year of one another, after living together in the bonds of matrimony more than fifty-seven years. The Duke's cousin, William, third Earl March, now became fourth Duke, familiarly known as old Q., a man of immense possessions and great eccentricities. As third Earl March he was descended from the first Duke, whose second son William became the first Earl and acquired Neidpath, that fine old estate, which he improved so much that it became quite the beau ideal of a place. The second Earl continued to reside at and to keep it up, but he had not the brains of his father. He had a town house in Peebles which he used for winter quarters, and was quite hand in glove with the citizens. On his riding to Edinburgh on one occasion, one of the old women fond of knowing everybody's business asked the Earl when he would be back. His reply was, "Gane Friday, Effy;" but alas on that very Friday he was brought home a corpse. His son was the third Earl and fourth Duke of Queensberry of whose wealth and eccentricities I have spoken. He lived in England, and allowed Neidpath to go to ruin, and besides he cut down all the fine old timber, leaving it in the language of Wordsworth,

> " Beggared and outraged."

He never married, and at his death his landed estates went in different directions, the Duke of Buccleuch getting Drumlanrig, as heir of line. His moveable property amounted to about a million, and was also divided, Lord Yarmouth being his residuary legatee.

It is worth noticing that the fourth and fifth Dukes of Queensberry possessed that ducal honour between them for ninety-nine years.

The male line of the Queensberry enjoys the Marquisate which is in the descendants of Sir William of Kilhead already mentioned.

THE MORTON BRANCH.

This branch sprung from Sir James Douglas of Loudon, a cousin of the Good Sir James, his second son being Sir John Douglas of Dalkeith. That property was acquired by the Douglas through marriage with Miss Graham its heiress, whose family had possessed it for about two hundred years. The Grahams of Dalkeith lived in great splendour, and were noted warriors, for up to a late period the family were still known as the gallant Grahams. Although Froissart, the chivalric historian, mentions having met James Douglas, afterwards of Otterburn fame, at Dalkeith when a boy of about twelve, the old Douglas line never possessed it. The first Earl Morton, created 1457, was Lord of Dalkeith. He married a daughter of James I., widow of the third Earl Angus. John the second earl was honoured with a visit at Dalkeith of James IV. and his royal bride-elect, when on their way to Holyrood to be married, their nuptials being celebrated by Dunbar in his famous poem the "Thistle and Rose."

The third earl was accused of writing some treasonable papers, but was acquitted. In his time the plague broke out in Edinburgh, and James V. then a boy, was removed to Dalkeith Castle for fear of infection, and he and his court remained there for some little time. This earl was in favour of Henry VIII.'s attempt to obtain Mary for his son Edward VI., to enforce which scheme the battle of Pinkie was fought, and Dalkeith, which contained a vast amount of property, deposited there for safety, was attacked and surrendered.

The third earl having no male issue, got the honours and estate transferred to his son-in-law, James Douglas of Pittendreich, who became fourth earl, and was an important historic personage. He filled several high offices, and finally became regent, but being accused of acquiescing in the assassination of Rizzio, and of being accessory to the murder of Darnley; he was arraigned on the latter charge, found guilty, and next day beheaded by the machine he caused to be introduced into Scotland—the maiden. Sir James Douglas of Pathhead, a relative of Morton, revenged himself on Stewart Earl of Arran, the profligate favourite of James VI., and the usurper of the principal offices of the government, for his persecution of the Regent, by killing him on the spot as he was riding in the neighbourhood of Douglas. The Earl of Arran was at that time stripped of his honours, and living as a private gentleman, but Douglas, although fifteen years had elapsed since the Earl of Morton's execution, did not forget Arran's share in the Regent's conviction and death, and took the earliest opportunity he had of showing his resentment by murdering him, and causing his head to be exhibited through the country. Douglas, however, suffered for this act of vengeance, for I find he was killed in Edinburgh, in the High Street, by a relative of Arran's, who pierced him through the body, to revenge his friend's death. Morton in early life lived in great obscurity. Owing to the attainder of his father and uncle the sixth Earl Angus, he was forced to live as he could, and adopted the feigned name of "Innes," under which he acted as a gentleman's factor. But on the attainder being cancelled, at James V.'s death, he returned home, threw off his disguise, and in due time married the heiress of Morton, adopting till he succeeded to the earldom, the title of Master of Morton. He had no family by his wife, and on his execution or decapitation, the estates and honours were forfeited, though after a time they were restored and given to the Regent's heir and nephew, the eighth Earl Angus, who, however, died childless, when they were inherited by William Douglas of Lochleven, the custodier of Queen Mary, and descendant of Sir John Douglas, who gallantly defended the castle in the minority of David II., against the English, but was afterwards assassinated. William Douglas' son and heir was drowned, and his grandson became eighth Earl of Morton, a man of very considerable talents and accomplishments, and the possessor of a large property, but espousing the royal cause when the Civil War broke out, he was involved in pecuniary difficulties, having made large advances of money to Charles I. In 1642 he was forced to sell the estate of Dalkeith, when the representative of Francis Earl of Buccleuch purchased it. The Earl of Morton got an assignment of the Islands of Orkney and Shetland for his reimbursement, and he retired to the Orkneys, where he died in 1648. His son only lived about a year after him, when his grandson became tenth earl, and obtained a fresh grant from the crown of the Northern Islands, though they were again taken away, but when the eleventh earl succeeded, being a zealous supporter of the Union, he obtained an Act of Parliament, vesting the islands in himself and heirs, which remained with the family till sold by the eleventh earl to Sir Laurence Dundas, ancestor of Lord Zetland, the present proprietor. The fourteenth earl was a man of great sagacity as well as of pre-eminent abilities. He had the honour of being elected President of the Royal Society, and was also made one of the Trustees of the British Museum. His grandson, Hamilton Douglas, second son of the fifteenth earl, was a most noted naval officer who perished at New York in 1783, in his twenty-first year, in the performance of a very bold and hazardous duty, which he, with others under his command volunteered, all being officers on board Sir Charles Douglas' man-of-war "Assistance." A monument at Sandyhook commemorates the loss of the gallant Douglas, who had assumed the name of Halyburton, and his comrades.

A very ancient cadet of the Douglas Burn Douglases, was the House of Pumpherston, a well-known and rather distinguished family in Linlithgowshire, a property which is now possessed by Mr M'Lagan, member for that County. One of the last of them was Sir Joseph Douglas, and one of his family married Andrew Riddell, Baron of Riddell. The fate of Sir Joseph was melancholy. He was one of the passengers in the Gloucester Frigate, which was wrecked in 1652, on her passage from London to Edinburgh, on the Yarmouth Sands. Besides Douglas one hundred and forty-nine other persons were drowned, many being notables. Among them was Robert third earl of Roxburgh.

Sylvester Douglas was created a Peer by Lord North, probably owing to his having married his daughter, who thus became Lady Glenbervie, the title of her husband.

Glenbervie's history is a little peculiar. Educated at Aberdeen, where he was a distinguished scholar, he became a Doctor or at any rate a student of medicine, which he afterwards renounced to go to the London Bar, but he acquired no fame as a barrister, except as a reporter of Lord Mansfield's legal decisions. This employment induced him to take for his motto *per varios casus*, which Lord Campbell, the Chancellor, remarked, was rather better than one adopted by a legal friend of his own, on launching his carriage, viz., causes produce effects, being much in the same style as "quack, quack," for the doctor whose crest was a duck.

Sheridan wrote a pasquinade on Glenbervie.

" Glenbervie, Glenbervie,
What 's good for the scurvy ?
For ne'er be your old trade forgot --
In your arms rather quarter
A pestle and mortar,
And your crest be a spruce gallipot,
Your crest be a spruce gallipot.
Glenbervie, Glenbervie,
The world's topsy-turvey !
Of this truth you're the fittest attestor ;
For who can deny
That the low become high,
When the King makes a Lord of Sylvester,
When the King makes a Lord of Sylvester.

Lord Glenbervie had a son an M.P., who published an essay

on several points of resemblance between the ancient and modern Greeks, but he is long since dead and the title extinct.

I have alluded to Sir Charles Douglas, captain of the man-of-war in which the noble and gallant Hamilton Douglas, of the Morton family, from which Sir Charles was descended, was an officer; and I must now say a little about the eminent commander himself, who was greatly distinguished during the American war, and particularly at Quebec, which he relieved when sorely pressed by the enemy. This officer, for his gallant exploits, which were numerous, obtained a baronetcy, and was succeeded by his son, also a distinguished naval officer; who again was succeeded by his brother, Sir Howard Douglas, a renowned soldier. Sir Charles Douglas was an accomplished linguist, having been able to speak six European languages.

DIVINES OF NOTE AMONG THE DOUGLASES.

The first in order is Gavin, son of the fifth Earl Angus, as already mentioned. He was a very eminent scholar and poet, and, as a brother bard says, he was—

> " More pleased, that in a barbarous age,
> He gave rude Scotland Virgil's page,
> Than that beneath his rule he held
> The bishoprick of fair Dunkeld."

He died of the plague in London, and is buried in the now beautiful church of the Savoy. Sir Robert Douglas, son of the ninth Earl Angus, is interred there also. The Savoy abounds with the remains of celebrities, amongst whom I may mention George, third Earl of Cumberland, one of Elizabeth's famous admirals, and father of the great Countess of Dorset, who, when Charles II.'s secretary recommended to her a candidate for Appleby, replied—" I have been bullied by an usurper, neglected by a court, and will not be dictated to by a subject. Your man shan't stand."

Then Robert Douglas, of the Glenbervie family, was bishop of Dunblane, but retired at the Revolution. I also mention John Douglas, Bishop of Salisbury, who was a man of ability and author of several literary works, that on "Miracles" being most noted, and a standard book. He was the son of a merchant at Pittenweem, in Fife, though descended from a branch of the old Douglases, and his grandfather was an eminent Episcopal Minister in Scotland, and the immediate successor of Bishop Burnet at Saltoun, East Lothian, from which living he was ejected at the Revolution, when Presbyterianism was established here. Bishop Douglas was a member of the celebrated club of which Dr Johnson, Sir Joshua Reynolds, Mr Burke, Mr Boswell, and Dr Goldsmith were members. He died at Windsor Castle in 1807, aged 86. He was tutor in Lord Bath's family, and was a warm and constant friend of his lordship. Lord Bath left him his library, but General Pulteney, not wishing to have it removed, gave the Bishop £1000 for it. On the General's death, it was again bequeathed to him, and he again relinquished it to another member of the Bath family for the same sum. Very good legacies for the prelate.

There was another Robert Douglas, said by some to be descended from royalty, an eminent Presbyterian minister, who was offered the Bishoprick of Edinburgh on the establishment of Episcopacy at the Restoration, but who refused it, and was afterwards deprived for non-conformity, though he was restored, and made minister of Pencaitland, where the famous Calderwood was before him.

Then, in later times, nearer our own day, there was the well-known Robert Douglas of Galashiels, the founder, as it were, of that prosperous town, the friend of Sir Walter Scott, and the proprietor of Abbotsford before Sir Walter, though under a less euphonious name.

There were also several other Douglases, ministers of the Kirk, too numerous to name. One was appointed to Ancrum, Hector, who on being examined on the rudiments of religion, was found *rude* thereon, which the clerical examiners must have intended for more than a piece of wit, for poor Hector was very *rudely* treated, being deprived of his appointment.

An Archibald Douglas, minister at Glasgow, a cousin of Morton's, was supposed to be concerned in Darnley's murder. He fled after the occurrence, but on his return was tried, though acquitted. The jury who sat upon him was packed, as it was thought he might be able to advance the king's prospects in England. You may remember that Bothwellhaugh, the murderer of the Regent Murray at Linlithgow, was let off, though an assassin, the King observing, " that if Murray had not been shot he would never have been king."

In connection with the Regent Morton, I may state that very different justice was dealt out to Andrew Douglas, minister of Douglas, who was actually tortured and then hanged for publicly rebuking Morton for some illicit amour.

Among the noted Douglas ladies not already mentioned were—

Lady Eleanor Douglas, who wrote " The Day of Judgment's Model," in 1646.

Mrs Douglas of Ednam House, who published early this century " The Life of Gellert," an eminent German poet and writer, with a course of " Moral Lessons," taken from a French translation of the original German ; and

Margaret Douglas. The latter was more noted for being the mother of that great philosopher, Adam Smith, who having lost his father soon after his birth, was watched over and fondly cared for by his excellent mother, whose kindness and love he repaid with the most filial affection, during the lengthened period of sixty years, her life having been long spared, while he only survived her a few years. She had the delight of seeing her son patronised by the wise and great— one of the highest compliments to him being shown at a dinner where Mr Pitt and other members of Government were guests. Adam Smith arrived late, and the company had sat down to dinner, but the moment he arrived, modestly apologising for being late, they all rose to receive him. He begged them to be seated, but they declined to do so till he took his chair, "because they were all his scholars."

THE SCOTT FAMILY.

I GIVE precedence to the Scotts over the Ker and other families, as I think they were first established in Scotland. Indeed they are indigenous, whereas the Kers are of Anglo-Norman lineage, having crossed the Border and domiciled themselves here in the thirteenth century. The derivation of the name of Scott is not very well-known—indeed that of Scotland is itself involved in obscurity. Originally it was, according to the Romans, Caledonia, which name it retained during the early centuries of the Christian era, after which it was called Scotia, from, as it has been said, Scota, wife of the chief of a tribe from Ireland who invaded the country, while it has also been called Scoty, and the people Scots, which it has been alleged was given by their enemies the Picts, the early occupants of the Lowlands, or rather the lands lying between the Tay and the Tyne, because they made great use of the strongbow, from Schotton, calling themselves Schots or Scots. But, however this may be, the country was finally named Scotland when Kenneth defeated the Picts, and established himself as Monarch of the united races. I have also seen it stated that Scot signifies in Gælic, "Wanderer," an appellation probably showing attachment to a hunting and warlike life of which this Border family was, at one time, particularly fond.

The founder of the great Border House of Scott was Uchtred, Filius Scoti, or Fitz-Scott, son of a Scotchman, probably to distinguish him from others of the same name. Mr Seton in his beautiful book on "Heraldry" is quite clear on the connection, adding that the same arms are carried with various suitable differences by most of the existing branches of the House of Scott, and Sir Bernard Burke in his "Heraldic Encyclopedia," says, the arms of the Murdistons were a bend between two crescents, one estoile; while others, I believe, hold that the Border Scotts never bore the three lions' heads as their paternal ensign. Uchtred was witness to the foundation charter of the Abbeys of Holyrood and Selkirk by David II., in 1128 and 1130.*

From Uchtred also derived according to some accounts, though the history of the Border family is silent on the subject, as a younger branch, the well-known race of Scott of Balwearie, of whom was the extraordinary magician,

"The wondrous Michael Scott,"

who, Sir Walter Scott says, "was a man of much learning chiefly acquired in foreign countries," adding that he wrote a commentary upon "Aristotle," and several treatises upon natural philosophy, from which he appears to have been addicted to the abstract studies of astrology, alchemy, physiognomy, chiromancy, passing for a skilful magician. Dante mentions him as a renowned wizard in his lines thus rendered by his accomplished translator Carey:

"That other, round the loins
So slender of his shape, was Michael Scott,
Practised in every sleight of magic wile."

"Quell altro chi ne fianchi e cosi poco
Michele Scoto fu, chi veramente
Delle magiche frode seppe il gioco."

and many popular stories are told of him to this day, of his commerce with evil spirits, and of the wonders which he achieved through their agency, even to the severing of the Eildon Hills from a single cone into three. He is also said to have been a prophet, and among other events to have foretold

* It is, however, believed that from the days of Kenneth III., the barony of Scotstown in Peeblesshire had been possessed by the ancestors of Uchtred, the first representatives of the family having come from Galloway. Some interesting memorials of Scotstown will be found in the "History of Peebles-shire," by William Chambers, pp. 475-6.

the union of Scotland and England. But such was the estimation in which he was held, that he was selected by the States of the country, as one of the two ambassadors sent to Norway to bring home Queen Margaret, the maid of Norway, granddaughter and heiress of Alexander III., who unfortunately died at Orkney on her way to Scotland.

Sir Michael Scott succeeded to the lands of Balwearie, in right of his mother, who was the daughter and heiress of Sir Richard Balwearie of that ilk, and dying not long after his return from his mission to Norway, was buried at Melrose Abbey. To his grave, according to the "Lay of the Last Minstrel," the aged Monk led William of Deloraine. Some authorities, including old Satchells, the Chronicler of the Scots, assert that the magician was buried in Cumberland, of which Sir Walter makes mention in his notes to the Lay. Other individuals soon arose, assuming the name of Scott, among whom were two Bishops and a Chancellor—all three mentioned by Douglas and Nisbet as parties to ancient charters. There was also the celebrated Duns Scotus, the subtle Doctor and learned Oxford Professor, a well-known borderer, though both sides claim him, Berwickshire, however, having, it is believed, the best right to consider him her son. Among the pictures at Windsor Castle there is one called Duns Scotus in the catalogue, in the Presence Chamber, said to have been executed by a Spanish painter, but Walpole considers it ideal.* Long previously to Duns Scotus, there was another learned Scotchman called Scotus, though some have called him Irish,

---

* John Duns Scotus was born about 1264, probably at Dunse, and studied at Merton College, Oxford, where he became so distinguished in scholastic theology, civil law, logic, and mathematics, that in 1301 he was appointed Professor of Divinity. He belonged to the Franciscan Order of Friars, and was the first to propound the doctrine of the Immaculate Conception of the Virgin Mary, which he defended in a public disputation, and having refuted two hundred objections, acquired the name of the most Subtle Doctor. He founded the sect of the Scotists, who divided the theological world in the middle ages with the Thomists, or followers of Thomas Aquinas. He died of apoplexy at Cologne in November 1308.

who gloried in the name of Johannes Scotus Erigena.* He translated the works of Dionysius the Areopagite into Latin at the request of Charles the Bald, King of France, whose love of learning made his Court the great resort of the scholars of Europe, and where Erigena resided, but having incurred the displeasure of the Pope Nicholas I. by his translation, he deemed it prudent to come to England, where, it is said, he assisted Alfred the Great in restoring learning at Oxford, though biographers differ on this point. Whatever was the fate of this good and learned man, after incurring his Holiness' displeasure, it seems clear he retreated from the Court of Charles. A complete edition of his works was published in Paris in 1533. But I return to the old Border house of Scott, the head no doubt of the Scott family generally, commencing with Uchtred's lineal descendant

RICHARD,† who really took the surname of Scott, and who married, as is well established, the daughter and heiress of Murdiston of that Ilk, taking the arms of his wife, a star between two crescents on a bend azure, and laying aside the lions' heads, which some say were his own cognizance, as they were of the Balwearie Scotts, and continue to be the arms of their representative, Sir William Scott of Ancrum. It is curious that an early ancestor of this latter family acquired Balwearie, as already mentioned, by marriage, as Richard Scott did Murdiston. Richard subscribed the Ragman Roll in 1296 with other celebrated Scotchmen, who thereby swore

* Some say he was a native of Ireland, some of Erigine, on the borders of Wales, but generally received opinion points to Ayrshire as the place of his birth. He was one of the most eminent scholars of his day, and besides original works showing great erudition, he translated from Greek into Latin certain theological treatises attributed to Dionysius the Areopagite, who was supposed to have been the first Christian preacher in France. His death occurred between 876 and 886, and is said to have been caused by his students in the Abbey of Malmesbury, who resented his strict discipline so strongly, as to stab him to death with the iron styles or bodkins used in writing.

† Between Uchtred and Sir Richard, who married the heiress of Murthockstone, there intervened two Richards and a William, about whom nothing particular is recorded.

D

allegiance to Edward I. of England. He died in 1320. The next member of the Border house was MICHAEL, the Christian name of the first Balwearie Scott, and he is mentioned by Dalrymple in his "Annals." He was present at the battle of Halidon Hill on the 18th July 1333, when Edward III. defeated the Scotch forces. Michael Scott served under Archibald Douglas, the regent for King David Bruce, and made a marvellous escape, considering the great slaughter, especially among the notables.

Michael Scott was not so fortunate at the battle of Durham in 1346, where he fell fighting for his country and his sovereign David II., who was present, and sustained a defeat, with a heavy loss of some 15,000 or 20,000 men.

The next supposed representative of the Scott family was ROBERT SCOTT,* but of him little is known.

WALTER of Murdiston in Lanarkshire, Rankleburn in Selkirkshire, and Kirkurd in Peeblesshire—the latter being confirmed in a charter by King Robert II. in 1389, comes next in order. The bravery of Michael, probably his grandfather, was fully sustained by Walter, who did good service on the Borders. He was at the battle of Homildon, near Wooler, where he showed his courage, and where some say he was killed, though others say he was alive in 1413, and on the 30th July of that year gave sasine to Andrew Ker of Auldtoune Burn of the lands of Lurdenlaw. This battle was fought on Holyrood Day, 14th September 1402.

ROBERT, described as of Murdiston and Rankleburn, his successor, was apparently a pious and peaceful man, though little is related of him except that he granted some property to the monks of Melrose for the repose of his soul.†

* Sir Michael Scott left two sons, of whom Robert, the elder, continued the main line of the family, while John became ancestor of the Scotts of Harden.

† Robert exchanged, in 1415, Glenkerry for Bellenden, and in the excambion was called Lord of Rankleburn. He likewise obtained from John Inglis of Manir half the lands of Branxholm, and the charter is dated at Manir Kirk on the last of January 1420. This was the first acquisition of Branxholm, which became for ages the family seat. Robert died in 1426.

WALTER, styled of Kirkurd, his successor, was a person of a very different mould, inheriting more of his grandfather's martial character, though he had not the same opportunity of showing it. His services, however, on the Borders, under the then Earl Douglas, one of whose supporters he was, and who rewarded Scott with the lands of Lempitlaw in 1426, were of a very marked character, and on the fall of the Black Douglas, a noble house which he aided in suppressing, he rose to great eminence, obtaining from his sovereign James II. the honour of knighthood, and a grant of various lands, including Buccleugh and the remaining half of Branxholm, in exchange for which he gave Sir Robert Inglis of Manir the lands of Murdiston. It has been said that Inglis was unable to brook the insults, or to protect himself against the plundering propensities, of the English Border thieves whom Scott found himself quite able to manage. Indeed, he coolly remarked that Cumberland cattle were as good as those of Teviotdale, and as coolly commenced his rieving habits. He had now obtained complete possession of· Branxholm, where he established himself, making it the chief seat of the family, which it continued to be down to the middle of the seventeenth century.*

I have mentioned that Sir Walter Scott acquired and was styled of Buccleugh. His son David, whom we shall next treat of, obtained a charter from James III. erecting into a free barony many of his lands, for payment of a red rose as blancheferme on the festival of the nativity of St John. From that time till the reign of James VI. the titles of Kirkurd, Branxholm, and Buccleugh were used indifferently, but ultimately

* He obtained also the lands of Eckford from King James II. on 3d May 1437, besides the lands of Abbington, Pharcholm, and Glendonanrig in 1458, as well as part of the barony of Langholm. Sir Walter died between 1467 and 1470, possessed of a great part of those pastoral lands in the counties of Roxburgh and Selkirk which still form a portion of the family estates. He had married Margaret, daughter of Cockburn of Henderland, the daring freebooter who was beheaded by James V. during his raid into Ettrick Forest.

Buccleugh was established. There is a tradition, as given by the old chronicler Satchells, that two brothers came to Ettrick Forest, and when one of the kings came to hunt there, that his Majesty pursued a buck from Ettrick Heuch to the glen now called Buccleugh, about two miles above the junction of Rankleburn with the River Ettrick. Here the stag stood at bay, when one of the two brothers seized the animal by the horns, and, being a man of great power, carried the stag to the sovereign, who was a little way off.*

The successor of Sir Walter was his son DAVID, who also aided materially in the suppression of the Douglas rebellion, and otherwise rendered important services to his sovereign James III., receiving in return additional lands, as well as the honour of knighthood—a mark of distinction which was frequently given to the heads of important families in ancient times.

The title of Buccleugh seems now to have been generally adopted, Sir David, in a record dated 1487, being described as Dominus de Buccleugh when sitting in the Parliament of that year. He enlarged and strengthened the castle of Branxholm, but in March 1492, he died, leaving by his wife, a daughter of Thomas, Lord Somerville, one of the ambassadors to England to treat for the ransom of King James I. of Scotland, three sons and two daughters. He had a brother, Alexander, who fought and fell at Sauchieburn in 1488, where James III. was defeated by an army raised by the supporters of the Duke of Albany, and headed involuntarily by his own son, the Duke of Rothesay, afterwards James IV.

Sir David's eldest son, already referred to, died in the lifetime of his father, and the succession devolved on his

* The king was on the top of a steep bank at a place called Cacra Cross. The king then exclaimed—

" And for the buck thou stoutly brought
To us up that steep heuch,
Thy designation ever shall
Be John Scott in Buckscleuch."

grandson, who also bore the name of WALTER, and who was served heir in 1492. Walter, who also was knighted, according to the Fœdera, was a witness to the infeftment of Margaret, daughter of Henry VII., and wife of James IV.

That monarch, according to general belief, fell at Flodden, whither he was accompanied by Sir Walter Scott of Buccleugh and a vast number of nobles, gentry, and citizens, in fact the bravest of Scotland's sons, in his foolhardy attempt of their king to subdue the English. Sir Walter Scott though in the thickest of the fight and quite close to his sovereign, escaped with his life, but was taken prisoner. He died in 1516, leaving a son by his wife, Elizabeth, daughter of Walter Ker of Cessford and widow of Philip Rutherfurd, younger of that ilk, who succeeded him, viz. :—

SIR WALTER of Branxholm and Buccleugh, served heir to his father in 1517. He was a brave and powerful Borderer, and was in great favour with James V., whom he aided in his endeavours to escape from the thraldom of his step-father, Angus. When the king was on a Border tour in 1526, he summoned to his councils the Laird of Buccleugh, who accordingly appeared near Melrose, accompanied by one thousand of his clan, James being determined then and there to strike a blow at the iron rule of Angus. A fierce conflict took place, when the party of Angus prevailed, though only for a time, for not long afterwards the king escaped from the bondage in which he was held. The contest near Melrose was the cause of a deadly feud between the Scotts and Kers, in consequence of Sir Andrew Ker, who supported Angus, having been killed by one of Buccleugh's retainers—an Elliot—it was supposed, but not clearly ascertained. Buccleugh was nearly related to Cessford, being first cousin, a fact which augmented the melancholy nature of the occurrence which was the cause of much blood being spilt on the Borders for a long time. An endeavour was made between the two clans to stop the feuds by a bond dated in 1529; but in spite of all the attempts to heal the rupture, the animosity continued, and in the end Sir Walter Scott himself fell in a nocturnal broil in Edinburgh some twenty years afterwards, the son of Cessford, who was killed at Melrose, being with other Kers concerned in the slaughter. This occurred on 4th October 1552.

After the battle at Melrose and a subsequent one at Linlithgow, where Sir Walter Scott was present, he was prosecuted for treason, but the prosecution was quashed on the king's getting out of Angus' grasp, and he was rewarded by his Sovereign with a grant of some of the confiscated property of this member of the Red Douglas family. Sir Walter Scott was, however, too impetuous, and afterwards incurred the displeasure of the king, notwithstanding his faithful services and many acts of devotion and gallantry. But his conduct had been misunderstood, and eventually he was restored to the full enjoyment of his property and honours, though the king was then dead, but had previously to his death ordered Buccleugh's restoration.*

* Previous to the king's death, viz., in October 1533, the Earl of Northumberland had, at the instigation of King Henry VIII. of England, invaded Buccleuch's country, plundered his lands, and burned Branxholm Castle, but failed in his chief object, which was to kill the chieftain himself or take him prisoner. Buccleuch retaliated by leading 3000 men into England, who ravaged Northumberland, returning home with a great booty. In 1529, only three years after the battle of Melrose, and one year after the king had escaped from the power of Angus, his Majesty undertook the memorable expedition to the Borders with intent, as he said, to "make the rush-bush keep the cow." Before setting out, the king imprisoned some of the principal Border chiefs who were known to afford protection to the marauders. The Earl of Bothwell was arrested, and confined in Edinburgh Castle. The Lords of Home and Maxwell, the Lairds of Buccleuch, Fernieherst, and Johnston, with many others, were shut up in prison. The king at the head of 10,000 men came suddenly into Ettrick Forest, where Cockburn of Henderland, and Adam Scott of Tushiclaw, "the King of Border Thieves," were publicly executed. The king then advanced to Carlenrig in Upper Teviotdale, where Johnie Armstrong, Laird of Gilnockie was induced to meet him, at the head of thirty-six horsemen, arrayed in all the splendour of Border chivalry. The king looked sternly at the hero, and said to his attendants, "what wants that knave that a king should have?" and ordered him and his followers off to immediate execution. Armstrong made great

Buccleugh was married twice or thrice, first to Elizabeth Carmichael, and lastly to Janet Betoun of Creich, the "Ladye" of the Poet's Lay, a woman of masculine spirit, as evinced by her riding in the front of her son's clan, after her husband's murder.

> "Of noble race the Ladye came ;
> Her father was a clerk of fame,
> Of Bethune's line of Picardie."

This family were of French descent, and derived their name from a small town in Artois. I have already said that Sir Walter was slaughtered at Edinburgh in a nocturnal broil with his relative, through his hereditary enemy, Sir Walter Ker of Cessford, which was a sad termination of a life of activity and offers to the king. He would sustain himself, with forty gentlemen, ever ready at his service, on their own cost, without doing wrong to any Scotchman ; and would pledge himself to bring any subject in England, duke, earl, or baron, dead or alive, to the king within a certain day. Seeing no hope, he said proudly, "It is folly to seek grace at a graceless face ; but had I known this I should have lived upon the Borders in despite of King Harry and you both ; for I know that King Harry would down-weigh my best horse with gold to know that I were condemned to die this day." Johnie and all his men were accordingly hanged upon growing trees at a place called Carlenrig Chapel, ten miles up the Teviot from Hawick, near the high road to Langholm. They were buried in a deserted churchyard, where their graves are still shown. The country people believe that, to manifest the injustice of the execution, the trees withered away. The tradition is versified as follows by Leyden :—

> "Where rising Teviot joins the frosty lee,
> Stand the huge trunks of many a leafless tree.
> No verdant woodbine wreaths their age adorn ;
> Bare are the boughs, the gnarled roots uptorn,
> Here shone no sunbeam, fell no summer dew,
> Nor ever grass beneath the branches grew,
> Since that bold chief who Henry's power defied,
> True to his country, as a traitor died."

Buccleuch was liberated shortly after the king's return from the Borders ; but was again imprisoned for a short time in 1535, because of alleged assistance given to the English in burning Cavers and Denholm. This accusation probably had its origin in the feuds between the Scots and the Kers which had continued since the battle of Melrose in 1526.

vigour. The event is referred to as follows in the "Lay of the Last Minstrel:"—

> " Bards long shall tell
> How Lord Walter fell !
> When startled Burghers fled, afar,
> The furies of the Border war ;
> When the streets of high Dunedin
> Saw lances gleam and falchions redden,
> And heard the slogan's deadly yell—
> Then the chief of Branksome fell."

His second, but eldest surviving son by his first wife, was WILLIAM, who died before him, having married Grizzel Betoun, sister of his step-mother, through whom the line was carried on, for their son WALTER succeeded his grand-father, and his widowed mother, Grizzel, married Andrew Murray of Blackbarony, becoming the ancestrix of several eminent families, and moreover the grand-mother of Margaret Murray, "Mucklemouthed Meg," who married William Scott, son of auld Wat of Harden, and his wife Mary Scott the "Flower of Yarrow."

The Betouns were of the same family as the persecuting Cardinal. There has been some uncertainty about two previous marriages that Janet, the heroine, is supposed to have made before wedding Buccleugh, but at all events one seems to have been authenticated, viz., that to Sir Simon Preston of Craigmillar, from whom she parted before marrying Sir Walter Scott. Her son David, by Buccleugh, was a distinguished soldier, and had a high and important command at Magdeburg in Prussia, a place which suffered much during the religious wars in Germany, and which afterwards, though of great strength, was taken and sacked by Tilley, the Jesuit and celebrated general, when the most frightful atrocities were committed. David Scott must have died long before Tilley's assault; but he settled abroad, having occupied the important position of President of the Court of Justice at the Hague, and left issue, a grandson. I must, however, return to Sir Walter, who was served heir to his grandfather in 1535, at a very early age. Melville describes him as abounding with the highest qualities.

Though at first he agreed to support James VI., then an infant, he afterwards adhered to Queen Mary, continuing his devoted attachment to her in her misfortunes, and in company with his brother-in-law, Sir Thomas Kerr of Fernieherst,—who married the eldest daughter of William Scott and Grizzel Betoun, also one of Queen Mary's trusty and personal friends, —invaded England, after the murder of the Regent Moray at Linlithgow in 1570, in the hope of advancing the interests of their unfortunate mistress. That invasion, during which Scott and Kerr plundered and destroyed the country most extensively, was followed by retaliatory measures on the part of Queen Elizabeth against the two Border Barons, for she did not think the Scottish nation generally concerned in their invasion. She accordingly despatched a force under Sussex and Scrope, who invaded our border-land and destroyed the Castles of Branxholm and Fernieherst. Buccleugh and Kerr still continued hostile to the king's party, and the latter making himself particularly conspicuous, was obliged to fly, and suffer forfeiture, while Buccleugh, surrendering himself to the new regent, was speedily released, for we find he very soon set about rebuilding Branxholm, according to the inscription upon it.* This, however, he did not live to finish, the completion being accomplished by his widow Margaret Douglas, daughter of Sir David Douglas of Pittendreich, who became seventh

---

* The following is the inscription upon a stone bearing the arms of the family,—"Sir Walter Scott of Branxheim, Knyt, yoe of Sir William Scott of Kirkurd, Knyt., began ye wark upon ye 24 March, 1571 zeir, quha departed at God's pleisour ye 17 April 1574. Dame Margaret Douglas, his spous, completed the foresaid wark in October 1575." Over the arched doorway at Branxholm are the following lines:—

"In . Varld . is . nocht . Natur . hes . vrought . yt . sal . last . ay .
Thairfor . serve . God . keip . veil . ye . rod . thy . fame . sal . nocht . dekay .
Shir . Valter . Scot . of . Branxholme . Knyght .
Margaret . Douglas,
1571."

Earl Angus of the Red race, so that the relict of Buccleugh was niece of the Regent Morton. The rebuilding of Branxholm was commenced in 1571, and completed in 1576, Sir Walter dying in 1574, during its progress. Though his widow seemed to respect his memory, she did not long mourn his loss, but soon lost her heart, and that to a comparative boy, Francis Stewart, Earl Bothwell, who was probably little more than fourteen when Lady Scott married him. He was the son of the Prior of Coldingham, natural son of James V., and cousin of the notorious James Hepburn, fourth Earl Bothwell, who married Queen Mary. The nearness of Stewart, Earl Bothwell to royalty, no doubt was his ruin, and having contemplated the treasonable design of seizing James VI., in his own Palace of Holyrood, he was forfeited, though most of his property was made over to his step-son, Sir Walter Scott of Buccleugh, who must have mourned his mother's unfortunate marriage. Though she lived to have six children to Bothwell, she had the misery of being connected with a man who not only conspired against his sovereign, but who exhibited the most dissolute conduct. As I have already said, most of Bothwell's property was made over to Sir Walter Scott, his grandson, the second Earl Buccleugh being confirmed in it, but it appears by public records the latter had to give up the whole, except the Liddesdale estate, to Bothwell's son, who got a rehabilitation, though he soon squandered all; and with his son, who was a trooper during the Civil Wars, the family became extinct, or at any rate sunk into oblivion.

Sir Walter Scott, son of Sir Walter and Margaret Douglas, and step-son of Bothwell, succeeded his father in 1574, when very young. Probably he was not much more than twenty when he was appointed Warden of the West Marches, showing at that early age all the courage of his race, and winning the title of the "Bold Buccleugh," by the subsequent gallantry and bravery he displayed, and finally a coronet, which he did not wear long, for he died in 1611, about five years after receiving the honour of the Peerage. Buccleugh married Mary Ker of Cessford, sister of Robert, well known as Habbie Ker, the valiant and resolute Warden of the Borders, who was created a Peer much about the same time as his brother-in-law. Buccleugh's wife was great-grand-daughter of Cessford who was killed at Melrose in 1526, when Buccleugh's great-grandfather fought against Cessford, whose son either murdered, or was accessory to the slaughter of Buccleugh in Edinburgh, in 1552, as before noticed. But I go on with the history of Lord Scott of Buccleugh, whose valiant conduct made a wonderful impression upon Queen Elizabeth, though she did not relish his acts. It is recorded with reference to his raid into England to rescue Kinmont Willie, that she asked him how he dared to undertake such a hazardous and bold enterprise, when he replied, "What is there, madam, that a man dare not do?" This answer so impressed Her Majesty, that she exclaimed, "This is a man indeed! With ten thousand such men our brother of Scotland might shake the firmest throne in Europe." This occurred during the concluding part of Elizabeth's reign, between October 1597 and February 1598, at which latter period our hero was in England; and even after King James' accession to the British throne in 1603, the Borderers, so long accustomed to rapine, were most difficult to be brought under authority, and in order to wean them from their predatory habits, Scott carried over a regiment of the bravest and most desperate of them to Holland, to aid Prince Maurice of Nassau, Governor of the Low Countries, in driving out the Spaniards. This being done, and other operations of the Prince who was the Wellington of his time, being accomplished, the Bold Buccleugh returned with great *eclát* to his native land, receiving a royal letter recognising the value and importance of his military services, which were more substantially rewarded by a further accession of land. But one of the most daring acts of this great chief, was the release of Kinmont Willie, who was imprisoned in Carlisle Castle in breach of a truce then existing. Buccleugh summoned his men to meet him at a spot close to the

Borders, and ten or twelve miles from Carlisle. The party was composed of Scotts, the only exception being Gilbert Elliot of Stobs, as the ballad says—

> "He call'd him forty marchmen bauld
> I trow they were of his ain name,
> Except Sir Gilbert Elliot, call'd
> The Laird of Stobs, I mean the same."

The Elliots were supporters or retainers of the Buccleughs, but Sir Gilbert having married one of the clan, the daughter of Wat Scott of Harden, of Border fame, this gave him a double claim to go to the rescue, especially as old Harden, his father-in-law, would be sure to be one of the band. They were successful in their mission, and so the ballad goes on—

> "We crept on knees, and held our breath,
> Till we placed the ladders against the wa';
> And very ready was Buccleugh himsell
> To mount the first before us a'.
> He has ta'en the watchman by the throat,
> And flung him down upon the head—
> Had there not been peace between our land,
> Upon the other side thou wad'st gaed;
> Now sound out trumpets! quo' Buccleugh,
> Let's waken Lord Scroop right merrilie;
> Then loud the warden's trumpet blew—
> O wha dar meddle wi' me.
> Then speedilye to work we gaed,
> And raised the slogan ane and a'*
> And cut a hole thro' a sheet of lead,
> And so we wan to the castle ha';
> Wi' coulters, and wi' forehammers
> We garr'd the bars bang merrilie,
> Until we cam' to the inner prison,
> Where Willie o' Kinmont he did lie—
> Then shoulder high, with shout and cry,
> We bore him doun the ladder lang;
> At every stride, Red Rowan made
> I wot the Kinmont's airms played clang.
> We scarce had won the Straneshaw bank
> When a' the Carlisle bells were rung,
> And a thousand men in horse and foot

---

* Bellenden, the war-cry of Buccleugh, because Bellenden was their usual place of rendezvous.

> Cam' wi' the keen Lord Scroop alang.
> Buccleugh has turned to Eden Water,
> Even when it flowed frae bank to brim;
> And he has plunged in wi' a' his band
> And safely swam them thro' the stream.
> He turned him on the other side,
> And at Lord Scroop his glove flung he—
> If ye like na my visit in merrie England,
> In fair Scotland come visit me."

The Bold Buccleugh, who was raised to the Peerage of Scotland, with the title of Lord Scott of Buccleugh, on the 16th March 1606, with the secondary title of Lord Scott of Whitchester and Eskdale, finished his active and distinguished earthly career on the 5th December 1611, having been longer lived than several of his predecessors. His son

WALTER, who also served with great distinction in Holland, where he had the command of a regiment under the States,—against the Spaniards who were conquered, and obliged to abandon the Low Countries,—married Lady Mary Hay, fourth daughter of the ninth Earl of Errol, and died in 1633.

He was a great favourite of King James I. of England, who advanced him to an earldom in 1619. No doubt there was an impression that his father's valour and magnanimity had not been sufficiently requited, for in addition to the earldom, he was endowed with other lands, and the patent of his Peerage was extended to heirs-*female*, the direct heirs-male of this and the previous generation being few. Indeed the earl and his father the Bold Buccleugh had only one son each, and the son and successor of the earl had but two daughters. He died of apoplexy in London, November 21, 1633.

FRANCIS, SECOND EARL, succeeded his father at about the early age of seven, and died when only twenty-four.* There

---

* It is thought by some writers that there must be some mistake about the age of Earl Francis, seeing that the dates of his first public appearances, the position he then at once took, and the number and ages of his children, seem hardly consistent with so youthful a career. He lost all the Bothwell estates, which were restored to that family, except the extensive domain of Liddesdale, but he acquired, besides Dalkeith, the large territory of Eskdale, and on the 7th of April 1643, had a charter of the barony of Langholm. At first

was therefore little time for the development of those rare qualities which were inherent in him. He was devotedly attached to Charles I., and in about two years after Buccleugh's death, which happened in 1651 very suddenly, the Protector imposed a heavy fine upon his property for his loyalty to his unfortunate sovereign. The fine was the largest made, being about equal to £200,000, according to the present value of money. No doubt he had large possessions, which had been much increased during his short incumbency, for he acquired the baronies of Dalkeith and Langholm—the former from the Morton family, whose principal seat it had been for centuries. Earl Douglas, during the reign of James II. of Scotland, tried to take it from his kinsman, in consequence of his having espoused the cause of the Monarch in opposition to that of the Douglases, the rivals of the throne, but did not succeed. It was the principal residence of the Regent Morton, in whose time it was called the "Lion's Den." But the old residence, formerly a fortress, gave way to the present magnificent palace, which was erected early last century, or at any rate then repaired and improved, when it was made one of the chief residences of the ducal family, as it has ever since been.

The widow of Earl Francis, a daughter of Lord Chancellor Rothes, and relict of Lord Balveny, became the third wife of David, second Earl Wemyss, by whom she had a daughter who became Countess of Wemyss; and her son, who

he took part with the Covenanters, in the Civil War, and in 1643, when he could be only seventeen years of age, he sat in the Governing Committee of Estates. In 1644 his regiment went with the Earl of Leven into England, where they took part in the battle of Marston Moor. In all public events of the period he acted a prominent part, on the side of the Covenanters, except that, under date 9th March 1649, Sir James Balfour says, "The Parliament of Scotland passed a most strange acte this monthe, abolishing the patronages of kirkes, which pertained to laymen, since ever Christianity was planted in Scotland ; Francis, Earl of Buccleuche, and some others, protested against this acte as wrangous, and altogether derogatory to the just rights of the nobility and gentry of the kingdom of Scotland, and so departed the Parliament House." The withdrawal must have been only temporary, as he continued to be one of the most trusted of the Presbyterian leaders, and was very active in bringing home the young King Charles II.

was the third Earl Wemyss, and Lord High-Admiral at the time of the Union, married Lady Anne Douglas, daughter of the first Duke of Queensberry, whose descendant, the ninth earl, succeeded, as heir-male of Lady Anne, to the large estates of Neidpath in 1810, on the death of the fourth Duke, called Old Q. The Earl Buccleugh had two daughters, Mary and Anne, who severally, in succession, inherited the honours and extensive property. The first was

MARY, born 1648, who succeeded as Countess of Buccleugh. Her grandmother Margaret Douglas, married a very young man, Francis Stewart Earl Bothwell, for her second husband, but Countess Mary wedded a young lad of only thirteen or fourteen, Walter Scott of Highchester, afterwards Lord Tarras, but she, unlike her ancestrix, was only eleven. This marriage, which was brought about by her mother, who, as already stated, became Countess of Wemyss, was no doubt prompted by the fear of abduction on account of the immense wealth of the young heiress. The minister of Wemyss married them by licence, without banns, the latter form being no great security, for a proclamation, though three Sundays are by law required for its performance, may, by custom, be reduced to one—so that a marriage by banns in Scotland, if qualified by residence, may be arranged and completed within twenty-five hours, or at the most forty hours, only a few persons knowing of it, for the precentor, if well paid, can get the proclamation published before the congregation assembles, for the first, second, and third time in one breath. This farcical proceeding, Lord Campbell thought might have been improved by publication on the *smiddy* door. The license under which Countess Mary was married, seems to have afforded little better security. The ceremony was performed in secret, and the Presbytery from which the license was obtained, was accused of irregularity for granting it, but on an appeal to a higher Court, absolution was given under an Act of Assembly, which it appears, allowed such marriages to be celebrated, on the ground of necessity, in the fear of rape.

Whether Walter Scott, the happy youth and bridegroom, was the nearest heir male of the family, I know not, as Scott of Scotstarvit claimed the honour, and considered the "liasance" lowering to Countess Mary's dignity, which he evidently thought would have been better consulted had she married into his family. After a good deal of opposition and discussion, the marriage was allowed to stand good, and as the Restoration had just taken place, the Countess Wemyss— her mother—took the young couple to London to be introduced at Court, soon after which the husband was created Earl Tarras * and Baron Alemore for life. But the youthful Countess was not destined to enjoy her Estates, or her marriage, for she died in the following year—1661, without issue, being only twelve years old, or as generally stated in her thirteenth year, her husband being but fifteen, or in his sixteenth year. Lord Tarras survived his young wife's death some thirty years, or more. He was accused of being implicated in the rebellion of Monmouth, who became the husband of his sister-in-law, Countess Anne, the successor of her sister in the honours and estates of Buccleugh, and was convicted and condemned, his titles and estates being forfeited—Lord Tarras was also a witness in the trial of his uncle, Robert Baillie of Jerviswood, in 1684, who was executed, but Lord Tarras escaped with his life, his forfeiture being also annulled, and he lived to see the Revolution accomplished, and to engage in it. His Lordship during his troubles, after being the widower of Countess Mary of Buccleugh, several years, married a second wife—another heiress, Miss Hepburn of Humbie, and by her had, with other children, a son Gideon, who succeeded to Highchester, but not of course to the titles, which were only for his life.

* From a stream which flows into the Esk, the name of which is commemorated—with reference to its rocky bed and precipitous falls in the following rhyme :—

"Was ne'er ane droun'd in Tarras, nor yet in doubt,
For ere the head can win doun, the harns are out.

The second daughter, Countess Anne, was born in 1651 at Dundee, a town at one time second only to Edinburgh, and which afforded shelter to many during the Commonwealth, but which was taken by Monk and plundered, having been a few years previously much injured by Montrose. It has again become one of the most important and wealthy towns of Scotland, and the British Association held its meeting there some years since, and was ably presided over by Countess Anne's great-great-great-grandson, the present much beloved and respected Duke of Buccleugh.

Anne succeeded her sister Mary when only ten years old, and she married in less than two years the Duke of Monmouth, who was but fourteen. They had six children, the first being born about nine years after their marriage, when the Duchess was twenty. Never did a handsomer couple appear at Hymen's altar, and their extreme youth added interest to the scene.

Monmouth was the son of Charles II. and Lucy Walters, a Welsh girl of great personal attractions, whom the king met with when a wanderer in Holland. Macaulay says that the lady had several admirers, and was not supposed to be cruel to any. The handsome Henry Sidney, First Earl Romney, who was in attendance upon the exiled Prince, was supposed, as says the National Portrait Catalogue, to have been the favoured lover of Lucy, and Father of Monmouth, both having had a mole on the lip. However that may be, he was the reputed son of Charles II., who, on His Majesty's restoration, treated him with the affection of a fond parent. Indeed it has been said, and some think truly, that Charles was privately married to Lucy Walters. The Duke of York did not of course favour this rumour, though when His Royal Highness became a Romanist, the story became important. A certain black box was said to contain the contract of marriage, but the deed never was forthcoming, and the king, no doubt pressed by his brother, declared to the Council that Monmouth had no claims to legitimacy, which of course

E

settled the question. Had it been otherwise, there was no Royal Marriage Act in those times to have prevented his being king, which the people would have hailed, for though a libertine, he had acquired great popularity with them by the possession of qualities always dear to a nation—generosity and courage, united to a handsome person, and affable and courteous manners. Queen Henrietta, who was fond of him, brought him to London in 1662, after which he was created Duke of Monmouth, and in the following year married the Countess of Buccleugh, one of the richest and finest women of her time. On his marriage he assumed the name of Scott, and was created Duke of Buccleugh, Earl Dalkeith, and Lord Scott. He had other high dignities conferred upon him, as well as an important military command, but he had a sad end, which the mistaken kindness of his friends helped to bring about, for it was folly, after Charles's solemn asseveration, to support the Duke in his foolish and rash enterprise, which was sure to cost him his life, as it did in 1685. Such was the devotion of the people to their hero, that many, after he was beheaded, believed he was living, that a person like him had paid the penalty for their Protestant Duke, and that his Grace would soon appear as Monarch. A knave took advantage of this and collected a large sum of money. Sundry ballads represented Monmouth as alive, and predicted his return—one being as follows:—

> Though this is a dismal story
> Of the fall of my design,
> Yet I'll come again in glory,
> If I live till eighty-nine;
> For I'll have a stronger army,
> And of ammunition store.

The Duchess of Buccleugh, Anne Scott, bore with extraordinary firmness, and composure, the tragical fate of her husband, but her youngest daughter and namesake, felt her father's sad end so keenly, though only a child of ten, that she pined and died a few weeks after him. Monmouth, or rather

Buccleugh, had not lived with his Duchess for some years, but he professed the greatest attachment to her Grace, who, he declared, was opposed to his designs and irregularities.

> For she had known adversity
> Tho' born in such a high degree;
> In pride of power, in beauty's bloom,
> Had wept o'er Monmouth's bloody tomb.

The interview with his family before his death was touching in the extreme, though all, except the daughter referred to, went through it with wonderful composure, but the harrowing accounts of the bungling manner in which the executioner (really called John Ketch) performed his duty, added keenness to their sorrow, as well as excited general disgust.

The king generously and feelingly gave the Duchess a gift of all the personal and real estates of the Duke, which had been forfeited; and after a time—say in about three years—she married Lord Cornwallis, ancestor of the great Marquis of imperishable fame, but the marriage was dissolved in about ten years, by the death of the noble Lord, to whom she had three children, one of whom—*Lady* Isabella Scott, succeeded to the Melrose *Lordship*,—her only brother having died,—including the Bailiery and Patronage of the Church, and, under the jurisdiction act of 1747, she got £1200 for her rights, instead however of £5000 being her full claim. She died very soon after the arrangement was made.

Her mother, the Duchess, survived her second husband some thirty years, residing occasionally at Dalkeith, where she lived in great splendour, conscious of her princely connection, and indeed Dr Johnson mentions that she was remarkable for inflexible perseverance in her demand to be treated as a princess.*

---

* In 1675, twelve years after his marriage, Monmouth, in order to stock the lands of Buccleuch on the Borders, got licence to import 4800 nolt of a year old, and 200 horses from Ireland, which was not then allowable by law. The Sheriff Depute of Roxburghshire, W. Scott of Minto, was cautioner that the number should not be exceeded, but as some of the oxen were more than

Dalkeith was occupied by Prince Charles in 1745 for two days when Edinburgh was taken by the Prince, whom the then Duke of Buccleugh opposed, and it has been honoured with more welcome visits from George IV., and our present gracious Queen, in 1822 and 1842 respectively.

The Duchess died in 1732, aged eighty, and was interred at Dalkeith. Her eldest son died young, but her second, James, Lord Dalkeith, grew to man's estate, and married Lady Henrietta Hyde, though he also died before his mother, the Duchess. He served in Flanders after the Revolution, but returned to Scotland, where he discharged the duties of his station with much credit, leaving a son FRANCIS who succeeded his grandmother, as Second Duke of Buccleugh.

But before saying anything about Francis, I must refer to his uncle, Henry Scott, third son of Monmouth and Duchess Anne, who was created Earl of Deloraine and Viscount Hermitage in 1706, which titles became extinct one hundred and one years afterwards, by the failure of issue on the part of the fourth

a year old, the Sheriff was fined £200 sterling. This importation of stock had become necessary to make up the loss sustained by the district in "the thirteen drifty days of March," which occurred in 1674. Another event of this kind is believed to have happened in 1620. The ground was covered with frozen snow when it began, and for thirteen days and nights, the drift never ceased, nor did the sheep break their fast. The cold was intense to a degree never before remembered. About the fifth and sixth days of the storm, the young sheep began to fall into a torpid state, and all that were so affected in the evening died over night. The intensity of the frost would often cut them off when in that state quite instantaneously. About the ninth and tenth days, the shepherds began to build up huge semi-circular walls of their dead, in order to afford some shelter for the remainder of the living; but they availed little, for about the same time they were seen frequently tearing at each other's wool with their teeth. When the drift ceased, there was, on many a high-lying farm, not a living sheep to be seen; and about nine-tenths of all the sheep in the south of Scotland were destroyed. In Eskdale Moor, which sustains 20,000 sheep, only forty young wedders were left on one farm, and five old ewes on another. The farm of Phawhope. remained twenty years without a tenant, after which it was let at the annual rent of a grey coat and a pair of hose. On Bowerhope, a farm pertaining to Sir Patrick Scott of Thirlstone, all that remained of 900 sheep was one black ewe, which some idle dogs chased into St Mary's Loch, where it was drowned.

Earl. The first Peer, Henry, occupied a distinguished position in the army, and otherwise, and was so noted for his polished manners that Dr Young in describing a conceited person says :—

> He only thinks himself, so far from vain !
> Stanhope in wit, in breeding Deloraine.

The last Earl of Deloraine, on the other hand, dissipated the family estates, and latterly subsisted on an annuity saved from the wreck of his property; his wife, by whom he had no issue, having been long separated from him, and dying in a Convent in France. I now revert to *Francis, second Duke,* whose amiable qualities, as well as zeal for the Protestant succession, are described on the occasion of his being restored, in 1743, to two of the forfeited honours of his grandfather. viz., the Earldom of Doncaster, and Barony of Tynedale, which enabled him at once to obtain a Seat in the House of Lords as a British Peer. This noble Duke married Lady Jane Douglas, daughter of James, second Duke of Queensberry, through whom the Buccleugh family succeeded, on the death of the fourth Duke, to Drumlanrig and other property in Dumfries-shire, as heir-of-line, and in virtue of an entail by the second Duke, and also to the Dukedom of Queensberry, the Marquisate and lesser titles, by the renewed patent of 1706, which extended the remaindership to the heirs male. or female, descended from the first Earl of Queensberry, going to his male kinsman, and heir-at-law, Charles Douglas of Kilhead, whose grand-nephew is now incumbent of the Marquisate.

Francis II., Duke of Buccleugh, was succeeded, 1751, by his grandson, Henry, the son of Francis, Earl Dalkeith, by Lady Caroline Campbell, eldest daughter and co-heiress of John. Duke of Argyll and Greenwich, who died *vita patris.* Their grandson,

HENRY, third Duke of Buccleugh, was distinguished for his agricultural knowledge and pursuits. He was the intimate friend of Dr Adam Smith, the philosopher and political economist, whose acquaintance and principles he valued; but what is better, he was the friend of the poor, who, notwithstanding his exalted rank, had easy access to him; and he was, moreover, always ready to take an active part in any scheme of benevolence and humanity which his princely income enabled him substantially to assist. He held various offices of trust and high position, and in the performance of the duties attached to them always showed the greatest attention and most courteous manners.*

The Duke married the only daughter of the last Duke of

* Henry, the third Duke of Buccleuch, was born on the 13th of September 1746, and succeeded to the title and estates at the age of six years, on the death of his grandfather in 1752. In 1755, the widow of Lord Dalkeith, and mother of the young Duke, married Charles Townshend, who interested himself greatly in the education of his stepson. The youthful Duke was first sent to Eton, and is mentioned with distinction by the Earl of Carlisle, who has left notes of his schoolfellows there. In March 1764, the Duke set out to travel on the Continent with Dr Adam Smith, of whom he afterwards thus kindly wrote :—" Having spent near three years together, without the slightest disagreement or coolness on my part, with every advantage that could be expected from the society of such a man, we continued to live in fellowship till the hour of his death; and I shall always remain with the impression of having lost a friend whom I loved and respected, not only for his great talents, but for every private virtue." On the 2d of May 1767, when he was twenty-one years of age, the young Duke married Lady Elizabeth Montagu, three years his senior, only daughter of George, Duke of Montagu; and in autumn of the same year the Duke and Duchess, with Lady Frances Scott, sister of his Grace, came to Dalkeith Palace, which the Duke had been prevented by Charles Townshend from visiting previously, lest he should become too fond of Scotland. The Duke's stepfather died just at the time, after an illness of only a few days, which tended to mar the festivities; but still there were great demonstrations of welcome all over the Buccleuch estates, which had been fifteen years without a resident owner. Dr Carlyle of Inveresk had traversed the route from Hawick to Langholm at the time when Eskdale and Liddesdale were all excitement over the coming ducal visit, and had written a copy of verses for the *Scots Magazine* as a kind of poetic welcome. The lines appeared anonymously, but Dr Gregory suspected the authorship, and it was admitted by Dr Carlyle. The poem is entitled, "Verses on his Grace the Duke of Buccleuch's Birthday, September 1767." Old Father Tweed is represented as hearing a great disturbance, on which he uplifts his watery head and asks what is the matter,

Montagu,* and their second son, Henry James, succeeded to the barony of Montagu which was revived, and to the property of the family on the death of his Grace of Montagu. In consequence of the Baron dying without male issue, the title became extinct, while the property, which was large, went to the eldest daughter, who married the Earl of Home, and who has since succeeded to the immense estates of the house of Douglas (so fiercely contested about a hundred years ago) in right of her mother, who was sister to the three last Lords Douglas, none of whom left male issue. Thus this branch of the Buccleugh family, and the main stem itself, have acquired large Douglas possessions.

CHARLES WILLIAM, Earl Dalkeith, succeeded as fourth Duke of Buccleugh on the death of his father in 1812. This nobleman suffered from delicate health, and having survived his father only about seven years, had little opportunity of distinguishing himself in the dukedom. There is, therefore, no occasion to dwell further on this amiable Duke, except to state that he married a daughter of Thomas Townsend, Viscount Sydney, and that by her he had three sons and six daughters. His eldest son, George Henry, a youth of much promise, died at Eton College in his eleventh year, in 1808. when his sons Yarrow, Ettrick, Esk, and Liddel, make reply. Yarrow is the first to speak and narrates his joyful tale in the following rhapsody:—

"A Scott ! a noble Scott ! again appears,
The wished-for blessing of thy hoary years !
Hark how the impetuous Esk in thunder roars !
Hark how the foaming Liddel beats his shores !
A Scott ! a Scott ! triumphantly they cry ;
A Scott ! a Scott ! a thousand hills reply ;
The night is passed, again the day 's at hand
To light this dark and long-deserted land.
Be glad ye hills, rejoice each living spring !
Ye muses wake, and every valley sing !"

* Dean Ramsay says she was remarkable for her dignity and affability. She was present at a dinner to the tenantry, and good-humouredly remarked to one of the guests, who was eating boiled beef without cabbage, that boiled beef and greens seemed naturally to go together, and wondered why he did not take it. The farmer, however, objected, remarking that your Grace " maun alloo it's a verra windy vegetable."

The Duchess was a lovely, intellectual, graceful, and benevolent woman. Sir Walter Scott bore enthusiastic testimony to her graces and merits, and all who came in contact with her spoke of her benevolence, which an author has stated gave more the idea of an angelic visitor than of an earthly being. She was, indeed, the prototype of Allan Cunningham's "Lady Anne." This peerless woman died a few years before her husband. Scott, in one of his letters to Miss Seward, observes that if requested by the Countess of Dalkeith (she had not then become Duchess) he would write a poem on a broomstick. Little did he think he would write her epitaph.

His second, Walter Francis, became Earl Dalkeith, and at his Grace's death in 1819 succeeded as

Fifth Duke of Buccleugh, being a nobleman devoted to his country's weal, and whose footprints bid fair to be left on the sands of time. He holds the second oldest dukedom in Scotland, but he ought to have been created a British duke long ere this, his high position and his singularly good and patriotic life entitling him to the highest place of honour in the country. He sits in the house of Lords as Earl Doncaster.

I have now done with what may be called the main or principal line of the great border family of Scott, and though it failed in the male side upon the death of Earl Francis in 1652, still his daughters, to whom the estates and titles could and did descend, as we have seen, became the representatives, and the issue of Countess Anne, the younger, who married, carried on the line, and having adopted the old family surname, the name of Scott will, it is to be hoped, long be perpetuated as the ducal house of Buccleugh.

Other Branches of the Scott Family.

I do not mean to go into the question of chieftainship since the failure, in 1652, of the male representation in the family of Buccleugh about which, according to a note in Sir Walter Scott's Life, there is great dispute among heraldic writers.

I shall only refer to some of the leading branches of the older Border Scott tree, the principal probably being that of Harden, descended through Sinton, but the Scotts of Ancrum, represented by Sir William, descend from Michael, the younger brother of Richard, the first of the old Buccleugh stock, as some writers have it—though here again there are differences of opinion—in the latter part of the thirteenth century; and several of that branch were distinguished. I should also mention that the Scotts of Scotstarvet, in Fifeshire, like the Balwearies, the original descendants of Michael, and ancestor of the Ancrums, came off later—say in the sixteenth century—from the Buccleugh stem, springing from David of Allanhaugh and Whitchester, who was the second son of Sir David of Buccleugh, the eleventh baron. Some of this branch—I mean the Scotstarvets—were celebrated; and there was also a noted woman of the race named Marjory, who married Lord Stormont. It is supposed she took with her the ability of her house, as she produced an illustrious Chief-Justice called the Silver-tongued Murray, who, on the Stormont side, sprung from an ordinary Scotch peer's family—the eleventh of a brood of fourteen children raised on oatmeal porridge—as it has been said.

Marjory was the daughter of David Scott of Scotstarvet, a man of great sagacity and prudence, and great-granddaughter of that eminent patron of literature, Sir John Scott, the author of the curious but sarcastically clever book called " The Staggering State of Scotch Statesmen."

Another was General Scott, M.P. for Fife, last male of the Scotstarvets, upon whose death his daughter, the Duchess of Portland, wife of the fourth Duke, succeeded to the representation and estates of the family, assuming the name of Scott, which that ducal house also took and perpetuates. But I revert to the early

HARDEN SCOTTS, descended from Buccleugh through the Scotts of Sinton—the latter's ancestor being, it has been thought, son or grandson of Michael; and though, by a note of Sir W. Scott's, the original stock of Sintons continued for some time, they ended in George Scott, who had no heirs.

WILLIAM SCOTT, first of Harden, was a younger brother of Walter of Sinton, from whom Harden was acquired, the superior being George, third Lord Home, who confirmed the grant in 1535. He died in 1563, and was succeeded by that renowned and jolly freebooter,

AULD WAT, of whom so many traditional anecdotes are extant. This old marauder married Mary Scott, the flower of Yarrow, remarkable for her beauty.

Walter Scott, commonly designated "Auld Wat," succeeded his father as Baron of Harden in the year 1563. The situation of his castle was one of the best on the Borders, and was immeasurably superior to either Branxholm or Hermitage. The high ground on the east side of Borthwick Water is broken up into promontories by the numerous streams which carry off the surplus water from an extensive moorland between the valleys of the Borthwick and the Ale. One of the deepest and darkest glens seems to have been so frequented by hares as to have acquired the name of Hare-dean, afterwards contracted into Harden. At the present day it is a darksome and eerie glen, with banks so steep as to be almost precipitous, which are overgrown with sturdy old trees and tangled underwood. Another glen of equal depth converges so as to form a tongue of high land on which is situated the house of Harden, so close to the edge of the precipice that one looks from the windows to a depth of probably two hundred feet. Just beneath the castle, the glen facing toward the south opened its capacious jaws to admit the cattle which Auld Wat and his followers were in the habit of driving from Cumberland. From the castle turrets, also, the old reiver could survey the hills as far southward as the English Border, so that when beacons were lighted, the lords of Harden were among the first to see, and were always foremost in the fray.

Though the house of Harden occupies the old situation, it is difficult to trace any remnant of Auld Wat's fortress; for though it is in the castellated style, and is of various ages, the oldest date about the building is 1671, more than forty years after the old hero was in his grave. Nor have we any portrait of the old warrior whose name has been the theme of so much ballad literature, and about whom his kinsman, Sir Walter, collected so many characteristic stories. In possession of Lord Polwarth at Mertoun House is a pair of gilt spurs, apparently more for ornament than use, which may have been the identical pair that the lady of the mansion was in the habit of serving up when it was necessary that her lord should ride for fresh provisions; and Lord Polwarth has likewise a huge horn which may have served as a bugle, though it looks more like a ponderous powder-horn, with a wooden stopper, now crumbling away with age. It used to be said that one of Auld Wat's spurs was used as a knocker for the door at Harden, and there certainly was an old knocker somewhat in the form of a spur, which is now at Mertoun House, but its peculiar form had only been due to a freak of the laird or the artist, as it had really never been used as a spur.

It was in the year 1563 that Walter Scott succeeded his father, William Scott, as Laird of Harden. In 1567 he married Mary Scott, the Flower of Yarrow, daughter of John, or, as others say, Philip Scott of Dryhope, near St Mary's Loch. By their marriage-contract the father-in-law was bound to find Scott of Harden in horse-meat and man's-meat at his tower of Dryhope for a year and a day; but five barons pledged themselves that at the expiry of that period the son-in-law should remove without attempting to continue in possession by force. A notary-public signed for all the parties to the bond, as not one of them could sign his name. Harden, on his part, agreed to give Dryhope the profits of the first Michaelmas moon—a curious illustration of the unsettled character of the age. By the Flower of Yarrow Auld Wat had six daughters and four sons, of whom the second was killed in a fray by one of the Scotts of Newhouse, or Gilmanscleuch. Harden's sons prepared to avenge their brother's death, but, according to tradition, the father confined them all in a dungeon of his tower, then hasted to Edinburgh, obtained a grant of the lands from the king, returned home, liberated his sons, and showed them the charter. Then he cried, "To horse, lads! and let us take possession. The lands of Gilmanscleuch are well worth a dead son."

The lands of Harden were extensive, but were not calculated to produce grain, or afford much wealth of any kind.

> "But what the niggard ground of wealth denied,
> From fields more bless'd his fearless arms supplied."

When the harvest moon shone clear and bright, the clang of the warder's horn was heard, and the men sallied forth to provide their winter stores. It is narrated that when the last bullock brought from English pastures had been consumed, the Flower of Yarrow placed on the table a pair of clean spurs, to indicate that her lord and his retainers must ride for their next meal. A characteristic trait of the old freebooter is mentioned by Sir Walter, in a note to the "Border Minstrelsy." On one occasion when the cows of the little settlement were driven out, the chieftain heard the cow-herd call on some one to let out Harden's cow. "Harden's cow!" echoed the affronted chief; "Is it come to that pass? By my faith, they shall soon say Harden's kye." The horn was sounded, and out sallied the raiders, who soon brought home a bow of kye and a bassened bull. When returning with his booty, the chief passed a large haystack, which he thought would be very useful for winter forage, but as no means of transport were at hand, he left it with the address, "By my saul, had ye but four feet, ye should not stand long there."

Auld Wat was prominent in several border frays. Somewhere about 1582, as narrated in a ballad in the "Border Minstrelsy," the captain of Bewcastle, in Cumberland, had ventured into Teviotdale "to drive a prey," and had carried off the kye of Jamie Telfer o' the Fair Dod Head, who complained to "auld Buccleuch" at Branxholm. Orders were forthwith issued to raise the clan, who were placed in command of Willie Scott, supposed to have been an illegitimate son of Buccleuch; and among other orders, they are told to

> "Warn Wat o' Harden and his sons,
> With them will Borthwick water ride."

Harden seems to have been second in command; for, when the reivers had been overtaken and attacked, and Willie Scott had been "stricken ower the head, and through the knapscap the sword has gane," it is added—

> " And Harden grat for very rage
> When Willie on the grund lay slain;
> But he's ta'en off his gude steel cap,
> And thrice he waved it in the air.
> The Dinlay snaw was ne'er mair white,
> Nor the lyart locks of Harden's hair;
> 'Revenge! revenge!' Auld Wat 'gan cry;
> 'Fye, lads, lay on them cruellie!
> We'll ne'er see Teviotdale again
> Or Willie's death avenged sall be.'"

He was one on whom Buccleuch chiefly relied in his famous raid into England to rescue Kinmont Willie from Carlisle Castle in 1596. The adventure seemed so desperate that the laird of Buccleuch desired to employ only the younger sons and brothers of the clan, but exceptions were made in the case of the lairds of Harden and Commonside, and Sir Gilbert Elliott of Stobbs. Previous to this date, however, in 1592, Auld Wat took part with Bothwell in the attempt to seize the King at Falkland, which was unsuccessful; and authority was given by the King and the Privy Council to Walter Scott of Goldielands and Gideon Murray of Elibank to demolish the houses and fortalices of Harden and Dryhope, belonging to Walter Scott of Harden. This order seems to have been effectually carried out: and though Auld Wat lived thirty-seven years afterwards, there is no evidence that he rebuilt the castle, though he probably did so in some shape. In 1603, when King James ascended the English throne, raids into England became less common, but for some time there were disputes on both sides of the Border. In 1611, for example, a fray took place between the Scotts of Harden and the followers of Sir Gideon Murray of Elibank, when the retainers of Harden were overpowered, and the heir-apparent, William Scott, was carried a prisoner to Elibank Castle, on the banks of the Tweed. Close to the tower stood the doomtree, on which it was decided that Willie Scott should be hanged till he was dead; but the lady of Sir Gideon considerately suggested that the culprit was handsome, was unmarried, and was the heir to a fine estate, and that they had three unmarried daughters not conspicuous for their good looks. The hint was approved, and it was agreed that young Harden's life should be spared on condition that he married the plainest of the three, who was conspicuous for her "muckle mouth," only her name was not "Meg," as is commonly believed, but Agnes. After some hesitation the young laird consented to link his fate with that of the lady, and the marriage-contract was instantly executed on the parchment of a drum. The marriage took place in 1611, and the offspring of it included four sons and three daughters. Auld Wat had married as his second wife, in 1598, Margaret, daughter of Edgar of Wedderlie, and relict of William Spottiswood of that ilk, by whom he had a daughter, Margaret, married to David Pringle, younger of Galashiels, and afterwards to Sir William Macdougall of Makerstoun. The veteran warrior was received with favour by King James VI., from whom he obtained several charters, dated 1603, 1607, and 1608. He lived to a great age, and died about the year 1629, twenty-six years after the accession of James to the English throne, having consequently outlived the time when raids into England were considered respectable. Of his surviving sons William was his successor at Harden, Hugh was progenitor of the Scotts of Gala, and Francis married Isabel, sister of Sir Walter Scott of Whitslaid, from whom are descended the modern family of the Scotts of Sinton.

The eldest son of the old Freebooter was WILLIAM, who

was knighted by King James during the life-time of his father, and who acquired Mertoun, sometime about the middle of the seventeenth century from the Hetlies, the latter family having got it from the Haliburtons, Barons of Mertoun and proprietors of Dryburgh.*

The first Sir William of Harden and Mertoun had a younger brother HUGH of DEUCHAR, who married the eldest daughter and heiress of Sir James Pringle of Galashiels and Smailholm, by whom he acquired the Gala property (the other being sold) which continues in his family, the present proprietor of Gala being his great-great-grandson. In right of their succession to the Pringle estate, the Gala family are the heirs-of-line of the oldest and main line of the House of Pringle, and while I refer to the Scotts of Gala, it is right I should mention that it produced a celebrated Admiral, Sir George Scott. The two elder lines of the family having expired, the descendants of the second Earl of Tarras became, and are now the representatives. They acquired the barony of Polwarth, the original but minor title of the Marchmont family by the marriage of Walter Scott of Harden, grandson of Lord Tarras, with Lady Diana Hume, third daughter of the third and last Earl Marchmont, which earldom is in abeyance. This alliance opened the succession to the barony of Polwarth, to the Hardens, and Hugh the only son of Walter and Lady Diana, after considerable difficulty, which was at one time thought to be insurmountable, obtained the title by an award of the House of Lords, while the earldom of Marchmont awaits the claim of the nearest male-heir, and the property went in another direction in consequence, it has been said, of a political affront having been offered by the Laird of Harden to the then

---

* During the Civil War he continued faithful to the King, and in 1654 he was fined £3,000 by Oliver Cromwell. His sons were Sir William, his heir, Sir Gideon Scott of Highchester, Walter, ancestor of the Scotts of Raeburn, James, ancestor of the Scotts of Thirlstane, and John, progenitor of the Scotts of Wool. He died in 1655 at an advanced age, leaving to all his sons considerable estates, and to his daughters handsome portions.

Earl Marchmont.* Hugh Scott, who became eighth Lord Polwarth, died soon after obtaining it, and was succeeded by his eldest son Henry Francis, the lately deceased Peer, well known and deeply regretted by the counties of Roxburgh and Selkirk, in whose affairs he took a most important part.

The first Sir William Scott of Harden was succeeded by his son, also Sir William, who had the honour of knighthood conferred on him by King Charles II., immediately after the Restoration. He had two charters under the Great Seal, to Sir William Scott of Harden, knight, of the lands and baronies of Harden, Mertoun, Kirkwood, &c., and had an annuity of six hundred merks yearly out of the lands of Makerstoun; and he seems to have transferred his residence to Mertoun on the banks of the Tweed. He died in 1680, and was succeeded by a third Sir William, who was engaged in Argyle's rebellion but obtained a remission from King James in December 1685. He died without issue in 1707, and was succeeded by his brother, who also died without issue in 1710, after which the honours and estates went to Walter of Highchester, second heir-male, and a lineal descendant of Sir Gideon, second son of the first Sir William Scott of Harden.

Gideon Scott had inherited from his father the estate of Highchester, and being a man of parts and merit, he was appointed by King Charles I., Sheriff-Principal of Roxburghshire. He married Margaret, daughter of Sir Thomas Hamilton of Preston, by whom he had several children, the eldest son being Walter, afterwards created by King Charles I., Earl of Tarras for life, but his honours did not descend to his posterity. It was he who, at thirteen years of age, married Mary, Countess of Buccleuch, elder daughter of Francis, second

* Lady Diana Scott who lived to a great age, appreciated the mighty minstrel of the clan, Sir Walter Scott, surviving till he reached the summit of his fame. She was a great treasure in Sir Walter's eyes, for having conversed in her early days with the brightest ornaments of the cycle of Queen Anne, and preserved rich stores of anecdotes, she would relate to the great gratification of Sir Walter, much that was deeply interesting to him. She was the only person who could give him personal reminiscences of Pope.

Earl of Buccleuch, then only eleven years of age; and in possession of Lord Polwarth at Mertoun House are a number of letters that passed between the youthful couple. The marriage took place in 1659, but the countess died without children very shortly afterwards. Had she lived, Walter Scott, Earl of Tarras, would have become Earl of Buccleuch, and proprietor of all the large domains of the Lords of Buccleuch, but those honours were reserved for James, Duke of Monmouth, who married Anne, younger and only sister of the Countess Mary, when she was only twelve years of age. In 1677 Walter, Earl of Tarras, married Helen, daughter of Thomas Hepburn of Humbie, by whom he had several children, but he died in 1693, at a comparatively early age. His place of residence was Harden, which he seems to have to a great extent rebuilt. The oldest date observable on the present edifice is 1671, and the next is 1680, when the Earl of Tarras would be thirty-four years of age, and had been three years married to Helen Hepburn of Humbie. All the old parts of the house bear marks of the Earl and Countess of Tarras. One of the bed-rooms is still known as Lady Tarras's room, and over the fire-place it bears a coronet, with the letters H.T. for Helen Tarras; outside the window of this room is a stone bearing the date 1680. This is on the second floor, and immediately below, in the same position, is the coronet, with the letters W.E.T., Walter, Earl Tarras. Outside the same room is a window recess, with a circular top, in which is a stone elaborately carved; on the face of it are the letters—

E. C.
W. T. H. T.
1691.

On the lower part of the stone are carved a large star, with the sun embraced within a crescent of the moon. The date is only two years before the death of Earl Tarras, and it is the latest on the building, which seems immediately afterwards to have been deserted for some other place of residence. Sir

Walter Scott paid a yearly visit to this historic place, and had obtained the consent of his kinsman, Mr Scott of Harden and Mertoun, to have it repaired and made habitable as a summer residence, but the building of Abbotsford otherwise absorbed his time and means. The late Lord Polwarth at different times made repairs and added conveniences, so as to make it habitable, somewhat in the style in which it was left by Earl Tarras, and in this condition it now remains. Walter, Earl of Tarras, was succeeded by his eldest son, Gideon Scott, and he by his son Walter, who died without issue, and was succeeded by his brother John, who died in 1734 without male-heirs, after which the estates devolved on Walter Scott, second son of the Earl of Tarras. He was four times married, and of his second wife Anne, only daughter of John Scott of Gorranberry, were born two sons and three daughters. In 1746 he died, leaving as his heir, Walter his eldest son, the fourteenth generation in a direct male line from the first Walter Scott of Sinton. He was elected Member of Parliament for the county of Roxburgh in the year 1747, and continued to sit in all the Parliaments till the year 1765, when he was appointed General Receiver or Cashier of Excise in Scotland. He married Lady Diana Hume, daughter of Hugh, third Earl of Marchmont, a lady who had sprung from a noble stock, and was herself worthy of her parentage. The first Earl of Marchmont was Patrick Hume, laird of Polwarth, who suffered persecution in the reign of Charles II., but was of great service to the Prince of Orange, afterwards King William III. After the Revolution a brilliant career was opened up for him. He was created a Peer by the title of Lord Polwarth, and was afterwards created Earl of Marchmont, Viscount of Blassonbury, Lord Polwarth, Redbraes, and Greenlaw, to him and his heirs-male, whatsoever. The great reputation of the first Lord Marchmont was sustained by his son, Alexander Hume, the second Lord Marchmont; and not less notable was Hugh Campbell Hume, the third and last Lord Marchmont. They were all devoted supporters of the House of Hanover.

The third Lord Marchmont married Miss Western of London, by whom he had one son who died young, and three daughters, of whom Lady Diana, the youngest, was married to Walter Scott of Harden. With the son Hugh and his wife, Lady Diana lived at Mertoun till 1827, when she died at the age of ninety-four. With this venerable lady, her daughter-in-law, and her son, Walter Scott, afterwards Sir Walter of Abbotsford, lived on terms of great intimacy, and from them he received unspeakable benefits, in the way of acquiring information and cultivating his style. It was in the autumn of 1799, when residing at Mertoun House that Walter Scott composed the ballad of "The Eve of St John." There are no fewer than four ancient towers or castles on Lord Polwarth's estate, all of them tolerably entire. These are Harden, Oakwood, Littledean, and Smailholm. The last-named is situated on the northern boundary of Roxburghshire, among the cluster of wild rocks known as Sandyknowe Crags. While residing at Mertoun in 1799, Walter Scott called the attention of his kinsman to some dilapidations in the tower, and suggested certain repairs. Harden playfully requested as the price of compliance that Scott should compose a ballad, having Smailholm Tower for its subject, and in response he composed "The Eve of St John."

Reverting to the family of Sir William and Mucklemouthed Meg, it may be mentioned that their third son was

WALTER SCOTT, FIRST OF RAEBURN, ancestor of the greatest man who ever bore the name of Scott, and moreover one of the most celebrated Scotchmen that ever lived, Sir Walter Scott of Abbotsford. The representative of the first Raeburn, who, with his wife, were Quakers, is Robert Scott of Lessudden House and Raeburn, while the Abbotsford family, now represented by an only great-granddaughter of the great novelist, descended from a second son of the Quaker Raeburn, viz., Walter, who was a singular character, being known as "Beardie" from a vow he had made not to shave till the restoration of the Stuarts. Beardie Scott's hirsute appendage would be more marked in that generation than our own, for as the pictures in the late Portrait Exhibition at Kensington prove to us, it was the universal custom in that age to have the chin entirely smooth. Though Quakerism did not convert Beardie, there was another link besides Raeburn, which connected Sir Walter with the society of friends in the person of his grandmother, Jean Swinton, great-granddaughter of John Swinton of Swinton, who had assumed the Quaker faith and garb. These Quaker connections made the illustrious Scott cherish a feeling of veneration for the body, and in his characters of Joshua Geddes and his sister, he has pictured the benevolence of the sect. Another of the name of John Scott of Leith became a Quaker, making himself notorious for brewing on Sunday, for which he was fined very heavily on the evidence of the Bailie and minister, with whom he was very angry, protesting that he might as well brew on the Sunday as the minister might take money for going up to a desk and talking, and throwing water in a bairn's face. He appealed in vain to the Privy Council. But to return to Beardie, who, though he did not turn Quaker, like his father, was a keen Jacobite, and moreover the friend of the great and witty Dr Pitcairn, a well-known Scotchman and partisan of the *exiled family*. Sir Walter Scott, who was Beardie's great-grandson, says, "It would have been well if his Jacobite zeal had stopped with his letting his beard grow, but he took to political intrigue, and lost all he had except his person and his beard," which were also nearly being annihilated, for he would probably have been hanged had it not been for the interference of Anne, Duchess of Buccleugh, who was the means of saving his life, and after this he subsisted chiefly on the fortune of his wife, Miss Campbell of Silvercraigs. Beardie's second son, Robert, Sir Walter's grandfather, was intended for a sailor, but an early shipwreck weaned him from a seafaring life, when he took to farming, getting from the laird of Mertoun, his distant kinsman, a lease of Sandyknowe, near Smailholm, in which farm he made a considerable sum of money. He commenced with £30 of capital borrowed from his shepherd, named Hogg, but he spent it all at Wooler fair, in buying a horse instead of sheep. His eminent grandson was fond of the neighbourhood of Wooler, not on account of its fair, but because it was situated amidst places renowned for the feats of former days, each hill being crowned with a tower, or camp, or cairn; and in no situation can one see more fields of battle—Flodden, Otterburn, Ford, Chillingham and Copeland castles, and many other scenes of blood are within the compass of a forenoon's ride. He had many other enjoyments in that to him, charming country, to describe which, such was the simplicity of the house he lodged in, that no pen could be found, and to enable our great Borderer to communicate with his friends, he had to shoot a poor crow to procure a quill. As Robert Scott, Sir Walter's grandfather, amassed a considerable sum by agricultural pursuits, he must have found other capital besides the £30 he invested in a horse to start with. He married a Haliburton of Newmains, a branch of the old baronial House of Mertoun, by whom he would get some tocher, and in consequence of that connection, Sir Walter chose their place of sepulture, at Dryburgh Abbey, as his last resting-place.* But before quitting the Raeburn branch of the Scotts, I must not forget the painful incident which occurred in the family early last century. Walter Scott the third laird fought a duel with Mark Pringle of Crichton,

* Sir Walter has furnished a picture of Sandyknowe farm-house as it existed about 1776, showing "old Mrs Scott sitting with her spinning-wheel at the one side of the fire, in a *clean* clean parlour," the grandfather a good deal failed, in his elbow-chair opposite; and the little boy, afterwards the great magician, lying on the carpet, at the old man's feet, listening to the Bible, or whatever good book Miss Jenny was reading to them. This family circle was often joined by Sir George Hay Makdougall of Makerstoun, who took special interest in little Walter Scott, who was then at Sandyknowe on account of delicate health. Some one had suggested that whenever a sheep was killed, little Walter, who was weak and lame, should be wrapped in the warm skin. Clothed in this Tartar-like habiliment, he was laid on the floor of the little parlour at Sandyknowe, when Sir George Hay Makdougall was wont to kneel on the floor, dragging his watch before the little *lamiter*, to induce him to crawl after it.

in a field at Selkirk, 3d October 1707, the scene of which has since been known as Raeburn's Meadow. The parties quarrelled the day before at a County Court, and they determined to settle the quarrel by a hostile meeting, which accordingly took place, when Pringle's sword caused Scott's death.

Pringle, who was the youngest son of Andrew Pringle of Clifton, immediately after, went abroad, and became a merchant in Spain, where he made a fortune, though he underwent many hardships and adventures during the early part of his expatriation, having been taken prisoner by the Moors, and kept in slavery. After the lapse of years he returned to his native country, and bought the estate of Crichton in Midlothian, surviving his purchase some thirteen years, and the duel with Raeburn about forty-four years. His grandson and namesake, Mark Pringle, M.P. for Selkirkshire, not only succeeded to Crichton and Fernielee (the latter being his mother's property), but to Haining and Clifton also, owing to the decease of all his original Clifton kinsmen. Mark's two sons, John and Robert, both of whom followed him, in turn, in the M.P.-ship, died *sine prole*, when their sister Mrs Douglas succeeded, on the death of the latter, to the family property in Selkirkshire, while Clifton, the largest estate, strictly entailed, passed to a kinsman, Mr Elliot, of Harwood, descended from Robert Pringle of Clifton, who lived early in the eighteenth century, and who no doubt made the entail. But I must not in giving an account of the homicide and his family, forget the unfortunate man Raeburn, who, though only twenty-four, had been some time laird, and who left three children by his wife, who was a daughter of Scott of Gala, and granddaughter of my ancestor, Sir Thomas Ker of Cavers, and who afterwards married Macdougall of Makerston and Hume of Eccles.

I ought to mention that, independent of the male relationship between the Raeburns and the illustrious Sir Walter Scott, there was a nearer tie of affinity, through the Haliburtons which made him and the late laird of Raeburn, long called

Maxpoffle, which he owned and where he once resided, first cousins.

Three predecessors of the Harden Scotts, the original Scotts of Sinton, married ladies of the House of Riddell of Riddell, while James the fourth son of Sir William Scott of Harden and Mertoun, by Mucklemouthed Meg, married Agnes, daughter of Sir Walter Riddell my ancestor. Another cadet of the old Sinton tree not to be forgotten, was the House of Satchells in Lilliesleaf Parish, whose ancestor was James, third son of Walter the sixth of Sinton, by his second wife, a daughter of James Riddell of that ilk, from whom descended the well-known Chronicler of the Scott family, Walter Scott of Satchells, who calls himself "Captain Walter Scott, an old Souldier and no Scholler,

"And one that can write nane,
But just the letters of his name."

One of the Satchell ladies, Jean Scott, was a sort of heroine. She went to the assistance of the *widow* of a clansman of her husband, Scott of Howpaslot (ancestor of the Thirlestanes), who owed a grudge at James Douglas of Drumlanrig (ancestor of the Dukes of Queensberry), who had acquired Howpaslot, probably by purchase, on the death of her lord. Desperate on being turned out of the property and her old home, the widow determined on wreaking her vengeance upon Drumlanrig. The ladies met at Hawick, and arranged with several parties of the name of Scott in that town to proceed to Howpaslot to punish the new proprietor, which they did by killing forty of his sheep and mutilating some twenty more. The three parties who committed the slaughter, for one of them relented after getting to the place, were hanged, and the fourth, who had turned king's evidence, was afterwards hanged for sheep-stealing. William Scott of Satchells was of the party, but seemed to escape punishment, which the heroine, probably his wife, no doubt secured. We may ask, however, why the ladies themselves did not suffer punishment?

Another cadet of Harden was the House of Woll, founded by John Scott, who was fined, like his brother of Harden, for his wife's non-conformity. The only member of the family I will specially notice is the late William Scott of Teviotbank (which he purchased and his son sold), who was an ornament of the Scott family generally, and had his son, the late John Scott of Rodono, been spared, a history of the whole clan would probably have been published in course of time. William Scott was well known, not only as a legal practitioner in Edinburgh, but as a writer on Phrenology and on Scripture History. An engraved portrait of him, Dr Rogers says, might be accepted as that of the author of "Waverley."

I now proceed to another branch, either of Harden or the main line, perhaps not yet fully ascertained, I mean the

SCOTTS of HOWPASLEY, GAMESCLEUGH, and THIRLESTANE, from whom the house of Dryhope (which produced the beautiful Mary, the Flower of Yarrow), Mount Benger, and Bowhill (not the ducal family now possessors of it) descend. The Scotts of Howpasley, or Thirlestane as I shall call them, produced several warriors, one of whom was the valued and faithful attendant of James V., who, for his loyal and gallant conduct, granted him an augmentation to his arms, with the motto, "Ready, aye Ready." John Scott was the only chief willing to follow James V. in his invasion of England, when the rest of the Scottish nobles, encamped at Fala, refused to accompany their sovereign in his expedition. In memory of Scott's fidelity, the augmentation in question was granted by charter.

A subsequent member of the Thirlestane family was an able public servant and M.P., and was created a baronet in 1660, as Sir Francis Scott, while his only surviving son, Sir William, was a poet. Sir William had no son, and his daughter Elizabeth, by his first marriage, carried the estate of Thirlestane to her son, the fifth Baron Napier, in whose family the representation rests.

There were also the Scotts of Tushielaw, of whom was Adam, the King of Thieves or Monarch of the Border. James V. was determined that Adam should be no longer sovereign, and he was accordingly deposed, captured, and executed along with his partner in crime, Cockburn of Henderland. It has been said there was an old ash-tree near Tushielaw Tower, on which Adam was suspended, and that on the same tree King Adam had previously hanged many a wight, but Pitcairn says that Adam was tried, convicted, and beheaded at Edinburgh on 18th May 1530, with his brother reiver Cockburn of Henderland, and adds, that the "heids" of both were fixed on the Tolbooth of Edinburgh. Adam had previously agreed to assist the Earl of Angus to stanch theft, reiff, and slaughter, but he was so habituated to crime that he was unable to abide by his resolution, and accordingly forfeited his life. There was another noted member of the Tushielaw family, John Scott, who married a sister of his neighbour Robert of Thirlestane, of which family we have spoken. The two lairds fought a duel, in which Thirlestane was slain. The alleged cause of dispute between the parties was the settlement on the occasion of the marriage of Miss Scott, a subject which often causes disputes even in our times, without, however, terminating in duels. Tushielaw conceived Thirlestane had not made good the endowment promised on his becoming his brother-in-law. The duel was fought near to Yarrow Kirk, opposite a pass in the hills from Ettrick, and two prominent unhewn stones, standing about one hundred yards from each other, commemorate the fatal affair.

There were also the SCOTTS of HASSINDEAN (off from Buccleugh in time of Sir W. of Kirkurd), an ancient branch, particularly mentioned by Old Satchells, and one of whose chiefs was summarily disposed of by Elliot of Horsliehill, previously a Scott property, as it afterwards again became. Verily human life was not much thought of or valued in olden times.

Another respectable branch of the great Scott family is

WAUCHOPE, descended from Howcleugh and Crumhaugh, of whom there are memorials at Hawick. Old Walter Scott of Wauchope and his wife, Miss Rutherfurd of Fernielie, were friends and patrons of the great poet Burns, who visited them at Wauchope, and whom he graphically describes in his journal thus, in 1787—" Mr Scott exactly the figure and face commonly given to Sancho Panza; very shrewd in his family matters, and not unfrequently stumbles on what may be called a strong rather than a good thing. Mrs Scott, all the sense, taste, intrepidity of face and bold critical decision, which usually distinguish female authors."

Then there were the Scotts of Whitehaugh, represented by Mr Chisholm of Stirches—the Scotts of Burnhead and Crawhill, of whom was Mrs Charters, the wife of Dr Charters of Wilton—the Scotts of Burnfoot, one of whose early members being lame, was sent to Glasgow to be educated, not being considered fit for border reiving, though a descendent of this student was, from his fellness and activity, called WATT THE RATTAN. This Rattan acquired Headshaw by marriage. Then there were the Scotts of Middlestead (before the Plummers, who are not so old a family), of Kirkhouse, Huntly, Whitslade, and Todrig. The last of the Whitslades was a Dr Robert Scott, described by an author as " a gentlemanlike-looking person in ruin, tall and meagre, the countenance of hunger and despondency." One of the Scots of Todrig, sold in 1748, cut, in 1622, his arms in wood on the family pew in the old church of Ashkirk, and the last member of the race was Thomas Scott, who probably was a marine, for he is somewhere described as a brave warrior both by sea and land.

Ashkirk parish was at one time nearly wholly in the possession of families of the name of Scott, and Old Satchells has minutely described them in his well known chronicle.

Other highly respectable families no doubt exist, who have sprung from some of the foregoing, but there are two men of the name, from whatever branch or source derived, who have shed lustre on the great family, whom I must commemorate.

They are Drs John and William Scott of Singlee, Ettrick, father and son.

Dr JOHN SCOTT, who was a distinguished Edinburgh physician, was well known and highly valued, and specially mourned in the Forest and in Tweedside, his skill, time, and means being always ready for any of the suffering natives of these districts. Dr Scott was singularly gifted as a discoverer and healer of disease. He seemed by a sort of instinct to get at the root of the mischief, and pointed to the cause as a pointer does to game—more than this, he was both pointer and shot. He was a most sagacious and successful practitioner, and one of the tenderest-hearted and most unselfish of men. His extreme modesty was the only thing in the way of his becoming the greatest physician of his time, and he was not only a doctor but a man of true literary faculty. He was a keen and retentive reader, and was alive to everything that could improve his fellows in mind, body, or estate.

Dr WILLIAM HENRY SCOTT, his son, was also an Edinburgh physician, but died at the early age of twenty-four, a short time after his father. This young man was a prodigy of knowledge, and his memory was almost miraculous. Indeed, he used to say, he did not know how to forget. But in addition to William Scott's vast general knowledge, he concentrated himself in numismatics, and also in the study of history and of languages. In the department of numismatics, he took high rank for so young a man, having made some primary discoveries. When a stripling of eighteen, he was the habitual correspondent of the chief savans of Europe, in their own languages; and when this marvellous youth died, letters came from all parts of the world full of amazement at his age. He had been thought a man of fifty from his accomplishments and scholarship. His knowledge of languages was quite as wonderful as his memory, and if his life had been spared he might have rivalled Scaliger or Milton.

In addition to the two Dr Scotts just sketched, and Dr Robert of Hawick, previously mentioned, there was another well known physician in Hawick, last century, named Dr William Scott, who wrote on several medical subjects. Then there was a distinguished soldier, named Scott of Hawick, whose name will ever rank among the heroes of Quebec.

Among others of the name are :

George Lewis Scott, F.R. and A.S.S., a gentleman of considerable talents and general learning, born at Hanover of Scotch parents, died in 1780. His wife, Mrs Scott, sister to the late Mrs Montagu, died in 1795 ; a lady of great acquirements, who published many works, all anonymous, the first of which was a novel called "Cornelia."

John Scott, the early printer at St Andrews and Edinburgh, who printed in 1561 the "Protestant Confession of Faith."

William Scott, schoolmaster, many useful class books, and "Beauties of Eminent Writers."

Andrew Scott of Bowden, and George of Lilliesleaf, poets.

I have now closed my brief but imperfect history of the families of Scott, bringing forward the salient points in the characters of those particularly distinguished. I have confined my history chiefly to the Scottish border house, and its branches, and borderers generally bearing the name, but before closing the chapter, I would mention some leading men of the name in other parts of Scotland, and then cross the Border to bring before you briefly our English friends of note who have gloried in the name.

Of the other noted *Scotch* Scotts there were in olden times a couple of Bishops, already referred to as witnesses to Charters—then there were several Professors, also John Scott the Hermit and miraculous faster—also Alexander Scott who flourished in the reign of Queen Mary, to whom he addressed a Poem, in which he styles himself—"her simple servant ; Saunders Scott." In Ramsay's "Evergreen" and other collections, his poetry is to be found—it was thought so good in past times he was called, "The Anacreon of Scotland." Then in later times, there was David a painter of ability, and a poet as well—another David, an historian, who suffered imprisonment for his attachment to the Stuarts—Michael the well-known author of "Tom Cringle's Log," and John, a Miscellaneous Writer, who fought and fell in a duel at Chalk Farm in 1821, his antagonist being a Mr Christie, and the cause a literary quarrel.

Then crossing the Border, and landing you in England, I have quite an array of celebrated *English* Scotts to present to you. There were several eminent Divines, the chief of whom was Thomas the Commentator, and in earlier times, Thomas Scott of Rotherham, who was Archbishop of York and Lord Chancellor in the 15th century. He was a munificent Prelate. There was also the well-known author of the "Christian Life," John Scott, whom the notorious Judge Jeffreys sent for on his deathbed to aid him in suing for mercy in heaven, which he so often denied on earth; then there was Samuel Scott, the Marine Painter, who is represented in the National Gallery; also Reginald the writer on Witchcraft whose opinions James the First in his demonology tried to refute; and John Scott the Poet of Amwell, who, like our friend Raeburn, was a Quaker; also a Col. Scott with a woman's name, Caroline, viz., Col. Caroline Scott. It has been said he was one of Hawley's officers, sent to put down the Scotch rebellion in 1746, when great cruelty was practised, but Scott's character was anything but cruel, for though brave and spirited, he showed the greatest gentleness of manners. He died moreover in India, in the Company's Service in 1755, which is rather against his having been at Culloden unless he had been on furlough and volunteered. I shall only mention two other celebrated English Scotts, and I am happy to say they may be called Borderers, though English ones. William, Lord Stowell, and John, Lord Eldon. William the elder brother was Judge of the High Court of Admiralty. He was an excellent scholar and profound reasoner, as well as a zealous supporter of the great Institutions of his country. It has been said his knowledge of international law, was unexcelled in Britain, and that he took rank with Grotius and other immortal Jurists. John Scott the younger brother, created Lord Eldon, was a distinguished statesman, as well as able lawyer. He attained the summit of the legal profession by reaching the Woolsack, where he sat for about twenty-six years as Lord Chancellor, the longest period the Great Seal was ever held by one individual. He was said to be slow, but in his day there were no assistant justices, and he evinced great anxiety to do justice in his judgments. Romilly said no man ever presided in Chancery who possessed more deep and various learning, and exhibited more humane attention to the suiters. Lord Eldon could relax in vacation time, when he participated in and enjoyed the sports of the field. On one occasion he was accosted as old Bags's keeper, but he told the man who accosted him, whom the Chancellor challenged for poaching, that he was "old Bags himself." There is an office in Chancery called the Bag office from which the nickname is probably derived.

THE KER FAMILY.

THE Family of Ker, a word which I believe signifies Strength, is of Anglo-Norman lineage, and the name stands in the earliest record of the Normans in this Country—the roll of Battle Abbey; an edifice founded by William I. to commemorate the victory which he gained over Harold II. on the 14th October 1066 (eight hundred years ago).

The name of Ker, or according to the Norman orthography, Karre, stands conspicuous on this roll of fame, as corroborated by the celebrated chroniclers Hollinshed and Duchesne. It has been said that the family was a noble and illustrious one in France before the Conquest, and that William's companion was one of its members who became the progenitor of the English and Scotch Kers, the former being no doubt the parent stock, which probably was settled at Kershall in Lancashire. Several of the name are mentioned by Prynne, and others appear on the Ragman Roll—that ancient document which contains a list of those who swore fealty to Edward I., 1272-1307. Two members of the family of Ker probably springing from the Lancashire stock came to Scotland about the close of the 14th century, where they settled in Roxburghshire, founding the two great families of Cessford and Fernicherst, or Kershaugh, or Kersheugh, as Fernicherst was first called. It is not known whether the two Anglo-Normans were brothers, but they were probably nearly related. Their names were JOHN and RALPH—the former being the ancestor of the Kers of Cessford, originally styled of Auldtounburn, and the Forest of Selkirk—the latter being the progenitor of the Kers of Ferniehirst, first styled Kersheugh. Both families were supporters of the great house of Douglas, at that time paramount on the Scottish Border. But a more ancient family than either, of the same name, whose original derivation probably is from the same Anglo-Norman race, existed in the West of Scotland at least 130 years before the two Border chieftains rose up. They no doubt, like the Ferniehersts, and also the Lancashire stock, called the property they acquired after themselves, for it was named Kersland, and to their honour and credit, they held it for at least a period of five hundred years, though during that time it twice went in the female line, through the failure of males, the name and title of Kersland being however continued by assumption, but owing to the improvidence and folly of the last John Ker, ironically called, honest Kersland, in that well-known Jacobite song called the "Awkward Squad," it was wasted.

Kersland was supposed to have acted a double part in the politics of the time, as he and David Baillie were accused of revealing to the Government all the secret proceedings of the Jacobites, whom they pretended to favour. At his death in 1726, the property of Kersland was judicially sold, and his widow and daughters were left in poverty. But before leaving this the most ancient of the Scottish family of Ker, of which some cadets still exist in the west, I think it right to mention that there were some conspicuous and worthy members of the main Kersland line, who figured in the history of the Reformation, and of the Covenant—one of them was Daniel Ker, a staunch adherent of Presbytery, who was killed at Steinkirk in Flanders in 1697, leaving behind him, according to his descendant John Ker, the character of a great soldier, a fine gentleman, and to crown all a good Christian. He carried his opinions against Popery, however, too far. For instance he joined a party who went to Traquair House from which they took a number of Romish wares and books, and burnt them at the Cross of Peebles. Amongst the books were no doubt many valuable missals, which would have been much prized now as works of antiquity and art. In this raid David, I think, tarnished his high character a little.

The arms of this ancient Kersland race, as exemplified on the Church of Dalry, the cradle of these Kers, are the same as the Border Kers, a Cheveron charged with three Stars or Mollets, the motto being, "Peace with God." The memoirs of John Ker of Kersland were published about one hundred and forty years ago.

I now proceed with the two great Border houses of Cessford and Ferniehirst, and, at the outset, I beg to state that the noble house of Lothian is derived from both—as Lothians they are of the Cessford stock, and being also Earls of Ancrum, they derive from and represent the Ferniehirsts through their Ancrum ancestor. In treating of the two great houses of Cessford and Ferniehirst, I give priority to the former, their chief being a duke—the Duke of Roxburghe — although during the warfare that so long existed between them, neither would concede the superiority to the other. I rather think, however, the Ferniehirst race can show the oldest charter, or at any rate they possess evidence of having the most ancient holding. A learned writer considers the Ferniehirsts the elder, because they carried the same arms with the Kers in England and France, without any difference of tincture or change.

THE KERS OF CESSFORD.

I have already said their first designation was Auldtounburn, which is situated on the banks of the Bowmont, about five miles from Yetholm; their charter of that place being granted in 1357, and afterwards confirmed by the superior, Archibald Earl Douglas. Their first charter of Cessford was obtained in 1446, having been granted by the same Earl of Douglas, afterwards Duke of Turenne. I begin with ANDREW,*

* The first notable personage of the family was "John Ker, of the Forest of Selkirk," who, in 1357, obtained from John de Copeland, an English warden, "all the lands and tenements in Auldtounburn, with their pertinents,

the fourth probably of the family, who had now acquired a considerable property, including Cessford, which was long the family fortress. He was esquire to the Earl of Douglas just mentioned, and died about the middle of the fifteenth century, leaving three sons—Andrew, his heir; James, of Linton; and Thomas, of Gateshaw. The descendants of the latter in the female line exist to this day, and possess Gateshaw. The Linton Kers have long since died out. There is a record of a quarrel in which one of the family was killed, and of a bond being taken in consequence from T. Ker, of Mersington; T. Ker, of Yair; A. Ker, of Newhall; and T. Ker, of Whitmuirhall, and others. ANDREW, the heir, and whom we shall call THE FIFTH, was infeft in other lands by William Earl Douglas—the forfeited Earl—who, after the decline of his power, went to Rome on an imposing expedition to the jubilee there, accompanied by a train of one hundred knights and magnates—Andrew Ker, or Karre, as I have seen him described, being one of the party. After our hero's return

---

which formerly belonged to Adam of Beale," and next year received from William of Blackdeane, "part of the lands of Mow and Auldtounburn" for himself and Mariote, his spouse. The designation Mow or Molle signifies a conical hill, and the territory of that name, which is still represented in the name of Mowhaugh, extended to the English border at the summit of the Cheviots. At that early date the territory supplied tribute to the monks of Kelso, Melrose, and Paisley, and the canons of Paisley. The monks of Kelso alone had land in the territory of Molle, at a very early period, sufficient to pasture four hundred sheep, sixteen nolt, two work-horses, and twelve swine, and latterly they had a good deal more. The "town" of Molle was of considerable size, and contained, as all towns did in those days, a "pele," with many fair houses around it. The monks of Kelso had fourteen cottages, each of which rented at two shillings a year, with six days' work, besides "the common easements of the town, and liberty to pasture cattle wherever the laird's cattle grazed." On the summit of a rising ground on the right bank of the Bowmont stood the church, close to which was the residence of the vicar; and the township had likewise those essential requisites of civilisation, a malt kiln and a mill. Further up the valley is a pass into Northumberland, the entrance to which was barred by the Cocklaw Tower, which had a standing garrison of trusty warriors. There appears to have been some wood in the district, as the tenants stipulated for wood to make their ploughs and to construct folds for their flocks.

from Italy, which he survived many years, he got a charter of Old Roxburgh, say in 1451, and became a man of mark, being conservator of truces with England, but he was forfeited, owing to his having been concerned with the Boyds in carrying off James III. from Linlithgow. Parliament, however, granted a remission, which he survived some years. He was twice married, having by his first wife, a daughter of Douglas of Cavers, several sons and a daughter, who married, as her second husband, William, third Earl of Errol, one of whose successors was James Lord Boyd, a descendant of the Boyds whom her father assisted in carrying off James III. Andrew's eldest son and heir was WALTER THE SIXTH, sometimes called " Wat Carre," who also got further possessions, including Caverton, which had been one of the possessions of the ancient family of Soulis. In 1488, Wat Carre got Roxburgh Castle, and the Maisons Dieu of Roxburgh and Jedburgh, from James IV., to whom he was esquire. The Castle of Roxburgh stands very beautifully on a prominent knoll of an oblong form, rising out of the plain, near to the junction of Tweed and Teviot. Judging from its outworks and massive fragments, it was doubtless a place of great strength. It was the scene of many a siege, and frequently changed proprietors. The good Sir James Douglas, " trustie and trew," the friend of Bruce, who sometimes held a Court at Roxburgh, took the Castle in 1313, but he did not hold it long, though it is on record that both castle and town were in possession of a descendant, who afterwards lost both. In 1460, James II. took the town and besieged the castle, which was then in possession of the English ; and while the King was observing the effects of his guns, then rude contrivances like Mons Meg, one of them called the Lion burst, and a fragment striking His Majesty on the leg, caused his death. His followers and supporters, however, encouraged, it has been said, by the Queen, went on with the siege, and razed the castle to the ground. James IV. gave the castle to Walter Ker, but it again got into the hands of the English, who repaired it, after which it was restored to the Cessford family by James V.; but by virtue of a treaty of peace with England, it was again demolished, and has since remained a ruin. Walter Ker, who like his father and grandfather, was a commissioner for settling Border disputes, appears to have been a religious man, for it is recorded that he built a chapel at Caverton

> pro salute corporis et animæ nostræ et pro
> salute animæ dicti Walter nuper defuncti.

His death occurred in 1501.

Walter Ker was twice married, first to Helen Ker, of whose derivation I am ignorant; indeed in some books where her name might be expected to appear, it is not given, but I have learnt it from the papers of the lamented and famous antiquary, John Riddell, who possessed a charter written on vellum by the abbot and convent of Kelso, in favour of Ellen, spouse of that honourable man, Walter Ker of Cessford, and Robert, their son and apparent heir of the lands of Halyden and Heathwood, in the barony of Bowden. The charter is dated 2d July 1481, and is signed by Robert, the abbot of the abbey, immediately before Thomas Ker, who will hereafter be mentioned. Walter Ker's second wife, by whom he had no family, was a daughter of Lord Chancellor Crichton, and widow of the second Lord Glammis. His children were by his first wife, Ellen Ker, and Robert, the eldest son, who was killed shortly before his father's decease; but by his wife Christian Rutherford, daughter of James Rutherford of that ilk, he had two sons. Robert had a brother, Mark of Dolphinston, ancestor of the Kers of Littledean, and a sister Elizabeth, who was married to Philip Rutherford, brother of her brother Robert's wife, and her daughter, as heir-of-line, carried the chief part of the Rutherford property to the family of Traquair, one of whose chiefs (killed at Flodden) she married. Great feuds took place between the Rutherfords, Traquairs, and Roxburghs, in consequence of the Rutherford property being carried away by the heir-of-line. Elizabeth Ker of Cessford, after losing her husband Philip

Rutherford, married Sir Walter Scott of Buccleuch, and was mother of the lamented Baron killed at Melrose.

I have said that Robert Ker, who was described as of Caverton, predeceased his father. He was a most distinguished man, and a great favourite of his sovereign James IV., whose chief cup-bearer he was. He was also Master of the Ordnance, and Warden of one of the Marches, in the execution of which latter office he was killed at Gamel's Path, about the year 1500, by three Englishmen named Heron, Lilburn and Starhead; and I presume it was in consequence of his slaughter and gallant resistance against the banditti, the family got a grant of fresh armorial bearings. The Cessfords previously had the field of their arms, gules or red, but in consequence of Robert Ker being killed in a green field, it was ordered that the bearings should in future be vert, and the livery also, in remembrance of the occasion. At the same time they got the *Unicorn's* head as a crest, being part of the royal arms and ensign, supported by two savages, with laurel leaves round the middle, holding batons over the shoulder, with the motto, *omne solum forti*—every soil for the brave.

One of the banditti who killed the gallant Ker was delivered up to the Scots. This was Lilburn, who died in prison; Heron, another, escaped; but Sir Andrew Ker, son of the murdered hero, captured, through the medium of some of his vassals, the third, Starhead, whom they decapitated, bringing his head in triumph to their master, who caused it to be exposed at the Cross in Edinburgh.

There is a tradition in Bowden that Habbie Ker struck the priest of that place, for which he atoned by giving his reverence a field north of the lade (burn), which was added to the glebe, the whole of which is on the south side of the stream, which would seem to favour the legend. It could not have well been Lord Roxburgh, the famous Habbie Ker, as he lived after the Reformation, and the occurrence taking place in Romish times, it must have been Sir Robert, who seems to have enjoyed the same soubriquet.

Sir ANDREW KER, son of Sir Robert, in consequence of his father's early and sad death, succeeded his grandfather, to whom he was served heir at his majority in 1511. He was then married, having wedded, at about eighteen, Agnes Crichton, daughter of Robert the second Lord of Sanquhar. This baron was very distinguished, but did not live long, having while in the Earl of Angus' army at Melrose, been killed by a follower of his brother-in-law, Buccleuch. His death was deeply lamented on both sides, and was the cause of a long and deadly feud, which ended in the murder of Buccleuch in Edinburgh.

I must now revert to Sir Andrew Ker's brother George of Fawdonside, whose descendants were conspicuous and survived for about a century, and had they continued would have been the male representatives after the Kers of Littledean now extinct.

George had a son, Sir Andrew Ker of Fawdonside, who is somewhere described as "a tall, thin-made savage looking man, his look and bearing being those of a Border freebooter." He was concerned with Ruthven and Douglas in Rizzio's murder, and is reported to have acted most barbarously to Queen Mary. This Sir Andrew had a son, who married the widow of the great John Knox, Margaret Stewart, daughter of the second Lord Ochiltree. She fell in love with the Reformer when he was nearly sixty, she being probably little more than twenty, and they had three daughters, one of whom married John Welch, at one time minister of Selkirk. John Knox had been a widower about three years, and his first wife, Marjory Bower, was of good family also, probably of the same stock as Mary Bower who married the ninth Earl Strathmore. By his first wife the Reformer had two sons, who were both graduates of Cambridge, and died unmarried, so that there are no *male* descendants of his body, though he had several nephews, who were, probably from Fawdonside connection, appointed to the benefices of Melrose and Bowden. The last of the Fawdonsides died in very indigent circumstances in the seventeenth century.

Sir Andrew Ker married Miss Crichton, and had five children, viz., three sons and two daughters.

Sir Walter,

Mark, Commendator of Newbottle, who was father of the first Earl Lothian,

Andrew, who left no male descendants. One of the daughters, Catherine, married Sir John Ker of Ferniehirst, and the other, Margaret, Sir John Home of Cowdenknowes.

Sir WALTER, the son and heir, married Isabel Kerr of Ferniehirst, his brother-in-law's sister. I conclude the Cessford family, in Sir Walter's time, lived occasionally at Halydene, for Dame Isabel Ker is commemorated by an inscription on a stone, now a lintel over the door of a small house there, viz., "Feer God—Flee from sin—Mak for the lyfe everlasting to the end. Dem Isabel Ker 1530."* On the north side of the farm-steading of Halydene there was, it is understood, a chapel and a burying-ground. There are no remains of either now, though from time to time handles of coffins and human bones have been dug up. Whether the family buried at Halydene or Cessford, before the vault at Bowden Church was first used as the place of sepulture, some time early in the seventeenth century, I do not know.

Sir Walter was served heir to his father in 1528, and had charters of various lands granted to him and his heirs, with

---

* In the centre of the Bowden Barony stood the ancient Castle of Halydean, a baronial residence of considerable splendour. There was a great deer park of about five hundred acres, surrounded by a dry stone dyke, six or seven feet high with copestones. The wall is said to have stood four hundred years, and part of it still forms a tolerable fence. The court-yard of the castle contained about three-quarters of an acre, and was surrounded by a strong stone and lime wall, four feet thick and sixteen feet high, with slanting holes about thirty feet apart, from which an arrow or a musket could be pointed in different directions. Upon an arched gateway in front there was a strong iron gate. Within the court stood two strong towers, the one three and the other five storeys high, consisting of eight or ten habitable rooms, besides porters' lodges, servants' hall, vaulted cellars, bake-houses, &c. The roofs and flooring were all of the strongest oak, and might have stood for a long time, but during the minority of John Duke of Roxburghe, the greater part of the edifice was pulled down to furnish materials for building a farm-house.

remainder to various members of the clan, which included Mark of Newbattle, Mark of Dolphinston or Littledean, and Andrew of Fawdonside. He with his brother-in-law of Ferniehirst had a remission for being art and part in the murder of Sir Walter Scott of Buccleugh in Edinburgh. He espoused the cause of James VI., and promoted the Reformation, dying in or about 1584, when he must have attained a considerable age, having been married upwards of fifty years. His eldest son Andrew died unmarried, in his father's lifetime, and he was succeeded by his only surviving one

WILLIAM KER, who was warden of the middle marches, but did not live long. His sisters respectively married Edmonstone of that Ilk, and the first Earl Home, while he himself wedded Janet Douglas, daughter of Drumlanrig and widow of Tweedie of Drummelzier, who bore him two sons and two daughters, viz., Sir Robert first Earl Roxburgh and Mark of Ormiston, who died without issue. One of his daughters, Mary, married the Bold Buccleuch, created Lord Scott, and the other Sir James Bellenden, whose son was created Lord Bellenden in 1661.

The second Habbie, Sir Robert Ker of Cessford, got fresh charters of the family estates, and acquired further property, and was one of the most celebrated men, as well as one of the ablest of the family. In 1585, when he was but fifteen years of age, he joined the army in driving the Earl of Arran from the councils of James VI., and in five years afterwards was concerned with others in the assassination of William Ker of Ancrum—a quarrel having arisen out of disputes about the seniority of the houses of Ferniehirst and Cessford ; but for this he obtained a remission under the great seal in 1591, the year after the murder. He was a Commissioner for the Scottish Borders, and his English antagonist seeing his value, characterises him " as a brave, active young man—wise and valiant, but somewhat haughty and resolute." For not delivering his prisoners, Sir Robert was made prisoner himself in England, but was soon released, and afterwards created a baron, but the patent has been lost, and the date cannot exactly be established. He accompanied King James to England in 1603, and was appointed by Parliament one of the Commissioners for a Union with England. In 1616, he was advanced to the Peerage, having been created Earl of Roxburghe and Lord Ker, to himself and heirs-male. He was made Privy Seal of Scotland, but was deprived of the office on joining "the engagement" for the rescue of Charles I. He was now getting old, and turned his attention to the settlement of his own affairs, his second, but last surviving son, Harry, Lord Ker, dying about this time, leaving three daughters and no son. The Earl accordingly got fresh charters enlarging his entail so as to admit his own nomination of heirs. By his first marriage with Miss M. Maitland of Lethington he had, besides a son who died early, a daughter Jean, married to James, third Earl of Perth, who had several sons, and upon the fifth son, the Honourable William Drummond, the Earl settled his titles and estates on condition of his marrying the eldest daughter of his son Harry, Lord Ker, by his second marriage with the sister of his son-in-law the second Earl Perth. This he accordingly did, the fresh entail including Harry, Lord Ker's other two daughters, and their descendants, before "heirs-male whatsoever," and from the younger of those two daughters, viz., Margaret, who married Sir James Innes, third Baronet of Innes, the present Duke descends. Such were his arrangements, which he probably made after seeing he was not likely to have issue by his third marriage, which he entered into, probably about the age of seventy-five, with a daughter of the seventh Earl Morton, who, after the Earl of Roxburghe's death, married the second Marquis of Montrose, who was no less than sixty years younger than her first husband, and by whom she had a son, the third Marquis.*

---

* Sir Robert, better known as Habbie or Hobbie Ker, occupies a place in the Roxburghe lineage somewhat similar to that of "Auld Wat" among the Scotts of Harden. He was the most renowned of all the Cessford Barons, one of the most powerful men of his time, and was the last noble occupant of

The Earl of Roxburghe's second wife, Miss Drummond, was a person of great abilities, and was appointed governess to the children of James VI., and was besides one of the ladies of the bed-chamber to Her Majesty, and there is a record by which it appears the sum of £3000 was given to her by the king, in consideration of long and faithful service done to the queen.

Cessford Castle, having lived till 1650, long after all Border feuds had come to an end. He was born at Cessford Castle in 1570, and his mother was a daughter of Sir William Douglas of Drumlanrig. He was Warden of the Marches, as deputy to his father, at a very early age; and was the first to communicate to King James VI. the information received through a trusty messenger that Queen Mary had been executed. As Scottish Warden, Habbie Ker had for his opponent on the English side Sir Robert Carey, who was no match for the active and sagacious laird of Cessford, whose men made continuous raids into England during the winter nights, driving off the cattle into Scotland. Carey said, "so powerful and awful was this Sir Robert Ker and his favourites, that there was not a gentleman in all the east march dared offend them." At length in 1597 a meeting of Scotch and English commissioners was held at Carlisle, when it was agreed that the wardens should deliver up certain offenders within their jurisdiction, failing which they were to surrender themselves. Against this arrangement Cessford and Buccleuch struggled hard; but were over-ruled. Sir Robert Ker, having failed to give up some others, surrendered himself to Carey, who writes :—" I lodged him as well as I could, and took order for his diet, and men to attend on him, and sent him word that (although by his harsh carriage toward me, ever since I had that charge, he could not expect any favour yet), bearing so much goodness of him, that he never broke his word, he would have no guard set upon him," and after mutual explanations the two wardens became so friendly that Cessford dined and supped daily, and went hunting thrice a-week with Carey. Sir Robert lived for some time in England, where he seems to have learned a good deal, and ever afterwards he was no less energetic in promoting peace between the two kingdoms, than he had been formerly in riding at the head of marauding expeditions. With him Cessford Castle ceased to be a residence of the barons, but it was habitable for some time afterwards; and within its walls Henry Hall of Haughhead and other covenanters were imprisoned in 1666. The Earl of Roxburghe spent much of his time in London, but when in Scotland his residence was at Floors. This part of the estate, with an old house thereon, had belonged to the Abbots of Kelso, and after 1587 was held by Sir John Maitland of Thirlstane, as commendator for King James VI., after which they came into possession of Sir Robert Ker. The earliest name of the place was "Flooris," and the old house remained till 1718, when it was removed, and a noble residence was built by the first Duke of Roxburghe, which has since been greatly extended and beautified.

The FIRST EARL OF ROXBURGHE died in 1650, aged 80. His coffin with his remains, is to be seen at Bowden, and there is a picture of him at Floors. His grandson, maternally, the Hon. WILLIAM DRUMMOND, was immediately served heir, took the name of Ker, and by his wife, Jean Ker, his first Cousin, he had four sons and one daughter. Before he became second Earl of Roxburghe he had acquired the reputation of being a brave man and gallant officer, having in his early life served in Holland. During the Civil War he joined the Royalists, and was heavily fined by Cromwell. He got a ratification from Parliament of the first Earl's entail, and an approval from Ker of Fawdonside, who was the male heir at the time, and died in 1675, when he was succeeded by his eldest son; his fourth son John becoming second Baron Bellenden.

ROBERT, THIRD EARL OF ROXBURGHE, did not very long enjoy the honours and estates, for he was lost with other Privy Councillors of Charles II., on coming down from London, with the Duke of York, afterwards James II., in the Gloucester Frigate. The melancholy accident happened near Yarmouth on the 4th May 1682. Several noblemen besides the Earl of Roxburghe perished, but the Royal Duke and Colonel Churchhill, afterwards Duke of Marlborough, made a narrow escape. By his wife, Lady Margaret Hay, a daughter of the first Marquis Tweeddale, he had three sons, two of whom were in turn Earls of Roxburghe, the third, the Hon. William Ker being a distinguished soldier, and attaining high rank and several important positions, being three times a member of Parliament. The Countess, the mother of the three sons, survived her husband more than seventy years, having died at Broomlands, near Kelso, in 1753, at the advanced age of ninety-five.*

* The *Gloucester* frigate, when proceeding from London to Edinburgh, with the Duke of York and his friends, was attended by some smaller vessels, and was wrecked on Yarmouth Sands, through a blunder of the pilot, one Aird of Borrowstouness, who had gone to sleep, and given wrong directions. A signal-gun brought boats from the other vessels to the rescue of the distressed party, by means of which the Duke of York and some others were saved. A

Her eldest son ROBERT, became fourth EARL OF ROXBURGHE, but he died under age at Brussels, when on a Continental tour, unmarried—being succeeded by his next brother

JOHN, who became FIFTH EARL OF ROXBURGHE. This Peer was a person of great learning and high accomplishments. An author states he knew "all the ancient languages thoroughly, and speaks most of the modern perfectly well—without pedantry—is a fine gentleman, and lives up to his quality. Hath a good estate, is handsome, brown complexioned, about twenty-five years old." He was appointed a Secretary of State in 1704, and having aided the Union, and favoured the Protestant cause, was made Duke of Roxburghe, with four subordinate titles in 1707, being the *last* creation in the Peerage of Scotland.

The Duke continued to fill important offices till the Cabal against Walpole, in which he joined, which cost him his Secretaryship.* He was Lord Lieutenant of the Counties of Roxburgh and Selkirk, and on the occurrence of the rebellion in 1715, distinguished himself greatly as a volunteer at the battle of Sherriffmuir. The Duke married Lady Mary Finch, only child of the sixth Earl of Winchelsea, an heiress, being the first Englishwoman married into the family. She had only one son by the Duke, viz. :

ROBERT, who succeeded as SECOND DUKE, and who was created before he was twenty, in his father's time, a British Peer by the title of Earl Ker. He only survived his father fourteen years, and died at Bath in 1755. In this Duke's

---

hundred and fifty persons, among whom were the Earl of Roxburghe, the Laird of Hopetoun, and Sir Joseph Douglas of Pumpherston, were drowned. The Earl of Roxburghe was heard crying for a boat, and offering twenty thousand guineas for one. His servant in the water took the Earl on his back, and was swimming with him to a boat, when a drowning person clutched at them, which caused the unfortunate Earl to fall off, and he was drowned. His servant escaped for the moment, but died an hour afterwards. The pilot was condemned to perpetual imprisonment.

* About the year 1720, the Duke, then resident in London, was in the habit of receiving one hundred pounds monthly by the waggon from Scotland for the maintenance of the ducal family in the Metropolis.

time, the Act abolishing Heritable Jurisdictions was passed, and his Grace got for the bailiary of Kelso £1300, and for his other bailiaries £800; in all £2100. He married his cousin, Lady Essex Finch, and by her Grace had two sons and eight daughters, one dying in infancy. The two sons were John, who became third Duke, the famous Book Collector; and Robert who was in the army, and who made an unsuccessful attempt to become M.P. for Roxburghshire in 1780. The two surviving daughters were Lady Essex and Lady Mary Ker, who were both bridesmaids to Queen Charlotte on her marriage in 1761, and Lady Essex, the elder sister, was a claimant of the Dukedom and Estates on the death of her kinsman William, the fourth Duke, in 1806.

JOHN, the THIRD DUKE OF ROXBURGHE, the great Book Collector, succeeded his father on the 23d August 1755, at the age of fifteen, having been born in London in 1740. This Peer was highly esteemed by George III., in whose Court he held high appointments, and by whom he was invested with the great distinctions of the Garter and the Thistle, the joint orders never having been conferred before on one individual since the reign of Queen Anne. His Grace possessed a remarkably fine physique and rare mental accomplishments. From his "Bibliotheca," the Roxburghe Club took its rise. The Duke was an extensive Book Collector, and his Town Library, which was sold off after his death, contained some very rare and valuable works.* Sir Walter Scott who had made great use of the splendid collecttion of books and documents, and who was disappointed he

* The library contained nearly ten thousand books, which were all sold by auction, and brought enormous prices. A copy of the first edition of the "Decameron" of Boccacio, printed at Venice by Valderfar in 1471, was bought by the Marquis of Blandford, afterwards Duke of Marlborough, for £2,260 sterling; a copy of the first work printed by Caxton, with a date, "Recuyell of the Historyes of Troye," (1461, folio), was sold for one thousand guineas, and a copy of the first edition of Shakespeare (1623, folio), for one hundred guineas. In commemoration of the event, the Roxburghe Club was founded for the collection of rare books, the preservation of curious manuscripts, and the reprint of scarce and curious tracts for the use of members of the Club.

had not the means of buying, says :—"The Roxburghe sale sets my teeth on edge, but if I can trust my eyes there are now twelve masons at work on a cottage and offices at this little farm which I purchased last year (the beginning of Abbotsford), then I have planted thirty acres, and am in the act of walling a garden—then I have a wife and four bairns crying as the old song has it, Porridge ever mair—so on the whole my teeth must get off edge as those of the fox and the grapes in the fable." His Grace never married, it was said from etiquette not permitting him to wed the sister of his queen to whom he was devotedly attached, as she was to him, and they both resolved therefore to die celibates.

At Duke John's death in 1804, which was caused by inflammation of the liver, the English titles expired, while the Scotch one and the Estates went to the heir of entail, William, seventh Lord Bellenden, a far off cousin, who had descended from John, second Lord Bellenden, second son of the second Earl of Roxburghe. His other property, amounting to upwards of £100,000, he left to three parties, one being the father of Mr William Scott, first, however, giving his two sisters the liferent over it. One of the sisters, however, was not satisfied with the liferent, wishing the fee as well, for she disputed the settlement, which was a death-bed one. It has been stated one of the witnesses who signed the Deed, gave up a Legacy of £1000 to give evidence, and the will was not only confirmed by the Law Courts, but by the House of Lords, to whom an appeal was made. The sisters survived their brother the Duke some fourteen years, and both died unmarried—one in 1818, and the other in 1819.

The death scene of "Elspeth Mucklebackit" in "The Antiquary," in which Edie Ochiltree appears, is said to have had a precedent in a striking incident which occurred at Duke John's funeral in 1804. An old and valued domestic named Archie, who had the charge of his Grace's Library, was himself, at that time, in the last stage of a liver complaint, of which the Duke died. He nevertheless determined on accompanying the Duke's remains to Floors, but was so exhausted on arriving, that for some days he was in a state of collapse. On the morning of the funeral, before it started for Bowden, a particular hand-bell used for summoning Archie to the Library was heard to ring—how it could not be found out, and the well-known sound having roused Archie from his stupor he called out in broken accents, "My Lord Duke, I will wait on you immediately," and with these words he fell back and expired.

As formerly stated, William Lord Bellenden became FOURTH DUKE OF ROXBURGHE. He was poor before inheriting the Dukedom, and on his getting the Barony of Bellenden, got a grant from the Crown of £250 as the salary of Usher of the Exchequer, which two previous Lord Bellenden's enjoyed. He was twice married, but left no surviving issue. His second wife and widow married, the year after the Duke's death, the Hon. John Tollemache. At Duke William's death the male line of William, second Earl Roxburghe became extinct. also the title of Lord Bellenden; and the Scotch Peerages were competed for by Lady Essex Ker as heir of line, by Sir James Innes as heir-male of Margaret, daughter of Harry Lord Ker, by General Walter Ker of Littledean, as heir-male of Habbie Ker, first Earl Roxburghe, and by Sir William Drummond as heir-male of the second Earl Roxburghe, each of whom petitioned the King, while the estates were respectively claimed by Lady Essex Ker, General Ker of Littledean, Sir James Innes, and Mr Ker Bellenden, the latter claiming, under Duke John, the fourth Duke's entail, which was set aside, as beyond His Grace's power to make. Lady Essex Ker's claim was also quashed, and the contest lay between Sir James Innes and General Ker. After a great and severe struggle, which lasted for some years, the case was decided in favour of the former, who accordingly succeeded to all the Estates and Scottish honours, except the original Barony of Roxburghe, which could not pass beyond the first Baron or heirs-male of his body, and in 1812 he accordingly became the fifth Duke of Roxburghe.

JAMES, FIFTH DUKE, who assumed the name of Ker, was, as Sir James Innes, descended from a long line of ancestry, the first of whom had a rather remarkable Charter in the time of Malcolm Canmore, 1154. But it is impossible to go into the history, interesting though it undoubtedly is, and of great antiquity. Suffice it to say that Sir James was the sixth Baronet of the title, which was one of the earliest created in 1625, and that soon after succeeding, he sold the Estate of Innes in Elgin, and went to reside at Innes in Devonshire till the lapse of the Dukedom brought him out. His was the twenty-second generation of the family in a direct male line, and according to a tradition, they were, in the long course of their succession, fortunate in three things, First, that their inheritance never went to a woman; next, that none of them ever married an ill wife; and thirdly, that no friend ever suffered for their debt. The Roxburghe inheritance, fortunately for the Inneses, did go to a woman, or at anyrate to her grandson in her right, and it is to be hoped it may long continue in the present line. Sir James Innes Ker, fifth Duke of Roxburghe, who was a fine old gentleman, died at an advanced age in 1823, leaving an only son, James Henry, sixth and present Duke, whom God preserve.

I have been told that Duke James wished to make a bargain with General Ker, that whoever gained the suit, should pay all expenses. General Ker objected, and his wife was indignant, saying she would be Duchess or nothing. Notwithstanding, the Duke maintained the General, who was ruined by the suit, Littledean being sold, and the family scattered.*

THE KERRS OF FERNIEHIRST, FORMERLY KERSHAUGH.

Having given, in introducing to you the Kers of Cessford,

* The wife of General Ker was the youngest daughter of Mr Forster of Bolton. She was alive in 1837, and it was said of her then, that "the loss of what the world most regards had in no degree lessened the sweetness of her spirit or the gaiety of her innocent mirth."

an account of the rise and domiciliation on the Borders of the two families generally, I now proceed to give details of this illustrious house from the time of its progenitor, Ralph's settlement on the banks of the Jed, which is supposed to have taken place somewhere about 1330, when he got possession of the lands now called Ferniehirst, called originally, by him, Kersheugh, and previously, before Ralph's day, called Scraesburgh, probably by the Earls of Douglas, who were the superiors.

It is supposed that RALPH lived, after acquiring the lands in question, some twenty years, and that he acquired Crailing from the Humes, and marrying, according to the Somervill History, a daughter of Mr Thomas of Carnwath, had two sons—Andrew, his heir, and John, who settled at Aberdeen, where he got some property, for which he obtained a charter from King David Bruce. Thomas's son and heir,

ANDREW, succeeded as third of Kersheugh, and was the first of the family introduced to court circles, when he obtained the appointment of cup-bearer to Robert III. Mackenzie states that he married a daughter of the then Edmonston of that ilk, by whom he had a son,

THOMAS, who succeeded as fourth laird, and marrying Elizabeth Hume, daughter of Sir Thomas Hume of that ilk, had three sons—Andrew, his heir; Thomas, noticed in a public document dated 1452; and James, also so noticed. Thomas died about 1430, and was succeeded by his eldest son

ANDREW, fifth incumbent, who was one of Earl Douglas's party in his imposing expedition to Rome, already referred to in the account of the Cessfords, whose chief was also one of the magnates forming the expedition.

Rymer mentions Andrew Ker of Kersheugh with other notables, and Mackenzie reports his marriage to Jane Crichton, by whom he had a son and successor,

RALPH, sixth laird, who married Mary, daughter of Toms of Innerleith, and dying about 1460, left by her two sons— Andrew, his successor; and Robert of Yair.

I have found several notices of the Kers of Yair and of Sunderland Hall, and also of Fernilie, all probably of the Yair stock. Thomas of Yair was a juror, with John Riddell of that ilk, on the retour of service of Walter Ker as heir of his father, Andrew of Cessford, in 1528; and again, Andrew Ker of Yair was party to a bond made at Melrose on the occasion of the quarrel, when Ker of Linton was killed in 1582. Then again I have notices of William and Andrew of Yair in 1633—father and son—the latter then coming into possession. How long after that the family held Yair I cannot say, though I apprehend but a short time, as James Pringle had acquired it some years before his death, which happened in 1667. Sunderland Hall, on the other hand, continued with the Kers till a later period, and did not leave the family, though failing in the male line—a daughter, the heiress, carrying it to her husband, Andrew Plummer of Middlestead, in whose family it continued till the death of the last Miss Plummer in the present century, when it went to a member of the Scott of Woll family.

The Kers of Yair are commemorated in a simple but striking form in Melrose Abbey, where there is a stone dedicated to them thus—

"Here lyes the race of the House of Yair,*"

or Yare. Another old family connected with the Yair one is that of Kippielaw, represented by the Rev. John Seton Karr. The elder brother of the Yair ancestor was

ANDREW, the seventh laird, who married the Honourable Mary Herries, by whom he had two sons—Thomas, his heir; and John, ancestor of the Kers of Greenhead, from whom the Kerrs of Chatto and Sunlaws are descended. Sir Andrew Ker of Greenhead was created a baronet in 1637, but dying *sine prole* in 1667, it became extinct. On Andrew, the seventh laird's death, he was succeeded by his eldest son

THOMAS, eighth laird, the first designated of Ferniehirst,

---

* This simple epitaph deeply impressed Washington Irving when he visited Melrose.

in place of Kersheugh. This laird or baron built the present residence, or castle, as it was called, say about 1490. He was a man of great consideration, and took an important part in the forays and wars of the Border. He got a new charter of his lands from Archibald, Earl Angus, the superior, which was confirmed to his son Andrew.

He married Catherine, daughter of Robert Colvill of Ochiltree, a man of name and fame, who fell at Flodden, and by his wife had only one daughter, who married a Ker of Smailholm, son of Cessford, and they had three sons—Andrew, his heir; Ralph of Cavers; and Thomas, Abbot of Kelso, 1507, died 1528; and another son, William.

Ralph Carre, the orthography adopted by the latter Ferniehirsts, as we shall see, was the first of Cavers, and the connecting male link between them and the old Border sept. A subsequent connection afterwards took place, through a marriage with a daughter of the second Lord Jedburgh, by which the Cavers family are the only descendants extant of the Lords Jedburgh, the Ferniehirsts proper.

I shall not go into the genealogy of the house of Cavers-Carre further than to say that it has produced men who have served their country as politicians, one having been M.P. for the county of Roxburgh; as soldiers and sailors, several having been in these noble professions; and as lawyers, one having reached the bench; and in all the varied relations of public and private life, the representatives of that house have been honoured and respected.

The third brother, Thomas, was abbot of Kelso for about twelve years, during which time he had important duties of a diplomatic as well as a spiritual character to perform. He died, as far as I can make out, a peaceful death, though another abbot of the Cessford family is stated to have been killed by his own kinsman. This latter officer, who must have been in charge of the abbey after the Reformation, and whose name was William Ker, could not have acted in an ecclesiastical, but only in a temporal capacity. I return to the father of Ralph of Cavers and Abbot Thomas, who died in 1499, when he was succeeded by his eldest son

ANDREW as ninth baron. He was a man of remarkable talent, great tact, and unbounded courage, and made a conspicuous figure in the reign of the Fourth and Fifth Jameses, when he was warden of the whole three marches—east, west, and middle—as well as one of the Commissioners appointed to treat for peace with the English, which they happily accomplished for a time in 1528. He was rewarded with the barony of Oxnam, and got fresh charters of Ferniehirst from James V., the former superior, Earl Angus, being forfeited, when the superiority reverted to the Crown. He also got the bailiery of Jedburgh Forest in 1542. He married Janet, daughter of Sir Patrick Hume, father of the first Earl of Marchmont, and had three sons and one daughter. The eldest son, Thomas, predeceased his father without issue; his third, Robert, acquired Ancrum, whose descendants, after the death of the last direct Ferniehirst—viz., Robert, third Lord Jedburgh, succeeded to the representation and estates, as we shall show at a subsequent period. The eldest surviving son,

JOHN, became the tenth baron. He was a valiant knight of the Borders, and did great service against the English, and well restrained their incursions. He married Catherine, daughter of Sir Andrew Ker of Cessford, killed at Melrose, and had three sons—Thomas, his heir, Andrew and William, of whom no issue survived. William was a great loyalist, and adhered firmly to the interest of Queen Mary, as his elder brother Thomas did, as we shall see, and in reward for his services William got a pension from James VI. Sir John Ker died in 1562, as stated by Douglas, but on a tombstone at Jedburgh the date is 1559. He was succeeded by his eldest son

THOMAS, also a knight, and eleventh baron. He was a man of commanding talents, and of sterling probity and honour. Like his brother William, he was a devoted friend and servant of Queen Mary, and in her greatest distress he never deserted her interest. He and Sir Walter Scott of Buccleuch —his brother-in-law—entered England with fire and sword, hoping, by sowing dissension and creating disturbances there, they might do service to their unfortunate Queen, of whom it is said that no person ever looked upon her beauty without admiration, or heard of her sorrows without pity.

Fernichirst was, it is said, concerned in the attack on the Parliament at Stirling, for which he was exiled, and forfeited. An author states :—

"He was accused of crime, and was committed to Dundee. He was a tall, stout, able warrior, ready for any great attempt and undertaking, and of an immovable fidelity to the Queen of Scots, and the King her son; having been once or twice turned out of all his lands and fortunes, and banished the sight of his country and children, which yet he endured patiently, and, after so many crosses falling upon him together, perished unshaken, and always like himself."

King James being perfectly sensible that the only crime alleged against him arose from his loyalty and devotion to Queen Mary, restored to him all his estates, and gave him a full and ample remission under the Great Seal in 1583. Soon after this, in acting on the Borders, an affray took place with the English, in which a son of the Earl of Bedford lost his life, and this exasperated Elizabeth so much that nothing would satisfy her but Fernichirst's capture. He was committed to Aberdeen, where he ended a life of great exertion and suffering in 1586.

Sir Thomas married twice; first Janet, daughter of Sir William Kirkaldy, another devoted friend of Queen Mary's, by whom he had one son Andrew, and two daughters (one married to Sir P. Hume of Polwarth); and second, Janet, sister of Sir Walter Scott of Buccleuch, by whom he had three sons—James of Crailing, Thomas of Oxnam, and Robert, the favourite of James VI., created Earl of Somerset.

As we shall speak of Andrew and James of Crailing as successors to their father in turn, I shall take up THOMAS of

Oxnam, and ROBERT the King's favourite. Thomas is easily disposed of, for he fell in a riot at Jedburgh, on Rood-day Fair, 1601, as set forth in Pitcairn, and as corroborated by Mr Jeffrey in his second volume; though in the fourth he makes Thomas Ker of Cavers the murdered man, forgetting what he said in his previous volume, *which is correct.* Thomas Ker of Cavers long survived the Rood-day Fair battle, as I know from family documents.

I now come to Robert the youngest son, the favourite of James I. of England, who became so notorious, though in my humble opinion the foolish conduct of the king towards him, and the designs of a profligate woman, caused his fall. It was said James, who was fond of handsome men, and took a fancy to Robert Carre (the new orthography which he adopted), appointed him to a situation in his Court, and afterwards raised him to exceedingly high positions, conferring a peerage—finally the Earldom of Somerset—upon him, and decorating him with the high honour of the Garter. The divorced Countess of Essex set her cap at Somerset, and he was weak enough to listen to her importunities, and to yield to her solicitations. A serious imputation rested upon them by the death of Sir Thomas Overbury, who advised Somerset not to marry Lady Essex. They had one daughter, Lady Anne Carre, who married the fifth Earl of Bedford, afterwards created Duke, and who, considering her mother's character and conduct, was a pattern of her sex.

Though Somerset never again appeared at Court, he was not altogether deserted by his sovereign, who saw him in private; but after James' death, he lived in complete retirement, and died in or near London, in 1645, and was buried at Covent Garden, where his son-in-law, the Duke of Bedford, had property (still in the family), and probably a vault, though the superb mausoleum of the Russells is at Chenies. In the exhibition of pictures in 1866 there was a portrait of Robert Carre, lent by the Duke of Devonshire, whose ancestor no doubt bought it with Chiswick House, which belonged to

Somerset, and which he sold in order to provide a suitable fortune for his daughter, Lady Anne.

The eldest son of Sir Thomas, Sir ANDREW, the twelfth baron, was a baron in every sense of the word, being created, in 1622, Lord Jedburgh, by King James, to mark his sense of his talents and usefulness, and no doubt of his father's devotion to his royal mother's cause. He got several charters of lands, with the Bailiery of Jedburgh, which had been held by his predecessors for three generations, and having married Anne, daughter of the Master of Ochiltree, left one son, Sir Andrew, who wedded Margaret Ker (Lady Yester), whose works of benevolence and charity are well known both in Roxburghshire and Edinburgh, in which city a church was built by her munificence, which bears her name. Sir Andrew was an Extraordinary Judge of Session and a Privy Councillor, but died in the prime of life, in 1628; his widow, who was daughter of the first Earl of Lothian, and relict of the seventh Lord Yester, surviving him many years. Sir Andrew also predeceased his father, Lord Jedburgh, at whose death, in 1631, without surviving male issue, he was succeeded by his half-brother

JAMES OF CRAILING, second Lord Jedburgh, the son of the same father, Sir Thomas of Ferniehirst, by his second wife Janet Scott, sister of Buccleuch. The circumstances of the family were now much reduced, and James was not ambitious about adopting the title. He, however, recruited the finances of the old house by marrying Marie Rutherfurd, heiress of Hundalee, and though living in retirement he well maintained the honour of the family. He died in 1645, and was buried in Jedburgh Abbey. He left one son and one daughter, the mother of John Carre of Cavers who died 1724.

The Son ROBERT became the Third Lord Jedburgh, and married Juliana Hamilton, widow of his cousin Sir Patrick Hume of Polwarth, but had no family by her, who, however, was the mother by her first husband of the Earl of Marchmont so distinguished in the annals of his country, especially at the revolution. There are no memorials of Robert, Lord Jedburgh, worth relating, and having no children, he got an extended patent to include the nearest male line, descended from his great-grand-uncle, Robert Ker of Ancrum, youngest son of the ninth Baron of Ferniehirst. My first Cavers ancestor was only one degree more remote in the *male* line, having been the son of the eighth baron, but his descendant John Carre the sixth of Cavers was nephew and heir-of-line of the third Lord Jedburgh, being the son of his lordship's only sister, the Honourable Jane Carre. Though Hundalee went to this nephew and his heirs under certain restrictions, it also followed, though in recent times, the same course as the Jedburgh title, by going to the representative of the male Ferniehirst line, who was at the time the third Marquis of Lothian, a remote cousin, while a sister of my grand-uncle, the last Cavers proprietor of Hundalee, survived him, but he felt he had not the power of altering the old entail.

I have noticed the change of the name to Carre in a late generation, and shall now more minutely explain the subject of the orthography.

At the outset of the family history, I stated that the Norman name was KARRE, and that when their descendants arrived in Scotland, they came as Ker, being the *Anglo-Norman* version of it, which still continues in one or more branches, though in various documents relative to the Scottish Border families, its metamorphosis to " Carre " * is frequently met with. But early in the seventeenth century the chiefs of the Ferniehirst Baronial house, beginning with the first Lord Jedburgh, usually adopted this new orthography, and I have seen a fac-simile of the signature of his only son, Sir Andrew Carre, Master of Jedburgh, and husband of Lady Yester, which was written in a strong, bold hand, with a K instead of a C as the initial letter, and the left limb of the K curled back both at top and bottom.

* An *e* was added to Carr, which accords with the universal spelling in old English, just as star was written *starre*, and bar *barre*.

The oldest Ferniehirst male line terminated in ROBERT, third Lord Jedburgh, and their successors of the House of Ancrum, did not adopt the new orthography, but continued the *Anglo-Norman* spelling, with the addition of an r, making the name Kerr, no doubt to distinguish the family from that of Cessford, from whom they descend as Lothians, who adopted Ker.

As already noticed, the male representatives of the House of Ferniehirst and Jedburgh, whose original line closed with Robert, third Lord Jedburgh, were the Kerrs of Ancrum, descended from Robert Ker, third son of the eighth Baron of Ferniehirst, and nephew of Ralph of Cavers Carre. The real heir was the great-great-great-grandson of this said Robert Ker of Ancrum, who was great-grand-uncle of the third Lord Jedburgh, which made the cousinship very remote, and was a great contrast to the Cavers Carre connexion, which was that of maternal nephew, of the said Lord Jedburgh, in addition to the previous male relationship. I must now carry on the male line through the Ancrums, which will finally bring us to the Lothians, and first:

ROBERT KER of Ancrum, before adverted to, was apparently a quiet, inoffensive character, who acquired a good deal of property, which he shared with his wife, Margaret Home of Wedderburn, by whom he had a son, who succeeded, viz. :

WILLIAM KER of Ancrum, who was assassinated when the disputes about the chieftainship of the two Houses of Ker ran high, in 1590. He was much lamented, and Archbishop Spottiswood remarks upon it: "A hateful fact it was ; for the manner in which it was done, and the loss the country sustained by his death, for he was a man generally well given, wise, of great courage, and expert beyond others in the laws and customs of the borders."

He married Miss Margaret Dundas of Fingask, and had children, two sons being particularly mentioned, viz., Robert, his heir, and William Kerr of Linton, the latter a man of great courage, who did good service on the Borders, and was very properly rewarded for his acts by the grant of a pension.

He was in the household of both James and Charles, and was married, leaving only one daughter. The eldest son and heir was

ROBERT, the third Laird, who, like his courageous and distinguished younger brother, was a great favourite at Court, having had many good qualities of head and heart to recommend him. He was a fair poet as well. But a sad circumstance arose which made it necessary for him to withdraw not only from his position at court, but from his native country. He accepted a challenge from Mr Maxwell arising out of a quarrel between the Maxwells and Johnstones, connected with the wardenship of the Western Marches, in which our hero was involved, slew his adversary in the duel which ensued, and though he was tried and acquitted, he was forced to conceal himself for a time. Being, however, recalled from the Continent, he was restored to his position at Court, and when Charles the First ascended the throne, he made him a Lord of the Bedchamber, and in a few years after, created him a Peer, by the titles of Earl Ancrum, and Lord Ker of Nisbet Longnewton and Dolphinston, with remainder to the issue male of his second marriage, failing which to his other heirs male. His son, by his first marriage, wedded the heiress of the House of Lothian, when he was created Earl. This explained the reason of his son by the second marriage getting the title of Ancrum, but little was eventually left to sustain that fine old place, and Ancrum was eventually sold to Sir John Scott of Kirkstyle, ancestor of Sir William Scott. The Earl of Ancrum sacrificed all his property for the sake of his royal master, Charles the First, to whom he was a firm and attached friend, throughout all His Majesty's troubles. On the king's death, the Earl retired to Holland, where he concluded his life in solitude and poverty, and his end was not a little embittered by the conspicuous part his eldest son, Lord Lothian, took against the king. He was noted for his correct taste in literature and the fine arts, but his poetry was not conspicuous, except for its plaintive character, which corresponded with his life, though he bore with fortitude and piety the misfortunes which accompanied his latter years.

The Earl of Ancrum married first Miss Elizabeth Murray, daughter of Sir John Murray of Blackbarony, and sister of the wife of Sir John Riddell of Riddell, and he married secondly, Lady Anne Stanley, only daughter of the sixth Earl of Derby, not the ancestor of the present Earl, though, of course, of the same family.

Lord Ancrum's younger son by the second marriage, succeeded him, as CHARLES, second Earl Ancrum, in terms of the patent, but dying without issue, it eventually merged in his brother, Lord Lothian's family. The second Lord Ancrum was a parliamentary speaker of note, having been long in the House of Commons, but he had little, beyond a pension he was allowed, to maintain his position and rank.

HOUSE OF LOTHIAN.

The first of this house was MARK, second son of Sir Andrew Ker of Cessford, who was Commendator of Newbattle after the Reformation, when he became a Protestant. He had previously been abbot, and was spiritual head of the abbey when the religious house was disestablished. He treated the monks with little commiseration, for he turned them out, when they complained that he would not give them a penny to live on. He was one of the few dignitaries of the Romish Church that espoused the doctrines of the Reformation. I suspect that Mark, though an abbot, had been an easy-going one, for he must have married while exercising his spiritual functions, which was against all rule. His marriage must have been before the Reformation, as his son in 1577 received a public appointment.

He had two other sons and a daughter who married Wm. Maxwell, Lord Herries. The Commendator was one of the three Commissioners or Judges on the south side of the Forth connected with the troublous times, and sided against Morton in 1578. He was also employed after the Raid of Ruthven, to propose terms to the conspirators, from which no good result followed. He died soon after, in 1584, and was succeeded by his eldest son, MARK, who got an appointment in 1577, and was made an extraordinary Lord of Session at his father's death, and in his room, his qualifications being thus stated: "The King is persuaded of the literature and good qualities with the quhilk he is endowit, and of the gude will and affection he bears to the furtherance of our service."

He got a charter of Newbattle Barony, including Prestongrange, in 1587, and in 1591 was made a Lord of Parliament by the title of Lord Newbattle, holding other high appointments afterwards, all culminating in the Earldom of Lothian, which he obtained in 1606, but he only survived this latter Peerage honour about three years. He married his cousin, Margaret Maxwell, daughter of John, Lord Herries, by whom Scotstarvit says he had thirty-one children, though ten only are given in Douglas. Sir John Scott adds that Lady Lothian was addicted to the black art, and that this proved fatal to the Earl. The Countess being afflicted with a cancer, implored the help of a notable warlock called "Playfair," who condescended to heal her, but on the condition that the sore should fall on the person she loved best, whereunto, she agreeing, did convalesce, but the Earl, her husband, found the boil in his throat, of which he died shortly thereafter, on the 8th of April 1609.

The Earl's eldest daughter, Lady JANE, married ROBERT, Master of Boyd, whose family once possessed great power and wealth, and one of whom, Mark Alex. Boyd, was a remarkable genius, and also an extraordinary person, for he was born with teeth.

The eldest son of Mark, the first Earl of Lothian, viz., ROBERT, succeeded as second Earl, but little is said respecting his life, though a melancholy account is given in a history of the Kirk of Scotland, by Calderwood, as follows:

"Upon Saturday the 6th of March 1624, Sir Robert Kerr, Earl Lothian, went up early in the morning to a chamber in the Place of Newbattle, pretending he was gone to lay accounts and write missives, and commanded that none come towards him for an houre. He barreth the chamber doore, and cutted his own throat with a knife, after he had given himself sundrie wounds with his dagger. Some imputed this desperate course to the great debtts which were lying in his hands, others to consulting with magicians and witches."

This unfortunate Earl married Annabella Campbell, daughter of the seventh Earl of Argyll, and by her he had two daughters only. Being therefore without male issue, he devised his titles and estates, with the king's permission, to his elder daughter, Lady Anne Kerr and her heirs, and at her father's death in 1624, she accordingly succeeded as

COUNTESS OF LOTHIAN. Her father's next brother, Sir William Kerr, disputing the arrangement, claimed the title of Earl Lothian, and continued to use it till interdicted in 1632, about eight years after the second Earl's death. Lady Anne was now fairly installed, and having married William Ker, elder son of Robert, the first Earl of Ancrum, he was created Earl of Lothian, which, of course, made him independent of Sir William Kerr's pretentions, and through him the junction of the Houses of Lothian and Ferniehirst took place. He may be called the third Earl of Lothian. He joined the Covenanters in 1638, and was actively engaged in behalf of their cause for some years.

He was President of the Commission despatched by Parliament to the King in 1646, with their final proposition, which was refused. He protested against the "engagement," and when it was declared unlawful, was appointed Secretary of State in room of Lord Lanark, then deprived of office, and was one of the Scottish Commissioners sent to avert the blow then impending over the King, for which they were arrested, but afterwards released, and finally he and Lord Cassillis were despatched to invite Charles the Second to Scotland, which was the last public act of his life, for though he lived about twenty-five years afterwards, he made no further prominent appearance. The Earl and Lady Anne, the Countess, had fourteen children. The eldest son was Robert, and he had another, Charles, ancestor of the Kerrs of Abbotrule, now extinct. The last of the Kerrs of Abbotrule—who was called the Abbot—was a great friend and admirer of Sir Walter Scott, anticipating for Sir Walter, when called to the bar, a splendid career, which, of course, he had, though not as a lawyer. One of the daughters, Lady Mary, who was married to Brodie of Brodie, was a zealous Covenanter. On her marriage "she subscribed her covenant to and with God, and became his, and gave herself up to him." Another daughter, Lady Henrietta, married in 1673 Francis Scott of Thirlestaine, and died at Edinburgh 1741, aged 90. Her grandson became Lord Napier.

ROBERT, the eldest son of the Earl and Countess, succeeded as fourth Earl. He served in Holland as a volunteer, with great credit, was a warm supporter of the Revolution, and of King William, who appointed him a member of the Privy Council. He held other appointments, and got extended patents, being finally advanced to the dignity of a Marquis. He married his kinswoman, Jean, daughter of the Marquis of Argyll, with whom his father served against Montrose in 1644, and by her had ten children, of whom I select the following for particular notice, viz.: WILLIAM, the eldest; Lord CHARLES; Lord MARK, and one daughter, Lady MARY KERR, who married James, Marquis of Douglas, and was mother of the rather foolish Duke of Douglas and Lady Jane, who was the subject of so much talk about the middle of last century, on account of the twins she had at the age of fifty-two, one of whom was finally found, not by the Court of Session, but by the House of Lords, to be the heir of the great Douglas estates. Lady Mary, the Marchioness of Douglas, was buried at Holyrood, where her ill-fated daughter, Lady Jane, was afterwards interred also.

LORD CHARLES, the second son, had numerous descendants. Two well-known citizens of Edinburgh—James Kerr of Bughtrig, M.P. for Edinburgh, convener of the trades there; and

Alexander Kincaid, Lord Provost of Edinburgh, and author of a history of that city, published 1787—married two of his daughters.

LORD JOHN KERR, the second son, was a gallant soldier, and died, a little above middle age, in command of the 31st Regiment.

LORD MARK, the third son, was also a distinguished son of Mars, and died at the ripe age of seventy-six, both being buried at Kensington. Lord Mark entered the army at seventeen, and served in various regiments, finally attaining the command of the 11th Dragoons in 1732, which he held for twenty years, dying in the command in 1752.

He was a gallant officer, and saw a good deal of active service in early life, as our military generally did during the reign of Queen Anne. He took part at the battle of Almanza between the Confederate army of English, Portuguese, and Dutch against the forces of France and Spain. Owing to the cowardly behaviour of the Portuguese, who deserted, the British were defeated with great loss, and Lord Mark Kerr was wounded. It has been commented on as singular that the Confederate army was commanded by a Frenchman, while the French were led by an English general—the Duke of Berwick. Lord Mark Kerr was also at the capture of Vigo by Lord Cobham, who carried off a large quantity of ordnance and other stores, and also a number of slave sloops.

Our hero, who lived in single blessedness, was a person of most peculiar and eccentric habits. He carried etiquette and punctiliousness to such an excess as gave an air of frivolity to his manners. But withal, he was a man of soldier-like appearance and high breeding. From his hastiness of temper, which he could not always restrain, he was frequently tempted to call out those who annoyed him or meddled with his peculiarities, and it has been said he fought several duels. In his time duelling was very common, and one of the most noted was the duel between the Duke of Hamilton and Lord Mohun, with swords, both being killed—the latter on the spot. This duel took place on a Sunday in Hyde Park, 15th November 1712.

Lord Mark held several important military appointments, and in 1745 had the command at Berwick, for he is mentioned in the Jacobite song of Johnie Cope, the English general who, after being defeated at Prestonpans, fled thither, as it is said—

> Sir John then into Berwick rode,
> Just as the deil had been his guide ;
> Gi'en him the world, he wadna staid.
> I have foughten the boys in the morning—
> Said the Berwickers unto Sir John,
> " O what's become of all your men ? "
> " In faith," says he, " I dinna ken ;
> " I left them a' this morning."
> Says Lord Mark Kerr—" Ye are na blate,
> To bring us the news o' your ain defeat,
> I think you deserve the back o' the gate ;
> Get out o' my sight this morning."
>   Hey Johnie Cope, etc.

ROBERT, the First Marquis of Lothian, dying in 1703, was succeeded by his eldest son

WILLIAM, the Second Marquis, who had succeeded previously to the Jedburgh Barony. He was a steady friend to the Revolution settlement, and a military man of note and rank, serving in the 7th Dragoons and Foot Guards in turn ; though owing to some offence he had given to the Tory Government he was obliged to retire from the latter corps. That was in 1713. Latterly, however, he had been restored, and held a high command in Scotland, but returning to London, died there in 1722. His funeral obsequies were performed with great pomp, and his burial place was in Westminster Abbey. He married his cousin, Lady Jane Campbell, from a principle of honour, feeling for the forlorn and poverty-stricken state of the Argyll family, owing to the forfeiture of the Ninth Earl (who was beheaded, as his father had been also), which the Marquis of Lothian thought undeserved. They had five children—one son, William, and four daughters.

All the latter married well, but there is no feature calling for special notice respecting their marriages, and I pass to their only brother William, after giving a rather curious extract from Mackay's "Memoirs," on the character of William the Second Marquis of Lothian.

" He hath abundance of fire, and may prove himself a man of business when he applies himself that way; laughs at all revealed religion, yet sets up for a pillar of Presbytery, and proves the truest card in the pack, being very zealous, though not devout. He is brave in his person, loves his country and his bottle; a thorough libertine; very handsome, black, with a fine eye. Forty-five years old."

He must have lived fifteen years after Mr Mackay made these observations, as he was sixty when he died in 1722. His only son,

WILLIAM, who succeeded as Third Marquis, in his father's lifetime, acquired from the last of the old Ferniehirst line the Barony of Jedburgh, which he adopted. When he succeeded to the Marquisate, he was elected, on the death of Henry Scott, Earl of Deloraine (son of Monmouth and the Duchess of Buccleuch), a Representative Peer, and was frequently chosen at subsequent elections, till he had completed a service in Parliament of upwards of a quarter of a century. He was for about six years Lord High Commissioner of the General Assembly of the Kirk of Scotland, and also held the office of Lord Clerk Register, so that his public services were important. He married twice: first, Miss Nicolson, by whom he had two sons and one daughter; secondly, his cousin Miss Kerr, daughter of Lord Charles Kerr, by whom he had no family. She survived him many years.

The two sons were both distinguished soldiers. The second, Lord Robert, joined the 11th Dragoons (the regiment of his celebrated grand-uncle the duellist). He fell at Culloden, the scene of the young Pretender's defeat, in 1746. The Duke of Cumberland commanded the Royal troops, and though he lost very few compared with the slaughter in the Pretender's army, Lord Robert was one. He died as a true soldier at the head of a company he commanded in Burell's Division. His elder brother, William Henry, who succeeded as Fourth Marquis of Lothian, was also a gallant soldier, and served under Cumberland at the bloody battle of Fontenoy in 1745, when the French, after a severe struggle, beat the allies. He served again under the Duke, at Culloden, being then Lieutenant-Colonel of the 11th Dragoons, and also in command of one wing of the cavalry. He had the pain of seeing his gallant brother fall; but being spared himself, though wounded at Fontenoy, he was enabled to give his active and efficient services on many future occasions, both in the field and in the Senate, and was rewarded with the Order of the Thistle. He died full Colonel of the brave Lord Mark, his granduncle's, 11th Dragoons, a regiment which may be called an heir-loom of the house of Lothian. The Marquis, when he entered the army, and married, took the title of the Earl of Ancrum, the eldest son's courtesy title which he was the first to assume. His wife was a descendant of the illustrious Duke of Schomberg, who was accidentally shot at the battle of the Boyne by the French refugees of his own regiment, and by her he had one son and two daughters. From one of the latter descends the present Duke of Richmond. The son,

WILLIAM JOHN, succeeded in 1775, at his father's death, as Fifth Marquis. He entered the army as a cornet in the heir-loom regiment, and finally got the colonelcy, though he served in several other corps besides, making his entire military service extend over the astonishingly long period of about sixty years. He married Miss Fortescue, a cousin of the Duke of Wellington, but she died early, and the Marquis survived her about thirty-five years, and continued a widower. They had five daughters, and four sons—three in the army, and one in the Navy—the latter, Lord Mark, being at the taking of the Island of Minorca in 1798, where he did good service. The two younger sons in the army acquitted themselves well and honourably, and the elder, William, Earl Ancrum, who succeeded as Sixth Marquis, saw a good deal of service in Ireland during the rebellion. He had the honour of commanding the Midlothian Cavalry Fencibles, who volunteered to go there, and afterwards to any part of Europe. His services were requited, though rather tardily, with a British peerage by the title of Lord Ker, and I believe he ordered the patent to be made out with one r, viz., Ker, the old Anglo-Norman spelling, though the family name has still the two r's.

By his first wife, who died in 1805, he had the late Marquis, Lord Hay, and one daughter, and marrying secondly in 1806, an aunt of the present Duke of Buccleuch, he left a number of children by her ladyship, who died in 1833, the Marquis himself dying in 1824.* His eldest son,

JOHN WILLIAM ROBERT, succeeded as Seventh Marquis, and died in the prime of life in 1841, being succeeded by his eldest son, William S. Robert, the Eighth Marquis. He was a distinguished scholar at Oxford, and gave promise of public usefulness, but lost his health, while yet a young man, died early, and was succeeded by his brother, Lord Schomberg Kerr, the present Marquis.

I have mentioned in the general histories of the great houses of Ker several branches, viz.: Fawdonside, Littledean, Greenhead and Chatto, Cavers Carre, Yair, Sunderlandhall, Fernielie, Linton, Abbotrule, and I may add the Kers of Graden, one of whose members was a brave soldier, as witness his riding under fire in front of the king's troops at Prestonpans, when engaged in reconnoitring for the Pretender, whom he served.

* Sir Walter Scott said of the late Marquis, in reply to a friend, to whom his Lordship had done a kindness, "Ay, Lord Lothian is a good man—he is a man from whom one may receive a favour, and that's saying a good deal for any man in these days."

THE ELLIOT FAMILY.

THE families of Douglas, Scott, and Kerr are three of the most distinguished, but not the most ancient, on the Scottish Borders, for in that respect the Soulises, Riddells, Corbetts, and others, bear away the palm for antiquity. I now take up the Elliots, who may be said to stand fourth on the historical roll. As far as I can ascertain, they came to Liddesdale towards the close of the fourteenth century. Their origin or derivation is uncertain. It is alleged by some that they, as well as the English Eliots—for the name is not confined to Scotland—are descended from one of William the Conqueror's band, viz., Monsieur Aliot, a distinguished soldier of the great Norman. A traditionary story is told that this warrior was with the Conqueror when he fell at his disembarkation, and exclaimed that the fall was a happy omen, as William had embraced the land he was to become monarch of, declaring with drawn sword that he would maintain the right of his Lord to the territory he had so embraced. After the conquest, it is further alleged that he added to Aliot's Arms a batten gules to a bend or on a field azure, and for a crest, an arm and sword, with the motto :

| Over rocks, through fires. | Per saxa, per ignes. Fortiter et recte. | Bravely and honourably. |

Some antiquarians think that the Scotch Elliots first settled in Forfarshire, on the river Eliot or Elot, in the parish now called Arbirlot, a contraction of Aber-Eliot, which refers to the circumstance of the stream passing through the parish and entering the sea, as it does, on its eastern side, and that from the river the family derive their name. Another authority thinks they came from Elliotston, in Renfrewshire, a place which I find belonged to Lord Semple's ancestors long before the period he mentions, and nearly two hundred years before the Elliots came to the Border, which seems against his view, as possessors at any rate of that place. The same authority states they were first called Ellwood in Liddesdale, which is also against their supposed Elliotston derivation. Ellwood is an English as well as an Irish name, and to an English Ellwood, the friend of the great Milton, we owe the immortal poem of Paradise Regained, which he suggested to the poet as a rider to Paradise lost. The late distinguished English physician, Dr John Elliotston, to whom the medical profession owes much for his scientific researches, is very likely, I think, to have had his derivation from Renfrewshire, but London claims him for her son, by birth, whatever may have been his descent.

It must be recollected that in early times the name of Eliot was distinguished in England, though with a different orthography. Willis states that early in the thirteenth century, Elliots were seated in Devonshire, and that from them several families descended, and one in particular which settled in Cornwall, in the sixteenth century, calling the place they acquired Port Eliot, after themselves—its previous designation being St Germans, the site of an old priory. This family produced some men of mark, the chief of whom was

SIR JOHN ELIOT, noted for his opposition to Charles the First, and his Court, and who suffered imprisonment for his conduct. After a time he was offered his freedom, but he preferred remaining in durance vile, which he did for some time, dying in 1632 in the Tower, where he was buried, the king refusing the petition of his son, to bury his father in his own county. Sir John Eliot was one of the most eloquent and popular of his party, and in Parliament he boldly stood up for the liberty of the subject, and though hot and impetuous in his temper, was a man of unimpeachable integrity. He was styled by a great writer Hallam, "the most illustrious confessor in the cause of liberty whom that time produced."

To show Sir John Eliot's style I now give his summing up on the impeachment of George Villiers, Duke of Buckingham, one of the favourites of James the First :

"I observe a wonder in policy and in nature, so dangerous to the state in *his immense greatness*, is able to subsist of *himself* and keep in being. To this I answer that the Duke hath used the help of *art* to prop him up. It is apparent that by his *skill* he hath raised a party in the court, a party in the country, and a main party in the *chief places of government in the kingdom*; so that all the most deserving offices, which require abilities to discharge them, are fixed upon the *Duke*, his *allies* and *kindred*, and thus hath he drawn to *himself*, his *family*, and *dependents*, the power of justice, the power of honour, and the power of command; and in effect the *whole power* of the kingdom, both for *peace* and *war*, to strengthen his allies; and in *setting himself* up, hath set upon the *kingdom's revenues*, the fountain of supply, and the nerves of the land. He intercepts, consumes and exhausts the *revenues of the crown*, not only to satisfy his *own lustful desires*, but the luxury of others; and by emptying the veins, in which the blood should run, he hath cast the body of the kingdom into *a high consumption.*"—*(See Rushworth's Collection, Anno* 1616, *p.* 350, *or No.* 1 *Scot.'s Mag. of* 1739*).*

During his long imprisonment, Sir John Eliot wrote the "Monarchy of Man," which a biographer declares, contains "specimens of thought and style, worthy of the best prose writers of that age."

I saw a picture of Eliot, painted in 1628 by Van Somer, in the National Portrait Exhibition at Kensington in 1866. He is there represented with "wide ruff, small peaked dark beard and moustache, with hair hanging down." When the picture, which belongs to the Earl of St Germains, his representative, was painted, Sir John would be under forty.

Before passing from Eliot, I would mention a curious scene which took place in the House of Commons, when he protested against the Tonnage and Poundage Bill of 1628. The

Speaker refused to put Sir John Eliot's resolution to the vote, when a violent outbreak of feeling was manifested. The door was barred, and the speaker held down by force in his chair, while Lord Hollis, another Cornish member, as well as a leader of the popular party, read the resolution to the House, amidst the most tumultuous applause.

Then again, branches of the ancient Devonshire Eliot tree were planted and took root in the East of England, and we all know that Essex gave birth to the celebrated

JOHN ELIOT, the missionary, born in 1604, it is supposed at Nazing. He has been deservedly called the apostle to the American Indians. Educated at Cambridge University, he afterwards took orders and became a famous preacher, and having derived his religious impressions from the great Richard Hooker, called the judicious Hooker, he was, no doubt, well skilled in theology. He, however, embraced Puritanism, and being fired with strong missionary principles, he embarked for America in order to devote himself to the conversion of the native Indians, among whom he laboured with success, obtaining much influence over the several tribes, and translating the Holy Scriptures, as well as other works, into their language. Richard Baxter, the celebrated Nonconformist, knew and appreciated Eliot. Indeed, he said, "there was no man on earth he honoured or loved more than him."

A copy of John Eliot's Bible was not long ago sold in New York, and purchased for a private library at the price of 1130 dollars, or say £282, 10s. Eliot's was the first Bible ever printed in any language in America. It took about three years to print, and when it appeared, it was dedicated to Charles the Second.

The Bible in question is the only monument of a tribe that no longer exists, and of a language no longer spoken. The apostle laboured for nearly sixty years in America, having arrived there in 1630 ; and he died in 1690, aged eighty-five. I have said his Bible was the first printed in America, and he himself was the first protestant minister who diffused the beams of evangelical truth among the benighted American Indians, and while labouring to enlighten their souls, he did all he could to improve their bodily and social condition. Through his means no less than fourteen different towns or settlements were established, to all of which he gave his unwearied attention, and in his journeyings, especially when engaged in his missionary work, he exposed himself to danger, as well as toil. But like a brave soldier, he fought the good fight of faith, bearing any suffering with cheerfulness, and any pain with resignation.

In one of his letters he stated that he had not been dry for several days together, and on stopping for the night he just pulled off his boots, and wrung his stockings, and in the morning put them on again, continuing his journey. At the end of one of his books, he added, " Prayers and pains through faith in Jesus Christ will do anything ; " and his laborious and successful life proved the truth of the saying. He outlived his wife and almost all his children, among whom were four sons, three having been in the ministry, and one of them his own colleague, on whose early death it was said by some one, " The father, having laid up in a better world a rich inheritance for his children, sent a son before to take possession of it."

I must add that Eliot's charity was unbounded, but in the distribution of alms he was profuse. He has been known to give away all his salary, and on one occasion the Treasurer of the bank, who paid him, tied up his money in his handkerchief, in order to prevent his using it before he reached home ; but visiting a poor family on his way, he gave them the handkerchief and its contents, so that the treasurer's kind intentions were defeated. A biographer states that benevolence was a " brilliant star in the constellation of his virtues, and the rays of it were various and extensive." That excellent Christian and great philosopher, Robert Boyle, was a dear friend of John Eliot's, and he was the means of getting for him an annual grant from one of the societies in this country, which aided the apostle in his benevolent schemes for the good of the poor Indians; and though, when near the close of his long and useful life, he found his understanding leaving and his memory failing him, he thanked God his charity still held out. Some of John Eliot's descendants in America have been distinguished, and one was noted for his skill in Natural Philosophy, being the first botanist in New England. Dr John Eliot, probably another descendant, compiled an interesting Biographical Dictionary of New Englanders—men honoured in their generation, and who were the glory of their times.

Previously, however, to the apostolic Eliot, upon whom I have been descanting, there lived in England

THOMAS ELYOT, who flourished in the sixteenth century, and who was held in high estimation by Henry VIII. on account of his learning, as well as his diplomatic talents. He was a moralist likewise. His writings are extensive and various. Some, however, are rather ludicrous, while others are profound. His dictionary, called the "Bibliothecæ Elyotæ," was, as Fuller says, "the stock on which the learned Thomas Cooper, schoolmaster at Oxford, and afterwards Bishop of Lincoln, grafted his 'Thesaurus;' and if not the first, was the best of the kind in that age." He also wrote a defence or apology for good women, which, as a sarcastic biographer very ungallantly and unfairly remarks, "are hardly found and easily defended." The first edition of Sir Thomas Elyot's book "The Governor," published in 1531, is a very scarce work, and so is the "Bibliothecæ Elyotæ," which appeared in 1533. Lowndes, an accoucheur of literature, pronounces the latter "a work of considerable ability, and deservedly held in high estimation as one of the earliest and best attempts in the promotion of lexicographical literature." A new edition of the learned knight's first work, "The Governor," was published in 1834 by Mr A. T. Eliot, Newcastle, and even that is scarce.

There are descendants of Sir Thomas Elyot, though with a

different orthography, and some have been noted. One accompanied Sir Thomas Drake in his famous voyage round the world; and another is supposed to have had granted to him a chapel in Godalming, Surrey, called the Old Mynster, which does not now exist, though lately some excavations were made which showed the foundations of the old building, skeletons being found, denoting where the burying-ground was.

In olden times there were two other Eliots of whom I have notes. One published a French grammar which, he said, "teacheth to speake truly, speedily, and volubly the French tongue;" the other, a book of satires, epigrams, &c. Then there was an anonymous poem, composed by nobody knows who, to be had everybody knows where, and for somebody knows what. I think, however, the name of John Eliot crops out somewhere in connection with this facetious announcement.

In later times, there have been other English Elliots who have added lustre to the name. Among these was an engraver, WILLIAM ELLIOT, who reproduced some of the works of the old masters about the middle of last century, and obtained from the Society of Arts a prize for a print of his own, which gained him considerable *éclat*.

Then there was GEORGE ELLIOT, who wrote a "Life of the Duke of Wellington," from his first achievements in India to the Peace of 1814. And there lived comparatively lately two Henry Elliots—one a civil servant of the late East India Company, and the other a clergyman of the Church of England.

HENRY ELLIOT, the Indian civilian, was an eminent public man, having obtained high rank in the Diplomatic Department of the Company's service—the treaty annexing the Punjaub to our Indian territory having been negotiated by him, for which he was honoured with the Knighthood of the Bath. He was also a distinguished literary man, especially in connection with Eastern lore; and when his health failed him, he had not completed a work connected with the ancient histories of India, which was looked forward to with much interest.

The other Henry Elliot was Henry Venn Elliot, the founder of St Mary's Hall or School for clergymen's daughters, and the respected pastor of the church in connection with that establishment for many years. Mr Elliot was a faithful and diligent servant of his Lord and Master; and if he did not make his talent ten, he certainly did not wrap it up in a napkin. He had varied intellectual gifts, and took high university honours. Mr Elliot had a charming wife, who was a poetess of no mean order.

It is alleged the Elliots came to Liddesdale to join the Douglases when their power was on the wane, but this cannot be vouched for. They were not a large body at first, but they soon multiplied, and became a considerable clan; and on the decline of the Douglases, they appear to have given their support to the Scotts. During the engagement near Melrose in July 1526, an Elliot got the credit of killing Andrew Ker of Cessford. It could not, however, have been an Elliot of Stobs, as often stated, because that family did not issue from Larriston or Redheugh for some time afterwards, and had not then acquired Stobs.* It might have been a Larriston, which property had been acquired by the Elliots sometime before the battle of Melrose.

I have already stated that the Redheugh or Larriston family was unquestionably the principal or chief one of the border sept. But the direct male line soon failing, the representation devolved upon WILLIAM ELLIOT of Stobbs, whose younger brother James, however, married the heiress. Much of the family history has, it is to be regretted, been lost by the burning of the various writs and documents by a great fire which took place at Stobs about the middle of the last century.

---

* Elliot of Redheugh appears to have been the Chief of the Clan during the sixteenth century, as the name frequently appears in historical documents in that capacity. Robert Elliot, last male heir of Redheugh, married Lady Jean Stewart, daughter of Francis Stewart, Earl of Bothwell, by Margaret Douglas, widow of Sir Walter Scott of Buccleuch, and daughter of David, seventh Earl of Angus, and niece of Regent Morton.

There were heroes among them, and the following verses, in imitation of an ancient ballad, from the pen of a learned and honoured friend of mine, the Rev. James Grey of Dumfries and Edinburgh, who became a clergyman and missionary of the Church of England in India, depicts one of the Larriston chieftains in a spirited manner. Another authority states the author was the Ettrick Shepherd :—

" Lock the door Larriston, Lion of Liddesdale,
Lock the door Larriston, Lowther comes on ;
   The Armstrongs are flying,
   The widows are crying,
The Castleton's burning, and Oliver's gone.
Lock the door Larriston ; high in the weather gleam,
See how the Saxon plumes bob in the sky ;
   Yeoman and carbineer,
   Billman and halberdier,
Fierce is the foray, and far is the cry.

Bewcastle brandishing high his proud scymitar,
Ridley is riding his fleet-footed grey ;
   Hedley and Howard, there,
   Wandale and Windermere,
Lock the door Larriston, hold them at bay.
Why dost thou smile, noble Elliot of Larriston ?
Why does the joy-candle gleam in thine eye ?
   Thou bold Border ranger
   Beware of this danger,
Thy foes are relentless, determin'd and nigh.

Jock Elliot raised up his steel bonnet and lookit,
His hand grasp'd the sword with a nervous embrace ;
   Ah, welcome, brave foemen,
   On earth there are no men
More gallant to meet in the fray or chase !
Little know'st thou of the hearts I have hidden here,
Little know'st thou of our mosstroopers' might ;
   Linhope and Sorby true,
   Sundope and Millburn too,
Gentle in manner, but lions in fight !

I've Mangerton, Gorranberry, Raeburn, and Netherby,
Old Sim of Whitram, and all his array ;
   Come all Northumberland,
   Teesdale and Cumberland,
Here at the Breaken Tower, end shall the fray.
Scowl'd the broad sun o'er the links of green Liddesdale,
Red as the beacon light tipt he the wold ;
   Many a bold martial eye,
   Mirror'd that morning sky,
Never more op'd on his orbit of gold.

> Shrill was the bugle's note, dreadful the warrior shout,
> Lances and halberts in splinters were borne;
>   Helmet and hauberk, then,
>   Brav'd the claymore in vain,
> Buckler and armlet in shivers were shorn
> See how they wane the proud files of the Windermere!
> Howard, ah! woe to thy hopes of the day;
>   Hear the wide welkin rend,
>   While the Scots shouts ascend,
> Elliot of Larriston! Elliot for aye!" *

Then the old chronicler Satchells, alluding to a Larriston, says:—

> "Could my unpractised pen advance thy name,
> Thou should be mounted on the wings of fame,
> Thy ancestors they were of good renown,
> They being all the Lairds of Larriston."

In Satchells' time, probably towards the close of the seventeenth century, the Elliots must have suffered an eclipse. For he adds:—

> "The Elliots brave and worthy men
> Have been as much oppressed as any name I ken,
> For in my time I have seen so much odds
> No Elliot, any heritage but Dinlabyre, Falnash, and Stobbs,
> Stobbs being *sine qua non* and obedient to the truth,
> A beloved sister's son to the family of Buccleuch."

---

* In the collected edition of the songs of the Ettrick Sheperd, published by Blackwood in 1831, appears the following note by Hogg:—"This border song was published in my own weekly paper, the *Spy*, March 30th, 1811, and found its way into the London papers, and partially through Britain, as the composition of my friend Mr Grey, now in India. I never contradicted it, thinking that anybody might have known that no one could have written the song but myself. However, it has appeared in every collection of songs with Mr Grey's name. Although I look upon it as having no merit whatever, excepting a jingle of names, which Sir Walter's good taste rendered popular, and which in every other person's hand has been ludicrous, yet I hereby claim the song as one of my own early productions—mine only, mine solely, and mine for ever." Mr W. Scott, schoolmaster at Burnmouth in Liddesdale, printed the ballad in the "Border Exploits," published in 1832, giving it as "from the forcible and energetic pen of Mr Grey, Master of the High School of Edinburgh." Thomas Grey, Esq., Melrose, nephew of Mr James Grey, has no doubt Hogg was the author, and says the ballad is utterly unlike anything ever written by his uncle. The ballad has been set to music by T. S. Gleadhill, with symphonies and accompaniment for the pianoforte, and published by Kerr and Richardson, 89 Queen Street, Glasgow.

This last line refers doubtless to William Elliot of Larriston's marriage with Mary Scott the sister of the "Bold" Buccleuch, their son being Gilbert Elliot, third of Stobbs, commonly called "Gibbie wi' the Gowden Garters."

The first known Border Elliot ancestor was Robert, who flourished at the end of the fifteenth and beginning of the sixteenth century, and was designed of Redheugh. It has been supposed he fell at Flodden. It is believed he had two sons, Robert and William, designed of Redheugh and Larriston respectively, but there seems to be a considerable hiatus in the subsequent pedigree, though William of Larriston had descendants who were William of Redheugh and Gilbert of Stobbs severally. The latter had only one male successor, Gavin; and the former carried on both lines, through his eldest son Robert, called of Redheugh, and through his second, William, designed of Larriston; and from the latter descend the present family of Stobbs and various other branches. From the former descended Robert of Redheugh and Larriston, who had no son, thus terminating the male representation of the elder branch which was transferred to his cousin Gilbert of Stobbs, his daughter, however, succeeding to the estates, and marrying James Elliot, a younger brother of Stobbs, and her cousin.

William Elliot of Larriston married Mary Scott, daughter of Sir Walter Scott of Buccleuch, by his wife Lady Margaret Douglas, daughter of the seventh Earl of Angus, and their son was Gilbert, third of Stobbs (and of "Garter" celebrity), while Robert Elliot of Redheugh married Lady Jean Stewart, daughter of Lady Margaret Douglas, widow of Buccleuch, by her second husband, that good-for-nothing man Francis Stewart, Earl of Bothwell, whose mother was a sister of the more notorious Bothwell, the husband of Queen Mary. Buccleuch, the first husband of Lady Margaret Douglas, died early, leaving a son, the "Bold" Buccleuch, who inherited in 1574, when his father died, and by a date on Branxholm House, I conclude his widow had not then remarried, but probably her second marriage with Bothwell took place soon after. There was a considerable disparity in age between Buccleuch's widow and her second husband, who was only about eleven when her first husband died.

Lady Jean Elliot and her children suffered much. Her husband, Robert Elliot, was suspected of being concerned in cattle-stealing with his servant Adam Usher, who was tried, condemned, and executed at Edinburgh, in 1624, for sundry acts of theft. Usher's son, a lad of tender years, was suspected, as well as the laird, of being an accomplice, but after several months' confinement in the thieves' hole, as the prison was called, he was let off with banishment, not, however, to return without licence. Mr Elliot, who is described as of Redheugh, suffered imprisonment likewise, on suspicion of being implicated in Adam Usher's delinquencies, but after a time was released without expatriation, for in November of the same year, when about to quit Edinburgh, on account of some infectious epidemic that prevailed, the Privy Council passed an order to relieve Lady Jean and children, who had been reduced to the greatest distress and wretchedness during her husband's incarceration; her ladyship having been actually compelled to sell part of her wearing apparel to supply her husband with some necessaries when in prison. The extent of the relief granted by the Council only amounted to 100 merks, with the addition of an allowance of about one shilling a-day in our money " during pleasure."

Robert Elliot and Lady Jean having no son, the property descended to his daughter and heiress, Mary, who married, as before mentioned, her cousin James Elliot, but they had no son either, and I presume after their deaths it was sold, as I can trace no successor to them. A long time afterwards, Larriston was acquired by a Colonel Elliot, whose birth was obscure, though it was supposed he was descended from the old stock, and who in early life served in a menial capacity, but going to India and getting into the army, he rose to distinction and affluence.*

* Of Colonel Elliot the traditional account is that he was the son of a young Elliot of Larriston, by a daughter of one of his father's retainers.

STOBBS.

The Elliots of Stobbs spell their name with one l and two t's. They probably acquired Stobbs some time before the close of the sixteenth century, though no doubt after the Reformation. They were in possession of it before 1596, for Gilbert Elliot of Stobbs, according to the famous ballad of Kinmont Willie, was at his rescue, by the bold Buccleuch, in that year. The ballad runs thus :—

> " He has called him forty marchmen bauld,
> I trow they were of his ain name.
> Except Sir Gilbert Elliot, call'd
> The Laird of Stobs, I mean the same."

It has been thought by some that Elliot of Stobbs was too young to have been at the rescue, and that it might have been a Larriston—perhaps William of Larriston, who shared in that glorious enterprise.

I have said the Elliots of Stobbs now represent the Border Clan, and the late Baronet, Sir William Francis Elliott, was authoritatively established as Chief, and in addition to the Arms of his ancestor, the first Baronet, Gules on a bend en-

Elliot had fallen in love with a young woman named Helen Kid, who lived with her father on the south side of the Liddel, directly opposite the present school-house of Saughtree, and consequently quite near the mansion of Larriston. The two were hand-fasted, and before the lapse of a year Helen presented her lover with a son. The young laird was more than ever resolved to wed the young woman, but his resolution was strenuously opposed by his kindred, and notably by young ladies of the Elliot connection who had aspired to the position which it now seemed likely that Helen Kid was to occupy. Remonstrances and entreaties were without effect ; and it is said they then changed their tactics, pretended great kindness for the prospective lady of the manor, invited her to a feast, and poisoned her. The son, who had been previously born, grew up and served in a menial capacity, having been stable-boy with his relative, Elliot of Stobbs. His master, who knew the connection, was in the habit of saying, as he mounted his steed, " Better he that holds the stirrup than he that rides." The young man entered the army, served with distinction in India, and, returning home a man of independent means, purchased his ancestral possessions. It is said that Robert Elliot of Larriston could travel from Larriston to Hawick, a distance of eighteen miles, on his own lands, with the exception of a narrow strip in one place.

grailed, or a bend azure, he got an augmentation of the Arms granted by the Crown to his celebrated kinsman, Lord Heathfield, applicable to his victory at Gibraltar.

The first of the family I begin with—having no precise information about the two first of Stobbs of the old line, so to speak—is GILBERT, second son of William Elliot of Larriston, and nephew of the bold Buccleuch, popularly known as "Gibbie with the gowden garters,"* who married Margaret Scott, commonly called Maggie Fendy, daughter of Auld Wat Scott of Harden, the celebrated freebooter, and by her he had six sons, the fourth being Gavin, who acquired Midlem Mill in the early part of the seventeenth century, and was ancestor of the Minto Elliots.

From WILLIAM, the eldest son—afterwards Laird of Stobbs, who married Elizabeth Douglas of Cavers—descended GILBERT, who was distinguished as a soldier during the Civil wars, and was honoured for his bravery, first with a Knight Baronetcy, and afterwards with a Baronetcy—the patent of the latter being dated in 1666. He married first Isabella Cranston, sister of the third Lord Cranston, whose family had, at an early period, large possessions in Roxburghshire, including Stobbs, her mother having been a daughter of Francis Earl Bothwell, by the widow of Buccleuch, and by this lady Sir Gilbert had one son, WILLIAM, his heir. By a second wife, Magdalene Nicolson, Sir Gilbert had several children; one daughter, Magdalene, marrying Sir John Pringle of Stichill, and was the mother of Sir John Pringle of medical and scientific fame, which procured him a Baronetcy.

Sir WILLIAM ELLIOT, the second of Stobbs, was married first to Miss Scott of Ancrum, and then to Miss Murray—the latter being the mother of his children. The eldest son was Gilbert second, who in 1699, at his father's death, succeeded as third baronet. He had a long incumbency—upwards of sixty-five years. Sir Gilbert married

* No record or tradition exists to account for the epithets bestowed on Sir Gilbert and his wife.

Miss Elliot of Wells, a property which, after the death, in 1818, of the Right Honourable William Elliot, was inherited by the Stobbs family, or rather its then chief, Sir William F. Elliot, in consequence of his kinsman, the second Lord Heathfield, who was before him in the entail, having died prior to Mr Elliot, unmarried. Sir Gilbert had a large family, being blessed with eight sons, the youngest, George Augustus, becoming most distinguished. Indeed, his career was brilliant, entitling him to be called the Wellington of our Border Land. He entered the army in early life, and saw much service, always making himself famous ; but his great and crowning success was his defence of Gibraltar, in the memorable siege which lasted from 1777 to 1782, and which preserved to this country that most important key to the Mediterranean. For his gallantry and generalship, George Augustus Elliot was created a Peer, by the titles of Lord Heathfield and Baron Gibraltar, which descended to his son, also a gallant soldier, at whose death, in 1813, the Peerage became extinct, though the property was inherited by his sister, Anne Elliot. She married Mr Fuller, a Sussex squire, who was created a baronet, an honour well bestowed, in recognition of his wife's descent from the gallant borderer, and also from the renowned navigator and warrior, Sir Francis Drake, both of whom the Fuller family represent, in right of Anne Elliot.

Lord Heathfield was no ordinary soldier and general ; one of his marked traits was his humanity to his enemies when vanquished, and his resistance to indiscriminate plunder on the part of his troops. To his own men he was most considerate, maintaining at the same time the highest discipline ; and when he received his several honours and distinctions, the pleasure of receiving the thanks of the two Houses of Parliament was enhanced by the fact that his heroic band was included. Like a true soldier, he was the faithful friend of his men, whose cheerful submission to the greatest hardships, as well as the matchless gallantry they exhibited during the long and arduous siege, made a deep and lasting impression upon him. He died on the 6th of July 1790, at the age of seventy-three.

My father-in-law, when a young man, and a lieutenant in the 73d Highlanders, was one of the heroic band of the gallant Elliot.

The well-known picture of Lord Heathfield by Sir Joshua Reynolds, representing the hero as holding the key of the fortress, is to be seen in the National Gallery, London.

I return for a little to the General's father Sir GILBERT, Bart., who was well known both in Edinburgh and this county. He had a house in Trunk's Close, Canongate, a popular situation at the time, which he acquired from Sir John Scott of Ancrum, and where he resided a good deal in the early part of last century, no doubt for the education of his large family of sons. In Sir Gilbert's day it was usual for country gentlemen, when dressed in fashionable costume, to wear a sword, and on the occasion of a public dinner after an election at Jedburgh in 1726, when he and Mr Scott, younger of Ancrum, were candidates, a fracas took place, which terminated in the death of Colonel Stewart of Stewartfield, now and previously called Hartrigge. Sir Gilbert was displeased that the Colonel had not voted for him, and expressing himself strongly, the latter was provoked, and taking up a glass full of wine, threw it in Sir Gilbert's face, upon which the baronet drew his sword and plunged it into Colonel Stewart's stomach, while he was sitting at the table. The Colonel then rose, drew his sword, and struck Sir Gilbert over the head once or twice, which wounded him, but friends interfering took the swords from the combatants, who however continued to struggle, Sir Gilbert losing his wig in the meleé. The result was, that Stewart died of his wound, and in a few days after, viz., 12th August 1726, the magistrates, consisting of the following country gentlemen, viz., Lord Minto, afterwards Justice-Clerk, Sir William Ker of Greenhead, Sir Walter Riddell of Riddell, called by mistake Sir John, Sir William Bennet of Grubbet, John Scott, younger of Ancrum, Archibald Douglas of Cavers, and Dr John Haliburton of Howcleugh, and others, met at Jedburgh, when, after hearing evidence, they ordered a copy of the precognition taken to be sent to the Lord Advocate, for a warrant to be issued for the apprehension of Sir Gilbert Elliot. He escaped to Holland, and remained there pending the enquiry, which ended in his pardon and return, and he survived the unfortunate event nearly forty years. Drs Andrew Rutherford, William Cranston, John Abernethy, and Mr James Rutherford were the medical men who examined Colonel Stewart, and gave evidence.

About the same time, and under somewhat similar circumstances, another melancholy occurrence took place near to Ancrum, Mr Haliburton of Muirhouselaw being stabbed by, it was supposed, Mr Rutherfurd of Fairnington. They had left Jedburgh together the previous evening, both under excitement caused by wine, and they were overheard disputing by the way. Earlier in the century, in 1707, a Pringle of Clifton killed Walter Scott of Raeburn in the vicinity of Selkirk, a quarrel having taken place at a county meeting, which ended in a duel, with swords, resulting in Raeburn's death.

SIR GILBERT ELLIOT of Stobbs died in 1764, and was succeeded by his eldest son SIR JOHN, who only enjoyed the title and estates about three years, his death occurring in 1767, or very early in 1768. He left two sons, SIR FRANCIS, his successor; and John, who entered the army, and became a captain of the 20th Dragoons, but dying early had not sufficient time to show whether he possessed any of the heroic qualities of his uncle, the gallant defender of Gibraltar.

SIR WILLIAM was the next incumbent of the Baronetcy, and held it and the estates for a long time, dying suddenly in 1812, and leaving a large family, whereof the eldest son was SIR WILLIAM FRANCIS, who succeeded. He married a daughter of the late Sir Alexander Boswell, who was shot in a duel by Mr Stewart of Dunearn. Boswell was the son of the celebrated biographer of Dr Johnson. The eldest son of this marriage is Sir William Francis Augustus Elliot, eighth Baronet of Stobbs.

MINTO.

We come now to the Elliots of Midlem Mill, from whom the noble family of Minto are descended. The first of the Midlem Mill Elliots was Gavin, fourth son of Gilbert of Stobbs, who probably acquired the estate in the early part of the seventeenth century, and whose descendants continued to hold it till about the middle of the eighteenth century, when it was sold by Robert Elliot, who was for some time chamberlain at Branxholm to the Duke of Buccleuch. The property was purchased by the Hunters of Union Hall, though I am uncertain whether there was not an interim proprietor for a few years in the person of Professor Stuart of Edinburgh, who at any rate lived for a short time at Midlem Mill. The Hunters, however, very soon acquired it, and as their estate of Union Hall was only separated from Midlem Mill by the river Ale, they took down their old mansion, which stood near to the present garden of Linthill, built a bridge and enlarged the house of Midlem Mill, which in the days of the Elliots had, I have understood, a thatched roof, calling the united properties Linthill, and there the Hunters resided, till the death of the last member of the family, the well known and justly popular Colonel Edgar Hunter, who was killed by a fall from his horse at Clarilaw Burn in 1807. Having died intestate, he was succeeded by his cousin and heir, William Riddell, whose father had married a sister of the Colonel's father. The Mill formerly stood near to the residence on the west side, close to the water and to a very large Ash tree, and was only removed to Toft Barns at the beginning of this century, some of the old stones with the Elliot initials and dates being preserved and inserted near to the large wheel in the present Mill. The following are the supposed letters and years on the stones:—

1601.	1677.	1730.
G. E.	R. E.	R. E. and K. E.

Gavin was the first of the Midlem Mill Elliots, as has been already stated, and he had two sons, GAVIN and GILBERT. The former carried on the line of the family, the last of whom in possession of the estate was Robert, who sold it as before mentioned. There are descendants of this gentleman in England, and he had a daughter Margaret, a maiden lady, who resided in Litchfield Street, London, and died there in 1804. She was well known and highly respected by the gentlemen of the Borders, some of whom put up at her house, when they visited the metropolis, Miss Elliot's finances being such as to make it desirable for her to supplement her slender means by letting apartments. Dr Somerville states that David Hume, the historian, always lodged at Miss Elliot's when he visited London. The Doctor was a particular friend of Robert Elliot's, and when they lived at Branxholm, at the time of his birth, which took place at Hawick in 1741, his father being parish minister, Miss Elliot carried him to church to be baptised.

GILBERT, the younger son, was founder of the now ennobled House of Minto. Gilbert had to push his own way in the world, and well and successfully he did so.* He embraced the legal profession, first becoming a writer and then an advocate. He had a large business, and accumulated a good fortune, which enabled him to buy first Headshaw and Shielswood, and afterwards Minto. He espoused, with great ardour, the cause of the Rev. William Veitch, the celebrated Covenanter, and was the means of obtaining a commutation of the sen-

* Lady Minto writes—"Gilbert Elliot of Minto was the first of the name who betook himself to the Law as a profession. That he did so with the true Border energy may be presumed from the fact of his having risen to its highest honours. His portrait at Minto gives the idea of a vigorous character. The strongly marked features, the bold open eye, and long upper lip bear a stamp of determination that might have become the leader of a foray as well as the Lord President of the Judges' Bench; and in the course of his career he found more frequent occasion for the exercise of qualities, such as had been exhibited by his forefathers, than a lawyer's life is apt to furnish."

tence of death which had been passed upon him for his participation in the rising at Pentland.*

He was accused, besides acting for Veitch, of assisting Argyll, and of furthering Monmouth's designs, and though he escaped for a time, he was at length caught and brought to trial, being condemned and forfeited, though afterwards obtaining a remission of his sentence. In 1685, when he was found guilty of treason, he was described in the process as a Writer in Edinburgh; but he soon determined on entering the higher branch of the profession, though difficulties seem to have interposed, for he was not called to the Bar till 1688. He was very successful as a counsel, and finally when he reached the Bench, his conduct as a Judge was marked by the strictest integrity. Soon after being called to the Bar he was appointed Clerk of the Privy Council, and received the honour of knighthood, which was followed — about ten years afterwards — by a Baronetcy; and in 1705, he was raised to the Bench under the courtesy title of Lord Minto—the estate of Minto having at that time previously been purchased by Sir Gilbert. But

* This he did by going to London, where he was successful in enlisting, on behalf of his client, the ardent support and co-operation of Shaftesbury, Monmouth, and other leaders of the Whig party, by whom an amount of pressure was brought to bear on the Government, under which, ultimately, its obduracy gave way. A royal order to stop all further proceedings against Veitch was forwarded through the Earl of Stair to Gilbert Elliot; and his success, which was contrary to all expectation, raised him to a high place in the estimation of the Whig leaders on both sides of the Borders. So marked an epoch in his history was that event that it has been made the subject of a humorous dialogue between Elliot and Veitch, when, subsequent to the Revolution, the one was Minister of Dumfries, and the other a Lord of Session, under the designation of Lord Minto. In a facetious manner, the Lord of Session had been heard to say, "Ah Willie, Willie, had it no been for me, the pyets had been picking your pate on the Nether-Bow Port;" to which Willie Veitch replied, "Ah Gibbie! Gibbie! had it no been for me ye would hae been yet writing papers for a plack a page!" Gibbie and Veitch had become acquainted while they were both young men, for Veitch was in 1660 tutor to a family in Roxburghshire, and a frequent visitor at Stobbs, along with John Livingstone and other eminent Covenanters. Young Gilbert is said to have passed much of his time at Stobbs under the roof of his grand-parents, Gibbie wi' the gouden garters and Maggie Fendy, when those eminent preachers were present.

his services as a Judge barely extended to thirteen years, his death taking place on the 1st of May 1718, when he was succeeded on the Bench by an eminent borderer and lawyer, Sir Walter Pringle, of the house of Stichill, uncle to Sir John Pringle, Bart., who married Magdalene Elliot of Stobbs. Sir Gilbert was strongly recommended for a Judgeship on the death of Lord Mersington, in 1700, by the celebrated Sir James Stewart of Goodtrees, the Lord Advocate, and though he also had the interest of Patrick Hume, Earl Marchmont, married to Grizzel Carre, the half-aunt of Lord Minto's second wife Jean Carre—who knew him well, and who spoke of him "as true, honest, just, and bold, of which he had given proof"— he did not then succeed, the President, Dalrymple, favouring another candidate, Sir Robert Stewart of Tillicoultrie, but his talents and services were soon after rewarded with a double gown.

Sir Gilbert Elliot married first Miss Stevenson, daughter of Dr Stevenson, by whom he had one daughter, married to Sir J. Elphinston of Logie; and secondly, Jean Carre, daughter of Sir Andrew Carre, yr. of Cavers, by whom he had his son and successor, Sir Gilbert, and other children. From the close proximity of Midlem Mill (now Linthill) to Cavers, the families of Carre and Elliot were on intimate terms, and Gilbert, on re-visiting his paternal roof, after his many adventures, renewed his acquaintance with the Carres, the friends of his youth, and selected the fourth daughter, Jean, for his wife. He had become a most successful man by the time he married a second time, and there was a tradition in my boyhood that he had the "siller" and his wife the "bluid." But Gilbert had bluid also; for though his father was the miller of Midlem Mill, he was nevertheless the laird, and as a cadet of Stobbs, well allied.

I have two amusing anecdotes to relate relative to the elder brother of Lord Minto, and of his lordship himself, when he was Clerk of the Privy Council. The first is that Gavin, the elder brother, and laird of Midlem Mill, one day came to Jedburgh when his brother was sitting as the Circuit Judge, and elbowing his way through the crowded court, some one called out, make way, make way for Lord Minto's brother, when Gavin replied, "Na, Na, Gibbie's my brother," thus proving that the Laird would not allow it to be forgotten that he was the senior.

The other story is that when Mr D. Douglas was one day preaching, he made some remarks touching the Clerks of the Council, exclaiming, "There is one Gibbie Elliot, Sirs, that has no charity nor discretion, for if we were all made up of dollars, he would swallow us up. Pray God to keep our purses from that false Lord Elliot."

The second Baronet of Minto, also Sir GILBERT, was born in 1693. He well maintained the reputation of his sire, whose profession he followed, rising almost to its highest pinnacle. He was admitted advocate in 1715, and in a little more than ten years was elevated to the Bench, in succession to Lord Cullen, who was called a living library. Sir Gilbert, like his father, took the judicial title of Lord Minto, though during the last three years of his life it merged in the higher title of Lord Justice-Clerk, to which office he was raised in 1763, holding it till 16th April 1766, when he died at Minto rather suddenly, aged seventy-three. Previously to his being raised to the Bench, he was a Member of Parliament for a short time, and was a warm supporter of John the famous Duke of Argyll, who had great sway in Scotland, and who was thus immortalised by Pope,—

"Argyll the States' whole thunder born to wield,
And shake alike the Senate and the field."

Lord Justice-Clerk Elliot made considerable improvements at Minto, and laid the foundation of its extensive library. He also contributed to the improvements in Edinburgh, which in his time were considerable, a number of important buildings being planned or erected; and he was the author of a pamphlet of proposals for carrying on certain public works in that city. The Justice-Clerk and his eldest son, Mr Gilbert

Elliot, were both on the committee for the improvements, and George Drummond, six times Lord Provost, founder of the Infirmary, was a member of it also, being perhaps the great mainspring of the movement. The Justice Clerk was a great enemy of the Jacobites, and when they traversed the country he had to hide in Minto Crags to escape their fury, and his daughter, Miss Jean Elliot * (to be noticed hereafter), was, like Lady Grizzel Hume, the means of saving her father from being captured.

To his other accomplishments, the Justice Clerk added a taste for music, in which he excelled ; and it has been said he introduced the German flute. I give a sonnet he composed in Italian, to be sung to the tune of "The Yellow Hair'd Laddie," to which I add a translation :—

> " Veduto in prato
> Il mio pastor,
> Il crin coronato,
> D' un serto di fior.
> Il sole negli occhi,
> La Fide nel sen'
> Ah ! dove s' asconde ?
> Il caro mio ben' !
> Al Bosco, al monte,
> La cereo in van,
> E, presso al Fonte,
> Non trove ch' 'il can ;
> Ah ! Cane Fedele
> Deh ! dimmi perche,
> Il mio crudele
> S' asconde di me ? "

---

* Lady Minto says Miss Jean received the unwelcome guests with courteous hospitality. She detained them within the house while her father found time to reach the refuge of some neighbouring craigs, and there he lay concealed among boulders, ivy, and brushwood, till the troopers had taken their departure across the Teviot. Though a kind father, he was very strict, as was the custom in those days. Hearing his son Andrew (afterwards Governor of New York) object to eat boiled mutton at dinner, the Lord Justice-Clerk turned to the servant who stood beside him, saying, " Let Mr Andrew have boiled mutton for breakfast, boiled mutton for dinner, and boiled mutton for supper, until he has learnt to like it." He did learn to like it, at least so he said to his children.—*Life of the First Earl of Minto.*

TRANSLATION OF SONNET.

"In the meadows I saw him,
My shepherd, my own,
He wore on his forehead,
Of sweet flowers a crown.
In his eyes was the sunshine,
Faith's home was his breast.
Ah ! where is he hiding ?
My loved one ! my best !
By stream, grove, and mountain,
I sought him in vain.
I found his dog Fido !
I found not my swain,
Ah Fido ! dear Fido !
Come tell me I pray
Why my cruel one shuns me,
What keeps him away."

The Justice-Clerk has left but few footprints on the sands of time, not having, like his friend, Lord Kames, been fond of publishing. One day, when complaining to Kames that he understood very little in a particular branch of political economy, expressing a wish at the same time for information, his learned brother told him the best way to understand it, *was to go and write a book upon it.* Kames was fond of writing, or as he said, "of spreading his sails on a wide ocean, not without hopes of importing precious merchandise."

Lord Kames was a great favourite of Lord Minto's, and when engaged as counsel (for though not much younger than Lord Minto, he did not get on the bench for about twenty-five years after him), in a cause in which he had written a paper of very considerable merit, Lord Minto, after hearing the arguments, came down from the bench, and shaking Kames, then Henry Home, by the hand, congratulated him upon his paper, observing that he had, like an able mathematician, thrown out all the useless quantities, and given only the equations. I have another anecdote to mention in connexion with Kames, who, when a depute-advocate, used, of course, to go the circuit, and when proceeding from Jedburgh to Dumfries, on one occasion, with Lord Minto, they stopped, as his Lordship was wont to do, at the house of Mr Armstrong of Sorbie. Armstrong, or Sorbie, as he was called, was always ready to welcome and receive his lordship with cordiality and hospitality, but was a little put out on the occasion referred to. Enquiring of Lord Minto "wha that lang, black, dour-looking chiel" was, whom he had "wi' him," and on being told that he was a man come to hang a' the Armstrong's, he retorted, "Then it's time the Elliot's were ridin'!"

Sorbie and the Justice-Clerk used to rate one another about the propensities of their respective clans of old. Sorbie confessed that as long as thieving was a *virtue*, the Armstrongs pursued the calling with uncommon vigilance, but as soon as it became a vice, they gave it up to the Elliots, whereby many of them were hanged for it.

Sir Gilbert Elliot, Lord Justice-Clerk, married Miss Helen Stewart of Allanbank, daughter of Sir Robert Stewart, and his wife, Miss Cockburn, of Langton, an ancestrix of the present Lord Chief Justice of the Queen's Bench, Sir Alexander Cockburn. By Helen Stewart, who, by the way, was of the royal Stuarts, notwithstanding the different orthography of her name, the Justice-Clerk had several children, of whom were Gilbert, Andrew, John, and Archibald; Anne, Eleanor, and Jean. Gilbert, the eldest, became Sir Gilbert, and will be taken up in his proper place hereafter.

His brothers, ANDREW, JOHN, and ARCHIBALD, were distinguished men. The first, named after his maternal grandfather, Sir Andrew Carre, was Lieutenant-Governor of New York before the American Independence, which took place in 1783, and while in that office was a staunch defender of British interests. He has been described as a man of strong sense, sterling loyalty, and high respectability. On returning to this country, Andrew Elliot settled at Greenwells, in Bowden parish, which, including Eildon Hall estate, which had then no mansion upon it, he purchased, and devoted himself to the improvement of his property, where, and in George Square, Edinburgh, he alternately resided. After his death,

Greenwells was sold to Mr Mein, and after passing through other hands, it was finally bought by the Duke of Buccleuch, who has rebuilt and extended the residence at Eildon Hall, first erected by Mr Mein, in supercession of the house at Greenwells, where Governor Elliot resided. Andrew Elliot married twice, his second wife being Miss Plumstead, an American lady of beauty, whose hand had been previously sought by the celebrated Washington. By this lady he had several children, his daughters being very beautiful, and making good alliances. One of them, Lady Carnegy, lived till 1860, when she died in the ninety-seventh year of her age, and fifty-fifth of her widowhood. She was spared to see the restoration of the attainted titles of Earl Southesk and Lord Carnegy to her grandson, in 1855.

JOHN and ARCHIBALD became flag officers of the Royal Navy, and the former was particularly distinguished, as the conqueror of Thurot. Thurot was an Irishman, his real name being O'Farrel, but in fighting under the French flag, he adopted his mother's name of Thurot, her family having been one of distinction in France. His object was to invade Ireland, and though before falling in with the gallant Elliot's fleet, he had landed at Carrickfergus and plundered the town, he could proceed no further, and was returning to France for additional help, when he was overtaken by Elliot, who engaged him, near the Isle of Man, capturing his fleet, which was also the terror of the British Merchant Service, and killing Thurot. This happened on the 28th February 1760, and for long the gallant Borderer's victory was commemorated by a ballad well-known and constantly sung throughout this district, though now it is nearly forgotten. The following is a copy of the ballad, copied from the "Genuine and Curious Memoirs of the Famous Captain Thurot. London, 1760." Reprinted for the Percy Society, 1847:

"The twenty-first of February, as I've heard the people say,
  Three French ships of war came and anchored in our bay;
  They hoisted English colours, and landed at Kilroot,
  And marched their men for Carrick, without further dispute.

"Colonel Jennings being there, at that pretty little town,
 His heart it was a breaking, while the enemy came down;
 He could not defend it for the want of powder and ball,
 And aloud to his enemies for 'quarter' he did call.

"As Thurot in his cabin lay, he dreamed a dream,
 That his grandsire's voice came to him, and called him by his name;
 Saying, Thurot, you're to blame for lying so long here,
 For the English will be in this night, the wind it bloweth fair.

"Then Thurot started up, and said unto his men,
 'Weigh your anchors, my brave lads, and let us begone;
 We'll go off this very night, make all the haste you can,
 And we'll steer south and south-east, straight for the Isle of Man.'

"Upon the next day, the wind it blew north-west,
 And Elliot's gallant seamen, they sorely were oppressed;
 They could not get in that night, the wind it blew so high;
 And as for Monsieur Thurot, he was forced for to lie by.

"Early the next morning, as daylight did appear,
 Brave Elliot he espied them, which gave to him great cheer,
 It gave to him great cheer, and he to his men did say,
 'Boys, yonder's Monsieur Thurot, we'll show him warm play.'

"The first ship that came up was the Brilliant, without doubt,
 She gave to them a broadside, and then she wheeled about;
 The other two then followed her, and fired another round,
 'Oh, oh, my lads,' says Thurot, 'this is not Carrick town.'

"Then out cried Monsieur Thurot, with his visage pale and wan,
 'Strike, strike your colours, brave boys, or they'll sink us every man,
 Their weighty shot comes in so hot, on both the weather and the lee,
 Strike your colours, my brave boys, or they'll sink us in the sea.'

"Before they got their colours struck, great slaughter was made,
 And many a gallant Frenchman, on Thurot's deck lay dead,
 They came tumbling down the shrouds, upon his deck they lay,
 While our brave Irish heroes cut their booms and yards away.

* "   .   .   .   .
         .   .   .   .
 And as for Monsieur Thurot, as I've heard people say,
 He was taken up by Elliot's men, and buried in Ramsey Bay.

---

* Here two lines are awanting in the original ballad.

"Now for to conclude, and put an end to my song,
To drink a health to Elliot, I hope it is not wrong ;
And may all French invaders be served the same way,
Let the English beat the French by land, our Irish boys on sea." *

Admiral Elliot was made Director of the Mint in Scotland, no doubt in recognition of his gallant services, and he died at Mount Teviot, which he rented, on the 20th September 1807. Two of his sisters married into good families—one of them was wife of John Rutherfurd, of Edgerston, a gallant soldier of the Independent Army at New York, who fell in battle in 1758. The third, Jean Elliot, never married. She was the constant companion of her father, and was no less distinguished for her heroism than her accomplishments, and was the authoress of one of the ballads of the Flowers of the Forest, which she composed about the middle of last century. It was published anonymously at first, and the authoress long remained unknown, but she was at length discovered, and Sir Walter Scott inserted it in the "Minstrelsy of the Border," his note upon it giving it high rank as a fine piece of elegiac poetry. It began as follows :

"I've heard them lilting at the ewe milking,
Lasses a lilting before the dawn of day ;
But now they are moaning on ilka green loaning,
The flowers of the forest are a wede away."

---

* "Thurot behaved with the greatest bravery imaginable ; had lost one of his arms near an hour, and received his death wound above half an hour before he quitted the deck.

"While he lived, he insisted on the ship being fought ; but as soon as the breath was out of his body, the whole squadron struck.

"Nothing could equal the courage of Captain Elliot, his Majesty's commander, but his humanity ; he would not suffer anything to be touched in Thurot's ship, made sacred by his dead body ; Alexander himself did not more bewail the death of Darius than Captain Elliot did the loss of Thurot.

"As soon as the shattered ships got to the Isle of Man, Thurot's body was taken on shore, and embalmed, after which he was buried with all those military honours which his courage and conduct so well deserved ; and Captain Elliot gave all his officers liberty to attend his funeral, himself walking in the procession."—"*Genuine and Curious Memoirs of the Famous Captain Thurot.* London, 1760." *Reprinted for the Percy Society,* 1847.

There is a similar composition by another Border lady of ability—I mean Alicia Rutherfurd of Fernilee, who married Mr Cockburn; and doubtless both ladies took as their text an old ballad called by the same name, a fragment of which only survives. Miss Elliot was a woman of general sagacity, and was a great and retentive reader. She was especially fond of French literature, but disliked the modern political principles of that nation. As regards her person, she is described as possessing "a sensible face—a slender, well-shaped figure. In manner grave and reserved to strangers. In her conversation she made no attempts at wit, and though possessed of imagination, she never allowed it to entice her from the strictest rules of veracity. She had high aristocratic notions, which she took no pains to conceal." Such is the description given of Miss Elliot by one who knew her in the latter period of her life. For many years she lived in Brown Square, Edinburgh, not very far from Minto House, the then town residence of the family; and in her lobby she kept her own Sedan chair, the last private one in Edinburgh.

Shortly before her death, which happened in 1805, she removed to the residence of her brother, Admiral John Elliot, at Mount Teviot, where she died.

SIR GILBERT, third baronet, carried on the line of the Minto family. Like his father and grandfather, he went to the Bar, and passed advocate in 1743. He did not follow up the profession, preferring to devote himself to politics, in which he was as successful as his predecessors were in jurisprudence. Sir Gilbert first represented Selkirkshire, and was afterwards elected for Roxburghshire—his Parliamentary career continuing for about twenty-three years, when his health broke down, and he died at the comparatively early age of fifty-four. Sir Gilbert held several important appointments, and was a Privy Councillor, standing very high in general estimation. He had good literary taste, and was an accomplished speaker. He was also a good writer of verses, having commenced versifying at fourteen. Several songs are attributed to him, among them the very good pastoral one beginning "My sheep I neglected," &c.

Sir Gilbert had the honour of holding several important appointments, and he was a member of the "Poker" Club, as well known then as the New Club is now. It was instituted in 1762, and continued for several years, being supported by some of Scotland's brightest stars, then brilliantly shining, such as David Hume, Adam Smith, and Adam Fergusson, who, I believe, invented its name, enigmatical to the public, though it had something to do with the militia question, the poker being an instrument for stirring up.

The third Sir Gilbert Elliot married in 1746, at the age of twenty-four, Agnes Murray Kynningmund, heiress of Melgund and Kynynmound, by whom he had several sons and daughters. The eldest, Sir Gilbert, fourth baronet, who more than sustained the reputation of his sires, will be referred to hereafter, while I now take up other members of the family, commencing with

HUGH, the second son, who was the "joy of his mother's life and the friend of her heart," and became a most distinguished man. He held several high diplomatic appointments, and finally became Governor of the important Presidency of Madras, about the time his elder brother concluded his service as Governor-General of India. The life of Hugh Elliot has been fully and pleasantly written by his grand-daughter, the Countess of Minto. Mr Elliot was twice married, and two of his sons, the Dean of Bristol and Admiral Sir Charles Elliot, are distinguished men; and his daughter Isabella married General Sir Thomas Hislop, the conqueror of the great Indian chief Holkar, who, for his brilliant achievements in India, obtained a Baronetcy and received the thanks of Parliament. Lady Minto is the daughter of Sir Thomas and Lady Hislop, and is consequently an Elliot maternally as well as by marriage. Hugh's younger brothers were

ALEXANDER and ROBERT. The former was a noted member of the East India Company's Civil Service, and at his death Burke, the statesman, paid a high compliment to his memory.

Robert was an English clergyman, and inherited the poetical genius of his ancestors. One of their sisters married the first Lord Monkland, and her son, the second Peer, became Governor-General of India some time after

LORD MINTO, the fourth Sir Gilbert Elliot, who was raised to an Earldom after his service in the high office of Governor-General of India terminated. Lord Minto entered public life soon after the death of his father in 1777, and became a member of Parliament. Previously, however, he made a tour of the Continent, visiting Paris, in the brilliant assemblies of which city he mixed. He was a marked favourite of the once beautiful, but ever witty and accomplished Madame du Deffand, a leading member of the literary fashionable circles of that city, and the friend of our best English letter-writer, Horace Walpole, with whom Madame maintained a close and interesting correspondence. After Sir Gilbert Elliot's return from the Continent he got into Parliament, having been elected at the age of twenty-three for Morpeth, and shortly after he was chosen for Roxburghshire without a contest, Lord Robert Ker, brother of John, Duke of Roxburghe, withdrawing in his favour. He was much esteemed in the House of Commons, and nearly carried the Speakership on one occasion. After a time he was sent to Toulon as Commissioner for the protection of the Royalists, and in the following year was despatched to Corsica, the people of that island having applied for British protection, and as Viceroy there Sir Gilbert showed so much judgment and prudence as to call forth the highest encomiums. Though an insurrection broke out, it was quelled before the island, which declared for the French, was delivered up. As a reward for his services, Sir Gilbert was made a Baronet of Great Britain in 1797, and at the same time got an augmentation of his armorial bearings of a Moor's head couped in profile, being the arms of the Island of Corsica.

After returning to this country he was not long inactive, for he was soon appointed Envoy at Vienna, in which office he continued two years, and then joined the All Talents Ministry

Minto was then appointed Governor-General of India, whither he went to practise the doctrine of non-interference ; but he very soon found, though he had joined in condemning " Warren Hastings' aggrandising and annexing tendencies," that the security of our Empire, as an author states, " depended upon the actual superiority of our power, upon the sense the natives entertained of that power, and upon the submissiveness of our neighbours." Still Lord Minto's rule in India was pacific, the great Mahratta War being over before he reached Calcutta ; but in the Indian seas he had much work; and his conquests there were considerable, requiring an extensive force and large means to carry them on. The Mauritius was conquered in 1810, and in 1811 Java was taken, the island capitulating to the British. Borneo, that nest of pirates, was subdued soon afterwards, our troops having made a successful attack upon it; and its recent history is well known under the Governorship of that devoted and patriotic man, the late Rajah Brooke.

Lord Minto went in person to Java with the expedition, and among the number of brave hearts which it included there was none more gallant or true than John Leyden of Denholm, who was in his ardour the first to land, and he was probably the first to die, for, owing to rash exposure, he was attacked by fever, which carried him off in three days, just on the eve of the battle that caused the capitulation of the island.

It has been already said that Lord Minto got two steps in the peerage for his services as governor-general, and he also received the thanks of Parliament, always a high honour to a public man. After an absence of about seven years, he returned to England ; but though the mansion house at Minto was completed and ready for his reception, he was not permitted to see it, having died on his way to Scotland on the 21st June 1814, aged sixty-three. He married in 1777 Miss Amyand, daughter of Sir George Amyand (whose ancestors were Huguenots or French Protestants), by whom he had several sons and daughters.

The sons were GILBERT, GEORGE, JOHN EDMUND, and WILLIAM, the three first being well known to many in the county now alive. Gilbert, the second Earl, will be afterwards noticed, and I now proceed with GEORGE, who was a distinguished naval officer. He was one of the heroes of Copenhagen in 1801, and accompanied his father, the governor-general, in his expedition against Java, and aided in its reduction. He also did good service against the pirates at Borneo. He obtained flag rank in 1837, and was for some time a Lord of the Admiralty; but went to sea again, commanding as Admiral on the African coast and at the Cape station. Admiral Elliot was made a K.C.B., and was elected the first member for Roxburghshire, after the passing of the Reform Bill of 1832, continuing to represent the county till 1835.

JOHN EDMUND, the third son, was long in the East India Company's Bengal Civil Service, in which he had a successful career, and some time after returning home he became member for Roxburghshire, retaining the honourable position for several years and discharging his duties to the satisfaction of his constituents generally. He was a genial, loveable man, and a universal favourite, full of anecdote and pleasantry. I have read an account of a party of notables assembled together on one occasion, John Elliot being of the number, and as usual the very life and soul of the meeting, at which personations were given, stories told, and a good deal of mimicry indulged in. One of Mr Elliot's neighbours at table was a certain old Scotch lady of eccentric ways. The conversation turned on the Minto estate of Melgund, which she told Mr Elliot was once the residence of Cardinal Beaton. He enquired if she knew it well. She said she did—and " Kenned a' the land thereabout frae the sooth side o' Seidlaw to the north o' the Grampians ;" and she told him how a living lobster had fallen out of a cadger's creel up about the parish of Lintrathen, and how a Highlandman had picked it up and carried it to the minister, and how the minister had put on his spectacles to see what kind of a beast it was, "and after long examination, and mony a reference to the Bible, he pronounced it to be either an *elephant* or a *turtle dove.*"

Mr Elliot in his turn related how a seafaring friend of his, in giving an order for provisioning the ship said, "I am resolved to have a *cow, for I am very fond of new laid eggs.*"

He then told her that a young lady had taken his purse the night before, and he would refer to her ladyship what punishment should be awarded. She said she would give the same judgment that the bellman of Arbroath did on a like occasion, when he happened to be the finder :—

> "John Elliot's lost his purse,
> And his money which is worse;
> Them that's found it let them keep it,
> Them that's lost it let them seek it.

John Elliot, who married Miss Cassmagil of Madras, had the pain of losing his eldest son, when commanding the 70th Regiment at Varna, during the Crimean War, the gallant officer's widow having had a son soon after her lamented husband's death.

The fourth son WILLIAM was also an officer in the Royal Navy, and died so far back as 1812, on his passage from India, being third lieutenant of the frigate " Fox."

Two of the Earl's daughters married respectively Sir Rufane Donkin, a gallant warrior, and Sir John Boileau, whose great-grand-father emigrated from France at the revocation of the Edict of Nantes in 1685, when many Protestants left France and came to England, and was no doubt a Huguenot like the ancestors of the Amyands. I now return to the eldest brother Gilbert, second Earl of Minto, who succeeded his father in 1814. Born in 1781, he was about thirty-two when he came to his dignities and estates, and living till 1858 he enjoyed them about forty-four years, attaining the age of seventy-seven. Before succeeding to the peerage, Lord Minto had been in the House of Commons as member for Ashburton, and like his father and grand-father, took a warm interest in political affairs. He held some important appointments, and became a Cabinet Minister in 1835, as first Lord of the Admiralty, and retiring in 1841 he remained out of office till 1846, when he became Lord Privy Seal with a seat in the Cabinet, which he held till 1852, when he retired into private life. He married in 1806 the elder daughter of Patrick Brydon, the traveller and author, son of the Rev. Robert Brydon, minister of Coldingham. She was a granddaughter of Dr Robertson, the historian, which connected Lady Minto with Lord Brougham, who was a grand-nephew of the historian. Robert Burns and Sir Walter Scott were friends of Mr Brydon, who is described in "Marmion" as the Pilgrim of Lennel.

OTHER BRANCHES OF THE ELLIOT FAMILIES.

An old cadet of the Elliot tree is the Brugh branch which merged in that of WELLS. The only noted member of the latter house was the Right Honourable William Elliot, who had settled his property first on Lord Heathfield, and failing him, upon the Stobbs family, who, in consequence of Lord Heathfield's death without male heirs, succeeded on the death of Mr Elliot in 1818. This gentleman, though born and educated in England, became the inheritor of Wells. He was long in Parliament and in office, having been Secretary for Ireland and a Privy Councillor. He was respected by Burke and Windham, but with him that bright brotherhood became extinct. His physique was peculiar, and he was almost like a living skeleton. He died at Minto House on the 26th October 1818, where there is a picture of him.

Among the old Elliot houses were the Horsliehills, Dinlaybyres, Falnashs, and Whitehaughs who have all disappeared. Then there are the Wolfelees and Borthwickbraes still in full vigour and well represented; but the Wolfelees descend from Stobbs two generations after the Mintos, and are now represented by Sir Walter Elliot, whose father had an elder brother who died in early life. I have no particulars of the old members of the family, and the first I have to notice is Cornelius, who was long at the head of the Roxburghshire Freeholders and also of the Writers to the Signet in Edinburgh. One of his daughters married first Sir John Gibson Carmichael, by whom she had an only daughter; and secondly, the first Lord Elphinston, by whom, curiously enough, she had an only son, the late Lord Elphinston, governor of Madras, and subsequently of Bombay, where his rule, especially during the mutiny in 1857, was characterized by much ability, and in reward for his services he was made a British Peer, but died early.

Cornelius Elliot had a brother, Thomas, a Scotch physician, who married Miss Elphinston of Logie, a family already referred to, but he only survived his marriage three weeks, and such was the inconsolable sorrow of his widow for his loss, that she never saw the sun for two years, till she yielded to the entreaties of her spiritual adviser, the eminent Hugh Blair, and once more emerged into Society, though she never recovered her former cheerfulness. She also had a narrow escape from being buried alive in a vault at Megginch Castle, when searching for old papers deposited there.

The Borthwickbrae Elliots, connected now by marriage with the Wolfelees, deserve notice next. They also descend from the old Elliot tree, through the Bewlie and Horsliehill branches. The Borthwickbraes are well allied, intermarrying with ancient Scotts, and the House of Cleghorn, which existed in the fifteenth century. One of the ladies of the family married Mr Simpson of Knowe, and was mother of General Sir James Simpson, for some time commander-in-chief during the Crimean War. The father of the present head of the family, Mr Elliot Lockhart, Lord-Lieutenant of Selkirkshire, was Member of Parliament for that county for nearly a quarter of a century. He had an elder brother who fell at Waterloo. The Peebles and Selkirk lines were of the old stock, and one or both may have been of the Horsliehill branch. William Elliot was Provost of Peebles early in the seventeenth century. His son, Hairie, was minister of Bedrule. He died in the prime of life, leaving a widow and seven children. Dr Scott mentions that she petitioned Parliament in 1662, showing that Mr Elliot "suffered so much persecution and affliction for defending His Majesty's interests and prerogatives in the pulpit both at home and abroad, publicly praying for His Majesty at the expedition of 1648, that he was driven from his charge, and lived in a most dejected, miserable, sad, and downcast condition, and that had it not been for the charity of some faithful, loyal, and well-wishing Christians, they had quite famished, and never been able to have subsisted." Parliament allowed the petition by granting £100 sterling out of the vacant stipends.

SELKIRK ELLIOTS.

About the same time, or shortly after, there lived Robert Elliot, minister of Lessudden, who, I suppose, was likewise from the Peebles stock. He was also cited before the Privy Council for dissuading the Magistrates of that town from taking the test, and was deposed for contumacy in 1690.

In the following century there flourished a celebrated man of the Peebles line, Sir John Elliot, who became an eminent London physician. He began in a very small way, and became surgeon to a Privateer, in which he obtained prize money, which enabled him to take out his diploma and embark, not in another Privateer, but as physician in the great metropolis, where he had as competitors Buchan of Ancrum and Armstrong of Castleton. All three did well in the profession, especially Buchan and Elliot. The latter was employed by families of rank and even royalty, and such were his fame, talents, and influence, he obtained a Baronetcy in 1778, but he did not survive his honours many years, for he died suddenly in 1786. When advanced in years, he made an unfortunate marriage with the notorious Grace Dalrymple, who got into some intrigue, which made Sir John divorce her, when I believe she entered a convent. No family resulting from this marriage, Sir John Elliot died without an heir to the Baronetcy, which consequently became extinct at his demise. Previously to Sir John Elliot, there were two well-known doctors of the name of Elliot in Edinburgh, who may also have come from Peebles, though I have not ascertained their derivation. Their names were Gideon and Robert, both members of the early Medical School of Edinburgh, and there is a picture of Gideon in the College of Surgeons. There was another Dr Robert Elliot, who died at Bilboa, at a very advanced age, early in this century.

INDIVIDUAL MEMBERS OF THE ELLIOT FAMILY.

I come now to notice individual Elliots, whom I cannot identify with any of the preceding families.

The first is a very historical name,

JOHN ELLIOT, of the Park, Bothwell's adversary. He lived in the middle of the sixteenth century and later, and was a desperate Freebooter. Queen Mary in 1566 appointed the notorious Bothwell, Warden of the Marches, which had been much disturbed by the feuds of the Liddesdale clans especially, and shortly afterwards, the Queen, accompanied by her Officers of State and Justice, visited Jedburgh for the purpose of holding a Court there. Bothwell in the exercise of his office as warden, made an attempt to capture Jock Elliot, whom he shot through the thigh, upon which the Mosstrooper assailed and nearly killed Bothwell. He was carried to Hermitage Castle, and it was upon this occasion Queen Mary visited him, having ridden from Jedburgh, a distance of nearly fifty miles there and back, exposed to danger from the fierce Borderers, besides being nearly lost in a morass, still called the Queen's Mire. An author states that the Queen was so much grieved in heart at Bothwell's accident, that she could take no rest till she saw the wounded Earl, and Lord Scrope states that she remained two hours at Hermitage, to Bothwell's great pleasure and contentment. This fatiguing ride and her distress of mind, another writer states, threw her into a severe illness, which detained her in Jedburgh for some time, in a house which still stands in Queen Street. Darnley was some time in visiting Mary, owing, as Birrell states, to his being long in getting intelligence, but when he did come, he only remained one night with her. But to return to Jock Elliot, who was the cause of Bothwell's illness, and indirectly of that of the Queen, I think he must be the person to whom the Border tune, which has been called the "Gathering of the Elliots," applies, and of which John Leyden was so passionately fond. It will be recollected that, when upon a sick bed in India, Leyden heard of the march of the volunteers to Hawick early this century, on the occasion of the then threatened invasion, to this lively air of "Wha daur meddle wi' me," he sprang from his couch, and with a strange melody, and still stranger gesticulations, sang aloud:

"Wha daur meddle wi' me,
And wha daur meddle wi' me."

Very little is known of this Slogan, or its origin, but as the following verses point to or fit the adversary of Bothwell, their quotation here is justifiable, and may be interesting:

"I vanquish'd the Queen's Lieutenant,
And gar'd his fierce troopers flee,
My name it is little Jock Elliot,
And wha daur meddle wi' me.
I ride on my fleet-futted gray,
My sword hanging doon by my knee,
I ne'er was afraid o' a foe,
And wha daur meddle wi' me."

The following verses, from Ayton's ballad, "Bothwell," relate to the Border Mosstroopers, and especially John of Park:

"Saint Andrew! 'twas no easy task
To hunt an Armstrong down,
Or make a Johnston yield his sword,
At summons from the Crown!

" Yet, ere a week had passed away,
    One half my work was done,
And safe within my castle lay,
    Whitehaugh and Mangerton.

" I had them all, but only one,
    John Elliot, of the Park,
As stalwart and as bold a man,
    As ever rode by dark.

" I sought him far, I sought him near,
    He baffled all my men ;
At last I met him, face to face,
    Within the Billhope glen.

" What parley passed between us twain ?
    ' Thou art the warden !'   ' Ay !'
' Thou Elliot of the Park !'   ' I am,'
    ' Wilt yield thee ?'   ' Come and try.'

" We lighted down from off our steeds,
    We tied them to a tree,
The sun was shining in the west,
    And all alone were we.

" Out flew the steel, and then began
    A sharp and desperate strife;
For Elliot fought to 'scape the cord,
    I fought for fame and life.

" Ha ! ha ! were he alive again,
    And on this dungeon floor,
What joy, with such a man as that,
    To cross the sword once more !

" The blows he fetched were stark and strong,
    And so were mine, I ween,
Until I cleft his head-piece through,
    And stretched him on the green.

" ' Wilt yield thee now !'   ' I will not yield,
    But an ye promise grace ;'
' That must you ask upon your knee,
    Before our Sovereign's face.'

" Blinded with blood, he struggled up—
    ' Lord Earl,' he said, ' beware !
No man shall take me living yet ;
    Now follow, if you dare.'

"I slipped upon the broken moss;
  And in the *sheugh* * we rolled,
Death-grappling, silent, heaving each,
  Within the other's hold.

" He passed above me, and I felt—
  Once—twice—his dagger drive,
But mine went deeper through his breast,
  I rose, but half alive!

" All spun around me, trees and hills,
  A mist appeared to rise;
Yet one thing saw I clearly yet,
  Before my fading eyes;

" Not half a rood beyond the burn,
  A man lay stiff and stark;
I knew it was my stubborn foe,
  John Elliot of the Park.

" I strove in vain to sound my horn,
  No further thought had I;
And reeling on that lonely glen,
  I fell, but not to die."

I now take up this hero's prototype, JOHN ELLIOT of Copshaw, who was quite as daring a freebooter. In 1568, he and his accomplices made a desperate raid on Torwoodlee, in Selkirkshire, killing the laird, George Pringle, when in bed; also destroying a great deal of property, and stealing a large amount of money. This Pringle of Torwood had been at the battle of Pinkie, and was ancestor of George, the distinguished adherent of the Royal cause during the Civil war, which entailed upon him great personal suffering—injuring his estate very seriously, though in a different manner to the raid on the first George by John Elliot of Copshaw, whose punishment was simply that of being put to the horn, and having his movables escheated.

Early last century there lived HENRY ELLIOT of Deadwater—a farm which belonged to the Duke of Northumber-

* Burrow or trench.

land—who was a shrewd but eccentric man. At a court held at Alnwick one May-day, the tenants being summoned to pay their rents, Elliot of course attended with the rest. It was after a very bad season, when many of their flocks had perished, and the tenantry were unanimous, except Henry of Deadwater, in pleading for a return, or an abatement of rent, in consequence of their heavy losses. Elliot told the agents he did not mean to whinge or cringe to them, and added, "Had I followed the plan of my neighbours, I cannot tell what the consequences might have been, for they no sooner saw a sheep dead than they skinned it; but I took another method, and ordered my shepherds not to skin one of them till the warm weather came, when to my great joy the most part of them came to life again." This *double entendre* excited much laughter, and Elliot got as large a reduction as any of the other tenants.

In the latter part of last century, there lived CHARLES ELLIOT, from Liddesdale, one of the most enterprising publishers in Edinburgh. He was, in fact, the John Murray or Blackwood of his time. He trained James Sibbald of Whitelaw, also a native of this county, who, like Elliot, had a great taste for literature, and who became as famous as his old master, for he was not only a great Book-seller, but a book writer.

THOMAS ELLIOT, Minister of Cavers from 1763 to 1809, deserves notice in the Elliot history. He was a man of intense modesty and gentleness, while he possessed considerable abilities as a mathematician and astronomer, of which he made little display.

He wrote an essay on astronomy, which appeared in the "Transactions of the Royal Society of Edinburgh;" and also the old statistical account of his parish. Mr Elliot had the honour of giving the celebrated Thomas Chalmers his first employment as a preacher, having appointed him his assistant about seventy years ago; and though his stay was but short, his ministry in our Border land is not forgotten. Chalmers was delighted with the beauty of Teviotdale, and his heart was quite won, as his biographer tells us, by the frank and intelligent cordiality of its families.

Although the Elliots were not much in record on the Borders before the sixteenth century, they distinguished themselves in their desperate calling—a calling of which an early Scottish poet says—

> " Of Liddisdale the common theifis
> Sa peartlie stellis now, and reifs
> That nane may keip
> Horse, nolt, nor scheip,
> Nor yett dar sleip
> For their mischiefis."

There was, however, neighbourly feeling in the hearts of some of the freebooters, for it is recorded of "Auld Buccleuch" that, when Jamie Telfer of the Fair Dodhead lost his cattle by an inroad of the English reivers, he sent Wat o' Harden and others to the help of Telfer, and had the honour of recovering his cattle that had been carried off. Jamie Telfer had paid black mail, or protection money, to Gilbert Elliot of Stobbs, and claimed his help before making application to Buccleuch at Branksome, but "Auld Gibbie Elliot" refused any assistance. In his great emergency Telfer applied to the Scotts, who, headed by Harden, came to his succour, and recovered his cattle. The story is well told in the ballad, of which a part is subjoined :—

> " It fell about the Martinmas tyde,
>   When our border steeds get corn and hay,
> The Captain of Bewcastle hath bound him to ryde,
>   And he's ower to Tividale to drive a prey.
>
>   .   .   .   .
>
> And when they cam to the Fair Dodhead,
>   Right hastily they clam the peel;
> They loos'd the kye out, ane and a',
>   And ranshackled the house right weel.
> Now Jamie Telfer's heart was sair,
>   The tear aye rowing in his e'e;
> He pled wi' the Captain to hae his gear,
>   Or else revenged he wad be.

The Captain turned him round and leugh ;
    Said—'Man, ther 's naething in thy house
But ae auld sword without a sheath,
    That hardly now wad fell a mouse.'
The sun was na up, but the moon was doon,
    It was the gryming * of a new-fa 'n snaw ;
Jamie Telfer has run ten myles a-foot,
    Between the Dodhead and the Stobbs' ha'.
And when he cam to the fair tower yett,
    He shouted loud, and cried weel hie,
Till out bespak Auld Gibbie Elliot—
    'Whae 's this, that brings the fraye to me ?'
'It 's I, Jamie Telfer o' the Fair Dodhead,
    And a harried man I think I be !
Ther 's naething left at the Fair Dodhead
    But a waefu' wife and bairnies three.'
'Gae seek your succour at Branxsome Ha',
    For succour ye 'se get nane frae me !
Gae seek your succour where ye paid black mail,
    For man ! ye ne'er paid mony to me.'
Jamie has turned him round about—
    I wat the tear blinded his e'e,—
I'll ne'er pay mail to Elliot again,
    And the Fair Dodhead I'll never see !' "

Telfer, in his difficulty, applies to Jock Grieve, his wife's brother-in-law, who lived at Coultart Cleugh, on the Teviot.

. . . .
" Then up bespak him Auld Jock Grieve—
    'Whae 's this that brings the fraye to me ?'
'It 's I Jamie Telfer o' the Fair Dodhead,
    A harried man I trow I be.
Ther 's naething left in the Fair Dodhead
    But a greeting wife and bairnies three,
And sax puir ca'as† stand in the sta'
    A' routing loud for their minnie.' " ‡

Though Jock Grieve pitied Telfer, he could do little for him, but, aided by another friend,

. . . .
" He 's set his twa sons on coal-black steeds,
    Himsel' upon a freckled grey,
And they are on wi' Jamie Telfer
    To Branxsome Ha' to tak the fraye.

---

* Sprinkling.   † Calves.   ‡ Mother.

> And when they cam to Branxsome Ha',
> They shouted a' baith loud and hie,
> Till up and spak him auld Buccleuch,
> Said—' Whae's this brings the fraye to me?'
> ' It's I, Jamie Telfer o' the Fair Dodhead,
> And a harried man I be!
> Ther's nought left in the Fair Dodhead
> But a greeting wife and bairnies three.'
> ' Alack for wae!' quoth the gude auld Lord,
> ' And ever my heart is wae for thee!
> But fye, gar cry on Willie,* my son,
> And see that he come to me speedilie!
> Gar warn the water, braid and wide;
> Gar warn it soon and hastily!
> They that winna ride for Telfer's kye,
> Let them never look in the face o' me.
> Warn Wat o' Harden and his sons,
> Wi' them will Borthwick water ride;
> Warn Goudielands and Allanhaugh,
> And Gilmanscleuch and Commonside.'"

Buccleuch's supposed son was most active in the pursuit, and lost his life on the occasion.

> " But Willie was stricken our the head,
> And through the knapscap the sword has gane.
> And Harden grat for very rage,
> When Willie on the grund lay slane.
> . . . .
> ' Revenge! Revenge!' auld Wat 'gan cry,
> ' Fye, lads, lay on them cruellie!
> We'll ne'er see Tiviotside again,
> Or Willie's death revenged sall be.'"

It was, indeed, revenged by the overthrow and death of upwards of thirty of the English reivers. The cattle were recovered, and

> . . . .
> " Whan they cam to the Fair Dodhead,
> They were a wellcum sight to see!
> For instead of his ain ten milk kye,
> Jamie Telfer has gotten thirty and three."

I must here observe that Sir Walter Scott intimates the supposition that there had been another ballad in which the same

---

* Supposed to be a natural son of Buccleuch's.

incidents are related, except that the merit of recovering Jamie Telfer's kye is ascribed to the Elliots, commanded by a friend of the Regent Murray, Martin Elliot of the Preahin Tower, whose son Simon is said to have lost his life in the fray. Sir Walter, however, suggests the possibility that both Scotts and Elliots might have been concerned in the rescue ; and if so, all honour to both clans.

CONCLUSION.

I have thus given you an imperfect sketch of the most distinguished of the Elliot name in various walks of life, on both sides of the Border. Those who have followed me in its details will agree, with respect to the Scotch Elliots, that few of the Border clans, as our Highland neighbours would call them, have contributed more useful or devoted citizens to the public weal. Like the Douglases, Scotts, and Kers, whose histories I have previously given, the Elliots long ago have sowed and reaped, and got rid of their wild oats, and have a goodly crop of faithful and disinterested labours to show as the credentials of their patriotism. They have exchanged

"Wha daur meddle wi' me?"

for a much more noble motto,

"Wha daur meddle with our country?"

Amongst the men of mark who have borne the name of Elliot stands conspicuous George Augustus, the hero of Gibraltar. The defence of this key to the Mediterranean—which may England ever retain—would of itself have been enough to have won for this Border sept lasting honour, had no other members of it been famed for public services; but when I have shown you that this is very far from being the case, the house of Minto especially having produced a number of distinguished men, abroad and at home, as governors of dependencies, as lawyers or members of the Senate, or last, not least, as country gentlemen living on their estates, they have played their part well. This, in conclusion, I may remark of them, as well as other families of our nobility or titled gentry : possessors of broad lands, or inheritors of honoured names, they have not been contented to rest solely on the prestige of ancestral distinction, but have felt that such advantages involve a responsibility to call out fresh exertions on their own part, acting on the French motto, " Noblesse oblige," which might be freely rendered, " We are noblemen ; we cannot help acting nobly." Such has been the conduct especially of the Minto family, some of whose good deeds I have brought before you. Such, with some few exceptions, is the case with the representatives of many a lordly name in this country still, and particularly with our Border Peers. While this spirit continues there will be little fear of levellers and ultra-republicans shouldering out our nobles and landed gentry. The people will look on them with respect and affection, and feel they claim their right of honour by services faithfully rendered, and achievements gallantly performed, for the country they love and which loves them.

We give on the next two pages a pedigree of the families of Redheugh and Larriston, furnished to the author by the Hon. George Elliot, brother to the Earl of Minto.

ELLIOTS OF REDHEUGH AND LARISTON.

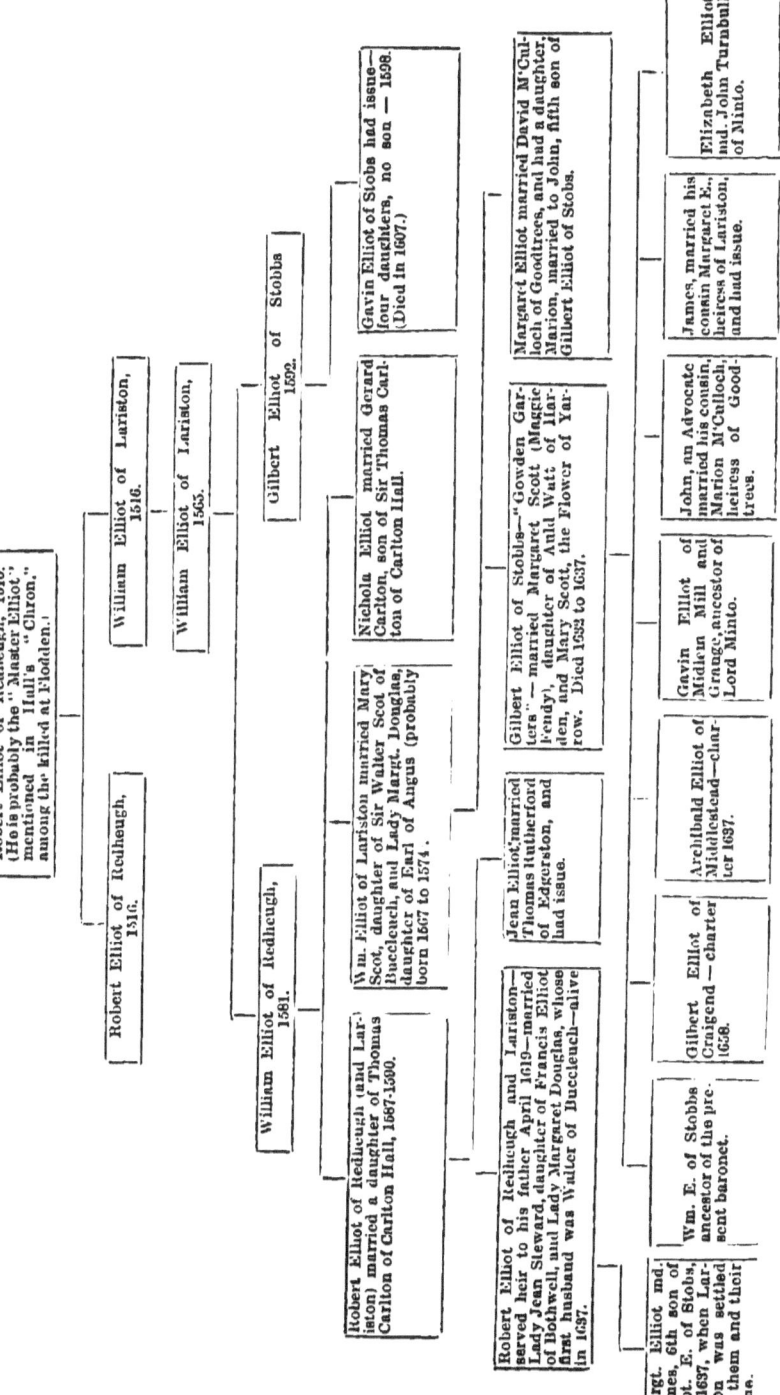

EARLY PEDIGREES OF THE ELLIOTS OF REDHEUGH AND LARISTON.

ROBERT of REDHEUGH, 1510, is mentioned in Pitcairn's "Criminal Trials," vol. i. p. 111.

ROBERT of REDHEUGH and WILLIAM of LARISTON, his brother, 1516, mentioned—*Ibid*, p. 232—as receiving a respite for them and their kinsmen on January 29th. Another respite, November 8, in same year, is addressed to William of Lariston alone. Had his brother Robert died in the interval?

WILLIAM of LARISTON, 1565, mentioned *Ibid*, p. 466. He is there called of Lameston—evidently a clerical error.

WILLIAM of REDHEUGH, 1581, mentioned in Nicolson and Burns "History of Cumberland," vol. i. p. 30.

ROBERT of REDHEUGH, 1587, *Ibid*, p. 32. In the map of 1590, given in "Jeffrey's Roxburghshire," vol. iv., the name of Robert Eliott of Lartison appears as the chief of the clan. This is, I believe, the same individual. Redheugh and Lariston seem to have been used indifferently as the designation of the chief.

ROBERT of REDHEUGH (and LARISTON), 1637—served heir to his father, Robert of Redheugh, April 20, 1619 (Retours)—by charter dated January 27, 1637, settled Lariston on his daughter and her husband (see paper of 1788, "Memories of Hawick," append).

GILBERT of STOBS, 1592, mentioned in case of Elliot against Elliot in "Morrison's Dictionary of Decisions," p. 8916. It appears from the case that he had a nephew, William Elliot, then a minor, and also a grand-nephew, then under fourteen. I do not find this Gilbert of Stobs mentioned elsewhere (of course he could not be the same as "Gowden Garters" who would then be a child); and it is very probable that Gilbert is a mistake for Gavin. [Such mistakes in names often occur in abbreviated reports, such as given in "Morrison's Dictionary." I will give an instance which has misled Wilson ("Memories of Hawick"), who, in a note to the pedigree of Elliots, says Gavin E. of Stobs' name occurs in "Morrison's Dictionary," vol. i. p. 201, date 1636. That is true; but in a fuller report of the same case in "Spottiswoode," p. 55, it appears that the name should have been Gavin Elliot of Burgh, and William Elliot of Stobs appears as the then proprietor.]

GAVIN of STOBS, 1598—Bond of that date referred to in the paper of 1788. He had four daughters as appears from the Retours of May 12, 1607, and January 21, 1621—no son.

WILLIAM of LARISTON, who married Mary Scott. I believe him to have been the William Elliot, nephew of Gilbert of Stobs referred to in case of Elliot against Elliot above mentioned. The "Robin Elliot, and Will, his brother"—"Nicolson and Burn," 31—were probably this William and Robert of Redheugh, 1587, above mentioned.

THE HOUSE OF RIDDELL.

I PROCEED to give a brief account of the Riddells of that Ilk and their branches, a house of even greater antiquity than those of Douglas, Scott, and Ker, though not so historically eminent. They seldom mixed themselves up with the contentions and forays of the sixteenth and seventeenth centuries, and until Covenanting times they were not very publicly known, though at that period two members of the family were noted for their defence of civil and religious liberty.

I shall first mention the rise of the Riddells in this country. They sprung from MONSIEUR RIDEL, who was a companion of William the Conqueror, and whose name appears with many other chieftains on the roll of Battel Abbey—the earliest record of the Normans—a table containing the names being at one time suspended in the abbey with the following inscription, viz. :—

> " Dicitur a bello, bellum locus hic, quis bello
> Angligenæ victi, sunt hic in morte relictis,
> Martyris in Christi festo cecidere Colixti,
> Sexagenus erat sextus millessimus annus
> Cum pereunt Angli, stella monstrante cometa."

Battel Abbey, which is a memorial of one of the greatest achievements in English history, was built on the extensive plain of Heathfield, a little to the north of Hastings, in fulfilment of a pledge given by the great Norman, prior to the battle which gained for him the crown of England. William had been named by Edward the Confessor, the last of the Saxon line, his successor, though Edgar Atheling was the next legitimate heir, and Harold had usurped the throne. But the battle of Hastings settled the point, and William, who there defeated Harold, was made king, having been crowned at Westminster in little more than two months after his arrival in England.

In Normandy the Riddells were a family of note, some members having joined a party of their fellow-countrymen—a most extraordinary and chivalrous people—who invaded Italy and eventually Sicily. Of these doubtless were Goffridus and Regnaldus Ridel, brothers—the first of whom figured there so very anciently as Duke of Gaeta in 1072, and the latter as Count de Ponté Carvo in 1093. Goffridus was a common Christian name in various families of Ridel in these early times, and the surname is precisely the same, the second *d* and the second *l* being additions in after times.

My late kinsman, John Riddell, the best antiquary that Scotland has had for many a day, found from Norman records proof of the existence of Gulfridus and Roger Riddell, possessors of estates in Normandy towards the end of the thirteenth century; and also two great stocks of the name in France, classed among its magnates there, being well allied, and designed of Baijerae in the thirteenth century, terminating in an heir-female.

William bestowed on his Riddell follower considerable landed property in England, and his descendants became celebrated, and one or two of them held high official appointments. An alliance by marriage was formed between them and the Bassits, a very old English family, lately represented by my old friend, John Bassit of Tohidy, who used at one time to come to Tweedside, where he rented Lord Polwarth's fishing water.

One of the English Riddells married Geva, the daughter of the Earl of Chester, one of whose descendants was Maud or Matilda, wife of David, Earl of Huntingdon, a maternal ancestrix of the Bruce.

Although the family were so prosperous in England some of its members emigrated to Scotland early in the twelfth century with David I., when Prince of Cumberland, who was a great colonizer. Gervasius was the elder, and he was a great favourite of the Prince, who appointed him in 1116 High Sheriff of Roxburghshire—the earliest on record. He must have been a constant attendant on royalty, for he is a frequent witness to crown charters, and especially to that celebrated commission for enquiring into the revenues of the Church at Glasgow in 1116, one of the most ancient Scotch records. Gervasius married and had family; a son Hugh is supposed to have been the ancestor of the Riddells of Cranston Riddell in Mid-Lothian. His wife, Christiana de Soulis, was a donor to Jedburgh monastery, and Gervasius, when advanced in life, assumed the ecclesiastical garb, and died at Jedburgh in the odour of sanctity. This was in accordance with a prevailing custom, namely, that those who had led a secular, and often a licentious and sinful life, sought to atone for the past by dying in a monastery. This was a practice followed by many whose lives had been peaceful and blameless. So great in these days was the reverence for religion, although a religion tainted with error.

Walter Ridel accompanied Gervasius in the suite of Prince David, and though younger doubtless, was not Gervasius's son, as some writers erroneously say. He was probably a brother or near relative. Like his kinsman, Walter enjoyed the friendship and patronage of Royalty. He too was also a witness to crown and other charters of importance, but that to himself from David I., of the lands of Wester-Lilliesleaf, &c., eclipsed them all, being the most ancient charter from a King to a Layman. The charter, which was dated between 1125 and 1153, included Whittun near the Cheviots, the lands to be held of the crown "per servitium unius militis sicut unus baronum meorum vicinorum suorum," &c. This ancient document became so frail that it was "legally" copied at Jedburgh about three hundred and seventy years ago, and the lands granted by it continued in the family for upwards of six hundred years without an entail, a fact highly honourable to all the members through whom they were handed down. Nisbet, the antiquary and herald, who flourished early last century, drew the copy. Besides this ancient charter, there was a Bull from Pope Adrian IV., nearly as old, confirming the properties vested in Walter to his brother and heir AUSKITTEL, Walter having no issue. The Bull must have been granted between 1154 and 1159, when Adrian was Pope, but the precise date is not given. Indeed in ancient Bulls the year was seldom mentioned. It runs thus :—" Adrianus Episcopus, servus servorum Dei, Auskittel Riddell militi, salutem et Apostolicum Benedictionem, sub Beati Petri et nostri protectione suscepimus specialiter ea quæ Walterus de Riddell testamentum suum ante obitum suum faciens tibi nosciter reliquisse, viz., villas de Wituness, Lilisclive, Brachebe, et cetera bona a quibuscunque tibi juste colate, nos authoritate sedis Apostolicæ integre confirmamus. Datum Beneventi Septimo ides Aprilis." There is another Bull from the Pope who succeeded Adrian to the same Sir Auskittel, and both documents, along with that formerly mentioned, were seen by Mr Nisbet.

The third laird was WALTER, son of Sir Auskittel, which is proved by the last named Bull. He married and had two sons, one of whom was

PATRICK, his heir, and RALPH, supposed to be the ancestor of the Northumberland Riddells, a highly respectable family of the Roman Catholic faith.*

PATRICK became the fourth Laird, and was knighted like his grandfather Sir Auskittel. After succeeding to his estates he made donations to the Abbey of Melrose, and to the monks serving God there. Sir Auskittel was a witness to a charter of confirmation granted to the Monks of Kelso in 1159 by Malcolm IV., the grandson of David I. Sir Patrick's son,

WALTER, the fifth laird, succeeded him, and seems to have

---

* The name of Ralph was not new in the family, for Gervasius had a brother called Ralph, who was a donor to Jedburgh Abbey.

been a pious Churchman, for he not only confirmed his father's donations to the convent of Melrose, but gave many benefactions himself, not only to the monks of Melrose, but to those of Kelso. His mother, Margaret De Vesci, also confirmed her husband, Sir Patrick Riddell's donations to Melrose. Miss De Vesci was, I believe, of the then Border family, one of whom was among the number of the feudal lords appointed to enforce the observance of Magna Charta, and who married a daughter of William the Lion, King of Scotland, brother of Malcolm the IVth., so surnamed from having introduced the lion as the armorial bearing of Scotland, and from this emblem the head of the Heralds' Office in Edinburgh is called "Lion King at Arms."

Walter, the fifth laird, now before us, had a brother William, who got part of Whittun on his marriage with Matilda Corbett, probably of the Makerstoun family of that name, very ancient proprietors, but it returned to the head of the family, as they had no issue. Walter having left two sons, William and Patrick, the former succeeded, viz.,

WILLIAM, who, like his grandfather, had the honour of knighthood conferred upon him. He was the sixth laird. William's succession is proved by a charter to Melrose Abbey, by which it appears there was a donation to the convent by Isabella:—"Uxor Wilhelmi de Riddell de alia bovata terræ in territorio de Whittun quam pater meus Wilhelmus, parsona de Hunam, emit a Ganfredo Coco"—the deed being made "pro salute animæ Domini Patricii de Riddell, and Walter, filii ejus, et Wilhelmi, sponsi mei." * It is witnessed by five members of the family, which proves four successive descents.

I pass over some of the next lairds, as I hardly know how to place them, antiquaries having misstated and miscalled several; but there are two before Quintin, next to be taken up, respecting whom and his successors who follow there is no

* "Isabella, wife of William of Riddell, gives this out of pasture land in the territory of Whittun, which my father, William, parson of Hunam, bought from Ganfred Coke, for the salvation of the soul of Sir Patrick de Riddell and Walter, his son, and of William, my spouse."

doubt. The two I refer to were clearly before Quintin's time, and were named Richard and Sir Robert, both of whom are proved by documents in the charter chest at Fleurs. Richard was a witness to two charters to John Ker of Auldtounburn, dated respectively in 1357 and 1358. This John Ker came from the Forest of Selkirk, and was the first ancestor of the Cessford or ducal family of Roxburghe, who acquired land in Roxburghshire. Sir Robert Riddell, on the other hand, was a witness to a charter to Kelso Abbey of land in Mow, and was cautioner for Mowe of Mains, who was a hostage in England on account of Border disturbances. While these charters throw light upon two Riddell ancestors well down their tree, the first to John Ker of Auldtounburn indicates the planting of the Roxburghe tree at a much later period.

QUINTIN, now to be noticed, is a new name in the family, and from whence derived I have not been able to make out, though a name of a saint in the Roman Calendar. He was the first designed of that ilk or *de eodem*, as far as the charters extant show. He was assuredly in possession in 1421, when a Court of Inquisition was held, and the Lilliesleaf lands were then called Riddell, though even after that date Lilliesleaf, no doubt an old and favourite name, crops up sometimes. Their own surname, however, had been regularly and officially given to the Lilliesleaf property (Whittun continuing as originally), deriving the baronial character from the tenure of the first charter by David I. to Walter, and hence the origin of the local name of Riddell, as denoting an estate, that previously was not Scotch or known in Scotland. The distinguished knightly and baronial family of Riddell of Cranston Riddell, with the latter adjunct was the first, and at a far earlier date designed of Riddell, similarly giving their name to their barony, which likewise held of the Crown, as the descendants of Hugh, supposed to be the son of the High Sheriff, Gervasius Riddell. This gave them an earlier position than the Lilliesleaf Riddells; but in little more than two centuries their male line became extinct, and the heir of the last proprietor, Isabella Rydell, dead in 1357, was a John Murray. Quintin was followed by his son, whose name is not given ; but his grandson, who inherited, was

JAMES, who was indisputably laird of Riddell and Whittun in 1493, and had a brother Thomas, who is particularly mentioned, and a son

JOHN, who succeeded his father in 1510. He had two sisters, both of whom married Scotts. There had been a previous marriage with the Scotts, as the widow of one of the Riddells, supposed to be a Ker of Fernilie, married a Harden. John granted a precept for infefting Patrick Earl Bothwell in a part of some lands at Lilliesleaf in 1534, which he held of the laird of Riddell. John died in 1542, and was followed by

GEORGE. This George is particularly mentioned in a legal transaction upon record affecting him, and left

WALTER, his successor, who married Mariotte, daughter of Hoppringle of Smailholm, and had a son, Andrew, and two daughters, one of whom married Thomas Ker of Cavers and Nether Howden. Walter was old when he died, and his son

ANDREW was served heir in 1592, obtaining a charter in 1595. Andrew was a man of much importance, and having acquired Haining from the Scotts, the first possessors of it, held large territorial possessions, and was called the Baron of Riddell. Though lordly in his position, he was a man of humility, for he was offered a Baronetcy, which he declined. He did not, however, prevent his eldest son, John, who was a person of considerable talent, accepting the honour, which was conferred on the 14th of May 1628, about three years after the institution of the order in Scotland. Andrew must have married first his cousin, Miss Pringle, daughter of James Pringle of Gallowshiells and Smailholm, and after her death he was united to Violet Douglas of Pumpherston, West-Lothian. He had a large family of sons and daughters, his eldest son,

Sir JOHN, being by his first wife. Other sons and some of the daughters were also by Miss Pringle, and some time ago I found a stone in the Abbey burying-ground at Jedburgh in memory of Jean Riddell, daughter of Andrew, born 1600, and died 1660. She is commemorated thus—

"Here lies a religious and virtuous gentlewoman, Jean Riddell, daughter of Sir Andrew Riddell of that ilk, who died in the year of God, MDCLX., and of her age 60.
    She lived a holy life,
    To Christ resigned her breath.
    Her soul is now with God,
    Triumphing over death!"

Andrew had, by Violet Douglas, his second wife, a favourite son called Andrew, on whom he settled Haining, which continued in this branch of the family till early last century, when it was sold to the second son of Pringle of Clifton.

Andrew of Haining married a Stewart of Traquair, and dying young, his widow married secondly Sir William Douglas, ancestor of the Marquis of Queensberry. His son and successor, John Riddell of Haining, was Sheriff Principal, and M.P. for Selkirkshire, and his grand-daughter, Magdalene Riddell, who married David Erskine of Dun, after succeeding to Haining, sold it, and the Marquis of Ailsa, as the heir of the Erskines, now represents the Riddells of Haining. But to return to Andrew, the Baron of Riddell, I would state that his tombstone in the aisle of Riddell gives his death in 1632, at the age of eighty-two. His second wife erected an additional stone to his memory, and there is also a stone to the memory of Andrew of Haining, whose life was "short but good," and with the exception of a more ancient stone, with a recommendation to pray for the soul, though no name is to be seen, there is no other memorial in the old aisle, which was once the choir of the ancient church, superseded by the present in 1771, over a century ago. One of Andrew's other sons was ancestor of the Riddells of Muselee. His daughters married respectively Rutherfurd of Edgerston; Robert Ker, brother of Sir Thomas of Cavers; John Baillie, ancestor, I believe, of the Baillies of Mellerstain; and Sir John Scott of Goldielands, while the pious Jean, already commemorated, lived in single blessedness.

Sir JOHN, first Baronet of Riddell, married Miss Murray of

Blackbarony, which brought the family further high connections, and had four sons and one daughter.

Three of his sons went abroad, two were captains in the Dutch service, while another, William, a youth of great spirit, was knighted at an early age, and was appointed Governor of Desborough, in Holland. His only daughter, by his wife, Miss Murray, married Sir Thomas Ker of Cavers, and by a second wife, the widow of the Honourable James Douglas, Commendator of Melrose Abbey, Sir John Riddell had another daughter. He was succeeded in 1636 by his eldest son,

Sir WALTER, who was knighted, like one of his younger brothers, in his father's lifetime. He married a very pious woman, Janet Rigg, the daughter of a worthy and godly man, William Rigg of Aithernie, Fife, by whom he had five sons and two daughters. Janet Rigg, Lady Riddell, was not only pious but accomplished, and her father was a man of high principle and character, and moreover, extremely wealthy. Mr Rigg was fined £50,000 Scots for opposing the introduction of the five articles at Perth, by James VI., and also suffered imprisonment in Blackness Castle. His sister, the aunt of Lady Riddell, Miss Catherine Rigg, who married Douglas of Cavers, was the celebrated Covenanter, and the ladies were descendants of Dr John Row of Perth, John Knox's coadjutor.

Two of Sir Walter's younger sons were ancestors of the Riddells of Glenriddell and Granton severally, respecting whom I shall have a good deal to say—especially about the latter—afterwards.

His daughters married respectively a brother of Sir William Scott of Mertoun, and son of Auld Wat, the Freebooter of Harden, and the Rev. Gabriel Semple of Jedburgh, a zealous Covenanter and field preacher at one time. His eldest son,

JOHN, succeeded as third Baronet. He is called in the family Sir John Bluebeard, because he had four wives, not of course at once, like Brigham Young.

His wives were—1st, Miss Scott of Harden; 2d, Miss Morrison, Prestongrange; 3d, Miss Swinton, Swinton; and 4th, Mrs Watt, formerly Miss Hepburn, married first to Mr Watt of Rosehill, and after his decease, to Sir John Riddell.

Sir John, inheriting his mother's religious zeal, became a zealous Covenanter, and suffered imprisonment for his defence of civil and religious liberty, and his nonconformity. He sat in several Parliaments for the county of Roxburgh. He got a remission from the king in 1687, and he died in 1700, a very short time after his fourth marriage. His son,

Sir WALTER, succeeded, from whom I directly descend. He married Miss Watt of Rosehill, a daughter of his stepmother, and had several sons and daughters.

His eldest son, John, who predeceased him, was an advocate, very clever and highly accomplished.

His second, WALTER, succeeded.

His third was Thomas of Camieston.

His sixth, Robert, was minister of Lilliesleaf from 1736 to 1760, and married his relative, one of the Granton Riddells.

His only daughter, Jane, married John Carre of Cavers.

Sir Walter was a very godly man, the piety of his grandmother and father having been imbibed by him. He did some eccentric things, however. When his son was preaching he is said to have stopped him, when, as Sir Walter thought, he was not stating the terms of the gospel correctly, or at any rate saying something which he disapproved of, telling him, "Robert, that won't do." He was recommended to stop so many people coming upon his property, but his answer was, "the earth is the Lord's." In his time the public road passed close to the back of Riddell House, and I daresay its nearness to the kind-hearted Baronet's mansion induced a good many "seekers," as beggars in his time were called, to visit him. His eldest son, John, having predeceased him, his second son,

WALTER, inherited, and became fifth Baronet. He was in early life a merchant at Eyemouth, probably a dealer in fish and spirits, brandy being no doubt largely imported there, and married a daughter of Mr Turnbull of Houndwood, near Eyemouth. It was a runaway marriage, but the lady had neither money nor rank. The rank was on his side, though from his being a trader at Eyemouth, the Turnbulls might have looked down upon him then.

Sir Walter Riddell's eldest son, Walter, died about ten years before his father. His second succeeded him, while two of his younger sons were respectively a soldier and sailor, James, a Lieutenant-Colonel in the Dutch service, and Thomas of Bessborough, a captain in the naval service of the late East India Company. General Henry James Riddell, Knight of Hanover, and Commander of the Forces in Scotland, who died a few years ago, was the latter's son.

JOHN succeeded as sixth Baronet. Being second son he was shipped off to Curacoa, where he was a merchant, but coming home before his father's death, married Miss Buchanan, eventually an heiress, but he only survived his succession to Riddell about three years. He left three sons—the youngest of whom was the late Sir John, who was posthumous. All three sons were Baronets in turn. The eldest, Sir WALTER, a delicate youth, died just about the time of his majority. The second, Sir James, who was a Lieutenant in one of the Guards, was drowned while bathing in the River Brunswick, aged nineteen, and the third, who finally inherited, was the late

Sir JOHN, ninth Baronet, known to many still alive. He was a man of the most polished manners, and had a commanding address. He was a precocious agriculturist—far too much so for his time, and his experiments, successful as regards the ultimate improvement of the property, ended in his ruin, and entailed distress upon many of his dependents and others. But in spite of his being the cause of loss to many families, his name is still much respected.

Sir John Buchanan Riddell, who was Member of Parliament for the Selkirk Burghs, died in April 1819, aged fifty-one, leaving by his wife, Lady Frances Riddell, daughter of the

Earl of Romney, three sons and five daughters, a son having been born some months after his death.

SOME CADETS OF THE OLD RIDDELL STOCK.

The first is the MUSELEE branch who claim to be, and are descended from, a son of Andrew, the powerful Baron and father of the first Baronet of Riddell. That son or ancestor obtained a charter of Muselee in 1618, and a descendant acquired BEWLIE, and both properties continue in the family, in the female line, being represented by Captain Hutton Riddell, whose father, Mr Hutton, a banker at Newark-on-Trent, married the niece and heiress of the last Riddell proprietor, viz., Charles Riddell, long chamberlain to the Duke of Buccleuch, at Branxholm, who died unmarried, 11th December 1849, aged ninety-five, or thereabouts.

The third Riddell of Muselee married Miss Eliott, a connexion of the Eliotts of Borthwickbrae, and their fourth grandson, William, was ancestor of the Riddells of Berwick, respectable and successful merchants there, and connected by marriage with the Curries, also merchants at Berwick, the ancestors of the large London Banking and Mercantile families, who have been so successful, and whose descendants occupy so many prominent positions in life, and are connected with the Lefevres, now represented by Viscount Eversley, late Speaker of the House of Commons. One of the Berwickshire Riddells —the Rev. Thomas Riddell, Fellow of Trinity College, Cambridge—was a good scholar, and a hard-working London curate for several years, at St Andrews, Holborn, a very large parish, and of which the Duke of Buccleuch is patron, but latterly he held a College Living at Masham, Yorkshire, where he died in middle life.

The Glenriddell family and the Riddells of Granton come next. They descended from two brothers, sons of the second Baronet of Riddell. Glen Riddell is in Dumfries-shire, but the first male occupants of it soon died out, and a daughter of the last heiress, who married Walter Riddell of Newhouse in Lilliesleaf, the son of the Rev. Simon Riddell, minister of Tynron, who married Miss Riddell of Newhouse—the heiress, I presume, of that place—carried Glenriddell to her husband, though some of the younger branches of the old Glenriddell males had families, and are now represented by a young gallant soldier. The Rev. Simon Riddell, whose original pedigree I do not at present know, was a man of some note. In 1715 he marched to Stirling with a portion of his parishioners, in defence of His Majesty and the Protestant interest, and in 1740 he was one of the fifteen ministers against deposing the eight seceders, of whom were Ralph and Ebenezer Erskine. Mr Simon Riddell's son, Walter Riddell, acquiring Glen Riddell through his wife, seems to have enjoyed it many years, being followed by his son, Robert, who was a most accomplished man, as well as a good antiquary. He was a great friend of the poet, Robert Burns, and was present at the celebrated convivial celebration connected with "the Whistle," as the following lines by the great bard imply:

"Three joyous good fellows, with hearts clear of flaw,
Craigdarroch, so famous for wit, worth, and law,
And trusty Glenriddell, so skilled in old coins,
And gallant Sir Robert, deep read in old wines."

The three were—Glenriddell; Fergusson of Craigdarroch; and Sir Robert Laurie. They were all connected. Fergusson was the hero of "the Whistle," having got through five bottles of claret at the sitting.

The Granton Riddells are next in order. Their chief, Archibald, third son of Sir Walter, second Baronet of Riddell, was ordained to the ministry, and, like his brother, Sir John, was a strenuous Covenanter, preaching in the fields, but neither of these committed any treasonable acts, and yet they both suffered imprisonment. Archibald was very severely dealt with. He was first imprisoned in Jedburgh, then in Edinburgh, and afterwards at the Bass. After a long incarceration, he was set free on a promise that he would go to America, which he did in 1684, remaining there till the Revolution, when he returned, but on his voyage home, the vessel he came in was captured by a French man-of-war, and Mr Riddell was again a prisoner. He was carried to Nantes, then to Rochefort, where he was placed in a common jail, with about two hundred prisoners, English and Dutch, and they were almost all sent to Toulon. They were chained two and two by the arm. Mr Riddell was chained to his son, a boy of ten years of age, for whom they were at pains to make three different chains, before they got one small enough for the lad's wrist. After this long and wearisome journey, and their detention at Toulon, during which there were several deaths, they were sent back to Rochefort, and afterwards to Douai, near to St Malo, where Mr Riddell continued more than a year in a vault of an old castle, with some hundreds of other prisoners. They lay on straw, never changed save once a month, and were oppressed with many disagreeables. It must have required great fortitude on the part of my kinsman and his son to have endured and survived such misery. But after twenty-two months, an author states : " Mr Riddell and his son were exchanged for two Popish priests, as proved by a royal letter to the Privy Council :

William Rex,

" Whereas we are informed that Mr Archibald Riddell, minister of the gospel, and James Sinclair of Freshwick, are prisoners in France, and are very hardly used, whom we resolve to have released by exchange with two priests now prisoners in Scotland, therefore we require you to call for the friends and nearest relatives of the said Mr Archibald Riddell, and James Sinclair, and signify our royal pleasure to them, in exchange of these two prisoners with the two priests, that shall be condescended upon, and authorise them not only to 'speik' with the two priests, but also to write to France anent the negotiating their friends' liberty, and that you cause the two priests to be condescended upon, be securely keeped, and make intimation to them that they shall be used in the same way and manner as the French King uses the said Scots prisoners, which they may be ordered to acquaint their friends in France with, that the exchange may be the more easily effected. For doing of which these presents shall be your warrant, and so we bid you heartily farewell. Given at our Court at Kensington, the 16th day of January 16$\frac{88}{89}$, and of our Reigne the first year. By his Majesty's command, here directed to the Privy Council of Scotland."

Archibald Riddell's trials being now ended, he passed the rest of his life in peace and security. Indeed, as Wodrow states, when he returned all his losses were made up, and he and his four children (for his wife died on the passage to America), were in better circumstances than if he had conformed, to which he had been instigated. He was appointed minister of Trinity College Church, that fine old church built by Mary of Guelders, now removed to make way for the North British Railway Station, but the stones are preserved to rebuild with, when a decision is come to. Mr Riddell died in 1708, and left a great reputation behind him. Dr Hew Scott says, "he was a singularly pious and laborious servant of Jesus Christ."

He left two sons, Walter and John—the former a most distinguished naval officer, and the latter a physician in Edinburgh. Captain Walter Riddell's conduct and bravery as a naval officer is noticed in a history of Europe, 1709, and he is also proved to have distinguished himself in captures of vessels and in opposing the rebels of 1715, stimulated, no doubt, by the treatment shown to his father in the reign of James II., as I have shown. I am not sure which of the two sons was chained to his father in the French prison, but I apprehend it was the elder, the naval officer, who, by the way, acquired the barony of West Granton, near Edinburgh.

The Granton Riddells were connected with the Dundas,

Barts. of Beechwood, and the Nesbitts, Barts. of Dean, the latter old family having become impoverished, and indeed extinct in the male line, and the fine old place of Dean was sold to the late Mr Learmonth, a celebrated coachbuilder in Edinburgh, and once Lord Provost.

The Granton Riddells are now represented by the Rev. James Riddell, of Balliol College, the father of the much-lamented James Riddell, a Fellow of the same college, and one of the best Greek scholars at Oxford in his time, whose early death has been much mourned.

I cannot, in justice to the memory of my lamented kinsman, pass on without further reference to his character and scholarship, which I can hardly find terms adequately to describe. His boyhood even was uncommon, and when at Shrewsbury School he was a favourite pupil of the master, Dr Kennedy, and he there obtained the highest honour, which was the Sydney Gold Medal. From Shrewsbury James Riddell was elected at the head of thirty candidates from the first schools in England to a scholarship of Balliol College, Oxford, in November 1841, being then eighteen. As an undergraduate he was beloved both by his seniors and cotemporaries for gentleness of manner and great amiability of disposition, and the heads of the college considered him one of the best and most promising scholars that Balliol ever reared. Having obtained a first-class in classics, he took his degree, and was made a Fellow of his college, taking holy orders. Shortly after, he was appointed one of the tutors, and in this sphere he was much respected by his many pupils. He was also made a public examiner, and in addition held other honourable appointments connected with the university, including a seat at the Hebdomadal Council, the governing body. He was also for one year a select preacher at St Mary's, and in 1864 was appointed one of the Whitehall preachers, both positions being alike honourable.

About the middle of the year 1866 his health, never very robust, and perhaps unfavourably acted upon by intense application to study for so many years, gave way, and alarming symptoms suddenly appeared, which ended in his death on the 14th September of that year, at the temporary residence of his family at Tunbridge Wells, where his remains were interred.

I said at the commencement that Mr Riddell was one of the best Grecians of his time at Oxford, the great seat of classical learning, and the "Reliquiæ Metricæ," published by Messrs Parker, contains translations of Greek and Latin verses by my friend, showing the high rank he took in such compositions; and it is not a little singular that the last production of his pen should have been a Latin translation of Watts' well-known hymn—

> "There is a land of pure delight,
> Where saints immortal reign;
> Infinite day excludes the night,
> And pleasures banish pain;
> There everlasting spring abides,
> And never-with'ring flowers;
> Death, like a narrow sea, divides
> That heavenly land from ours."

It was said of Mr Riddell, by one capable of judging, that he was admired and loved as the very model and ideal of a Christian scholar and gentleman in the University of Oxford, of which he was a chief ornament. And the Rev. Canon Liddon, in lately replying to my request for a sketch of his friend for this lecture, said that stress of work obliged him to decline; for even if he could feel at all sure that he could do his dear friend's character anything like justice, it would require much more careful consideration than I took for granted; and to write about the holy dead, except with great care and conscientiousness, was to do them and others no little wrong. Canon Liddon adds:—"The salient features of his character—his courage, his purity, his tenderness, his delicate and far-reaching conscientiousness—were sufficiently obvious to all who knew him; but to show the relation of these virtues to his great intellectual life, and to mark the finer shades which would have to be distinguished, is, I fear, beyond anything that I could at present, if ever, attempt."

Three brothers of the Rev. James Riddell, senr., who still survives, have lately died in Scotland—John, Robert, and Henry—the latter minister of the Parish of Dunse, in Berwickshire. John was the celebrated genealogical scholar and antiquary, being without a rival in Scotland in his branch of law, though, being a kinsman, I shall not individually further sound his praises, but allow Lord Lindsay—now Earl Crawford—to speak in his behalf, by quoting from his lordship's testimony to Mr Riddell's great eminence :—" The genealogical knowledge, which gave weight and value to his (Mr Riddell's) opinions, was vast and profound—the gathered stores of a life-time spent among public and private records, almost every principal charter-chest in Scotland having at one time or other passed under his review. But this vast knowledge would have been little serviceable towards the great purposes to which he devoted it had he not possessed that thorough familiarity with the law—feudal, consistorial, genealogical, and heraldic—and not of Scotland and England only, but of foreign nations, which determined the value and regulated the application of the facts ever present before his mental eye. It was from this lofty eminence of principle and precedent that he was enabled to survey the length and breadth of Scottish genealogical antiquity, assign its limits to undue family pretension, recall forgotten rights of representation to public recognition, and point out in many instances the means through which unsuspected or neglected hereditary honours might be legally claimed and vindicated. And it was from the full concurrent perception of the extent of the difficulty always attendant on such processes, more especially before the House of Lords, that, acting under the impulse of that honesty which is always allied with the love of truth, as well as in accordance with his chivalric sense of honour and his extreme disinterestedness on the point of professional remuneration, he carefully and distinctly, before engaging in such undertakings, pointed out the adverse considerations likely to attend upon them, whether through deficiency of evidence or irregular and fluctuating procedure in the tribunal where the claim must necessarily be prosecuted—anxious ever that his client should not commit himself to the pursuit without full warning of what it might entail upon him. But when once engaged in it he gave his whole soul to the object before him ; and it was a beautiful and inspiring thing to witness the play of his thought during the evolution of his argument ; the historical breadth of his views, and their ready convergence to the required focus, however minute and particular ; his subtlety of legal discrimination ; his fertility in illustration ; his extraordinary readiness of resource ; his untiring patience and industry in working out his results, contrasting with the eager impetuosity of utterance which accompanied their birth ; and lastly, the genuine professional courage, springing again, as before, from his manly honesty and love of truth, with which he never evaded, but boldly faced and combated every difficulty. I speak (says Lord Lindsay, now Earl Crawford) to all this from my own experience during the prosecution of the minute and complicated Peerage claims."

Again :—" I have seldom witnessed more touching examples of that beautiful humility which is generally the sister of mental strength and moral dignity than in Mr Riddell. His pride was far more in the fame of his great predecessors in the same studies, and in that of the historical families of Scotland, more especially those with whom he had become professionally related, than in his own reputation. He was as unselfish in that respect as he was disinterested (as I before incidentally remarked) in regard to the remuneration of his labours."

And again :—" Everything he wrote was stamped with the power bestowed by profound legal knowledge and a boundless command of facts ; and his works will be continually resorted to as a store-house of information on matters of genealogy and Peerage law by future generations."

Such are some of Earl Crawford's views of Mr Riddell's

great professional acquirements and character, and I need not further enlarge except to say that he had a strong affection for the ancient classic literature, but as the Latin epitaph on his tomb in Dean Cemetery, of which I read a copy, refers to this, I say no more :—"John Riddell, Esquire, advocate, a man imbued with the literature of every age, who, in antiquities, and especially that branch of them which relates to the origin of families, by recalling it to the truth of fact, was prodigal of labour, and, moreover, felicitous. This pursuit he illustrated by his writings, being an author of the greatest weight, as all admit. In this land, once the property of his ancestors, he was buried. Born 4th October 1785. Died 8th February 1862. He lived seventy-six years." I before alluded to the Dean (a portion of which property was sold to the cemetery company), having been the property of the Nisbetts, his ancestors, which accounts for what is stated in the epitaph.

With reference to his brother, Robert Riddell, also an advocate and Sheriff-Substitute of Haddingtonshire, who died suddenly, not long after his brother John's death, and the day after that of his elder brother, the Rev. Henry Riddell, minister of Dunse. He possessed considerable professional acquirements, and made a most efficient magistrate, and combined with these qualifications no ordinary degree of literary attainments, especially in that department of law and research in which his brother John was so famous. As John said to me once, " he was tarred with the same brush."

The next branch to be sketched is the Camieston, its ancestor being Thomas, third son of Sir Walter, the fourth Baronet, for whom that property was acquired in his youth, being now possessed by his great-grandson, General William Riddell. Thomas married the youngest daughter of the Rev. William Hunter, minister of Lilliesleaf, and laird of Union Hall, which is part of the present Linthill property, Midlem Mill estate on which the present mansion-house stands having been acquired by Dr Hunter, the minister's son, who conveyed it to his son, Colonel Edgar Hunter, a very popular country gentleman who was killed by a fall from his horse in the prime of life, and unmarried. At his death, the succession went to his first cousin, William Riddell of Camieston—well-known to many still alive—whose father married one of Colonel Hunter's sisters. The Hunters were well descended, and the minister was a singularly good and pious man. He was one of the supporters of the Marrow of Modern Divinity, which raised a controversy which lasted for some time in the Church of Scotland, but without leading to the secession of any of the thirteen ministers who supported the Marrow. There were three supporters of it in this neighbourhood besides Mr Hunter, viz., the Rev. Thomas Boston, the Rev. Gabriel Wilson of Maxton, and the Rev. Henry Davidson of Galashiels. I may add before leaving the Hunters, so intimately connected with the Camieston Riddells, that the eldest daughter of the Rev. William Hunter married the Rev. Adam Milne, minister and historian of Melrose, whose book about the antiquities of the abbey and parish is one of the best that has been written, and is the text-book of many subsequent historians. Mr Milne's only child, a daughter, having died, the Linthill property passed to Mr Riddell, as the son of the younger sister. But that gentleman soon sold it, being a good deal embarrassed, when the late Mr Currie bought and entailed it. It may be worth noticing that Midlem Mill was formerly the property of the Elliots, a branch of the ancient House of Stobs, and that Gilbert Elliot, a younger son of the first Elliot of Midlem Mill founded the House of Minto, which was subsequently ennobled.

Among the other members of the Camieston branch, entitled to be named, and also eulogised, was Robert the fourth son of the first laird, and grandson of Sir Walter, fourth Baronet, a lieutenant on board the Honourable East India Company's ship, Duchess of Athol, which was burnt in 1783 in Madras Roads, a fire having broken out in the vessel. Robert Riddell was the officer in charge of the ship, the commander being on shore, and though all the crew were saved, and Riddell could have escaped also, he declined to leave the vessel, though

death stared him in the face, and, of course, fell a sacrifice
—a noble sacrifice to duty. His namesake nephew, my
late uncle, Admiral Robert Riddell Carre, was a sailor also,
and no smarter or more gallant officer ever trode a quarter-
deck. He was at Copenhagen under the illustrious Nelson,
and at Algiers under the brave Exmouth, and I possess his
medal, recording both victories. · And then the Admiral's two
nephews were officers in the East India Company's Service,
Thomas and Robert, the latter the Admiral's namesake, and
following him as a sailor, having been in the Indian Navy.
He was known, though young when he died, for his good
qualities as a seaman, and what is still better, for being an
earnest disciple of the Lord Jesus Christ.

The next branch I have to notice is that settled at Ber-
muda, in the West Indies, its chief being William, fourth son
of the fourth Baronet, but it soon became extinct, though I
am in possession of a medical thesis written by one of the
family, which showed a desire to benefit humanity.

The last branch to be noticed, and which has only lately
died out, is the Bessborough family, and in consequence of its
extinction, the Camieston Riddells stand next to the main
line, which still flourishes in England, though deprived of all
their Scotch property.

The ancestor of the Bessborough family—in fact, their
father—was Thomas, who also was a gallant sailor, and a
captain in the Honourable East India Company's Naval Service, commanding the " Bessborough," in which ship he made
money which he invested in land in Berwickshire, altering the
name of the estate from Kaims to Bessborough, after the vessel
he commanded. He married Elizabeth M'Lauchlan, of the
Fassifern family in Argyleshire, the aunt of my late wife, and
by her he had five daughters and two sons, all of whom died
unmarried. The two sons were soldiers, one of them, the late
General Henry James Riddell, at one time commander of the
forces in Scotland, already noticed.

I have some information about descendants of the old

house, who flourish in Ireland, as well as in America, but I cannot say when or how they came off the parent tree.

The Irish Riddells settled in Ulster, and intermarried with the Morrisons, who were forced to leave Scotland for their adherence to the royal cause after the battle of Worcester.

There were, not very long back, four Riddells, though they seem to have called themselves Riddall, brothers, two of them distinguished men—Sir James, who was knighted, and General William, who was a knight of Hanover—and formerly in the 62d and 18th regiments of the British army. Strange to say, the four brothers died without issue, though one only was a bachelor.

With respect to the American Riddells or Riddles, as they are so numerous, and their history is so replete with interest it would be quite impossible on the present occasion to do more than introduce them as a family, however derived, of importance, and well entitled to honourable mention.

Having previously alluded to the Northumberland Riddells, I would here pay a tribute of respect to one of their number, who, though a Roman Catholic, as the family all are, was a most devout servant of God. The gentleman I mean was Dr Riddell, Roman Catholic Bishop of the Northern District of England, who died of typhus fever, caught at Newcastle in the performance of his duty, in 1847, in attending and solacing the poor in the hour of sickness and suffering.

I may also refer to the other Scotch family of Riddell raised to the Baronetage in 1778. They were originally connected with Edinburgh, but purchased a large property in Argyleshire, most of which has been sold. They at one time claimed descent from the Riddells of Riddell as set forth by Douglas, but finding the descent could not be proved or authenticated, they issued a new pedigree, which far eclipsed in grandeur the first descent they claimed, to the astonishment of a good many antiquarians who could not understand it.

Before closing my remarks on the far-descended Riddells,

I would for a few minutes draw your attention to their ancient seat :—

> "Ancient Riddells' fair domain
> Where Aill, from mountains freed,
> Down from the lakes did raving come ;
> Each wave was crested with tawny foam
> Like the mane of a chestnut steed."

Sir Walter Scott has a note in connection with the first of the foregoing lines, highly complimentary to the ancient seat, though I must respectfully differ, however bold it may appear to do so, with the illustrious author of the "Lay of the Last Minstrel." He endeavours to establish the family as being domiciled at Riddell long previous to the time they acquired it, though that period is quite far enough back, as you have heard, to show their antiquity, and to entitle the great ministrel to call them "ancient Riddell." As I have told you, they acquired the property under the designation of Wester-Lilliesleaf in the reign of David I., not long prior to 1153, and having held it till 1823, they were in possession for the lengthened period of six hundred and seventy years. It was not called Riddell for a long time after their first occupancy, though they at length called it after themselves, an unusual occurrence in the history of landed families, who generally took their names from their lands instead of giving it to them. The earliest date mentioned by Sir Walter Scott is 727, and he alludes to the year on the aisle of Lilliesleaf church-yard, as being 1110. No doubt these memorials are to be seen on the south wall, but they do not possess a sufficiently antiquated character to represent such a far back period, though it is true they may have been fresh cut in after times. But be that as it may, I cannot appropriate the date as attaching to my ancestors, as the first did not get possession for some years after. As, moreover, there was an ancient church or chapel on the Wester Lilliesleaf or Riddell estate, said to have stood at or near the old Ash tree, not far from the last gate leading from the Easter-Lodge to the mansion-house, not a great way south from the old castle which stood in the wood a little above where the old Lilliesleaf road to Selkirk passed. At what period the old castle, which probably was a place of great strength and security, was built it is quite impossible to say, but it is probable that the family erected it soon after acquiring the property in the twelfth century. It is also difficult to say when the present mansion superseded the old castle as a residence, though it gives evidence of great antiquity also. On the occasion of the present respected proprietor preparing for the addition he erected in the western side of the mansion, an old stone with the Riddell arms on one side of the shield, and what I suppose to be the Carre arms on the other, though the stars are not on a chevron according to the heraldic cognizance of that family. If I am right in the interpretation of the stone, I think I may state its date to be at the close of the fifteenth century, when a Riddell of Riddell married a Ker, who survived her husband, and afterwards married a Scott of Harden. The stone may therefore be nearly 400 years old, and besides it, an arch was discovered giving evidence of antiquity, as the walls also did, from their hardness, caused no doubt by hot lime having been used, as was frequently the case in olden times. With reference to the aisle in the churchyard which was not reserved when the estate was sold, but which was generously restored to the old family by the kindness of Mr Sprot, it is impossible to say when it was first used by the Riddells. No doubt they were buried on the property in early times, probably at the chapel, where bones have been known to have been dug up, but in process of time the aisle would no doubt be used, in fact when it was part of the old castle which stood till 1771, the year of the erection of the present one, having just completed its centenary. I have evidence of the place of burial being in the choir of the old church, which I apprehend is just where the aisle now stands. Whether that church was the original one, I cannot say, but it was no doubt a pre-reformation one, and it was thatched with broom, as was the custom in mediæval times.

EMINENT ROXBURGHSHIRE MEN.

I NOW proceed to give a biographical sketch of the celebrities and worthies of Roxburghshire of the past, including not only natives of the county, but eminent individuals identified with Tweedside and Teviotdale by residence and ancestral ties, as well as by professional duties, and without depreciating the earlier history of our county, I propose to begin with the sixteenth century, or very little antecedent thereto. I have selected as first in order the

LEGAL CELEBRITIES.

And I would premise that the supreme legal tribunal in Scotland, viz., the Court of Session, was established in the early part of the sixteenth century, in the reign of James V. At first the judges were composed of ecclesiastics, as well as laymen, the aggregate number being fourteen, with two chiefs —one called the Lord Chancellor, an office of great antiquity in Scotland, and the other the Lord President. The office of Lord Justice-Clerk was not originally established, though it has now been in existence for a long time, the judge holding it, being President of the Criminal Court. It is, however, comparatively lately, viz., on the separation of the court into two divisions, that the Lord Justice-Clerk was established as head of the second division, and ranked accordingly.

At the institution of the Court of Session, Gavin Dunbar, Archbishop of Glasgow, was Lord High Chancellor, and an ecclesiastic, named Alexander Mylne, Abbot of Cambuskenneth, near Stirling, was the first President. In addition to the number of judges just mentioned, there were extraordinary ones, whose number was not limited. The appointment of ecclesiastics to the bench continued till about 1640, when an act was passed, by which the judges were to be wholly temporal.

The earliest judges connected with Roxburghshire were

RICHARD BOTHWELL (son of a provost of Edinburgh), Rector of Ashkirk, appointed at the institution of the Court in 1532, and died in 1547.

ANDREW DURIE (son of the laird of Durie in Fife), Abbot of Melrose, appointed in 1541, and died 1558.

Durie seems to have been a great ally of the Pope, for he was made Abbot of Melrose in spite of the efforts of the Court to procure the office for another, and he held it from 1526 till after he was made one of the extraordinary judges in 1541, shortly after which he resigned the abbacy, upon being further advanced to the Bishoprick of Galloway, and getting a pension. King James V., no doubt got all this arranged, in order to procure the office for his natural son, James Stuart, who, though a minor, was appointed Abbot in 1541.

Durie died in 1558, his death being occasioned by a fright, which he got on the 1st September of that year, when a mob interrupted the procession in honour of St Giles, broke the image of the Saint, and ill-treated the priests. John Knox, who hated Durie, gives an account of his death, and also of his principles, which, according to the Reformer's statement, were very bad, but allowances must be made, considering the difference in their religious faith.

MARK KER, commendator of Newbottle, second son of Sir Andrew Ker of Cessford, appointed in 1569, who died in 1584, comes next, but is noticed in the family of Ker, as is likewise his son Mark Ker, also Commendator of Newbottle, who was made a judge on his father's death in 1584, and was afterwards created first Lord Newbottle and then Earl Lothian.

His son Robert, the second Earl, was likewise noticed in the family history as is Sir Ambrose Carre, master of Jedburgh, likewise an extraordinary judge, and Andrew Ker, who was appointed upon the close of the Commonwealth under Cromwell. The Elliots of Minto are likewise noticed in the history of that noble family, and therefore are omitted here.

DAVID MACGILL of Nisbet stands next in order. He owned the estate of Cranstoun-Riddell in Mid-Lothian as well, and before being elevated to the bench in 1582, was Lord Advocate, the yearly value of that office being then only £40! In Sir James Melville's diary there is an account of this judge, who at one time seems to have had no sense of religion, though before his death, which happened in 1596, he became a changed character, and died happily, with these words in his mouth—the words of the Psalmist—"Lord in thy light, let me see light."

Other noted men connected with the county were made judges during the past century, and four of them were Pringles, a name historically eminent. The first was

Sir WALTER PRINGLE, of Newhall (second son of Sir Robert Pringle, first baronet of Stichill, a baronetcy created in 1683), who succeeded the first Lord Minto in 1718, and died in 1736. Lord Newhall, for this was Sir Walter Pringle's judicial title, was a man of pre-eminent abilities and high moral character. There is a portrait of Lord Newhall in the Parliament House, Edinburgh, the walls of which are adorned with the pictures of many legal celebrities.*

The next of the Pringles was JOHN PRINGLE, Lord Hain-

* Walter Pringle of Lochton was admitted advocate 10th December 1687, constituted a Lord of Session, as Lord Newhall, 6th June 1718, at the same time appointed a Lord of Justiciary and knighted. He died 14th December 1736, and his funeral was attended by the other judges in their official robes. On the same occasion the Faculty of Advocates met, and an eloquent eulogium on Lord Newhall's character, written by Sir Robert Dundas of Arniston, then Dean of Faculty, was ordered to be engrossed in the Minutes. A poetical epitaph, written by Hamilton of Bangour, is published among the works of that poet.

ing (second son of Andrew Pringle, of Clifton, in this county), the purchaser of Haining, from the Riddells of Haining, cadets of Riddell of that ilk, to whom Haining for a time belonged, having been acquired early in the 17th century by Andrew Riddell, Baron of Riddell. Haining was sold by the Riddells about 1702, and purchased by John Pringle, who accordingly took the judicial title of Lord Haining, when raised to the bench in 1729. Lord Haining had, for many years previously, been member of Parliament for Selkirkshire, both before and after the union, and continued a member of the British Senate till he was raised to the office of judge, which he held for upwards of twenty-five years, his death occurring on the 19th August 1854, when in his 80th year. His successor on the bench was Thomas Hay, Lord Huntington, who enjoyed his seat little more than two months, having died suddenly while sitting in court. Shortly after Lord Haining's death,

ROBERT PRINGLE, of Edgefield, grandson of Sir Robert Pringle, first Bart. of Stichill, and nephew of the celebrated Lord Newhall, was made a judge by the title of Lord Edgefield, having previously been Sheriff of Banffshire. Promoted to the bench on the 20th November 1754, he died on the 8th April 1764, so that he was barely ten years a judge.

I come now to the last, but not the least distinguished of the Pringles, as judges, though hardly to be compared to Lord Newhall—ANDREW PRINGLE, of Haining, who was made a judge not long after the death of his father, Lord Haining, and who assumed the title of Lord Alemore.

Properly speaking, Lord Alemore was a Selkirkshire man, but, being the grandson of Andrew Pringle of Clifton, in this county, I cannot refrain from sketching his offices and character. He was called to the bar in 1740, appointed, first, Sheriff of Wigton, then of Selkirkshire, which latter sheriffdom he held at his father Lord Haining's death. Afterwards he became Solicitor-General, which office he held for nearly four years, attaining the ermine in 1759, when he got a double gown, which he held for upwards of sixteen years, till his death, which took place at Hawkhill, near Edinburgh, on the 14th January 1776. Of Lord Alemore it was truly said, that his abilities " as a lawyer, and his integrity as a judge, have been long admired. His decisions were the result of deliberate consideration, founded on law, tempered with equity, and his opinions were delivered in such an easy flow of eloquence, and with such a dignity of expression, as captivated every hearer, and commanded attention."

The last Scottish judge connected with Roxburghshire was a kinsman of my own, GEORGE CARRE, of Nisbet, in Berwickshire, fifth son of John Carre, of Cavers, Nisbet, and Hundalee. Lord Nisbet—for this was George Carre's judicial appellation—was raised to the bench a few years before Lord Alemore, whom, to keep the Pringles together, I have sketched first. Lord Nisbet was called to the bar in 1725, and received the appointment of Sheriff of Berwickshire in 1748, being elevated to the bench in 1755, a seat which he occupied till his death, which took place at Edinburgh, 21st February 1766.

His father, John Carre, of Cavers, was twice married. His son by his first marriage inherited Cavers and Hundalee; while George Carre, Lord Nisbet, his surviving son by his second marriage, finally got Nisbet. The Nisbet Carres are long since dead, and the two last, who were ladies, bequeathed the property to the late Lord Sinclair, who possessed it for nearly fifty years, and who died lately at the advanced age of ninety-four.

Though I have only as yet given, as legal celebrities, those of our county who have risen to eminence by obtaining seats on the Scottish bench, there have been doubtless able and learned advocates as well, but it would be quite impossible, and it would not harmonize with the object in view, to bring forward such, unless they have signalised themselves in some remarkable manner. The only two I can think of who have so distinguished themselves are

Sir PATRICK SCOTT of Ancrum, and WALTER PRINGLE of

Graycrooke. Sir Patrick was eminent as a lawyer about the time of the Revolution, and was summoned to the Scottish Convention in 1688, by the Prince of Orange. Sir Patrick succeeded his father, John Scott of Kirkstyle—descended from the great author and magician, Michael Scott of Balweary—who purchased Ancrum from the Kers of Ancrum, and was made a baronet a short time before the Revolution.

WALTER PRINGLE of Graycrooke, grandson of Robert Pringle of Bartingbush, a Writer to the Signet, who, by a successful professional career, was enabled to purchase the fine estate of Stichill and other lands, stands next on the list. Walter Pringle is supposed to have been the distinguished counsel of the Covenanters who were tried as rebels, a short time before the Revolution, his uncle being Walter Pringle of Greenknowe, the noted Covenanter. Mr Pringle of Graycrooke's eminence as an advocate is commemorated by Wodrow.

Before dismissing the Legal Celebrities, I have to bring to notice a lately deceased nobleman, who rose to the highest law-office in the State. I mean

Lord Chancellor CAMPBELL. This extraordinary and highly talented man was suddenly summoned to appear before his Maker. Seated quietly in his chair, and having up to the last discharged his high and important duties with wonderful ease and also with consummate ability, his spirit, as it were at a moment's call, winged its way to the unseen world. I may mention a striking circumstance connected with his death, which the Bishop of London communicated to me. The Lord Chancellor had invited the Bishop to dine with him a short time before his death, and the invitation being a long one, the Lord Chancellor had died and was buried ten days before the day named for the entertainment had arrived, thereby solemnly verifying the statement, that "in the midst of life we are in death." A day or two before his death, and when talking of that part of the Litany, in which we pray to be delivered from "lightning and tempest; from plague, pestilence, and famine; from battle and murder," "and from sudden death," he remarked that it would be well to pray also to be delivered from lingering illness.

Born at Cupar Fife in 1778, and educated at St Andrews, Campbell went to London, and was called to the Bar in 1806, but was long in making way in his profession, and in order to increase his means of living, took to writing in the public journals. But John Campbell's power as an advocate gradually became known, and a large business then flowed in upon him. His success was promoted by his marriage, in 1821, with Miss Scarlett, the elder daughter of Sir James Scarlett, Lord Abinger. John Campbell's first honour was obtained in 1827, when he got a silk gown, being then close upon fifty years of age. In 1832 he was made Solicitor-General, when he had the honour of knighthood conferred upon him. In 1834, he was made Attorney-General; in the same year he became one of the members for Edinburgh, which city he represented in three Parliaments till 1841, when he was created Baron Campbell, receiving at the same time the appointment of Lord Chancellor of Ireland, which he held for some time. He afterwards returned to England, and was made chancellor of the Duchy of Lancaster, with a seat in the cabinet, but in order that his great legal knowledge should not be lost to the country, he was made Lord Chief-Justice of the Queen's Bench. On the retirement of Lord Chelmsford with his party in 1859, he was raised to the Woolsack, which he occupied till his death, on the 23d June 1861. Both Lord Campbell and Lord Chelmsford (Sir Frederick Thesiger) were, what is called common-law lawyers, in which branch of the profession, and as advocates, they had no superiors; but both shed lustre on the Woolsack, where equity as well as common law is required, and the public services of Lord Campbell were almost unparalleled.

The only other Scotchmen that I am aware of that ever held the Great Seals were,

Alexander Wedderburn, Lord Loughborough, from 1793 to 1801.
Thomas Erskine, Lord Erskine, from 1806 to 1807.
Henry Brougham, Lord Brougham, from 1830 to 1834.

Lord Campbell produced during his long period of judicial life, the "Lives of the Lord Chancellors," as well as those of the Chief Justices—works which must have cost him great labour and much research. And in addition to his employment as an author, his reading must have been extensive, down even to the magazines of the day. The "Recreations of a Country Parson," which appeared in *Frazer's Magazine*, so pleased his lordship as to induce him to obtain the name of the author, and to offer him a living, but not being in English orders the offer could not be accepted by the writer. He was invited, however, to Hartrigge to partake of his lordship's hospitality and good will. On his arrival, the Chancellor, who could unbend and enjoy the innocent amusements of life, was playing bowls, and he immediately introduced the Rev. author to the bowling-green and to the recreations of a Lord Chancellor.

Lord Campbell and Lady Stratheden, his wife, who predeceased him, are both buried in the Abbey of Jedburgh.

It is said that a *post-mortem* examination of Lord Campbell took place, and that the weight of his Lordship's brain was enormous, being $53\frac{1}{4}$ ounces, and, what was considered very remarkable, it was found to be in a perfectly healthy state. Cuvier, the great French naturalist, writer, and statesman, had the largest brain ever known, being 59 ounces, but it was not healthy like Lord Campbell's. The average weight of brain is about 46 ounces.

DIVINES.

I now take up the Divines. Keeping as near as possible to the period already mentioned, the first of the divines to be noticed is

GAVIN DOUGLAS, who flourished at the latter end of the fifteenth and the early part of the sixteenth centuries, and who was for a time Rector of Hawick, which entitles him to be noticed.*

JOHN RUTHERFORD was born at Jedburgh, in the early part the sixteenth century. He became minister of Cults immediately after the Reformation received its legal establishment, in 1560. He was also Provost of St. Salvator's College, St. Andrews, where he was a colleague of the great Buchanan. In 1570 he had the honour of having for a pupil James Crichton, afterwards known as the admirable Crichton, a man of the highest intellectual endowments, and of the greatest personal accomplishments; and though Rutherford never attained the eminence of his pupil, he had the reputation of being a distinguished man in his time. He was an author of some note, one of his works being a " Treatise on the Logic and Poetics of Aristotle." He was of course a good deal absent from his parish in consequence of his duties at the college, and the Assembly threatened proceedings against him; but no steps seem to have been taken, as his successor at Cults was not appointed till a year after his death. Next in order is

WILLIAM FOWLER, who is stated to have been Rector of Hawick towards the close of the sixteenth century, and by the ecclesiastical records of 1612 he is noted as then dead. There seem to be no further traces of his ministerial connection with Hawick, and it has been surmised that he may have enjoyed the benefice, at that peculiar time of the Church's history, as a layman, without being called upon to qualify or reside. But be that as it may, Mr Fowler has at any rate left some traces of his having dedicated himself to the muses, though his poetical works are not of great importance.

THOMAS FORRESTER was the third Protestant minister of Melrose. Mr Pont was the first, and Mr Knox, nephew of

* A sketch of him will be found in connection with the Family of Douglas.

the Reformer, who died 1623, the second. Forrester, the third, seems to have had "a bee in his bonnet," though a man of no mean ability, and abounding with humour and satire. His theology seems to have been of a very milk-and-water description; and, though professedly a Protestant, he was accused of Popery. During Charles the First's efforts to establish Episcopacy, Forrester seems to have favoured the sovereign's attempts towards that end, and it is presumed he was called to account for this, and above all for the laxity of his opinions and conduct, for it is stated, on unquestionable authority, that he was deposed from the office of the ministry by the Glasgow Assembly in 1638. Forrester held that prayer was the chief part of public worship, and more important than preaching, an opinion which many in our day will endorse, but which, no doubt, added to the charges which contributed to bring about his deposition. Forrester was a keen satirist, and composed a mock litany ridiculing his enemies, which made a great noise at the time, and is noticed by Bishop Guthrie, and Adam Milne the historian of Melrose, one of Forrester's successors in the pastorate of that place. Milne states that in his time (1711-1747) there was a lady who remembered parts of it, such as where he prayed to be delivered

"From the Jesuit knave in grain,
And from the she-priest crack'd in brain,
From her and a' such bad lasses,
And a' bald ignorant asses,
Such as John Ross, that donnard goose,
And Dan Duncanson, that duncy ghost."

The Jesuit knave was one "Abernethy," who had turned a zealous Presbyterian; and the she-priest was a Mrs Mitchelson, who was looked upon as inspired.

Forrester further prayed in his litany to be delivered from

"Dickson, Henderson, and Cant,
Th' apostles of the Covenant,"

and
"From all the knockdown race of Knoxes."

Forrester's successor was Alexander Scott, who died the year of his admission; and after him came David Fletcher, who seems to have been even more fickle than Forrester, for he was Episcopalian before he came to Melrose, and when there was a zealous Presbyterian—though after the Restoration he again became Episcopalian—finishing off as Bishop of Argyll, and dying, according to Milne, in 1665. It was in Fletcher's time that the statues in the Abbey were demolished, but previously, at the Reformation in 1560, the venerable building was greatly destroyed, and Cromwell completed the work of destruction by bombarding it.

DAVID CALDERWOOD, the next divine to be noticed, was born in 1575. He was descended from a good family, heraldically speaking, and was an ancestor of Sir William Calderwood of Polton, a Lord of Session, 1711-1733. Personally he was a good man, possessing, however, a good share of obstinacy, and exhibiting, occasionally, a warm temper. But the best of men err sometimes in these respects, and much need have we all to say, with the Psalmist—

"Set a watch, O Lord, before my mouth;
Keep the door of my lips."

Calderwood was Minister of Crailing, to which incumbency he was appointed in 1604. Soon afterwards he took a very prominent part in Church politics, and was one of the warmest defenders of Presbyterianism. The Reformation was accomplished in 1560, after which there was for some time a mixed government in the Reformed Church, its governors being superintendents; but after a time the system was changed and the Presbyterian form substituted, agreed to by King James the Sixth in 1586, and ratified by Parliament in 1592, when it was fairly established. Although James consented, he did not personally like the new constitution of the Church, and even before he ascended the English throne, which he did in 1603, he got the consent of the Scotch clergy to the Parliamentary Jurisdiction of Bishops, and in 1606 prevailed on them to receive such bishops as visitors or moderators, till

1610, when a reformed Episcopacy on liberal principles was recognised; and in the same year the General Assembly at Glasgow voted by a large majority in favour of it, though Dr M'Crie states that the basest means were used to bring about that decision, which, he adds, was a blot upon "the escutcheon of the Church of England."

Calderwood, then in full force and vigour, inveighed against their proceedings, and being a Member of the Assembly, as well as an inveterate opponent of the new form of church government, he was, on account of his opposition, excluded from all ecclesiastical courts, and ordered "to be put to the horn" along with the minister of Ancrum,

GEORGE JOHNSON; and had it not been for the intercession of powerful men in the state,* both would have been severely punished, whereas their punishment was restricted to confinement within their respective parishes.

In 1617 King James visited Scotland for the first time, after ascending the English throne in 1603, but CALDERWOOD was not to be overawed by the presence of royalty, and, continuing his opposition, was in the following year ordered to prison † (caption now succeeding the horning), from which he was only released on his promising to emigrate, which he did after a time, proceeding to Holland, where, during his banishment, he gained much information which was of use to him in his future career. Thus, rendered more able for controversy, he returned to his native land in 1624, one year before King James died, and joined with earnestness the ranks of the Covenanters, who, in 1638, in the reign of Charles the First, set up Presbyterianism. Calderwood about this time was appointed Minister of Pencaitland, in Haddingtonshire, where it is supposed the greater part of his famous work—

* Chiefly Mark, Earl of Lothian.
† He signed the Protestation in behalf of the Liberties of the Kirk, 27th June 1617, and on the 12th of July following was deprived of his office by the Court of High Commission, was imprisoned in St. Andrews, and subsequently in Edinburgh, till he had to find caution to depart furth of the realm, which he did on the 27th August 1619.

the History of the Church of Scotland—was written. This history occupied him many years in its preparation; and Irving states that the General Assembly, in 1648, urged him to complete the design, and voted him a yearly pension of £800, but his death, which occurred soon after—viz., on the 29th October 1650, at Jedburgh, whither he had retired while Cromwell's army occupied the Lothians—prevented its publication. The original manuscript is in the British Museum, an abridgement of the work only having been published, though a copy of the author's manuscript, taken under the eye of Wodrow, another intelligent church historian, is among the archives of the Church. Calderwood's death saved him the pain of seeing Presbyterianism again overthrown, and Episcopacy established, which existed till the Revolution in 1688, when Presbyterianism was again set up and confirmed by Parliament, being subsequently secured by the treaty of the Union with England in 1707.

SAMUEL RUTHERFURD was born at Nisbet, then, I believe, a parish, but afterwards annexed to Crailing, about the time of Calderwood's appointment to the incumbency of the latter place. Rutherfurd was "a very powerful and heart-stirring" writer, as well as a man of most earnest piety, and of great devotion to his work. It has been said his flock were the object of his tears, cares, fears, and daily prayers, and that he laboured among them early and late. His great zeal, doubtless, exposed him to the taunts and indignation of those in authority, and on his death-bed a charge of treason was brought against him, but his summons to a higher tribunal saved him the pain of being dragged before an earthly one. Such was his earnestness in his Master's service, that he would rise at three o'clock in the morning to pray, before beginning laborious duties he had to perform.

It is related that an English merchant happened to visit Scotland, and having heard three of Scotland's worthies preach, of whom Rutherfurd was one, describes them thus:—
"First I heard a sweet majestic-looking man (Mr Blair), and

he showed me the majesty of God. After him I heard a little fair man (Mr Rutherfurd), and he showed me the loveliness of Christ. And then I heard a well-favoured old man, with a long beard (Mr Dickson), and that man showed me all my heart."

Rutherfurd, who had been one of the Assembly of Divines at Westminster, was finally made Principal of St. Mary's College, St. Andrews, at which city he died on the 20th March 1661. His well-known book, entitled "Lex Rex," the text-book of the Covenanters, was publicly burnt—a work which Wodrow said "it was much more easy to burn than to answer," and which, on Charles II. reading it, he remarked with his native shrewdness, "that it would scarcely ever get an answer." The burning of the book in question was accompanied by the confiscation of his stipend, and a summons to appear before Parliament on a charge of high treason, but his death occurred before the meeting of the legislature.

It has been said that "books have souls as well as men, which survive their martyrdom, and are not consumed but crowned by the flames that encircle them;" and surely Rutherfurd's are of that class. When dying, he remarked, "it is no easy thing to be a Christian; but I have gotten the victory, and Jesus Christ is holding out both his arms to receive me." And his last words were "Glory! glory dwelleth in Immanuel's land."

JOHN LIVINGSTONE, whose memoirs have been published, is well known, and was inducted as Minister of Ancrum in 1648. He was not unfrequently called "the Godly Livingstone." Those who have read his life may remember a singular account given of his courtship.*

* He had formed an attachment to the eldest daughter of Bartholomew Fleming, merchant in Edinburgh, "of most worthy memory." The young lady was also recommended to him by the favourable speeches of many of his friends. Yet he spent nine months in seeking direction from God before he could make up his mind to pay his addresses. "It is true," he says, "I might have been longer in that darkness, except the Lord had presented me an occasion of our conferring together, for on November 1634, when I was going to the Friday meeting at Antrim, I forgathered with her and some

GABRIEL SEMPLE was well born, being descended from Sir John Semple of Sempil, created by James the IV., in 1489, Lord Semple, who fell with his sovereign at Flodden.*

other young brethren, and propounded to them, by the way, to confer upon a text whereon I was to preach the day after at Antrim; wherein I found her conference so just and spiritual, that I took that for some answer to my prayer to have my mind cleared, and blamed myself that I had not before taken occasion to confer with her. Four or five days after, I proposed the matter, and desired her to think upon it; and after a week or two I went to her mother's house, and being alone with her, and desiring her answer, I went to prayer, and desired her to pray, which at last she did; and in that time I got abundant clearness that it was the Lord's mind that I should marry her, and then propounded the matter more fully to her mother, and, albeit, I was thus fully cleared. I may truly say it was about a month after before I got marriage affection to her, although she was, for personal endowments, beyond many of her equals, and I got it not till I had obtained it by prayer; but thereafter I had greater difficulty to modify it." John Livingstone was born on the 21st of June 1603, at Kilsyth, in Stirlingshire, where his father was minister, but from which place he was, in 1614, translated to Lanark. He was licensed to preach in 1625, and for some time officiated for his father in Lanark and in other places about. In 1627 he became chaplain to the Earl of Wigton, at Cumbernauld, and while there was instrumental in promoting the great revival of religion of the Kirk of Shotts. On Sunday June 20th, 1630, the communion had been held, and there was a great assemblage, including many women of rank, in that part of the country. The impression produced by the solemnities of the day was so great that many did not depart, but spent the whole night in prayer and conference, and among those who did so was John Livingstone. The bedroom of Lady Culross was filled with people, to whom she prayed "three large hours' time," as we learn from Livingstone's memoirs. It had not been customary to have service on the Monday, but as multitudes of people still lingered, John Livingstone was requested to preach, which he did from Ezekiel xxxvi. 25, 26. Having got good assistance for an hour-and-a-half, he continues, "in the end, offering to close with some words of exhortation, I was led on for about an hour's time, in a strain of exhortation and warning, with such liberty and melting of heart as I never had the like in public all my lifetime. The effect of the address was "an extraordinary appearance of God and downpouring of the Spirit, with a strange unusual motion in the heavens," in so much that five hundred, as it was calculated, had at that time a discernable change wrought upon them, of whom most proved lively Christians afterwards.

* Gabriel Semple was minister of Kirkpatrick, in Durham, from which he was ejected by the Act of Glasgow, 1662, after which he withdrew to the house of Corsack, in the neighbouring parish of Parton, where he was hospitably entertained, along with Mr John Welch of Irongray, by Mr. John

ARCHIBALD RIDDELL.—Having from family papers got some interesting records of his chequered life, I will detail a few. Riddell was an ordained Minister of the Kirk, and incumbent of Kippen; but, being a zealous man, he also preached in the fields, and likewise in private houses, for which he was imprisoned and banished, his brother, Sir John Riddell, then member for Roxburghshire, being also prosecuted for favouring Archibald's practices.

Mr Riddell was confined to the Bass Rock for three years, and was only released upon condition that he would expatriate himself. This he agreed to do, and accordingly sailed for New Jersey in America, where he remained till the revolution in 1688, when profiting by that favourable juncture, he, with others, embarked for England, but on the voyage home, they were unfortunately captured and carried to France as

Neilson. He preached in the house, and then in the garden, to such as came to hear, but on the third Sunday the crowd was so great that they had to retire to the fields, making, according to Woodrow, the first field meeting or conventicle in Scotland. The rising of the Covenanters, which ended at the battle of Pentland Hills in 1666, was abetted and promoted both by Welch and Semple, the latter of whom preached to the army of the Covenanters at Tarbolton and Lanark. After the defeat of the Covenanters Semple was declared a rebel, and, to escape the peril which awaited him, he took refuge in the north of England, where he became minister of Ford, in Northumberland. The gospel had extraordinary success in that neighbourhood and all along the borders. Having ventured across the borders, he was apprehended and lodged in the Canongate jail, but was liberated on account of sickness, after which he again returned to the north of England. After the Revolution he was settled as minister of Jedburgh, where he continued in the zealous discharge of his sacred duties till the year 1706, when he died, at a very remarkable old age. He had married a daughter of Sir Walter Riddell of Riddell, and left behind him several children. Mr Semple was anxious that Thomas Boston should have been appointed his colleague and successor in Jedburgh, but could not manage it. On the 27th of February 1703, Boston preached for Semple forenoon and afternoon, and in his autobiography, says of Semple :—" The congregation being convened again about a quarter of an hour after, he, from the reader's desk, made a short discourse from the fifth command, particularly the duties of husbands and wives. The things he insisted on were indeed common and ordinary, but they were delivered in such a manner, and such power accompanied them, that I was in a manner amazed, and they ran out through me and in through me, so that I said in my heart, 'Happy are they that hear thy wisdom.'"

prisoners, where they underwent sufferings of a very aggravated kind. They were carried first to Nantes, then to Rochfort, where Mr Riddell was deposited in a common jail with two hundred English and Dutch prisoners. They were afterwards sent to Toulon, where they were chained two and two by the arms. Mr Riddell was chained to his son, a boy of ten years of age, for whom the jailor was at pains to make several chains before he could get one to fit. At Toulon several of the prisoners died, and after a time the remainder were sent back to Rochfort, and finally they were despatched to Douai, where Riddell continued more than a year, in a vault of an old castle, with some hundreds of prisoners. They lay on straw, never changed save once a month, and were oppressed with everything that was disagreeable. It must have required great fortitude on the part of my kinsman and his son to have endured such extreme misery. But after nearly two years' cruel suffering, they were relieved by being exchanged for two Romish priests, who were prisoners in Scotland. Of this last fact a striking confirmation, honourable alike to the sufferers and the sovereign, was discovered some time ago by one of the family in the State Paper Office, London, being no less than a Royal Letter, issuing directly from the sovereign, William III., and directed to the Privy Council of Scotland, being to the following effect :—

"WILLIAM REX, Right Trusty and Entirely Beloved. Whereas we are informed that Mr Archibald Riddell, Minister of the Gospel, and James Sinclair of Freshwick are prisoners in France, and are very hardly used, whom we are resolved to have released by exchange with two Priests now Prisoners in Scotland, Therefore, WE require you to call for the friends and nearest relations of the said Mr Archibald Riddell and James Sinclair, and signify our Royal Pleasure to them in exchange of these two Prisoners with the two Priests that shall be condescended upon, and authorise them not only to speik with the two Priests, but also to write to France anent the negotiating their friends' liberty, and that you cause these two Priests to be condescended upon and securely keeped, and make intimation to them that they shall be used in the same way and manner as the French King uses the said Scots Prisoners, which they may be ordered to acquaint their friends in France with, that exchange may be more easily effected. For doing of which these Presents shall be your Warrant, And so we bid you heartily farewell.

"Given at the Court of Kensington this 16th day of January 1689, and of our Reign the first year.—By His Majesty's Command, (Signed) MELVILLE."

All Mr Riddell's afflictions were now over; and on his return to Scotland, his losses consequent upon his non-conformity were made up. He was appointed minister of Trinity College Church, Edinburgh (that late fine piece of Gothic architecture) in which charge he died, in 1708, and his remains were deposited in the Greyfriars Churchyard, where the bodies of many eminent servants of God are buried, and where his brother, Sir John Riddell of Riddell, had been previously interred.

The late eminent and distinguished advocate, John Riddell, Edinburgh, whose fame as a peerage lawyer and an antiquarian is well-known, was the representative, being the great-great-grandson of Archibald Riddell. Contemporaneously with Mr Riddell, was

ALEXANDER ORROCK, Minister of Hawick, born 1659, died 1711. He was a man of note and great benevolence, as a tablet erected to his memory amply testifies. He also suffered imprisonment for his opinions, but ended his career in peace, after an incumbency of twenty-two years.* He is

---

* Orrock was licensed in 1687, and in a sermon called the king an idolater, and declared that Episcopacy was not of God's planting. He was seized by command of the Archbishop of St Andrews, when attempting to preach in that city, and was removed to Edinburgh by order of the Privy Council. The whole case was referred to His Majesty, but the revolution followed, and nothing was done. The author of the "Fasti Ecclesiæ" says, "He protested against an act of the synod of Merse and Teviotdale asserting their principles with respect to the established government of the church, and concurring

reported to have been a rigid disciplinarian, and as an instance of this, he summoned the magistrates before him for some offence, which he would not overlook, till upon bended knees they asked pardon of God, and also of the Kirk Session. Notwithstanding his austerity, he must have retained the sincere respect of his people, for they urged him to decline a call he got to Kelso (approved by the church courts), which he did, thereby reciprocating the good feeling of his flock.

WILLIAM CRAWFORD, born at Kelso, was minister of Wilton. He was the author of some small works—"Dying Thoughts and Sermons,"—and was generally esteemed, being described "as a master of great and good qualities in a very uncommon degree." Mr Crawford died in 1742.

ADAM MILNE, is well entitled both as minister and historian

---

with other two brethren, he complained to the General Assembly, 1705, against the acts passed by certain synods as tyrannical impositions. Not being a member of Assembly he was refused a hearing, and was seized by the officers. The commissioner (William, Marquis of Annandale), stated that he was sorry one bearing the name of a minister of the gospel should suffer himself to be a tool to serve the interests of the enemies of His Majesty's government, and of the prosperity of the church, and ordered the disturbers to remove. Mr Orrock and his associates, however, remained till a second order was issued from the throne, when they went off undaunted, were insulted by a mob at the door, and reproached as incendiaries." Referring to this matter, Boston of Ettrick says, "in the month of March 1702, met the first General Assembly in the reign of Queen Anne, of which Seafield was the commissioner, and Mr George Meldrum, moderator. The asserting of the intrinsic power of the church was then the great point that some laboured for ; but in vain, it was told them by their brethren they had it, and what then needed the passing of an act asserting it ? The Assembly having sat several days, were upon an overture for preventing Protestants marrying Papists ; in the time whereof, a whisper beginning about the throne, and a motion being, I think, made for recommitting the overture, the commissioner, rising from his seat, instantly dissolved the assembly in His Majesty's name." "In April following, the synod meeting at Dunse, entered on making an act asserting their principles with respect to the government of the church, against which Mr Alexander Orrock, minister at Hawick, a man of vast parts and the greatest assurance I ever knew, protested and left the synod, pretending the same to be a raising of groundless jealousies against the magistrate." With him joined Mr Robert Bell, Cavers, Mr Robert Cunningham, Wilton, and Mr Robert Scott, Roberton.

of Melrose, to commendation, on account of the faithfulness of his ministerial labours, as well as for his general good abilities. Mr Milne's "Description of Melrose" stands unrivalled, and has been the text-book of later writers. Though a small work, it has received a large amount of public favour, and is now scarce. Mr Milne, after a ministry of about thirty-six years, closed his career by death on the 8th June 1747, "to the great grief and universal loss of his congregation," as the session record states, and was succeeded by the Rev. James Brown.

Mr Milne married Alison Hunter, elder daughter of the Rev. William Hunter, minister of Lilliesleaf and laird of Union Hall, now called Linthill, though the mansion-house of Union Hall stood on the south side of the river Ale, the property on the north side, where the present house of Linthill stands, having been purchased afterwards by Mr Hunter's son, being then called Midlem Mill. The united properties were then named Linthill, and after the death of the Hunter family they were inherited by William Riddell, of Camieston, my grandfather, whose father, a member of the house of Riddell of Riddell, married Margaret, the younger daughter of the Rev. William Hunter. But Mr Riddell did not retain the estate long, for in 1822 he sold it to Mr Currie, the father of the present William Currie, Esq. of Linthill.

WILLIAM HUNTER was Incumbent of Lilliesleaf, and one of the leading men engaged in the Marrow Controversy, which agitated the Church for some years—say from 1717 to 1723. Gabriel Wilson of Maxton, Henry Davidson of Galashiels, and Thomas Boston of Ettrick, all members of the Selkirk Presbytery, like William Hunter, were also prominent movers in this controversy. Mr Hunter was a man of great devotion to the work of the ministry, and died at the advanced age of seventy-eight, "in the sure and certain hope of a joyful resurrection.*"

* Regarding the preaching powers of Mr Hunter, we have the testimony of Boston, who wrote in 1727 :—" Mr Hunter preached after Mr Wilson, on

JAMES RAMSAY, Minister of Kelso, and formerly of Eyemouth, died about the middle of last century, after a lengthened career in the service of the Kirk. He was not over choice in his vocabulary, for I have somewhere seen it stated, that when he was preaching from the 148th Psalm—where all creatures and things are summoned to join in a concert of praise to their Creator—he remarked that married women were not distinctly mentioned, unless they were included among dragons or fiery serpents.*

the Monday, on these words—'He is faithful who hath promised.' I was so refreshed with that sermon that I found my body in good condition when he was over."

* Mr Ramsay was born about the year 1669, and was minister first at Eyemouth and then at Kelso. Frequent mention is made of him in the Memoirs of Thomas Boston, whose worth he seems early to have appreciated, and whom he on various occasions warmly befriended. "When I entered on the study of theology," says he, "Mr James Ramsay having put the book in my hand, viz., 'Parens on Ursin's Catechism,' the which I read over three or four times ere I went to the school of divinity." It was "through the interest of Mr James Ramsay aforesaid, and other friends," that when minister of Simprin he was chosen Clerk to the Synod of Merse and Teviotdale. His entering on the duties of the office he describes with that *naïveté* which imparts so great a charm to his whole narrative:—"When I first took the seat among them, and stood up for to read, being in great confusion through my natural diffidence and timorousness, I blundered; but recovering myself, in much ado made it out. Upon which occasion Mr Ramsay did seasonably express his confidence in me notwithstanding. The oath *de fideli administratione* I declined, and they were pleased to accept of my promise to serve them faithfully and keep their secrets, which I strictly observed." Boston and Ramsay, however, frequently differed on public questions, especially as to the oath of abjuration and the Marrow doctrine. Being the leading man in the Synod, Mr Ramsay took an active part in conducting the process against Boston's friend, Mr Gabriel Wilson of Maxton, accused of venting certain heterodox sentiments in a sermon preached before the Synod in October 1721. Messrs Ebenezer and Ralph Erskine went to Kelso to be present at the trial, and it is to Mr Ramsay that the latter is said to have addressed the *impromptu* couplet, when asked by him to give a specimen of his poetic powers :—

" We be two angels who did ride and run
 To see the angel *Gabriel* fight and win."

He was twice Moderator of the General Assembly, and the only person put on the leet along with him the second time was Mr John Hepburn, one of the ministers of Edinburgh; but, though the former had filled the chair so lately

ROBERT RICCALTON, Minister of Hobkirk from 1725 to 1769, in which latter year he died, aged seventy-eight. Mr Riccalton was a person of original genius, but had some peculiar notions derived from Hutchinson the English philosophical and critical author, of whose writings he was an admirer. He was, however, a man of great worth, liberal

as the year 1738, he was again elected. His concluding address is the shortest we find on record, being comprised in this one sentence :—" It is with pleasure I can observe that the affairs of this Assembly have, by the good hand of God upon us, been managed with great decency and remarkable unanimity." Mr Ramsay died on the 3d July 1749, being upwards of eighty years old.

Mr Ramsay was a man of great natural gifts, of a sturdy bodily frame, and much shrewd common sense, together with a great deal of humour. It was customary with him to walk from Kelso to Edinburgh, a distance of over forty miles. As specimens of his character, we take the following from a book entitled "The Kelso Records," which is now out of print :—

" About the period when Thomson was the guiding star of literature, Mr Ramsay was parochial minister of Kelso. He was a man of high original powers, a leader in the ecclesiastical courts, a quick discerner of men's parts, and possessed of great humour and ready wit. His settlement was not a harmonious one. He learned that a leading elder—one of the discontented—had absented himself when he was placed. After proper consideration, he waited upon this person—a shopkeeper—and was received in a manner which would have disconcerted an ordinary man. Ramsay persevered, and having exhausted the ordinary topics of the day, he observed—' I hae na been lang amang ye, Mr ——, but I hae been lang enough to ken ye hae the best hame-brew'd o' the toun. Noo, as I am unco fond o' gude ale, I sud like to try it.' This self-invitation, without extreme rudeness, could not be declined. The minister was requested to walk into the parlour, where a foaming tankard was speedily produced. Under the mild potency of the generous liquor, and the conversation it induced, the reluctant host gave way. Watching his opportunity, Ramsay remarked—

"'Though I be a young man, I'm nae spendthrift. I hae saved a little siller, which I should like to place in a safe hand; and I am told that you are the best qualified man in the parish to direct me where I ought to place it.'

"'I'll no deny that I ken my neighbours well enough, but I'm no inclined to be *caution* for ony o' them !'

"'Just what I said. Mr —— is a prudent man, and without any *caution* I'll trust to your judgment. But, my good man, why no take the siller yersel? Rich as ye are, money ay produces money; and the little I hae may whiles be turned to good account. Take it, therefore, yersel !'

"'Weel, weel ! I hae nae objections ; but we maun hae another tankard.'

sentiments, and warm affections, and John Newton, the poet Cowper's friend, of Olney Hymn celebrity—no mean authority —speaks of him as a masterly writer. Riccalton published in early life an essay entitled "A sober enquiry into the grounds of the present difficulties in the Church of Scotland," and afterwards, "An Enquiry into the Spirit and Tendency

"The ale did its good work, until Mr Ramsay felt himself justified in saying—

"'Oh! Mr ——, I was sair grieved in hearing ye were absent frae the kirk last Sabbath. Your example is a great effect, and I hope ye'll be in the elders' seat next Sunday.'

"'I will, Mr Ramsay! You are not the cause of the Law of Patronage, and ought not to be a sufferer because such a law exists.'

"Although decidedly popular as a preacher, Mr Ramsay knew that he was in the habit of giving utterance to expressions which, though they might startle or even delight his own congregation, would, if published, offend the eye of the fastidious, and was therefore jealous of any person who attempted to take a transcript of his discourse. One day he observed an excise officer who had recently been placed in the town, whom he knew to be a Highlander, busily employed in taking notes. Ramsay was discoursing upon the work of regeneration, when, darting his eye to the gallery, he exclaimed— 'I tell you, my brethren, that unless you be born again it is as impossible for you to enter the kingdom of Heaven as it is for a Highlander not to be a thief. Man wi' the keel-o'-vine, do ye hear that! Dinna forget that; but be sure to write *it* down.' The keel-o'-vine disappeared, and never again offended the sight of the minister.

"The Highlanders, with the Stuart Prince at their head, marched through Kelso in the year 1745. During the progress of the Rebellion, it is well known that many persons in various parts of the country were apprehended on suspicion of being favourably disposed to the cause of Charles, and either imprisoned or forced to give security, under a heavy penalty, for their loyalty. Mr Ramsay, among others, received a communication from government, requiring him to consult with the well-informed of the inhabitants, and report whether or not there were any Jacobites in the place. Ramsay was decidedly loyal. He was in the habit of visiting all classes of his parishioners indiscriminately, and knew how many of them wished the Stuarts to succeed in the enterprise; and though he knew from the character of those persons that they would never actively assist Charles, it was necessary that he should obey the commands of government. Accordingly, he sent for the most eminent of the disaffected party to his house, and put into their hands the dispatch he had received. These gentlemen stared upon each other with looks of consternation, and Mr Ramsay asked—'What return shall I make to this order of the government? Do you know of any disaffected persons among us?' It will readily be believed that every individual assured of Letters of Theron and Aspasio, with a View of the Law of Nature, and an Enquiry into Letters on the Law of Nature," and, after his death, three volumes of Sermons, and Essays on Human Nature and on several of the doctrines of Revelation, were published. But Mr Riccalton was a poet besides, and his kindness to the author of the "Seasons," James Thomson (whose father was minister of Southdean, in which parish

him that all their acquaintances were decidedly loyal. 'Well, well, I am exceedingly glad to hear so. Had there been any disloyal persons in the place I am sure *you* must have known them; and I shall now acquaint the Privy Council that I have consulted with the most intelligent of my parishioners, who assure me that the people here are all well affected to His Majesty's Government.'

"That Ramsay judged aright in the matter is evident from what was afterwards said by the Prince. When in Kelso he was waited on by some of the most zealous of his partisans, who assured him of their firm attachment to his service, as a mark of which they never met together in an evening without drinking prosperity to his Royal Highness and the good cause. 'I believe you, gentlemen, I believe you. I have drinking friends, but few fighting ones, in Kelso.' Indeed, not an adherent joined his ranks; and such persons as were pressed to convey the baggage returned home as soon and safely as they could.

"Sometime about the year 1740, when the country was so agitated about the question of Church patronage, the living of Maxton became vacant, and the parishioners expressed their determination to resist the settlement of the person appointed to the charge. Accordingly, when the Presbytery met to ordain the minister, they were grossly assaulted, several of them severely hurt, and the whole of the body forced to fly, while the ordination was taking place. Another day the meeting was appointed, and in order that the clergyman might then be inducted, the presbytery were accompanied by a troop of dragoons. On approaching the village the malcontents were observed in considerable numbers, drawn up so as to oppose the clergy and their escort. Seeing this, Mr Ramsay, whose convivial powers rendered him very popular, but who had, nevertheless, suffered severely in the first skirmish, prevailed on the commanding officer to order the soldiers to halt, and then rode forward himself among the rioters. 'What is all this, masters?' cried he: 'What is all this? Do you always expect to have the upper hand? You beat us last time; and, my wig being lost, I had to ride home with a *bare pow*. But to-day I am better provided—I have got a spare one in my pocket.' Thus saying, he pulled out a wig and exhibited it to the crowd. This ludicrous sight, with the unexpected speech by which it was accompanied, disarmed their wrath. A loud laugh was raised; no further opposition attempted—the minister was ordained, and lived long harmoniously with his parishioners."

•Riccalton lived, before he was appointed to Hobkirk in 1725, the year Thomson went to London), is much to be praised. Riccalton composed a poem on Winter, which Thomson well knew, though it was never published, except, I believe, in Magazines, but I have looked in vain for it in the *Scots Magazine*. Thomson's own words are—" Mr Riccalton's poem on Winter, which I still have, first put the design into my head. In it are some masterly strokes that awakened me." Thomson means that Mr Riccalton put the design of writing the "Seasons" into his head, so there is an overpowering debt of gratitude due to the minister of Hobkirk for prompting such an immortal poem.

GEORGE RIDPATH, minister of Stichill, must have died about the same time as Riccalton paid the debt of nature. I have no particulars as to his professional career, but he was an author of repute, his "Border History" being a most interesting and instructive book, especially to the antiquary and genealogist. The work, which is posthumous, was published by his brother Philip Ridpath, minister of Hutton in Berwickshire, an author himself, in 1776, and dedicated to Hugh, second Duke of Northumberland, the descendant of the Percys renowned in the Border, as well as in the general history of the country.

There was another George Ridpath, who, it is supposed, wrote several historical works which were published anonymously, very early last century, and it is possible he may have been the father of the two ministers.

JOHN HOME flourished in Ridpath's time, and long afterwards, for he lived to a great age.* He was ordained parish minister of Athelstaneford, where the poet Blair had previously been the incumbent, in 1750, having been licensed as a preacher on the 4th April 1745. His great dedication to tragic verse was a bar to his success in the clerical profession,

* He was born in 1722, and died at the age of eighty-six, in the year 1808, having outlived all his eminent contemporaries, save Dr Ferguson, who died in 1816, aged ninety-two.

and though he continued for some time in the ministry, he at length abandoned it, and resigned his living, which stopped the proceedings that were being taken to depose him.

Mr Home's celebrated tragedy of "Douglas" was first acted in Edinburgh in 1756. Several clergymen attended the performance, which led to an ecclesiastical conflict. But a love for theatricals in those days was not the only clerical inconsistency. There was a great deal of drinking, and I have read that a minister, who would have been ashamed to have been seen at the play-house seeing the performance of "Douglas," would nevertheless sit at his cups till he had consumed five bottles of wine, which earned for him the soubriquet of Dr Magnum Bonum, or rather Bonum Magnum. John Home sustained no pecuniary loss from the resignation of his benefice, for he got government employment and a pension, the latter being his mainstay, and he was enabled to live in comfort, and to enjoy the society of his literary friends in Edinburgh, where he finally located himself; and at that period, it must have been truly an enjoyable place for a man of letters. David Hume was one of John's most intimate friends, and there never was a difference between them except on the subject of wine and the spelling of their names. The philosopher liked port, then but lately introduced into Scotland, and the poet preferred claret; and with respect to the orthography of their surnames, David preferred *Hume*, and John, *Home*. Both are pronounced Hume, and in point of euphony, the philosopher had the best of the argument, which his own family must have thought, for instead of being Home of Ninewells, it is now Hume. A number of the class, and especially the head of it, still stick to the *o*, though in all cases, I believe, the name so spelt is pronounced as if spelt with *u*. In the same way Ker, the orthography of which has been referred to, is pronounced as if spelt Carre.

Two authors—Maunder and Haig—make John Home to be a Roxburghshire man, and born at Ancrum, while others describe him as being born at Leith. I do not profess to settle this point, but whether born at Ancrum or Leith, he was descended from the older Border family of Home of Cowdenknows, through their ancient cadets the Homes of Bassendean, and, moreover, his wife, who was his cousin, was the elder daughter of the Rev. William Home of Fogo, who became the representative of the house of Bassendean on the death of the descendants of his elder brother, and whose fifth son, John, purchased the estate from his cousin, bequeathing it to his son, the late General Home of the Grenadier Guards. With this pedigree, notwithstanding the uncertainty of Home's birth-place, I think he is well entitled to shine among the Roxburghshire stars.

JOSEPH LECK was minister of Yetholm for some time after he middle of last century. I bring this divine before you as a man who appears to have been much respected by, and well known to, his parishioners—even the gypsies, a class of notables, who will hereafter be introduced to you in their proper place. The anecdote which I wish to relate proves how much he was respected by that dusky band, and also verifies what is said in "Guy Mannering" about them, viz., that though "they're queer devils, there's baith gude and ill about the gypsies." Mr Leck on one occasion had been visiting his friends across the Border, and on his return in the evening, got benighted on a drove track in crossing the hills on horseback. Coming upon an old shepherd's cot, said to be haunted, Mr Leck, though a man of nerve and not easily frightened, became somewhat afraid when he saw a grim looking visage peeping behind a curtain which acted as a door to the cot, and his alarm increased when he saw outside hazel-looking figures prowling about. Mr Leck felt himself in an uncomfortable position, especially when his dusky friend bolted out upon him from the cot, seized his horse's reins, and demanded his money. He, however, soon recognized his tawney parishioner to be gleed-neckit Will, the gipsy chief, when the following colloquy took place:—

"Dear me, William," said the minister in his usual quiet manner, "can this be you? Ye're surely no serious wi' me?

Ye wadna sae far wrang your character for a good neighbour for the bit trifle I hae to gie, William?"

"Lord saif us, Mr Leck," said Will, quitting the reins of Mr Leck's horse, and lifting his hat with great respect, "whae wad hae thocht o' meeting you out owre here away? Ye needna gripe for ony siller to me—I wad nae touch a plack o' your gear, nor a hair o' your head, for a' the gowd o' Teviotdale. I ken ye'll no do us an ill turn for this mistake, and I'll e'en see you safe through the eerie staw. It's no reckoned a canny bit, mair ways than ane, but I wat weel ye'll no be feared for the dead, and I'll take care o' the living."

Will accordingly gave the Rev. Mr Leck a safe convoy through the haunted pass, and notwithstanding this ugly mistake, continued ever after an inoffensive neighbour to the minister, who on his part observed a prudent and inviolable secrecy on the subject of the rencontre during the life-time of gleed-neckit Will.

DAVID CLERK, Minister of Maxton, deserves a passing remark. He was a man of lively manners, and of great wit, which of course made him a most agreeable companion.

Matthew Henry says—"Innocent mirth, soberly, seasonably, and moderately used, is a good thing; fits for business, and helps to soften the toils and chagrins of life; but, when it is excessive and immoderate, it is foolish and fruitless." Alas! I am afraid poor David Clerk, by indulging in too much hilarity, verified the learned divine's remark, for he became imprudent and embarrassed, the result being, as Dr Somerville states, "a depression of spirits, bad health, and a premature death." As far as I can ascertain, Mr Clerk must have died somewhere about 1776, when

STEPHEN OLIVER was appointed, having been translated from Innerleithen, where he had been Incumbent for twenty years. He continued at Maxton for twenty-seven years, dying in 1803, aged eighty-nine. He was noted for his fidelity, diligence, and zeal; was a man of practical piety; like Enoch, walked with God; and when his body was committed to the dust it was followed by a large and sympathising body of friends and people.

Dr JAMES MACKNIGHT, who was for a short time Incumbent of Jedburgh, comes next, to which place he was translated from Maybole, and afterwards became one of the clergy of Edinburgh, where he died on the 13th July 1800. Dr Macknight was well known as the author of the "Harmony of the Gospels," and a translation and commentary upon the apostolic epistles. A celebrated biographer says the latter "was the result of an almost unremitting labour for nearly thirty years, and is a work of theological diligence, learning, and piety, not often paralleled." *

Dr THOMAS SOMERVILLE followed Dr Macknight at Jedburgh, where he was settled in 1772, having been translated from Minto, to which latter parish he was ordained in 1767; and as his death did not take place till the 16th May 1830, Dr Somerville's life and ministry were extended to an unusually long period. Few ministers enjoyed so much respect as the Doctor did. His genial nature and catholic spirit drew around him men of all classes and opinions, and he went to the grave honoured and esteemed "for his public services and private worth."

Dr Somerville was an author of some note, but is best known as the historian of Queen Anne, the youngest daughter of James II., and the last of the Stuarts.

Dr Somerville sprang from the Somerville who was one of the companions of William the Conqueror, and who settled in Staffordshire.

Dr Somerville was otherwise well connected, and he had the honour of having for his daughter-in-law Mrs Mary

* Dr Macknight came to Jedburgh in 1770, and was the first who introduced the white kidney potato to the district, having brought some with him from Maybole. He was a most excellent and respectable minister, but a dry preacher; and some one of his hearers jocularly remarked, when the Doctor was in Edinburgh getting his "Harmony of the Gospels" printed, that he had gone to Edinburgh for the needless purpose of making harmony among four evangelists who had never cast out.

Somerville, one of the most profoundly scientific ladies of the present age. She was, besides, the niece of Mrs Somerville, senior, whose sister married Admiral Sir William Fairfax, the father of the talented authoress of the "Mechanism of the the Heavens," and other works of great fame, for which she received many well-deserved acknowledgments.

THOMAS ELLIOT, Minister of Cavers, was a contemporary and great friend of Dr Somerville's, besides being one of his nearest clerical neighbours when at Minto. Mr Elliot was a man of such intense modesty that for a time he concealed his knowledge of mathematics and astronomy, which was very superior; but at length he produced an essay connected with the latter science, which the editor of Dr Somerville's "Life" says was printed in the "Transactions of the Royal Society of Edinburgh." He died at Kelso in 1808, after having for many years had assistants in the parish, one of whom was the afterwards celebrated Dr Thomas Chalmers.

During Mr Elliot's Incumbency at Cavers, THOMAS DYCE was Minister of Teviothead Chapel, a place of worship intended for the parishioners of Cavers and Hawick, in the western district of those extensive parishes. The old chapel, or rather barn, which had existed for many years, was of a very humble description. I have heard there were no seats, but only bare benches, which chiefly rested on piles of turf; but there is a nice modern erection now.

Mr Dyce was a singular character, and I apprehend not of very extensive erudition; but he might have been useful in his way, and suited to his people. His congregation consisted chiefly of shepherds and dogs. The latter sometimes fell out and became combatants, and on one occasion the noise was so great, Mr Dyce was compelled to stop. He must have known all the dogs as well as their masters; and he had a favourite called "Gary," whose success in the combat he was anxious about, for on pulling up, he called out "a guinea on Gary's head." As I am discussing the dog fight, I may relate a little anecdote connected with Mr Dyce's canine friends.

They were as well aware as their masters when the minister was drawing to a close, and exhibiting, by whirring and fretfulness, great impatience when the blessing was about to be given, during which the people stood up, it was arranged between Mr Dyce and the shepherds that the congregation should sit still when the blessing was being given. This, which acted favourably, was very well when Mr Dyce officiated, but upon the occasion of a stranger preaching one day, there was a little scene. The people sat still, and the stranger who represented Mr Dyce, not being in the secret, extended his arms in vain, till a shepherd rose and explained the arrangement as to sitting at the blessing, adding that it was done to cheat the dogs.

Mrs Dyce aided her husband's small income by keeping a chool, and he died at Hawick on the 6th of February 1808.

Dr SAMUEL CHARTERS, the intimate friend and companion of Dr Somerville, and cousin of his wife, was appointed Minister of Wilton in 1772, just about the time Somerville was translated to Jedburgh, and he lived to complete his ministry of about fifty-three years at Wilton, a long pastorate, but not quite so long as that of his old friend referred to. He was the intimate friend of that eminent judge and scholar, Henry Home, Lord Kames, and his acquaintance was sought by many literary people, who were delighted to have intercourse with this wise but humble and good man. Dr Charters was an author of respectability, and was celebrated for his composition, which was chaste, if not eloquent.

WILLIAM CAMPBELL of Lilliesleaf, who was Incumbent of that parish from 1760 down to the early part of the present century, was well known as a popular preacher. On one occasion, when officiating in the Abbey Church of Melrose, he was supposed to be reading his sermon, for a man in the gallery, which came down nearly to the pulpit, eyed Mr Campbell very keenly, when the minister pulled up, and addressing himself to the person who stared, whose name was Taket, said, handing him the hieroglyphical notes which the minister had before him, "Tak it man, Tak it, I can do without it."

Mr Campbell was a very large man, and calling one day at a farmhouse with a neighbouring minister, found the host from home, and the woman who opened the door, asking Mr Campbell, who was spokesman, for his name, that gentleman replied, telling her just to say, " Twa o' the Lord's trumpeters ca'ad," on which she rejoined, " I just thocht sae, your cheeks are sae swalled wi' blawing."

Mr Campbell must have had wonderfully strong lungs, for he could preach to a well-packed congregation inside his church, and to a dense crowd outside at the same time, selecting a window for his pulpit.

There is a man in Dr Carlyle's autobiography called "Lungs," because he preached so loud, and the worthy minister of Lilliesleaf was of that class, though his soubriquet was even less elegant, being "roaring Campbell."

Mr Campbell's companion on his visit to the farm-house was

JOHN SCADE, Minister of St Boswells, a man who, though he has left nothing more behind him, that I am aware of, as a memorial of his abilities, than the Statistical Account of his parish, which he wrote for Sir John Sinclair's work, requires notice on account of his very peculiar physique. He was one of the smallest men imaginable, and when he preached in other churches he required to be mounted on an especially high footstool (of course he had one in his own pulpit, and at Lilliesleaf one was kept for Mr Scade's special use when he preached there). On one occasion, when so mounted, in the adjoining parish of Bowden, the footstool—a three-legged one—capsized, and down he went. A remarkable circumstance connected with this catastrophe was the fact of Mr Scade's uttering at the time it happened the words, "And they shall see me no more," his disappearance actually taking place then, to the astonishment of the people. He was a man of extraordinary bashfulness, which his dwarf-like appearance may in part have caused, and was of the most retiring habits. This probably caused him to marry his housekeeper, a most respectable person, though I have heard he wedded her out of gratitude for her kindness, and in order to place her on the Ministers' Widows' Fund, on which fund she was an annuitant for upwards of forty years.

Mr Scade died at St Boswells, on the 2d February 1810, after a ministry probably of about a quarter of a century.

ANDREW THOMSON was appointed by John, Duke of Roxburgh, Minister of Sprouston in 1802, where he remained till 1808, when he went to Perth, and finally to St. George's Church, Edinburgh, where he died in 1831, very suddenly.

This talented man and great orator was an honour to the Church of his fathers, having been one of her most devoted sons and greatest champions. He was specially noted for the part he took in the Apocrypha and Slave questions, and also in the Erskine Controversy. There is no man since the days of Knox on whom the words of the Regent Morton over the Reformer's grave could with more appropriateness be pronounced than o'er Andrew Thomson's—

"Here lies one who never feared the face of man."

To show the courage and lion-heartedness of the man, as well as his patriotic feelings, I may mention that on the threatened invasion of this country in the early part of the present century, Dr Thomson led a body of volunteers from Sprouston to Kelso, there to await orders for their future movement, had such been necessary. Thus the faithful soldier of the Cross could, in the hour of need, be the faithful soldier of the country that gave him birth.

I have mentioned Andrew Thomson as being of Anti-Apocrypha note, and I trust we may never think of lowering the Bible, the writers of which were holy men of God, and spake as they were moved by the Holy Ghost, by comparing the uncanonical with those undoubtedly inspired; for, as the Church of England says, the Apocrypha is only to be read for example of life and instruction of manners, and not to establish any doctrine. The immortal John Bunyan who, as an eloquent writer says, was as great in grace as in godliness, made a curious mistake as to the Apocrypha. He was in the depths of distress and had given up all hopes of life and blessedness, when the sentence, "Look at the generations of old and see, did ever any man trust in God and was confounded." He had thought the inspired Bible spoke these words of comfort to him, but he could not find them there, and when he made this discovery, after a long search, he found them to be in the Apocrypha. Nevertheless he took comfort, and blessed God for the consolation he derived from the verse in question, which was often his solace afterwards. Now it is singular that Bunyan confounded the Apocrypha with the canonical Scriptures, for the latter have the impress of the Deity upon them, while the former show they are from the pen of man. Many of the precepts are excellent. For instance, what can be more beautiful than the verses in Tobit:—

"Give alms of thy goods, and never turn thy face from any poor man; and then the face of the Lord shall not be turned away from thee."
"Be merciful after thy power. If thou hast much, give plenteously; if thou hast little, do thy diligence gladly to give of that little, for so gatherest thou thyself a good reward in the day of necessity."

About the time when Thomson became Incumbent of Sprouston, or a little earlier, the ever to be lamented

DR CHALMERS was for some time minister of Cavers parish, but only remained a very short time, obtaining a presentation to the parish of Kilmany in his native county, where he settled in 1803.

He was on intimate terms with many whose names are familiar to the inhabitants of Roxburghshire, viz., Dr Charters, of whom I have given a sketch, Dr Hardie of Ashkirk, Mr Arkle of Hawick, and Mr Paton of Ettrick. He was especially intimate with Charters, to whom, as he states, "he became bound by the tie of a very sincere admiration of his character and talents, as well as a lively gratitude for the kindness shown to him at this early period of his life."

ROBERT STORY, afterwards of Roseneath, was born at Yetholm, 3d March 1790. Few men have left more pleasant memories behind than Robert Story, not so much on account of any particular talent he possessed, as on account of his true nobility of character and greatness of soul. Story was the friend of many whose names were associated with what is great and good in the land. He was intimately acquainted with Chalmers and Irving. He was also the early friend and companion of Thomas Pringle. And amongst others, Dr Norman Macleod and Dr Robert Lee were not only his friends, but admirers. I do not enter upon the Row and other controversies he was mixed up with, but refer you to his Memoirs lately published by Macmillan, concluding with two verses applied to him by a friend whose name is not given :—

> "In these ears till hearing dies,
> One set slow bell will seem to toll
> The passing of the sweetest soul,
> That ever looked with human eyes.
>
> I hear it now, and o'er and o'er,
> Eternal greetings to the dead :
> And ave, ave, ave, said,
> Adieu, adieu, for evermore !"

DIVINES AMONG THE DISSENTERS.

JOHN HUNTER was ordained to the congregation at Gateshaw, in Morebattle parish, on the 17th October 1739, the celebrated Ralph Erskine, brother of the founder of the seceding body, preaching on the occasion.

Mr Hunter was a man of talent, but his career was a very short one, for he died the following year, viz., in 1740. Principal Robertson, the historian, once heard Hunter preach, and the earnest and impressive style of the preacher made a

lasting impression on his mind.* Mr Hunter was succeeded at Gateshaw by
JAMES SCOTT, son-in-law of Ebenezer Erskine, founder of the Secession body.†

* John Hunter was a native of Roxburghshire, and was for some time assistant teacher at Linton. He studied theology in connection with the Established Church, but was not licensed by the Presbytery of Kelso, because of some objections to his views on the "Marrow" controversy. Being recommended by the Rev. Gabriel Wilson of Maxton, he seceded to the Associate Presbytery, and studied under the Rev. William Wilson of Perth. At Orwell, on the 8th June 1738, he was licensed to preach, and was the first licentiate of the Associate Presbytery. On the 17th October 1739, he was ordained as minister of the united congregations of Morebattle and Stitchel, when the ordination sermon was preached by the celebrated Ralph Erskine of Dunfermline, from Luke xiv. 23. Prominent among those at Stitchel who joined the Associate Presbytery was Sir Robert Pringle, whose name was included among the first five elders constituted into a session by the Rev. Messrs Moncrieff and Fisher as reported to the Associate Presbytery at Perth on the 12th of October 1737. At Stitchel the first church was built in 1740, and at Morebattle or Gateshaw in 1749, so that Mr Hunter had to preach at both places in the open air, and his ministry was attended by large crowds. He died on the 7th of January 1740, before completing the twelfth week of his ministry. After Mr Hunter's death a small volume was published containing four of his sermons, and the sermon preached by Ralph Erskine at his ordination. The title of the volume was "The Bush Burning but not Consumed," and in a postscript to his sermon Mr Erskine says, "He was indeed a burning and a shining light, that burned so fast and shone so bright, it is less to be wondered that he did not burn and shine long." Principal Robertson who, when a young man, had heard Mr Hunter preach, said long afterwards, "Even yet when I retire to my studies, the recollection of what I then heard thrills through my soul."

† James Scott was born at Africa, a small estate in the parish of Ancrum, of which he was afterwards proprietor, and on the 13th May 1742 he was ordained as Hunter's successor at Gateshaw. For seven years Mr Scott preached in the open air on what is still known as Gateshaw Brae, and it is one of the traditions of the district, that though in winter they sat among the snow, none of his hearers suffered in health from the exposure. Mr Scott prepared his sermons with great care, writing out with exactness all he intended to deliver; and their elegance is apparent from a volume published after his decease. He was noted for punctuality in all things, and was very attentive to all his ministerial duties. Mr Scott married a daughter of the Rev. Ebenezer Erskine. In 1747, when the Secession Church became divided into the Burgher and Anti-Burgher sections, the Erskines, Ralph and Ebenezer, took part with the Burghers, but Mr Scott took the other side. When Mr Scott had reached his home at Gateshaw after the meeting of

THOMAS BOSTON was son of Thomas Boston of Ettrick, where he was born, in 1713, and where he succeeded his eminent father as parish minister in 1732 or soon after, being then very young. After a time he was translated to Oxnam, where he continued till 1759 as parish minister, though in 1755 when a vacancy occurred in the parish of Jedburgh by

Synod at which the breach took place, his wife remained silent for a while, but at length ventured to ask what had been done. She was told that the Burghers had been excommunicated, She replied, "If you, James Scott, have excommunicated my father and uncle, I can no longer wait on your ministry." Nothing farther was said, but thenceforth Mrs Scott rode every Sabbath to Jedburgh, where she attended on the ministry of Mr Shanks. This produced no alienation of affection, for Mr Scott regularly saw her off on horseback on the Sabbath morning, and duly waited her return in the evening. One of Mr Scott's elders, who came from the west, was wont to meet Mrs Scott on her way to Jedburgh, but never looked at her. In the afternoons he met her returning home to her husband, a dutiful act which he uniformly recognised by lifting his hat. Mr Scott died on the 6th of February 1773, and was buried in the churchyard of Ancrum. Mrs Scott afterwards removed to Edinburgh, where she lived to a great age, and was connected with the congregation of Bristo Street. She was fond of elegance and even finery in dress, a circumstance on which her minister, Dr Peddie, made some remark, when she replied, that in her opinion the temple of the Holy Ghost should have suitable outward adornment.

George Coventry, from Kinross, was ordained as Secession minister at Stitchel on the 18th of June 1755. He was twice called to Stirling, but continued at Stitchel, where he died on the 30th of June 1795, in the sixty-ninth year of his age and the forty-first of his ministry. A picture at once of the man and his times is furnished by the Rev. Dr Waugh of London, who, in his latter years, referred with much feeling to his recollections of summer sacraments at Stitchel, and specially to the tent gatherings on such occasions on Stitchel Brae. His words were, "Oh that I could again sit among them, and hear good old Mr Coventry give us as much sound divinity in one sermon, as is now found in ten volumes! It was a scene on which God's eye might love to look. Such sermons! and such prayers! none such to be heard now-a-days. What are your cathedrals, and your choirs, and your organs? God laid the foundations of *our* temple on the pillars of the earth. Our floor was nature's verdant carpet; our canopy was the vaulted sky, the heaven in which the Creator dwells. In the distance, the Cheviot-hills; around us, nature in all her luxuriant loveliness. There fields ripening into harvest; here lowing herds in all the fullness of supply for man. On the banks of that little rivulet at our feet, lambs, the emblem of innocence, sporting in the shade, and offering to heaven the only acknowledgment they could, in the expression of their happiness and joy. The birds around warble praises the decease of the pastor, the Rev. James Winchester, the people unanimously desired the appointment of Mr Boston in his place. The patronage belonged to the crown, and the first person named was Mr Bonar, Cockpen, who declined. The next was Mr Douglas, Kenmore, who accepted though he had only five signatures affixed to his call, and so the wishes of the parishioners were not complied with. This induced Mr Boston and his friends to relinquish the establishment, and to erect a new place of worship at Jedburgh, independent of the General Assembly, who after considerable discussion ordered the settlement of Mr Douglas. This new place of worship was finished in 1759, when Mr Boston demitted his pastorship of Oxnam parish, and entered upon the ministry of the new chapel, and having joined Mr Gillespie and Mr Collier, who both likewise seceded, the three constituted themselves into a presbytery of relief.

Mr Boston was an earnest and devout man, but like his father his career was cut short by a comparatively early death, for when he died in 1767, he was only fifty-four.* Notwithstanding his high character, it is said that he disobeyed his father in three particulars—first, in publishing his memoirs; secondly, in marrying Miss Anderson of Tushielaw; thirdly, in leaving the Established Church; but his father did not live to know of these several acts of disobedience.

to Him who daily provides for all their wants; the flowers and green fields offering their perfume; and lovelier still, and infinitely dearer to Him, singing His praises in grave sweet melody; perhaps to the tune of 'Martyrs.' 'Martyrs,' so sung on Stitchel Brae, might almost arrest an angel on an errand of mercy, and would afford him more pleasure than all the chanting, and all the music, and all the organs in all the cathedrals of Europe."

* His health seems to have broken down owing to the great physical exertions of ministering to a congregation of two thousand people, when he had not ministerial help even for his communions. The first sacrament in Jedburgh was dispensed, and the whole service conducted by himself alone, and in the open air, on the Ana, by the side of the Jed, he addressed an immense audience for a whole summer day. His preaching powers were highly estimated by Bogue, of Gosport, who testifies that, "next to Whitfield, Thomas Boston was the most commanding preacher he had ever heard."

By Miss Anderson, his wife, Thomas Boston had several children, and amongst them a son called Michael, who likewise married a Miss Anderson. Michael edited his grandfather, Thomas Boston of Ettrick's "View of the Covenant of Works," and though I find little is known of him, he seems to have done honour to the name. He was for a few years—at the commencement of his ministry—at Alnwick, in Northumberland, from whence he went to Falkirk, where he became "Relief" minister; but his useful career was cut short by death at an earlier age even than his father and grandfather, for he was thirty-nine only. Thomas Boston, of Jedburgh, was buried in the abbey there, where a slab is erected to his memory, and the following lines are inscribed to him:—

> "The sweet remembrance of the just
> Shall flourish while he sleeps in dust.
> With heavenly weapons Boston fought
> The battle of the Lord;
> Finish'd his course, and kept the faith,
> And waits the sure reward."

And the tablet erected to the memory of his son Michael, at Falkirk, where he died 5th February 1785, states that—

> "The distinguished peculiarities of the scholar, of the gentleman, and Christian met in him, and formed his character. Having discharged with fidelity and general approbation the pastoral duties of the congregation for seventeen years, he fell asleep in the hope of a glorious immortality."

ALEXANDER SHANKS was minister for nearly forty years of what was then known as the Burgher Meeting House of Jedburgh, and died in 1799. He was ordained on the 15th October 1760; resigned on account of declining health in 1795, and died on the 5th October 1799, in the sixty-eighth year of his age, and the thirty-ninth of his ministry. He was a man of great simplicity of character, but very considerable talents. He wrote with ease, and not a little vigour. He published several sermons, and one on "Peace and Order" was particularly noted. It attracted the attention of those in authority, and in consequence Mr Shanks was offered a pension; but such was his disinterestedness, he refused it, hinting, at the same time, that it would be well bestowed on the parish minister (Dr Somerville), whom he considered more in need of it than he was, having to support a numerous family. Mr Shanks' noble reasons for declining the offer of a pension ought to be stereotyped, being as follows, viz.—

"I am loyal from conscience—a seceder from principle—I have done nothing more than my duty—I take no reward."

Mr Andrew Moir, father-in-law of the late Dr Lawson, his predecessor as the minister of the Associate Congregation at Selkirk, preached the sermon at Mr Shanks' ordination, at Jedburgh, on the 15th October 1760, and delivered the charge. Mr Moir selected a peculiar text for his discourse, viz., "What will this babbler say?"

Dr JOHN YOUNG was appointed Anti-Burgher Minister at Hawick, 7th October 1767, in which charge he died on the 25th March 1806, aged sixty-two. Dr Young was a man of mark and popularity; indeed he was highly distinguished, both as a writer of sermons and essays. The latter, which were on political subjects, were ingenious, and had a most extensive sale. The Lord Chancellor of the day, Lord Loughborough, a man distinguished by great powers of reason and eloquence, thought Dr, then Mr Young's, essays the best he had seen (and a number were produced by the French Revolution), and recommended the same very warmly to the heads of the church. Such a deep impression had the secession minister of Hawick made by his writings, and so acceptable were they to the rulers of the country in the alarming times that then prevailed, there is no wonder that Dr Young was rewarded with a pension.*

* Dr Young had the offer of a pension, which he declined, requesting that it might be given to the parish minister of Wilton, which was done. His widow is said to have got the pension after his decease. Dr Young published three volumes of sermons chiefly preached on communion occasions, and a history of the French War in two volumes. A memoir of Dr Young, edited by Sir Walter Scott, would have been given to the world had the design not been averted by illness, which ended in Sir Walter's death. Connected with this a melancholy incident is recorded, as follows, in Lockhart's "Life of

Dr ALEXANDER WAUGH, who finished his career in London, where he acquired much popularity, was for some time minister of the Dissenting Chapel at Newtown, St. Boswells. Dr Waugh's merits are well known, and one of his best acts was the construction of the Constitution of the London Missionary Society, the extension and usefulness of which he long and successfully laboured to promote.*

Scott":—" On the 15th of February 1830, about two o'clock in the afternoon, he returned from the Parliament House, apparently in his usual state, and found an old acquaintance, Miss Young of Hawick, waiting to show him some manuscript memoirs of her father, a dissenting minister of great worth and talent, which he had undertaken to revise and correct for the press. The old lady sat by him for half-an-hour, while he seemed to be occupied with her papers. At length he rose up to dismiss her, but sank down, a slight convulsion agitating his features. After a few minutes he got up, and staggered to the drawing-room, where Ann Scott and my sister Violet Lockhart were sitting. They rushed to him, but he fell at all his length on the floor before they could reach him. He remained speechless for about ten minutes, by which time a surgeon had arrived and bled him."

* Alexander Waugh was born on the 16th August 1754, at East Gordon, in Berwickshire, where his father, Thomas Waugh, had a small farm. Both parents were most excellent and industrious and pious people, and Thomas Waugh belonged to the Secession Congregation of Stitchel from the date of its formation. Alexander was destined from his childhood to the holy ministry, and received his preliminary education first at Gordon and afterwards at Earlstoun, the Grammar School of which place he entered on the 1st of January 1766. He was the best scholar and the most active boy in the school, his hours of recreation being spent in excursions over the classic scenes by the banks of the Leader and the Tweed. Among his chief friends was Mungo Park, the African traveller. In 1770 he became a member of the Secession Congregation at Stitchel, and continued in the membership till 1779, when he was licensed to preach the gospel, after having studied in the Universities of Edinburgh and Aberdeen, and in the Theological Hall under the Rev. John Brown of Haddington. He was ordained minister of the Secession Church at Newtown, on the 30th of August 1780, but was translated to London in 1782, after having been three times called. His brief ministry at Newtown was remarkably successful; and his services at the only communion he had there were so remarkable that Mr. Coventry, formerly his minister, said to some one—" Oh, what lofty expressions! what exalted views of the perfections of the Almighty; and what a bright star this young man promises to be!" Among many other excellences he had a happy talent of interposing a jocular anecdote to terminate a debate that was kindling irritation. It is narrated that on one occasion some one in his company was getting hot in a discussion upon Church Establishments, when Dr Waugh set all

ROBERT HALL was the second minister of what was then the Burgher Associate Congregation at Kelso, having succeeded, in 1786, Mr Nichol, who was the first minister of the body settled in that town. Mr Hall was a strong-minded and outspoken man, and had great and most attractive conversational powers. He sounded the praises of his namesake, Robert Hall of Leicester, the Jeremy Taylor of English Dissenters, whom he admired, as every one must who can appreciate great gifts nobly employed in the service of the great Giver. Robert Hall, of Kelso, possessed a genial and loving nature, and was at all times anxious to do good, especially by setting a good example. As an illustration of this, when he was travelling on one occasion he visited a public coffee-room where were seated three other individuals, two of them being companions engaged in conversation, during which Mr Hall heard one of them swear, when he took leave to speak to them, introducing himself as the Rev. Robert Hall. He expostulated with them on the impropriety of swearing, more to the delight of the

parties in good humour by the following anecdote:—"I remember when I returned home at the vacation of Earlstoun school, I frequently went out to the muir to have some talk with my father's shepherd, a douce, talkative, and wise man in his way, and he told me, a wondering boy, a great many things I never had read in my school-books. For instance, about the Tower of Babel—that
"Seven mile sank, and seven mile fell,
And seven mile still stands, and evermair sall."
And about the craws, that they aye lay the first stick of their nests on Candlemas Day, and that some of them that big their nests in rocks and cliffs have siccan skill of the wind, that if it is to blaw mainly frae the east in the following spring, they are sure to build their nests on what will be the bieldy side; and mony a ane that notices it can tell frae that the airth the wind will blaw. After expressing my admiring belief of this, I thought as I had begun the Latin, and was therefore a clever chield, that I wadna let the herd run awa' wi' a' the learning. It was at the time when the alteration of the style had not ceased to cause great grief and displeasure to many of the good old people in Scotland, and I knew the herd was a zealous opponent of the change, so I slyly asked him, "Do the craws count Candlemass by the new or the auld style?" He replied with great indignation, "D'ye think the craws care for your acts of Parliament?" After a career of great eminence and usefulness, Dr Waugh died in London on the 14th of December 1827.

third individual—who did not come in for a share of the rebuke—than the two who did. The third party referred to turned out to be a Liverpool merchant, who, I suppose, was so pleased with Mr Hall's pluck, that he spoke to him and invited him to dine with him at Liverpool, or where his house was. Robert Hall accordingly accepted the invitation and went. On being ushered into the drawing-room, he found himself environed with the fashion and elegance of the place; but having understood his host was not a religious man, or at any rate did not say grace before his meals, he went up to him and said he could not sit down to dinner unless a blessing was previously asked. Oh, said his friend, the hospitable landlord, he would be most happy if Mr Hall would officiate, which he was of course most delighted to do.*

JOHN PITCAIRN, the first minister of the Relief Church in Kelso, did much to awaken a taste for pulpit oratory. His preaching was characterised by much faithfulness. Pitcairn was very young when he came to Kelso, and the precociousness of his powers was quite remarkable. His health gave way when in middle life, and it is rather singular that much about the same time both Mr Pitcairn and his fellow labourer, Mr Hall, were laid aside from preaching, the former from debility and the latter from old age.

* Mr Hall was born in 1757, at Cathcart, and the farm occupied by his father had been in the family for several generations. His father found the site for the first Secession Meeting-house in Glasgow; and his mother, whose paternal property lay contiguous to Kirkintilloch, presented the Seceders of that place with a site for their church. His brother was Dr James Hall, of Rose Street, and afterwards of Broughton Place, Edinburgh, one of the most exemplary ministers of his time. Robert Hall was called to Kelso in 1786, when Mr Dick, afterwards Dr Dick, Professor of Theology, was proposed and supported by a minority of the congregation, some of whom afterwards formed the Relief congregation. Mr Hall is well remembered for his peculiarities of manner, but scarcely less remarkable were his force of character, his intellectual acumen, and his great devotion to evangelical preaching. In 1814 he published a discourse entitled, "The State of the Heathen World Disclosed," which was criticised in "The Christian Instructor:" but the critic was ably answered by Mr Hall in some "Addenda" to a subsequent edition. Mr Hall died on the 7th of July 1831.

Dr ALEXANDER PRINGLE was also an eminent man among the Dissenters, and a native of Blakelaw, in Linton parish, where Thomas Pringle, the Poet, was also born, and who probably was a kinsman of the minister. Dr Pringle attached himself to the Anti-burgher party, and was ordained in 1777 to the ministry of the congregation of that body at Perth, continuing its pastor for the long space of sixty-one years—yea, till his death, which took place on the 12th August 1839.

Dr Pringle's congregation consisted of about 3000, being one of the largest in the Secession, or in any other body in those days; for till Mr Spurgeon became so eminent, such a congregation was very uncommon in later times.

Dr Pringle was well known as a writer, and when he had reached the ripe age of eighty-three he composed the greater part of a volume called "Scripture Gleanings," which was published only a few months before his death. He promoted the union of the Burgher and Anti-Burgher parties in 1820, and became an active and auspicious member of the United Secession body. But he did not live to see the Relief party come within the pale, when the triple body became the United Presbyterian Synod, so denominated in 1848.*

The Doctor was walking one day, when he met two thoughtless young men, who accosted him, and pompously enquired if he could tell them the colour of the devil's wig. The Doctor, having surveyed them attentively a few seconds, replied—" Truly, here is a most surprising case: two men have served a master all the days of their life, and can't tell the colour of his wig."

MEDICAL MEN.

Dr Scott of Thirlestane, in Ettrick parish, flourished in the seventeenth century. He was a medical adviser of Charles

* He had the degree of D.D. conferred upon him by Marischal College, Aberdeen, in 1819; and was Moderator of the Synod in 1821.

II., which shows he had a good medical reputation. He was a Professor of Alchymy—the romantic forerunner of chemistry; and at Thirlestane he prosecuted his experiments. There was an apartment in the ancient house there, called the "warlock's room," in which it has been said necromancy was practised, and where Dr Scott used to carry on his alchymical studies, or surveyed, according to the rhyme—

> "His copperplates, with almanacks
> Engraved upon't, and other knacks;
> His noon dial, with Napier's bones,
> And several constellation stones."

Dr THOMAS WILSON, son of the Rev. Gabriel Wilson of Maxton. Dr Wilson was a celebrated physician in London, in the early part of last century. He was also an eminent and zealous Christian.

When visiting Maxton on one occasion, his father, the minister (who died about 1740), was taken suddenly ill one Sunday morning, which incapacitated him from officiating, and seeing the people, some of whom came from a great distance, had assembled, the Doctor regretted they should be allowed to disperse without some religious exercises, and accordingly proposed to his father that he should take his place. The old minister, who was rather lax, after adopting the "Marrow" views in his notion of Church order, though a most worthy man, consented, and the physician, who, I suppose, was equally lax, on the score of Church government, clothed in his father's coat (probably the gown was not generally worn at that period), ascended the pulpit and commenced divine service, which he conducted to the great satisfaction of the congregation, one of whom declared, as I have seen it stated, "That he never witnessed a greater day of the Gospel at Maxton."

Sir JOHN PRINGLE, fourth son of Sir John Pringle of Stitchel, by Magdalen, daughter of Sir Gilbert Elliot of Stobs, was a very eminent member of the medical profession.

Sir John, at first Dr Pringle, was an ornament of his noble

profession, and also a distinguished philosopher. After studying at Leyden for some time, he returned to his native land, and settled at Edinburgh, where, in 1734, he was made Professor of Moral Philosophy, in which professorship he continued till 1742, when he received a high medical appointment with the British Forces on the Continent, which he held for some time, giving the greatest satisfaction, and obtaining still higher preferment as a reward for his eminent services.

Dr Pringle returned to Scotland during the rebellion in 1745, and attended the Duke of Cumberland, then in command, resuming his duties on the Continent when the rebellion was put down, and he finally settled in London, where appointments and rewards were heaped upon him, the dignity of a baronetcy being conferred upon him by George III.

The Doctor's writings were numerous, but his celebrated work was his "Treatise on the Diseases of the Army," which was translated into several foreign languages. He accumulated considerable wealth, the bulk of which he bequeathed to his nephew, the late Sir John Pringle of Stitchel, who succeeded to his uncle's British baronetcy, Sir John dying without issue.

Although Sir John Pringle's religious views were at one time unsettled, he afterwards became a diligent student of Holy Scripture, and could adopt the Song of Simeon, and say, "Now lettest thou thy servant depart in peace, for mine eyes have seen thy salvation."

Sir John was buried at St James's, Piccadilly, but a monument, with a medallion of him, is erected at Westminster Abbey, commemorating his fame and virtues, and intimating his birth and death as happening respectively in 1707 and 1782.

Dr JOHN ARMSTRONG was born in the parish of Castleton in 1709, of which parish his father and afterwards his brother were ministers. After completing his medical studies in Edinburgh, Dr Armstrong went to London to follow up his profession, but his practice was much interfered with by his versifying tendencies, and he left the Metropolis in 1760, to join the

British army on the Continent as physician, continuing with it for about three years, till peace was established, when he returned to London, where he finally settled, in 1768, employing his time as a practitioner and author till his death in 1779.

Dr Armstrong was a poet of some celebrity, though from his intimacy with Thomson and other geniuses his fame may have been unduly extolled.

Dr WILLIAM BUCHAN was born at Ancrum in 1729. He was originally designed for the Church, but his heart being set on following the medical profession, he accordingly did so, abandoning the study of divinity. After completing his medical studies in Edinburgh, he went to Yorkshire, where he obtained a practice, interesting himself most deeply in a foundling hospital there, which gave him extensive knowledge in the diseases of children. He afterwards returned to Edinburgh, where he devoted himself to the important work which made him so justly celebrated, the "Domestic Medicine," his *magnum opus*. For that work, which was first published in 1771, it is said he did not get much, though the publisher for many years realised annually what he gave for the copyright. It is stated, however, that the publisher, much to his honour, presented Dr Buchan with a handsome compliment on the revisal of every edition of the work, which was so popular as to run through some twenty or thirty editions.

The work, which [was also translated into many foreign languages, gained the Doctor such *eclat* that he was induced to go to London, where his great and popular reputation and pleasing manner gained him an extensive practice; and after a long residence in the Metropolis, he died on the 25th February 1805, in his seventy-sixth year, and his remains were interred in the cloisters of Westminster Abbey, amongst those of the great and learned of the land.

Dr RICHARD HALL was born at Haughhead, Eckford parish, and was descended from Hobbie Hall, of Haughhead. Dr Hall received the rudiments of his education at Jedburgh, and completed his studies at Edinburgh, where he became a member of the medical profession. He afterwards entered the Royal Navy, in which he served for some years as a surgeon, until the peace, when he returned to Edinburgh and graduated as a physician. He then proceeded to and settled in London, where he commenced a literary life which did not add to his wealth. On the contrary, he got into pecuniary difficulties, which compelled him to accept of a medical appointment abroad; but, meeting with an accident on his travels, that, together with the climate, so affected his health as to oblige him to return to England, and he died at Chelsea on the 24th May 1824.

Dr JOHN LEYDEN was born at Denholm in 1775. After becoming a member of the medical profession, he proceeded to India in the service of the East India Company. That service opened up for Dr Leyden a wide field in which to display not only his professional knowledge and skill, but also his literary attainments, and, above all, his talents as a linguist; but at the early age of thirty-five, when fortune was smiling upon him, he was seized with fever, which carried him off in a few days.

Lord Minto, then Governor-General of India, and a warm friend of Leyden, thus wrote of him:—

"No man, whatever his condition might be, ever possessed a mind so entirely exempt from every sordid passion, so negligent of fortune and all its grovelling pursuits—in a word, so entirely disinterested—nor ever owned a spirit more firmly and nobly independent. I speak of these things with some knowledge, and wish to record a competent testimony to the fact that Leyden never in any instance solicited an object of personal interest, nor, as I believe, ever interrupted his higher pursuits to waste a moment's thought on these minor cares. Whatever trust or advancement may at some periods have improved his personal situation have been, without exception, tendered, and in a manner thrust upon his acceptance. To this exemption from cupidity, was allied every generous virtue worthy of those smiles of fortune which he disdained to court. And amongst many estimable features of his character an ardent love of justice and a vehement abhorrence of oppression were not less prominent than the other high qualities I have already described."

There are other pleasing and touching testimonies to Leyden's hallowed memory from brilliant men of his time, and among them there is one from Sir John Malcolm, and there is an anecdote touching his love for the place of his birth, which amounted almost to a passion with him. Sir John went to visit him when he was ill, and on that occasion told Leyden he had news from Eskdale (the place of Sir John's birth), on the mention of which he inquired what they were all about on the Border. Sir John's letter noticed a surprise the Liddesdale people had had, in consequence of a fire at one of the beacons, which caused the volunteers to assemble with promptitude and march to Hawick, which they did to the tune of the "Gathering of the Elliots," on hearing which Leyden sprung from his sick couch, and with melody of the strangest character, and movements still more extraordinary, repeated that Border ditty—

"Wha dar meddle wi' me,
And wha dar meddle wi' me,
For my name it is little Jock Elliot,
And wha daur meddle wi' me?"

to the astonishment of those present, who thought his brain affected.

I have made every effort to obtain the whole of this ballad, I mean the ballad of the great Little John Elliot. No one that I have met with seems to know it in full, and I suspect even the great Leyden only knew the verse—which seems to be a chorus—that he quoted. The late Mr Telfer, not long dead, knew more about the Border ballads than any one now living; but from what I can learn from a friend, who communicated with him on my behalf, he only knew another verse, as follows, viz.—

"In raids I rode always the foremost,
My *straik* is the first in melée';
My name it is little John Elliot,
And wha daur meddle wi' me."

There is another anecdote communicated by Sir John Malcolm, and though it is about Leyden's father, it is worth giving, as being so deeply interesting as well as so highly characteristic of the fine old man. It speaks volumes, and proves what a noble person he was, truly worthy of having such a gifted son. There was necessarily some delay in winding up the accounts of his son's estate in India, and in preparing his manuscripts, which were committed to the care of Mr Heber, the talented brother of the able and amiable Reginald Heber, Bishop of Calcutta, for publication, for the benefit of Leyden's family. On this being explained to the old man he showed no wish for what many would have urged and coveted, a speedy and successful outturn from both, but with sublime pathos exclaimed, " God blessed me with a son, who, had he been spared, would have been an honour to his country. As it is, I beg of Mr Heber to think more of his memory than my wants. Money may be a comfort in old age, but thanks to the Almighty I have good health, and can still earn my livelihood."

This fine old man has, like his gifted son, passed " to that bourne from whence no traveller returns;" but in the language of Scripture, " He being dead yet speaketh."*

* A monument to Leyden has been erected on the green of his native village. This was accomplished chiefly through the efforts of a local committee consisting of Mr Haddon, farmer, Honeyburn ; the Rev. James M'Clymont, of the Free Church, Denholm, the late Mr James Duncan, Denholm, and some others. The monument is in the Venetian-Gothic style, and represents an ornamental pyramidal structure, chiefly of freestone, but the shafts of the pillars consist of polished red granite from Peterhead. On each of the four sides is a suitable inscription. The foundation-stone was laid with a good deal of ceremony on Saturday the 3d of August 1861 by the Rev. James Duncan, the Rev. James M'Clymont having first offered prayer.

On the 4th September 1875 the centenary of the poet's birth was celebrated at Denholm, under the auspices of the Edinburgh Border Counties Association. It should have been on the 8th, but circumstances rendered the 4th more suitable. The demonstration was very successful ; and there was a great gathering of people, including some from London, and many from Edinburgh and Glasgow. The village was gaily decorated ; and in all the neighbourhood it was a holiday. The scenes described by the poet were visited with interest by strangers from a distance. There was a procession.

Dr THOMAS TROTTER of Housebyres, near Melrose, was an eminent Naval Surgeon, having attained the rank of Physician to the Fleet. He introduced important alterations in the medical department of the Royal Navy, highly beneficial to the service, which in these days would no doubt have procured him some distinction or decoration, but he got nothing, except the approbation of an enlightened conscience, which after all is the good man's best reward. He held, it is true, two high official medical appointments connected with the Navy, but from these he retired, and settled at Newcastle-upon-Tyne, where he terminated his earthly career in 1832.

Dr WILLIAM TURNER was a Naval Surgeon of distinction. Having entered the Royal Navy when young, his career was a long one, during which he saw a great deal of active service. He was one of the few officers who attended Nelson when he received his death wound at Trafalgar on the 21st October 1805. Indeed the gallant doctor assisted in extracting the fatal ball from the immortal Nelson's shoulder.

ARMY AND NAVY.

I come now to the last, though not the least honourable of the professions, I mean that of arms, and I include, of course, the Naval as well as the Military service of the country, omitting those already noticed in connection with particular families.

Sir THOMAS MACDOUGALL BRISBANE of Makerston.

This gallant officer and able astronomer was son of Thomas Brisbane of Brisbane and Eleanor Bruce, descended from a common ancestor with the "Brus of Bannockburn," was born

There were addresses delivered in the open air, and there was a dinner in the school, at which Lord Neaves presided, and in which various eminent literary men took part. Two or three editions of Leyden's works were published on the occasion, and one of them, published by Messrs J. & J. H. Rutherfurd, Kelso, contained a number of illustrations of much interest not previously familiar to the public.

in 1773. He married Miss MacDougall of Makerston, daughter and heiress of Sir Henry Hay MacDougall, through whom he got that property, and whose name he assumed.

Sir Thomas's services extended over a lengthened period. He entered the army in 1790, served in Flanders, and afterwards through the Peninsular War, and a few years after that memorable campaign, he was appointed Governor of the important colony of New South Wales, where he remained some time. In token of his long and meritorious professional services he was made a baronet by King William IV.

SIR ADAM FERGUSSON, son and namesake of the Philosopher, was like his brother, Admiral Fergusson, one of Sir Walter Scott's earliest and dearest friends, and the intimacy continued through life.

Sir Adam had another brother, Colonel James Fergusson, who lived for a time at Huntly Burn.

Sir Adam joined the army and saw considerable service, but retired ere he got field rank, and settled at Toftfield, afterwards called Huntly Burn, this more euphonious name being given to the place from the brook which passes through its garden—celebrated traditionally as the scene of Thomas the Rhymer's interviews with the Queen of Fairyland.

Sir Adam was called by Sir Walter the "Noble Captain Fergusson," and you may remember the jolly account he gives of the veteran's marriage, which took place in 1821, and which Sir Walter attended. After their marriage Sir Adam and Lady Fergusson removed to Gattonside, not much further from Abbotsford. In the following year George IV. visited Scotland, when Fergusson, who was Deputy-Keeper of the Regalia, received the honour of Knighthood, along with Raeburn the great portrait painter, who died soon after, and whose last picture was one of Sir Walter Scott for Lord Montagu, then Lord-Lieutenant of Selkirkshire, of which county the baronet was Sheriff-Depute.

Sir Adam was a very joyous man, full of fun and humour, and always adding to the hilarity of a party by singing a good

R

song or producing a real laugh, which Sir Walter says is a thing as rare as a real tear.

NAVAL HEROES.

The Royal Navy may be considered as having been first established in the early part of the sixteenth century, when an office to govern it was formed, but at that time the ships of war did not exceed eleven, the largest being named the "Great Harry," after Henry VIII. It gradually increased, and now consists of several hundred vessels, and it is to be hoped its efficiency may not be impaired by any false economy, as "on our wooden," or now rather our "iron walls," depends, under Providence, much of our security in this our sea-girt island.

I have looked in vain through "Campbell's Lives of the Admirals"—an old book now, it is true—for Roxburghshire men, but without finding any. In later times, however, there have been several flag officers and some of distinguished note. The first is

Sir JAMES DOUGLAS of Springwood Park, great-grandson of Andrew Douglas of Friarshaw, Lilliesleaf parish, a property which does not belong to the family now, though it was at an early date in their possession.

Sir James was a naval officer of celebrity, and was knighted for bringing home advices of the storming of Quebec in 1759, where the great British General Wolfe lost his life in the hour of victory.

"Brave Wolfe a chief invincible in war,
Brittania's darling son, a friend to all."

Admiral Douglas was subsequently raised to the baronetage for various other achievements. He commanded at and took Dominica, and also assisted at the siege of Martinique, thus terminating a successful professional career. Next in order is,

ADMIRAL JAMES DOUGLAS, second son of the foregoing, who was born in 1755, and after a meritorious service died in 1839.

The family of Dickson of Sydenham, near Kelso, produced three admirals in the persons of
Admiral WILLIAM DICKSON,
Admiral ARCHIBALD DICKSON, and,
Admiral ARCHIBALD COLLINGWOOD DICKSON.
Admiral Archibald Dickson was so distinguished that he was created a Baronet in 1802, in acknowledgment of his important services, with remainder to his nephew in case of failure of issue, that nephew being Admiral Archibald Collingwood Dickson, who succeeded to the baronetcy accordingly on the death of his uncle, which happened very soon after he got the title.

Sir Archibald Collingwood Dickson received his first naval commission in 1791, and was lieutenant on board the flag ship of Sir Alexander Hood (afterwards Lord Bridport), which was in the memorable action of the 1st June 1794, when Lord Howe totally defeated the French fleet, took six ships of war, and sunk several. Sir Archibald Collingwood, now captain of the " Veteran," sixty-four, assisted at the capture of the Dutch fleet in the Texel, in 1799, under Admiral Mitchell, and joined Sir Hyde Parker's fleet employed against the Northern Confederacy, in 1801. Afterwards, during the greater part of the war, he commanded the " Orion," a seventy-four, till put out of commission in 1813. His last command was the " Rochfort," eighty guns, soon after giving up which, he was promoted to the rank of Rear-Admiral. He died suddenly at Tichfield, Hampshire, in 1827, and was succeeded by his son, who is in the Royal Navy.

Admiral Sir WILLIAM GEORGE FAIRFAX went to sea about the middle of the last century, and at his death, in 1813, had been about sixty years a naval officer. He saw a great deal of active service, and was captain of the admiral's flag ship the " Venerable," at Camperdown, Duncan's celebrated battle fought on the 11th October 1797. Duncan, who for his victory over the Dutch fleet on this occasion, which was considered one of the greatest achievements of the war, was created a peer, did not fail to recognise Fairfax's services in that important engagement, not only by highly complimenting him, but by sending him home with his despatches for the government, on which occasion he was made a *Knight Banneret.* This is an order of knighthood very ancient and very venerable—strictly, however, the honour ought to be conferred under the Royal Standard on the field of battle. As Shakespeare says :—

> "A soldier by the honour giving hand
> Of Cœur de Lion knighted on the field."

The last Knight Banneret made in due form was at the battle of Edgehill in 1642, the first important battle in the Civil War, which was a drawn one; but George III. renewed the honour in a certain form, by making several. William IV., our Sailor King, however, thought Sir William Fairfax ought to have had an hereditary title for his important services, and in order to do justice to "departed worth," conferred the dignity of a Baronet on his son, Colonel Sir Henry Fairfax of St Boswells.

Admiral ROBERT ELLIOT of the Harwood family and brother of General Henry Elliot, deserves honourable mention. He entered the navy in 1781, passed lieutenant in 1788, but owing to the difficulty of getting employment he joined the Swedish marine for a time, in which service he saw and participated in a good deal of fighting. He returned to England in 1793, when he got employment. He distinguished himself by capturing two French privateers. He was afterwards attached to the Egyptian expedition, and got, with others, a Turkish gold medal in acknowledgment of meritorious services.

Admiral Lord MARK ROBERT KERR, third son of the fifth Marquis of Lothian, who was born in 1776, entered the navy when young, for I find him distinguished at the action off L'Orient in 1795, when the French fleet was defeated by Lord Bridport, and three ships of war captured. He is next found in the Mediterranean under Jervis, who made him captain of one of the large prize-ships taken off St Vincent, and afterwards he was at the reduction of Minorca under Duckworth, and he finally commanded the "Fisgard" frigate, in which he cruised with activity and success. Lord Mark married Charlotte Countess of Antrim, and died in London on the 10th September 1840.

Admiral JOHN MACPHERSON FERGUSON was called generally Jock Ferguson, and with his brother Sir Adam, resided near Melrose. Both these gallant men were intimate friends of the great Sir Walter Scott. They accompanied the Baronet, then plain Mr Scott, to England in 1797, and on their way south they spent a few days in Peeblesshire with Dr Adam Ferguson, father of Sir Adam and Jock. It was when visiting the Doctor, Scott met with Ritchie, the original of the Black Dwarf, in 1797, but a more important occurrence took place when on this tour, for when they reached England, Sir Walter first met with Miss Carpenter, with whom he fell in love, and afterwards married. But to return to Jock Ferguson, who Sir Walter says was Nelson's favourite lieutenant, a feather in his cap, I have to state that he was made commander in 1808, and afterwards appointed to the "Pandora" brig, with which vessel he captured a French privateer; but not long after his ship was stranded off Jutland, when several of his men were drowned, some were saved, including himself, but were made prisoners by the Danes who saved them, treated them kindly and afterwards released. This circumstance did not bar his promotion or further employment, for he had two commands afterwards. His Post-Captaincy was obtained in 1817, and he had been some time a Rear-Admiral ere he died in 1855.

Admiral ROBERT RIDDELL CARRE of Cavers, my worthy uncle and predecessor in the old family place, comes now to be noticed. Admiral Carre entered the navy in 1796, joining the "Albatross," commanded by Captain Scott of the Gala family, afterwards Admiral Sir George Scott. Previously to his leaving the "Albatross" the crew mutinied, but were put down by the spirited conduct of Captain Scott and his officers, and they afterwards assisted in the capture of two privateers. He afterwards served in the North Sea and Baltic stations, proceeding after those services were over to the East Indies in Sir Alexander Collingwood Dickson's ship the "Sceptre," seventy-four. But I should state that Admiral Carre had shared in Nelson's celebrated battle of Copenhagen. After his return from India, and further service in the Baltic and North Sea, he got the command of the "Britomart" in 1812, and in that vessel he was at Algiers, taking part in that brilliant and successful battle. He was promoted to the rank of Post-Captain in 1819, and finally to that of Rear-Admiral. He was the recipient of a medal with bars for Copenhagen and Algiers. Admiral Carre died in 1860 at his residence of Cavers Carre, where he had long been settled, and his life in his retirement was like his death, calm and peaceful.

Captain ROBERT CAMPBELL, son of the Rev. William Campbell, minister of Lilliesleaf, deserves special notice, not only for his gallantry, but his extraordinary good fortune. Captain Campbell ran a small French fleet into a harbour in the Mediterranean, and made them all captures. His senior officer on the station claimed the prize, but Campbell disputed the claim, and succeeded at any rate to the extent of about £70,000. But alas his surviving family spent it all.

POETS.

JAMES THOMSON, the celebrated and justly-popular author of the "Seasons," was born in 1700, at Ednam, in Roxburghshire, where his father was parish minister—the first after the Revolution—though he was translated to Southdean, also in the county, soon after the poet's birth. His mother's name was Beatrice Trotter, of Fogo, in Berwickshire.

Thomson's early studies, which commenced in Jedburgh, and concluded at Edinburgh University, to which he had a bursary from the Presbytery of Jedburgh, were at first directed towards the Church, but the speedy development of his poetical talents made him relinquish all idea of entering the ministry. One of his best and earliest friends was the Rev. Robert Riccalton of Hobkirk; and another great friend and patron of the poet's was Sir William Bennet of Grubet, to whom Thomson was much attached, and at whose house at Marlefield he visited.*

Lord Chancellor Talbot made the poet one of his secretaries. Frederick Prince of Wales, son of George II., and father of George III., noticed Thomson in a very marked manner, his Royal Highness making a handsome settlement upon him, which, with an appointment given him by Lord Lyttleton, of literary celebrity, placed him in tolerably easy circumstances during the latter period of his life, though at times much in want of money, which he never seemed to know the value of.

It ought to be mentioned, to the honour of Quin, the celebrated actor and elocutionist, one of Thomson's best friends, that on visiting him during a period of his greatest embarrassment, he told him he had come to square accounts with him. This Thomson did not understand, and, exhibiting a most astonished look, Quin immediately explained himself by saying—"The pleasure I have had in perusing your works I cannot estimate at less than £100, and I insist upon requiting that debt," upon saying which Quin laid down that sum and took his leave.

It has been said that a poem composed by Riccaltoun, on a

* After his father's death Thomson went to London, where his college friend, Mallet, procured him a situation of tutor to the son of Lord Binning. His poem of "Winter" appeared in March 1726, and for the copyright the poet received only three guineas. A second and a third edition appeared the same year. "Summer" appeared in 1727, and in 1728 he issued proposals for publishing, by subscription, all the four seasons, at a guinea each copy. The number of subscribers was 387, but Pope took three copies, and others took more than one.

storm gathering round Ruberslaw, suggested the idea of the "Seasons;" but it appears by a letter from himself to Dr Cranston, son of the Rev. Mr Cranston, minister of Ancrum —the original of which was, I believe, sent as a wrapper to a pair of candlesticks forwarded to Kelso, but was afterwards recovered—that the idea of his Winter was suggested by a poem of Mr Riccaltoun's on the same subject. The letter referred to had no date affixed to it, but was posted at East Barnet, Hertfordshire, where Thomson resided in 1725, as tutor in the family of Charles, Lord Binning, a poet also, and author of the pretty pastoral "Ungrateful Nanny," and at whose house Thomson wrote his Winter, as the letter states, for he says—"Mr Riccaltoun's poem on Winter, which I still have, first put the design into my head. In it are some masterly strokes that awakened me, being a present amusement, till ten to one but I drop it whene'er another fancy comes across."

I shall now give you a few anecdotes of Thomson, which were collected by David Stewart, Earl of Buchan, a peculiar but talented man, who was passionately fond of the poet, and who instituted a commemoration of him at Ednam, where an obelisk was erected to his memory, and who erected a bust of him at Dryburgh, and also placed a brass tablet to his memory at Richmond, where Thomson was buried. The poet's grave, owing to an alteration in the church since he was buried, is partly inside and partly outside the church, in the north-west corner. The anecdotes were collected from a barber at Richmond, by name "Will Taylor," who said he had taken Thomson many hundred times by the nose. Taylor, or "Will" as the poet called him, said that Thomson was corpulent, with a long face, like a horse's, and long hair as soft as a camel's. He was rather slovenly in his attire, and stooped a good deal in walking, as though he was full of thought. He was a good pedestrian, and would sometimes walk to and from London in a day. Thomson, the professional stated, wore a wig, in which kind of head-dress he was very extravagant, for he had known him to spoil a new wig in walking from London. The poet kept a good deal of company "of the writing sort," and he remembered to have seen Pope, Paterson, Malloch, Quin, Lyttleton, Armstrong, and Andrew Millar, at his house. Pope was described by "Will" as a strange, ill-formed figure of a man; and Quin was a great lover of punch, of which Thomson was also very fond, frequently writing with a punch-bowl before him. He further stated that Thomson was very cheerful and good-tempered, indeed one of the best natured men possible, and when he had money he would send for his creditors and pay them all round. "Will" continued to attend Thomson till the day before his death, which happened in 1748, and concluded his communication to the Earl of Buchan by giving a hearty encomium on his character.*

SIR WALTER SCOTT was one of the greatest men of modern times. Sir Walter, who was born in the College Wynd, Edinburgh in 1771, was son of Walter Scott, Writer to the Signet, and Ann Rutherfurd, his wife. His grandfather was Robert Scott of Sandyknowe, Smailholm, and his grandmother was Barbara Haliburton of the Newmains family, a very ancient one, and formerly possessors of Dryburgh and Mertoun; and his greatgrandfather was Beardy Wat, of whom there is a picture at Abbotsford, who was so named from a vow he made not to shave till the Stuarts were restored. His great-great-grandfather was Walter Scott of Raeburn, who embraced Quakerism, third son of Sir William Scott of Harden, the uncle of Walter Scott of Highchesters.

Sir Walter Scott was fond of family pedigrees, and everything connected with heraldic and antiquarian pursuits, and I have had the pleasure of seeing him at his own beloved Abbotsford, and hearing him point out and explain the curiosities and antique reliques in that great museum collected by himself.

* The poet died on the 27th of August 1748, from a fever, caught by sailing in a boat from Hammersmith to Kew, after he had got heated by walking from London. No poet was ever more deeply or sincerely lamented.

He was unfortunate in his family, and it is one of the inscrutable dispensations of Providence that the whole of the children of Sir Walter, whose fond wish was to perpetuate his name at Abbotsford, the place of his own creation, have all passed away, and the baronetcy granted to him in 1820, being the first conferred in the reign of George IV. and the only one in that year, is now extinct, and the heiress of Abbotsford is a great-granddaughter.

Sir Walter's early days were passed among the hills and valleys of the Borders, where, as Allan Cunningham has well said, "almost every stone that stands above the ground is the record of some skirmish or single combat, and every stream, although its waters be so inconsiderable as scarcely to moisten the pasture through which they run, is renowned in song or in ballad."

This residence, so delightful and congenial to the illustrious novelist and poet, in a district so replete with legendary lore, has enabled him to bequeath a legacy to posterity far above all price. As long as the hills, dales, and streams of Tweedside, Teviotdale, and Liddesdale last, so long will Scott's fame be imperishable.

It is close upon sixty years since the Minstrelsy was commenced, and from that time * down to about 1830 his brain and his hands were constantly at work, and poems, ballads, novels, and other works were produced, of which in the aggregate there is scarcely any parallel in the annals of this country.

His Novels are generally considered his "chef d'œuvres," being preferred to his poetry, but English romantic poetry has perhaps nothing more beautiful than his "Marmion" or "Lady of the Lake." †

---

* The first two volumes were published in 1802.

† On the 21st of September 1832 the great man breathed his last in presence of all his children.

Lockhart says, "It was a beautiful day—so warm that every window was wide open—and so perfectly still that the sound, of all others most delicious

THOMAS PRINGLE of Blakelaw, in Linton parish, possessed high general attainments, and was a poet of very considerable merit, and though, not connected with the Pringles so historically eminent, he keeps up the credit of the name, and indeed adds to it a lustre.

Pringle's life was a very chequered one, and though he was always employed, what with literary, philanthropic, and editorial work, he determined on emigrating, with his household and other members of his family circle, to the Cape of Good Hope, which he accordingly did in 1820; but his worldly affairs not having been bettered by that step, he returned to England, and became secretary of the Anti-Slavery Society till the Negro Emancipation Act was passed in 1833, which deprived him of his situation, the society being no longer necessary. Mr Pringle renewed his literary occupations, upon which he now depended entirely, and he continued the same till his death, which happened on the 5th December 1834. He died of pulmonary disease in his forty-sixth year, and was interred in Bunhill Fields burying-ground, London, not very far from John Bunyan's tomb.

Pringle's grave may still be seen, over which there is a flat stone with an elegant but too lengthy inscription upon it; but alas it is beginning to show the effects of time, and requires renovating.*

to his ear, the gentle ripple of the Tweed over its pebbles, was distinctly audible as we knelt around the bed, and his eldest son kissed and closed his eyes."

* Pringle was born at Blakelaw on the 5th of January 1789, and was the son of a respectable farmer. In infancy his hip-joint was dislocated by some accident, and the fact was culpably concealed by his nurse till it was past remedy, so that all his life he was a cripple compelled to use crutches. After preliminary home education, he went for three years to the Grammar School of Kelso, and thereafter to the University of Edinburgh. He betook himself to literature, but to maintain himself worked as a clerk in the Register Office. In 1811 he published, in conjunction with a literary friend, a poem, called "The Institute;" and in 1816 was a contributor to "Albyn's Anthology," and the "Poetic Mirror." He is described by Mr P. Gillies, in his "Memoirs of a Literary Veteran," as "a young man of excellent literary tact, and of most amiable disposition, mild, prepossessing, persevering, patient,

WILLIAM KNOX is well entitled to follow Thomas Pringle, and like him was born in 1789, being a native of Firth, in Lilliesleaf parish. Knox's father, Thomas Knox, married Barbara Pott, widow of —— Pott of Todrig, she being previously Barbara Turnbull of Firth, and William was their eldest son.

His life was a chequered one like Pringle's, though spent in his native land and latterly in Edinburgh, whither he went for the purpose of gaining a livelihood by literature, to which he was much devoted, agricultural life, in which he at first engaged, not suiting him. But, alas, the temptations of the metropolis were too strong for him, and, mixing much in society, his health could not stand the excitement to which he exposed himself, and at the early age of thirty-six he was suddenly carried off in 1825.

Knox was a man of great hilarity, and possessed a large amount of wit and humour, and many now living amongst us will no doubt remember him, as well as his excellent songs and anecdotes.

The great Southey, Poet Laureate for about a quarter of a century, had a high opinion of Knox's paraphrases, and thought them well suited for a collection of hymns which Bishop Heber, the author of the well-known poem, Palestine,

and industrious." He was likewise well supported by literary friends, including Lockhart, John Wilson, Cleghorn, Dr Brewster, James Hogg, and even Sir Walter Scott, but his schemes never appeared to prosper. His father and five brothers, who were agriculturists, were not more fortunate; and in 1820, Thomas Pringle, with his wife and family, his father, two brothers, and several friends, in all twelve men, six women, and six children, emigrated to the Cape of Good Hope. Fortune favoured him for a while, but again the sky was overcast, and on the 7th July 1826, Pringle, with his wife and sister-in-law, arrived in London, without means, and with a heavy burden of debt. Afterwards, through the influence of Messrs Z. Macaulay and Baxter, he was appointed Secretary of the Anti-Slavery Society, and continued so till the slaves were emancipated, on the 27th of June 1834. His work on earth was done. On the day after the important document had been published a crumb of bread had passed down his windpipe, which caused such a fit of coughing as to rupture a small blood vessel, which led to consumption. He died on the 5th of December 1834, in his forty-sixth year.

and the devoted Bishop of Calcutta, had intended publishing, and to whom Southey offered to forward them, but both Knox and Heber were soon afterwards called away, the former by paralysis and the latter by apoplexy, the bishop being at the time on an arduous ecclesiastical and missionary journey.

ROBERT DAVIDSON was born at Morebattle, in humble life, which he never quitted, as a man of his talents ought to have striven to do. Indeed his poverty was at times so great as to induce him to accept public relief. Davidson's poetry takes a good place in modern Scottish minstrelsy, and some of it is of no mean order, as will appear from the following verses in his " Farewell to Caledonia : "—

" Adieu ; a long and last adieu,
   My Native Caledonia !
For while your shores were in my view
   I steadfast gazed upon ye O.

" Your shores sae lofty, steep, an' bold,
   Fit emblem of our sires of old,
Whose valour, more than mines of gold,
   Has honoured Caledonia.

" My fancy haunts your mountains steep !
   Your forests fair, an' valleys deep ;
Your plains, where rapid rivers sweep,
   To gladden Caledonia.

" In vain I'm told a vessel hies
   To fertile fields an' kindly skies,
But still they want the charm that ties
   My heart to Caledonia.

" Oh, land of heroes, famed an' brave—
   A land our fathers bled to save,
Whom foreign foes could ne'er enslave—
   Adieu to Caledonia ! "

WILLIAM LAIDLAW was the faithful and confidential friend of Sir Walter Scott, and deserves honourable mention, not only as such, but on account of his own poetical and general acquirements. Laidlaw's family being once tenant-farmers in

Tweedside, added to his long domicile at Abbotsford, entitles me to include him among the Roxburghshire notables.

Laidlaw and the Ettrick Shepherd were inseparable friends, and in 1801 the former was introduced to Sir Walter Scott, at which time the great poet was in pursuit of matter for his Border Minstrelsy. Leyden, who was then assisting him, was the cause of the introduction, thinking Laidlaw, who was so fond of ancient ballads, would just suit Sir Walter. He afterwards became Sir Walter's steward, at Abbotsford, where he officiated till Sir Walter's embarrassments commenced, when he informed Laidlaw of his inability to continue his services. This led Laidlaw to withdraw from Abbotsford, to avoid being a burden to his attached friend and employer, who wrote to him about his misfortunes and his consequent difficulties, adding—"You never flattered my prosperity, and in my adversity it is not the least painful consideration that I cannot any longer be useful to you. But Keaside, I hope, will still be your residence, and I will have the advantage of your company and advice, and probably your services as amanuensis." Laidlaw accordingly left Abbotsford some time about 1827, but in 1830, when Sir Walter anticipated the return of brighter days, he got his old steward back again, his absence having been, as he said, "a most melancholy blank." Laidlaw, however, returned principally to act as amanuensis, but his services in that capacity even were not long required, for the great author was soon struck down by illness, during which his faithful friend Laidlaw was his constant attendant, a source of great satisfaction to the noble sufferer. On the death of Sir Walter, on the 21st September 1832, or soon after, Laidlaw bid a final adieu to Abbotsford, receiving from his late dear friend's son and his wife, the present of a brooch which the great novelist wore, and which Laidlaw prized and wore till his own death, which took place in 1845, at the age of sixty-four.

William Laidlaw was a man of considerable acquirements. He was scientific, statistical, and poetical. His last ballad is called "Lucy's Flitting," in the style of "Robin Gray," but though not so able as Lady Anne Lindsay's, it is like it, and is very touching.

Miss JANE ELLIOT was no less distinguished for her heroism than for her accomplishments. One of the songs styled the "Flowers of the Forest" was composed by her, and although it was published anonymously, and the authoress remained long unknown, she was afterwards discovered, and the ballad was rendered famous by Sir Walter Scott, who inserted it in his "Border Minstrelsy," his note upon it giving it high rank as a fine piece of elegiac poetry. A short time before her death she returned to Roxburghshire, and resided with her brother Admiral Elliot at Mount Teviot, where she closed her mortal career, on the 29th March 1805, at an advanced age, having nearly reached eighty years.

The depopulation of the youth, or "Flowers of the Forest," at the fatal battle of Flodden, no doubt was in Miss Jane Elliot's mind in writing her charming ballad; and it is rather singular that much about the same period another lady wrote a ballad called by the same name, to which Sir Walter Scott has likewise given a place in the Minstrelsy, prefacing the elegy with a very pretty compliment to the writer. She was Alicia Rutherfurd of Fairnilie, Galashiels parish, wife of Mr Patrick Cockburn, advocate, a most distinguished lady, as regards both her genius and her charms.

ELIZABETH RUTHERFURD, of Capehope, niece of Mrs Cockburn, and wife of Walter Scott of Wauchope, in this county, composed "The Lover's Address to a Rosebud," commencing—

"Sweet nursling of the tears of morning."

She wrote other poems, chiefly elegiac, and was generally accomplished.

Dr Blacklock, the poet (was a minister of the Church of Scotland, but being blind, was objected to, and obliged to retire from the parish of Kirkcudbright, to which he had been presented), mentions Mrs Scott with high praise; and from his excellent knowledge of poetry his opinion must carry weight. The great poet of nature, Robert Burns, also was her friend and correspondent, and he paid her a visit on his Border tour in 1787, for he says in his journal—"Set out next morning for Wauchope, the seat of my correspondent, Mrs Scott. Mr Scott, exactly the figure and face of Sancho Panza; very shrewd in his farming matters, and not very infrequently stumbles on what may be called a strong thing, rather than a good thing. Mrs Scott, all the sense, taste, intrepidity of face, and bold critical decision, which usually distinguish female authors."

JOHN HOY of Gattonside, near Melrose, who died in 1781, at an early age, deserves notice. A book of poems which he composed and published, exhibits poetical talents which, had the author been spared, might have been succeeded by productions of a higher order. His love of poetry and song was very marked, and the rapture with which he read Milton and Pope was quite extraordinary. Our own highly gifted Thomson was also one of his favourite authors; and Hoy, too, composed upon the Seasons.

ANDREW SCOTT, the self-taught bard of Bowden, where he was sexton for many years, is next in order.

He was born in 1757, and died in 1839. His occupation at first was that of a herd, no doubt a favourable pursuit for anyone of poetical tendencies, which showed themselves in Andrew at a very early age; and though he joined the army and went to America, he continued to string his lyre in that country, no doubt to the pleasure and gratification of his comrades.

At the conclusion of the American War in 1792, he returned to his native place, but for a time he laid down the lyre, taking to daily labour for the maintenance of his family. After a time, however, he renewed his acquaintance with the muses, and was advised to publish, which he did; but though he did not make much as an author, he had the satisfaction of ranking among his supporters and admirers many by whom it was an honour to be patronised.

I shall give a few lines from Andrew Scott's "Fiddler's Widow":—

> "There was a musician who played a good stick,
> He had a sweet wife, and a fiddle,
> And in his profession he had right good luck,
> At bridals his elbow to diddle.
>
> But, ah! the poor fiddler chanced to die,
> As a' men to dust must return,
> An' the poor widow cried, wi' the tear in her eye,
> That as long as she lived she would mourn.
>
> Fair shone the red rose on the young widow's cheek,
> Sae newly weel washen wi' tears,
> As in cam' a younker some comfort to speak,
> Wha whispered fond love in her ears.
>
> The young widow blushed, but sweet smiling, she said,
> Dear sir, to dissemble I hate,
> If we two thegither are doomed to be wed,
> Folks needna contend against fate.
>
> He took doun the fiddle, as dowie it hung,
> An' put a' the thairms in tune,
> The young widow dighted her cheeks, an' she sung,
> For her heart lap her sorrows aboon."

Some twenty years after Andrew's birth, was born GEORGE SCOTT, at Dingalton, Melrose, who was for many years Parish Schoolmaster at Lilliesleaf.

George Scott was a fair poet, and a good scholar for his station, and was patronised by the elite in the neighbourhood, which showed the respect entertained for him and also for his acquirements. The late Sir John Riddell and Sir Walter Scott were two of his patrons, and to the latter Mr Scott showed the manuscript of a Statistical Account of Roxburghshire which he had prepared, and which was well thought of, but never published. He issued, however, a small volume of poetry, called "Heath Flowers."

Contemporary with Andrew and George Scott, was JOHN YOUNGER of St Boswells. Though the younger in age of the three, to pun upon his name, he was the senior in general natural talents, which, however, he did not nurture sufficiently, or turn to the account he might, and though long resident at Lessudden, he was born, in 1785, at Longnewton, once a parish, but now annexed to Ancrum.

John Younger was a man of great intelligence, and much general information. His Prize Essay on the Sabbath gained him great fame far and near; and his poetry, which more concerns me now, is by no means contemptible. Since his death, a book of his on angling, of which he was once very fond, has been published.

ALEXANDER HUME, a native of Kelso, was born in 1809, his father having been a respectable tradesman there. His history is full of interest. About the age of fifteen, Hume was missing one day, and it was afterwards discovered he had joined a band of strolling players, with whom he continued some months. He was very popular with the Coryphœus of the band, being a good singer, actor, and dancer, but conscience soon upbraided him for leading such a wretched life (and, my friends, can you witness a company of strolling players and not feel the degradation of such an occupation?), and he returned home to his family, who had, in the interim, removed from Kelso to London. He now determined to turn over a new leaf in his history, and at length became a most respectable and respected young man, entering into commercial life in London; and such was the opinion of his employers that the fidelity bond they took on his entering their service they soon voluntarily cancelled, to show their regard for him, as well as to mark their sense of his probity and good conduct. At the same time, while going on steadily with his mercantile pursuits, he was cultivating, during his leisure hours, his musical and poetical talents, which were of a high order.

His first song was sent to one of the London Magazines, but the editor, not being able perhaps to appreciate a true Scotch lyric, threw it aside. It was, however, soon rescued from the editor's basket of rejected compositions by one of the staff who had been better acquainted with our national poetry, and he pronounced it fit for the public eye by certifying it "as musical as is Apollo's lute." This little episode is interesting, especially as the occurrence was the cause of inducing Hume to persevere, and finally to become a graceful writer, his poems abounding with not a little pathos, and being marked by no inconsiderable talent.

The author was short-lived, having in early life fallen into bad health which he at first tried to remove by change to a foreign land, but though he returned greatly benefited the improvement did not long continue, for in a few years he was threatened with a renewal of his old complaint, which induced him to cross the Atlantic again, and though the voyage and change stayed the progress of his disease for a time, he afterwards, on his return, gradually declined, and died in 1851.

For some years before his death he had written but little, in consequence of his state of health requiring all his time and strength for the maintenance of his family.

Hume was buried at Northampton, where he died.

WILLIAM B. C. RIDDELL was a son of a poet, the Rev. Henry S. Riddell, author of the "Songs of the Ark." This precocious and lamented young man was born at Flex, near Hawick, in 1835, and was chiefly educated at John Watson's Hospital, Edinburgh. This promising youth was there apparently during the whole of the allotted period, from seven to fourteen years of age, and on leaving entered, as a bursar, the College of Edinburgh. His studies at the University were more than diligently pursued, for after a time his health became impaired by too great application, and he was forced to relinquish them altogether, and return to his father at Teviothead, where, after trials borne without a murmur, he died in 1856, aged twenty, thus closely resembling the gifted and unfortunate Henry Kirke White, who also died an untimely victim to excessive study. The precociousness of young Riddell was somewhat remarkable, for at a very early age his compositions in prose and verse were far beyond his years. He was not only a good classical scholar, but well up in history and philosophy. And with all these high attainments he possessed still higher, being well acquainted with the Holy Scriptures, which are able to make us wise unto salvation. He could read the sacred volume in the original, and he found unspeakable comfort from its study, dying in the faith which it reveals, and in the hope of a joyful resurrection which it inspires.

The following verses were composed by this amiable youth at the age of thirteen, and called the "Lament of Wallace":—

> "No more by thy margin, dark Carron,
> Shall Wallace in solitude wander,
> When tranquil the moon shines afar on
> Thy heart-stirring wildness and grandeur.
> For lost are to me
> Thy beauties for ever,
> Since fallen in thee
> Lie the faithful and free,
> To awaken, ah! never!
>
> "And I, thus defeated, must suffer
> My country's reproach, yet, forsaken,
> A home to me nature may offer
> Among green forests of braken.
> But home who can find
> For heart-rending sorrow?
> The wound who can bind,
> When thus pierced is the mind
> By fate's ruthless arrow?
>
> "'Tis death that alone ever frees us
> Of woes too profound to be spoken,
> And nought but the grave ever eases
> The pangs of a heart that is broken.
> Then oh! that my blood
> In Carron's dark water
> Had mix'd with the flood
> Of the warriors shed
> 'Mid torrents of slaughter.
>
> "For woe to the day when desponding,
> I read in thine aspect the story
> Of those that were slain when defending
> Their homes and their mountains of glory.

> And curst be the guile
> Of treacherous knavery,
> That throws o'er the isle
> In its tyranny vile
> The mantle of slavery."

ROBERT BOWER, son of Sir Walter's friend, "Johnie Bower," custodier of Melrose Abbey, deserves notice as an author of ballads and lyrics, from which I extract the following on "Liberty":—

> " Liberty ! how dismal, melancholy, dark
> Were we among the wretched but for thee—
> Without one cheering ray—one glimm'ring spark
> Of solace, heaven, hope, divinity.
>
> "O Slavery ! what a loathsome thing art thou :
> Thy abject nature stamped upon thy brow ;
> All the sad ills humanity can know
> Walk in thy wretched train a ghastly show.
>
> " Liberty ! thy votaries ever eminent
> For virtues free-born to the world were sent.
> Slavery ! thy victims, with a sullen glare,
> Crouch, striken and supine, near misery and despair."

Robert Bower was educated for the law, and at his death was procurator-fiscal for the district of Melrose.

JAMES TELFER, among the Border poets, was not the least remarkable. Indeed Telfer's death breaks a link that bound us to the older and greater ballad writers of the Border ; and over and above his talents for poetry, which were respectable, he was, as Rogers says, an ingenious prose writer. He was a native of Southdean, and for long was master of a school at Saughtree, in Liddesdale, where he died on the 18th January 1862, of paralysis, having barely reached the climacteric period of man's life. Though he never emerged from humble life, in which he was born, or courted popularity, he had a considerable circle of literary friends on both sides of the Border by whom he was greatly appreciated. Laidlaw and the Ettrick Shepherd were also friends of Telfer's, and he had a passionate love for Hogg's muse. Telfer was a frequent contributor to periodicals, and was a good letter-writer, his correspondence being both clever and entertaining. His Border ballads and other pieces were published at Jedburgh in 1824, and dedicated to his friend the Ettrick Shepherd in the following lines :—

> " O Cheviot's fell is rudely wild and blue,
> No warbling chorister, nor blooming spray;
> The sun in silence drinks the purple dew,
> Without a strain to hail him on his way.
>
> " Oh, favourite bard, accept my wilding lay,
> The first rude efforts of my minstrelsy;
> And, if my simple toil thou wilt repay
> With kind perusal, it is all to me,
> The only boon I ask, oh tuneful swain, of thee."

Another volume of "Tales and Sketches" was published by Mr Telfer about 1855.

There are two classes of notables deserving of notice— "Gypsies," and "Fools" or "Innocents." The Gypsies predominate at Yetholm—

> " On Yeta's banks the vagrant Gypsies place
> Their turf-built cot—a sun-burnt swarthy race;
> From Nubia's realms their tawny line they bring,
> And their brown chieftain vaunts the name of king."

Leyden in these lines intimates that Africa was their cradle, but it is supposed by others that they are descendants of Hindoos, and were expelled from India by Timour, about 1400 A.D. No doubt they came from Egypt latterly, passing from thence to Europe, where they arrived in the fifteenth century, giving out that they were Christian pilgrims, and had been banished from that country by the Saracens for their adherence to the true religion. They soon came on to England, where an act was passed against their itinerancy, and they were not long in finding their way to Yetholm. When they first came to Scotland, which they did early in the sixteenth century, they enjoyed a good deal of liberty. Sir Walter

Scott says they were acknowledged as a separate and independent race by James V., but that afterwards they were less favourably distinguished. Indeed, for long they have been looked upon as vagrants and thieves, though professedly engaged in some kinds of handicraft, and in the sale of coarse earthenware. However, they possess some accomplishments, for they are fond of music and out-of-door sports; and they delight in fortune-telling, though the wildness of their original character continues, and, like the Jews, in manners, habits, and physiognomy, they are unchanged. How long they will continue a separate people God only knows, but it is hoped the Bible, which I am glad to find has been translated into the Gypsy dialect, may both humanise and Christianise them. With these prefatory remarks I proceed to notice

JEAN GORDON, that singular heroine upon whom was founded the character of Meg Merilees, born at Yetholm about 1670, and who married Patrick Faa, a well-known Gipsy chief. Jean had a large family. Her eldest son was murdered, and the extraordinary pains she took, and the fatigue she endured in tracking the murderer—which she did like a bloodhound—sound like a romance, though by capturing the murderer she was repaid, for he was sentenced to be hanged at Jedburgh in 1727, which, however, his escape from prison prevented. The other sons must have perpetrated some foul deed, for it is related that they were all condemned to die at Jedburgh the same day, which Jean had the misery of hearing, for she lived for some time after, and she herself afterwards met an untimely death, having been murdered by being drowned in the Eden, some little time after the rebellion 1745, when between seventy and eighty. Whether any of Jean's descendants are now alive I don't know, but about the end of last century one survived, who was the chief, and a chief in wickedness, I presume, for he was called " the Earl of Hell." He was tried for a robbery at Dalkeith, but owing to a failure of proof was not convicted, though the judge, in dismissing him, said "that he had rubbit shouthers wi' the gallows that morning." Whether Esther Faa Blythe, who was some years since elected queen, is a descendant of Jean Gordon, *alias* Meg Merilees, I have not been able to ascertain. There are Gypsies in other counties, and Galloway, it is well known, was their stronghold in the west, where occurred the celebrated intrigue of Johnie Faa, in the seventeenth century, with Jane Hamilton, sixth Countess of Cassillis. It has been alleged that she married the earl called "the Grave and Solemn Earl," contrary to her inclinations, having previously become enamoured of Sir John Faa of Dunbar, called Johnie Faa, who was not only handsome but gay and cheerful. It has been further alleged that when Lord Cassillis was absent on a mission from the Scottish to the English Parliament, or as a member of the Westminster Assembly, Faa and his attendants carried on their intrigue, which ended in the Countess eloping with Faa, who of course used the charms, philters, and glamours of his wicked race to accomplish his purpose. Happily, however, the return of the earl enabled him to catch the fugitives before they crossed the Border, and on the return of the Countess, scatheless, from her perilous flight, she lived in retirement—indeed in confinement—at Maybole, during which she worked a piece of tapestry which is still preserved at Colzean. By the Earl of Cassillis, ere the elopement, she had two daughters—one married to Bishop Burnet, the well-known historian, and the other to Lord Cochrane, and one son who died unmarried.

But to return to the Gypsey enchantments, of which song was one. I shall give a few verses of the ballad which was used as one of the charms on the occasion of the intrigue:—

> " The Gypsies they came to my Lord Cassillis' yett,
>   And oh, but they sang bonnie ;
> They sang sae sweet, and sae complete,
>   That down came our fair ladie.
>
> " She came tripping down the stairs,
>   And all her maids before her ;
> As soon as they saw her weel faur'd face,
>   They coost their glamourie owre her.

> " She gave to them the good wheaten bread
> And they gave her the ginger ;
> But she gave them a far better thing—
> The gold ring off her finger."

I have only further to say that fifteen Gypsies formed the band of abductors, if I may coin such a word, and that they all lost their lives for their wicked conduct, as the following verse states :—

> " They were fifteen valiant men,
> Black, but very bonny ;
> And they lost all their lives for one—
> The Earl of Cassillis' ladie."

I come now to the "Fools," or "Innocents," or "Jesters." A jester or merry-andrew may not like to be classed with "Fools" or "Gowks," but I don't think there is much difference between them. Well, a "jester has been described as a witty and jocose person kept by princes to inform them of their faults and those of other men, under the disguise of a waggish story." About the courts of the ancient kings, especially of the Tudor line, jesters were kept ; and the two first of the Stuart kings, James I. and Charles I., had jesters or merry-andrews, the latter name being applied to a buffoon after a physician of some fame in the sixteenth century, whose real name was "Andrew Borde," a man of intense humour, and author of many quaint works. There were no licensed jesters about the court after Charles I.'s reign ; but in our own country the custom of keeping fools about noblemen's establishments was not given up till late in the last century ; and Sir Walter Scott tells us that at Glammis Castle is preserved the dress of a jester, very handsome, and ornamented with many bells ; and he moreover adds that it is not above thirty years since such a character stood by the sideboard of a nobleman of the first rank in Scotland, and occasionally mixed in the conversation, till he carried the joke rather too far, in making proposals to one of the young ladies of the family, and publishing the banns betwixt her and himself in the public church. The gowk I have now to bring to your notice is

ANDREW GEMMELL. I need not attempt to describe this character, so graphically drawn in his representative David Gellatley, of the admirable Romance "Waverley." Andrew cannot be recollected by many of us, for he died in 1806, and his remains lie in Roxburgh churchyard, where a stone is erected by Mr Thomson commemorative of Andrew—his poke and his dog. Though no doubt a half-crazed simpleton, he had sharpness enough to keep on the windy side of insanity; and withal he had warm affections, an almost superhuman memory, and a good musical ear, though perhaps not so good as Jock Gray, the gowk of Selkirkshire, upon whom I must not enlarge here, though well known in, and a frequent visitor of, our county.

EMINENT SELKIRKSHIRE MEN.

I PROPOSE to bring before you the noted characters of Selkirkshire who have flourished from about the beginning of the sixteenth century, and who have also passed away.

The period I start with brings forcibly before me the fatal battle of Flodden, fought in the early part of the sixteenth century, in which the men of Selkirk took so brave a part, and I cannot do better than begin with the

WARRIORS of the Forest. Flodden was a battle provoked by the Scotch monarch, James IV., by his having taken part with Louis XII. of France, against his uncle Henry VIII. of England. The result was truly disastrous to Scotland, for James himself, with many of his nobles, and upwards of ten thousand of his army, were slain, while the English forces, commanded by the Earl of Surrey, lost a comparatively small number. Though the contest terminated in defeat, it was unsullied by disgrace, and however serious the result was to our native country, it was no fault of the brave men of Selkirk. Of one hundred denizens of the Forest who accompanied James under the command of William Brydon, town-clerk of Selkirk, not more than a twentieth part returned, but that little band of which the renowned town-clerk and captain was one, brought with them in proof of their valour a standard taken from the English by one of the weavers, which is still in existence, though at least three hundred and eighty-four years old, and which used to be carried in the processions of the corporation among the insignia of the town.* As the brogue,

* The descendants of Brydon are also in possession of the basket-hilted sword he used at Flodden.

or single sole shoe trade was then in activity, it is probable that some members of that as well as the weaving craft, took a distinguished part in the fearful conflict. As a further proof of the importance and ability of the souters, it is authentically recorded that, when the highland army in 1745 commanded the magistrates of Edinburgh to supply six thousand pairs of shoes, Selkirk was called upon to furnish no less than one-third of the number. This was done with alacrity; but the trade is now nearly extinct. The souters, notwithstanding Dr Johnson's contemptuous observations, are a very ancient craft, for in 1426 the Abbot and Convent of Melrose let to John Brydinson and Thomas Robynson, shoemakers, or the longest liver of them, a certain tenement of theirs lying on the north side of the town of Selkirk, and within the same town, and a croft of three acres pertaining to the foresaid tenement, with liberty of folding and pasture, and all pertinents.

It is considered doubtful whether the celebrated song "The Souters of Selkirk" had reference to the battle of Flodden, or to a football match between the souters and the men of Hume, which I suppose means the Merse of Berwickshire, the county of the Humes. We subjoin the lyric :—

> " Up wi' the souters of Selkirk,
>   And down wi' the Earl of Hume ;
>   And up wi' a' the braw lads,
>   That sew the single soled shoon.
>
> " Fye upon yellow and yellow,
>   And fye upon yellow and green,
>   But up with the true blue and scarlet,
>   And up wi' the single soled shoon.
>
> " Up wi' the souters of Selkirk,
>   For they are baith trusty and leal ;
>   And up wi' the men of the Forest,
>   And down wi' the Merse to the deil."

One reason alleged against the song being applicable to Flodden is, that there was then no " Earl " Hume, the earldom not having been created till 1604, nearly a hundred years afterwards. There was a barony of Hume (created 2d August 1473), long before the battle of Flodden, and at that frightful conflict, where according to the old poem :—

> "The English line stretched east and west,
> And southward were their forces set;
> The Scottish northward proudly prest,
> And manfully their foes they met."

Alexander, Lord Hume, took a most distinguished part, though taxed with being the cause of the defeat, as well as of the death of the king.

Though the gallant bearing of the souters on the field of battle awoke the implacable resentment of the enemy, who soon reduced their town to ashes, it kindled in the breast of James V. of Scotland warm feelings towards Selkirk, and he granted to the town an extensive portion of forest and other privileges, besides knighting the town-clerk, though the charter conferring the honour of knighthood upon that official for the bravery of William Brydon, and the valour of his fellow-townsmen seems to have been lost. King James also granted arms to the burgh, viz., a woman in a forest lying dead at the root of a tree, with a living child at her breast, the wife of one of the burghers whose husband was at Flodden, having wandered out in hopes of meeting him, and having died in the position represented.*

* It seems to be uncertain whether William Brydon was knighted before the battle as a proof that King James appreciated the spirit and bearing of the Foresters when mustered for the expedition, or after the battle, in which case the honour must have been conferred by James V., and not by James IV., who had fallen in the fight. Certain it is that most of the privileges were conferred on the town by James V. The burgh is understood to be of ancient foundation, but the oldest charter preserved is one granted by King James V., dated March 4th, 1535. It proceeds on a narrative that the charters of the ancient foundation of the burgh, and liberties thereof granted to the burgesses and community by his majesty's progenitors had perished; as they may have done when the town was burned by the English after the battle of Flodden, and so the king grants anew the privileges of an annual fair, with a court, gallows, and other liberties, and to hold burghal courts, and full privileges of trade, as any other burgh in the kingdom, all to be held in free burgage, for payment to his majesty of the burghal firms and

The Selkirk archers played a prominent part also in the battle fought by Wallace against Edward I. of England at Falkirk, some two hundred years previous to the battle of Flodden; but there, also, the result was disastrous, though the men of the Forest fought courageously, many falling round their brave leader, Stewart of Bonkhill, as thus described by a modern poetess :—

> " The glance of the moon had sparkled bright,
> On their plumage green and their actions light;
> The bugle was strung at his hunter's side,
> As they had been bound to the chase to ride;
> But the bugle is mute, and the shafts are spent,
> The arm unnerv'd and the bow unbent,
> And the tired Forester is laid
> Far, far, from the clustering green shade.

other duties used and wont. At the same date a precept under the great seal was granted, upon which sasine followed, and the instrument dated 22d March, infefts the burgh *inter alia*, in the south and north commons of the burgh. The Flodden flag is now in possession of Mr James Brown, manufacturer. It had been reduced to mere shreds, and has been repaired by pasting these on to a cotton cloth, which gives cohesion to the fragments. As seen upwards of forty years since it is described as " of green silk fringed round with pale silk twist, about four feet long, and tapering towards the extremity most remote from the staff. Some armorial bearings, such as an eagle and a serpent, were once visible upon it, but scarcely a lineament can be discerned amidst the tatters to which it is now reduced." At this day there are no armorial bearings visible, but there is the appearance of two shuttles passing each other, which must have been made at some later date than the battle of Flodden. The story is that the flag was brought home by one of five brothers named Fletcher. The king had summoned all the male inhabitants of mature age to join his army, excepting the eldest of each family, who was to remain and guard the women and children. Of the Fletcher family the youngest feared to go, and his elder brother went instead. He was the only one of the family who returned, and he carried with him the pennon of some English leader, which he gave to the incorporation of weavers to which he belonged. For ages it was kept by the deacon of the weavers, and was produced only on great occasions, such as riding the marches. So faded and insignificant did it appear, that the boys in derision called it "the weavers' dishclout."

Among the few who returned from Flodden was William Brydon, the town-clerk, whose sword is still carefully preserved by his descendants. It is a light basket-hilted blade, and near the hilt, on one side, is engraved the word "Andrea," and on the other " Ferrara."

> Sore have they toiled—they are fallen asleep,
> And their slumber is heavy, and dull, and deep ;
> While over their bones the green grass shall wave,
> When the wild winds over their tombs shall rave,
> Memory shall lean on their graves, and tell
> How Selkirk's archers bold around old Stewart fell."

I now proceed with the individual heroes of the Forest, whom I shall take up as near as I can in the order of time in which they flourished, keeping the military and naval officers separate. I begin with the former ; and the first is

COLONEL WILLIAM RUSSELL, son of James Russell of Ashiesteel, and his wife, Jane Boston, the favourite daughter of that devoted soldier of the Cross, the Rev. Thomas Boston of Ettrick. This distinguished man entered the British army as an ensign in the 8th Foot, and had the honour of serving under the illustrious Wolfe :

> "Brave Wolfe, a chief invincible in war,
> Britannia's darling son."

After very important services rendered by Colonel Russell, the peace of 1763 arrived, and, fearful of being thrown out of employment by the probable reduction of the 79th Regiment, which he had joined, he determined on entering the service of the Honourable East India Company. This opened up to Colonel Russell, as it has done to many subsequent heroes, a vast field of glory, and the gallant Forester ably conducted himself, assisting in memorable battles, which were fought and won under the leadership of those Indian warriors, Clive, Sir Eyre Coote, and Laurence.

Colonel Russell retired from active service in 1790, and settled at his paternal estate of Ashiesteel, where he died in 1804, having married in 1779, Jane Rutherfurd, daughter of Dr John Rutherfurd, and aunt of Sir Walter Scott, by whom he had several sons, his eldest son and successor being the lately deceased Sir James Russell, also a distinguished officer of the same Honourable Service, to whom I shall now refer.

GENERAL SIR JAMES RUSSELL, born 1781, succeeded his

father, Colonel William Russell, in the estate of Ashiesteel in 1804, being at that time in India, whither he had proceeded nine years previously. Sir James Russell, who was an officer of the Madras Cavalry, saw a great deal of service. He was at the taking of Seringapatam, which was stormed and carried by General Baird in 1799, under the commandership-in-chief of General, afterwards Lord Harris, when Tippoo Saib and the greater part of his garrison, amounting to 8000 men, were killed. General Russell commanded a brigade in the Deccan, during the Pindaree war, when Holkar was defeated by Sir Thomas Hislop, then commander-in-chief of the Madras Presidency. For his distinguished services, Sir James Russell was created a Knight Commander of the Bath; and he had attained the rank of full General some years before his death.

I come now to the family of Napier, whose connection with Selkirkshire arose from the marriage in 1699 of Elizabeth, the Mistress of Napier, with William Scott, son of, and successor to, Sir Francis Scott of Thirlestane. By him, she had an only son, Francis Scott, who inherited the Barony of Napier, on the death of his grandmother, Margaret, Baroness Napier, in 1706, his mother having died the preceding year. He assumed the surname of Napier. He also succeeded, on the death of his father, Sir William Scott, in 1725, to the Baronetcy of Scott, and also to the estate of Thirlestane—a property acquired by David Scott of Howpasley, his grandfather, from the Abbacy of Melrose. Francis Scott or Napier became fifth Baron Napier, and marrying twice, had ten sons, some of whose descendants became celebrated, and will be afterwards noticed.

THE NAPIER FAMILY.

The Napiers were originally settled in Dumbartonshire, but after the lapse of a few generations, they came to Edinburgh, when Alexander Napier figured as Provost of that city in

1437. This Alexander acquired, early in the fifteenth century, the lands of Merchiston, which gave the title to the family. His grandson, John, was Provost of Edinburgh in 1484, and passing over the next three generations, we come to

JOHN NAPIER of Merchiston, the inventor of Logarithms.* He published his great work on Logarithms, styled " Mirifici Logarithmorum Canonis Descriptio," in 1614, when he was upwards of sixty years of age. The publication of this most useful invention gave unbounded joy to the savants of the age, and to none more than Dr Briggs, the Oxford Professor of Geometry, who was greatly enraptured with the discovery. He came to Scotland twice to see and confer with Napier on the subject of his invention, and in a few years afterwards, published, with the aid of that profound mathematician and divine, " William Oughtred," (who died of joy at hearing of the restoration of Charles II.), a work rendering Napier's system more compendious, and the great astronomer, Halley, who was also Professor of Geometry at Oxford, afterwards contributed further improvements, facilitating its operation. Napier only lived about three years after the publication of his invention, but his last work, called " Rhabdologice," † familiarly known as " Napier's Bones," was not issued till after his death, which took place at Merchiston in 1617. He was an elder in the West Church, and was buried in the north-east corner of the porch or entrance hall, west side; and the Royal Society not long ago erected a monument to him, bearing an inscription in Latin, which may be Englished thus:— " Nearly on this spot was laid the body of John Napier of Merchiston, who earned the everlasting remembrance of future time by his wonderful invention of Logarithms. He died 8th of April 1617, aged sixty-seven. In honour of so great a man, this tablet was erected 1847."

* Born at Merchiston in the year 1550.
† Describing the mode of performing the operation of multiplication and division by means of a number of small rods.

Before Napier's famous work on Logarithms appeared, he had employed himself in matters connected with the sciences, and propounded theories which were at times akin to divination. He had also shown himself alive to religious questions, and in 1593 published a book called "A Plaine Discovery of the whole Revelation of St. John," set down in two treatises; the one searching and proving the true interpretation thereof; the other applying the same paraphrastically and historically to the text. There is a dedicatory epistle to King James VI., dated in 1593, by John Napier, Peer of Merchistoun. This work was extremely popular, and was translated into several European languages. Unfortunately for Napier's character as a prophet, he affirmed that the day of judgment was to happen at a given time, which has long since gone by; another proof how dangerous it is for even the highest human intellect to meddle with prophetic interpretation.

The adoption by Napier of the designation of "Peer" or "Baro Merchistonie," led some to think that he was ennobled, but his son was the first of the family ennobled by rank, though the inventor of logarithms was ennobled by fame. It was a common thing in olden times for extensive proprietors to be denominated barons or feudal lords. There were "Barones Majores," and "Barones Minores," the former being summoned to Parliament by the King and the latter by the Sheriffs, and I presume the Peer of Merchiston was one of these barons, though from his profound intellect and mighty invention he was well worthy of the highest honours.

This celebrated man, who was married twice, had a numerous family, and his son, Archibald, who succeeded him, reaped the benefit of having had such a father, for he was created first a Baronet and then a hereditary Peer.

He was a great loyalist, as was his son, Archibald, the second baron, and both suffered great hardships from the Covenanters.

The first baron, having been a Lord of Session, will be noticed under the legal celebrities.

His half-brother, the third son of the great Philosopher, chiefly inherited his father's mathematical talents, and published his posthumous works, among which were three Latin treatises relating to logarithms and spherical trigonometry.

The third baron, and third Archibald in succession, succeeded his father, who died in 1660, in Holland, whither he had retired. Being a bachelor, and the peerage being to male heirs only, he resigned the honours and got, in 1677, a new patent from Charles II., with whom he was a favourite, extending the remaindership to heirs female or general, on condition of the name and arms of Napier being assumed. This (the third) peer died in 1683, and was succeeded in the barony by his elder sister's son, Sir Thomas Nicholson, who became fourth Lord Napier, while the baronetcy passed to Robert Napier of Culreugh, whose descendant, the present Sir William Milliken Napier, is the male representative of the inventor of logarithms.

The fourth baron, Sir Thomas Nicholson, died young and unmarried in 1686, and at his death there appears to have been a lawsuit as to the Nicholson estates, and a dispute took place amongst his heirs as to who should deposit his head in the grave. His uncle, Lord Linlithgow, was selected to carry and deposit his head, which, Fountainhall says, was adjudged to a male. The honours, however, went to his aunt, Margaret, second sister of the third baron, who had married John Brisbane, British resident at the Court of France; and his daughter, Elizabeth, married to Sir William Scott of Thirlstane, Selkirkshire, became Mistress of Napier, or next heir. Having died before her mother, she did not inherit the title, but her son, Francis Scott, succeeded to his grandmother in 1706, when an infant, and became the fifth Baron Napier. He enjoyed the honours for the long period of sixty-seven years or thereabouts, but his son, William, the sixth baron, did not enjoy them two years; while on the other hand his son and successor, Francis, seventh lord, held the title nearly fifty years. This peer entered the army at an early age, and served under General Burgoyne during the American War of Independence, and was with that General when he capitulated at Saratoga in 1777. Lord Napier, after a slight detention as a prisoner of war, came home, but continued in the Army till the year 1789, when his Lordship sold out, having obtained the rank of Field officer. After quitting the Army he devoted his time to important duties in his native country,* and he became respectively Lieut.-Colonel of the Hopetoun Fencibles, a Representative Peer of Scotland, Lord Lieutenant of Selkirkshire, and Lord High Commissioner to the General Assembly of the Church of Scotland, which latter office he held for about twenty years.†

Though not distinguished as a statesman, Lord Napier was a warm supporter of his own order, and was a man of the highest integrity. In person he was about the middle size, and was well-proportioned. He was noted for an eagle eye and prominent nose. He had great taste in dress, which, at the period of his manhood, was rather gaudy; the garments of a gentleman often consisting of a crimson or purple coat, green plush waistcoat, black small clothes, and white stockings.

Lord Napier died in 1823, and was succeeded by William John, the eighth baron, who died in the prime of life, after an incumbency of barely eleven years. He was a spirited agriculturist, and was especially celebrated in store farming, on which subject he published a book in 1822, which does him credit.‡

* He laid the foundation-stone of Edinburgh College, as Grand Master Mason of Scotland.

† He was first nominated as Lord High Commissioner in 1802. In 1805 he became President of the Society for propagating Christian knowledge; and in 1806 he was appointed a member of the Board of Trustees for the encouragement of Scotch fisheries and manufactories.

‡ The book is entitled "A Treatise on Practical Store-Farming, as applicable to the mountainous region of Ettrick Forest, and the Pastoral Districts of Scotland in General. By the Honourable William John Napier, F.R.S. Edin., Post-Captain in the Royal Navy, etc. etc., Edinburgh, Printed for Waugh & Innes, 1822." And it is dedicated to the Pastoral Society of Sel-

Subsequently, in 1834, when the exclusive privileges of the East India Company in China ceased, Lord Napier was appointed Chief Superintendent of British Commerce there, but he died shortly after reaching the country, falling a sacrifice to the arduous duties of his office, aggravated by the harsh treatment he experienced from the Chinese.

I now turn to the descendants of Francis Scott, fifth Baron Napier, who had ten sons, some of whom had large families, several members whereof being grandsons of that peer and third cousins of the present, distinguished themselves most highly. The first I have to notice is

Sir CHARLES JAMES NAPIER.* This distinguished soldier's career was one blaze of military glory. He commenced his soldier life at the time of the Irish Rebellion in 1798, and his services were brought into play during the Peninsular War, when he showed the stuff he was made of. The deeds of daring he performed there will not easily be forgotten. In the performance of those valorous deeds he was dreadfully cut up, and nearly lost his life while suffering from his wounds, which almost completely disabled him, and threw him into the hands of the French. He would have been severely handled, had it not been for the intervention of a drummer, at whose instance he was placed in safety, as a prisoner of war. Marshal Soult, however, treated him kindly, and allowed him to visit England, as soon as his wounds were sufficiently cured. On his arrival in this country he found his friends clad in mourning for him, believing him to be dead, and actually engaged in taking out letters of administration to his estate.

When sufficiently recovered, our hero returned to his duty in the Peninsula, acquiring further glory, but sustaining

kirkshire, of which he was a Vice-President. It contains much curious information about the prices and management of sheep, and about mountain storms, his chief informant regarding which was an intelligent shepherd, William Laidlaw of Bowerhope.

* He was a son of Colonel George Napier by Lady Sarah Lennox, and was born at Whitehall, London, on the 10th of August 1782.

another wound which might have cost him his life, for a bullet lodged behind his ear, and before he could get it extracted he had to proceed to Lisbon, a distance of one hundred miles. After participating in other Peninsular exploits and glories, and not being appointed to take any part at Waterloo, we next find him in the Mediterranean, on Staff and Government employ, on the termination of which he returned to England, where he obtained the command of the troops in the Northern District. But such a sphere was of too limited a character for Sir Charles, and soon afterwards he was despatched to India, where he added fresh lustre to his military fame. He was the conqueror of Scinde, where he broke the power of the Ameers. In this campaign his bravery and generalship called forth the praise of the illustrious Duke of Wellington. After acquiring Scinde he was appointed governor of the province, and his administration was so satisfactory and successful as to elicit the commendation of a great Indian authority, Lord Ellenborough, who said—"There never has been, is, or will be, any name so great as Sir Charles Napier's in Scinde, because no name but his is associated with justice, and justice to all in the exercise of it."

Well did this distinguished man deserve a monument in the Metropolitan Cathedral of Great Britain, which, as also a statue in Trafalgar Square, Charing Cross, was erected after his decease. He died on the 29th of August 1853, at the age of seventy-one.

GENERAL SIR GEORGE THOMAS NAPIER, brother of the hero of Scinde, entered the army in 1800, when he joined the expedition to Sweden. Thence he went to the Peninsula, where he was present at many of the battles, serving as aide-de-camp to the illustrious Sir John Moore at Corunna, under the walls of which his chief was killed. Sir George was wounded on several occasions, and lost his right arm when leading the storming-party at Ciudad Rodrigo. For his distinguished military services he received a gold medal for Rodrigo, and the silver war-medal with three clasps. In after-life he was for some time Governor and Commander-in-Chief at the Cape of Good Hope.

GENERAL SIR WILLIAM FRANCIS PATRICK NAPIER, also a brother of the Conqueror of Scinde, entered the army in 1800, and soon saw important service. He assisted at the siege of Copenhagen under Lord Cathcart, in 1807, and he fought at the battle of Kioge; also in Denmark, the same year when the Danes were defeated and their town taken. General Napier is next found in the Peninsula, and was present at Corunna, under Sir John Moore. He was likewise in several other Peninsular battles, including Salamanca, Nivelle, and Nice, and received a gold medal and two clasps, also the silver war-medal and three clasps; and he was wounded on several occasions. Later in life he was for some time Governor of Guernsey. Besides having a long distinguished professional career to boast of, there are few sons of Mars that have enjoyed such a high reputation as a writer. His works are not only numerous but important, his "chef d'œuvre" being the history of the Peninsular War from 1807 to 1814. This admirable book, consisting of six volumes, is a standard work, and it is a most valuable record of the scenes it depicts. It goes 'home to the soldier's heart, and often were its tales recounted in the trenches at Sebastopol, the effect ever being to "warm the heart, fire the mind, and nerve the arm." Sir William dedicated his history to the Duke of Wellington, in the following brief but spirited terms :—" This history I dedicate to your Grace, because I have served long enough under your command to feel why the soldiers of the 10th Legion were attached to Cæsar."

The 10th Legion included the bravest troops in Cæsar's army, and they were attached to him because he had led them to victory in so many battles.

NAVAL HEROES.

I now come to the Naval Heroes connected with Selkirkshire :—

JOHN BOSTON, son of the Rev. Thomas Boston of Ettrick, entered either the naval or marine service, and attained a high rank. It is understood he settled abroad.

SIR GEORGE SCOTT, second son of John Scott of Gala, was born in 1770. The services of Sir George extend over a very long period. He entered the navy in 1780, at the age of twelve, and attained the rank of Rear-Admiral in 1825. He had previously been made a C.B., and Colonel of Marines, and finally got a K.C.B.-ship in 1831. When a lieutenant, Scott took a part in Lord Howe's actions of 1794, which were so important and successful as to receive the approbation and thanks of Parliament. The ship in which he held a commission—the "Bellerophon"—was particularly conspicuous in the actions.

Captain Scott having been appointed to the command of the "Albatross," received the thanks of the Marine Society of London for his efforts to counteract the mutiny at the Nore in 1797, and after other successes and commands, he is found, in 1807, in full command of the "Horatio," 38-gun frigate, in which he engaged a French frigate of the largest class, and obliged her to surrender. His engagement with the Frenchman was of the severest kind, and much skill and bravery was shown on both sides, but Captain Scott was victor, though at a heavy cost, for he had seven men killed and twenty-six wounded, including himself. In the French frigate, 136 were killed and wounded, including, among the latter, her commander, who afterwards died. Captain Scott, for his very gallant conduct, received high encomiums, and a pension, which was well-earned, for his wound disabled him from holding subsequent commands. Admiral Scott died on the 21st December 1841.

SIR CHARLES NAPIER of Merchiston, Hampshire, was

grandson of Francis Scott, fifth Baron Napier. Sir Charles was born in 1786, and must have joined the navy when very young, for he was not twenty when he received his lieutenancy.* He saw a great deal of service, and was the deserved recipient of many honours, British and Foreign. His last command in the Baltic did not add to his fame, for after promising much, he performed little; but he may have been fettered by Admiralty instructions, and for any great good that was done, beyond the blockade, the fleet might as well have remained at Spithead. Nor did he add to his fame by his various conflicts with the Government, or by his Parliamentary tactics; but his professional career was, in the main, characterised by unrivalled valour and irresistible decision of character. Sir Charles Napier had attained the rank of Vice-Admiral, when he died on the 6th November 1860.

JAMES PRINGLE of Torwoodlee, joined the navy at an early age, and obtained his lieutenancy in 1804, getting the two higher steps quickly, and finally his flag rank on 1st October 1846. Admiral Pringle, though not lucky enough to have been at any of the great naval battles, did good service in his profession, and was several times noticed in the public Gazette—his good conduct having elicited the praise of the authorities.

WILLIAM JOHN LORD NAPIER entered the navy when young, serving part of his time as midshipman with Lord Cochrane, in the "Imperieuse," and commanding one of her boats at the attack on Arcasson in 1807. After getting his lieutenancy, he served, for a time, with Admiral Pringle of Torwoodlee, then Captain of the "Sparrowhawk," on the Mediterranean station. On getting his commandership, he was appointed to the "Goshawk," in which he was wrecked. He was not long in being again employed, for he is found in the following year in command of the "Erne," of twenty guns; and almost immediately after, he obtained his post commis-

* He was born at Falkirk, was educated at the High School of Edinburgh, and at the age of thirteen joined the "Martin" sloop of war, as a first-class volunteer, and went to the North Sea.

sion, on getting which he was unemployed for some years, and it was then no doubt that he devoted himself to agricultural pursuits.

DIVINES.

JOHN WELCH was minister of Selkirk some time before the close of the sixteenth century—say about 1590. He was the son of a landed proprietor in Dumfriesshire of some note and standing in the county. When a youth, Welch deserted his father's roof, and joined a party of freebooters, with whom he continued for some time, till his conscience smote him, on account of the profligate life he was leading, when he determined to amend his ways and return home. . How to face his distressed and afflicted father was his great difficulty, when Agnes Forsyth, of Dumfries, a relative of his father, prepared the way for the prodigal's return. This worthy woman received the heart-sick lad into her house, after he gave up his wretched life, and she took the first opportunity of breaking the subject to his afflicted parent, using the utmost tact, and not forgetting to remind him of the scriptural story of the Prodigal Son. So moved was the old man by the touching narrative, that he consented to see his son, who was accordingly ushered into his presence, and after suitable reproof from his father, and heartfelt sorrow being expressed by the son, a reconciliation took place. Young Welch, like the great apostle of the Gentiles, was determined, by an increase of diligence and zeal, to make up for mis-spent and lost time—his future conduct proving the honesty of his determination. His father, having yielded to his entreaties to be sent to College, in order to prepare for the holy ministry, had the high satisfaction of finding his indulgence well repaid, not only by the devoted diligence of the youth, but by his rapid proficiency in learning. Such was his amazing progress, that in a very short time young Welch was found to be duly qualified for the ministerial office, and he was licensed to preach the gospel, and ordained as minister of the parish of Selkirk, being then only in his twentieth year.

John Welch entered upon the duties of his sacred calling with a degree of zeal and devotion not to be surpassed. He performed divine service every day, and spent several hours besides in prayer.* Not content with his daily devotions, he snatched several hours from his nocturnal rest for the purpose of pouring forth his soul to God; and in the history of the Church it would be difficult to find one who took greater delight, or spent more time, in the discharge of his pastoral duties than Welch. But notwithstanding his unparalleled devotion in his Master's service, and his increasing watchfulness over the flock committed to his care, the discouragements he met with were so great that he left Selkirk; and such was the unaccountable apathy of the people that, when this man of God quitted the town, there was only one man, named Ewart, who offered to assist him in his removal.†

Mr Welch, after leaving Selkirk, was for a time at Kirkcudbright, but soon got a call to Ayr, whither he went in 1590, conceiving, as it was a place of considerable importance, it might be a greater field of usefulness for him; but he found it quite as difficult work breaking up the hard and stony ground of Kyle as he did that of the Forest. He pursued, however, the same arduous round of devotional exercises, and although at Ayr they were a very factious and quarrelsome people, he tried to produce among them harmony and good will, his endeavours being signally blessed. His career of usefulness was cut short by the attempt of King James, soon after ascending the English throne in 1603, to introduce a modified episcopacy, which, with the suppression of the Assemblies, so irritated Welch and others as to cause them to assume a hostile attitude, for which they were brought to

* He is said to have spent seven or eight hours out of the twenty-four of each day in prayer.

† The special cause of his removal was that Scott of Headshaw, having taken up some ill feeling, cut off, by himself or others, the rumps of two horses belonging to Mr Welch, after which he would not remain in the place.

trial and found guilty of treason. The sentence of death was recorded against them, but this was afterwards commuted to banishment. Mrs Welch, who was the daughter of John Knox, and inherited some of his fiery spirit, must have cheered and encouraged her husband under his misfortunes. It is reported that instead of lamenting his fate she praised God for giving him fortitude to uphold his Master's cause, and when driven to exile of course shared in his banishment.

France was selected as the place of expatriation, and thither Welch sailed from Leith, in November 1606, accompanied by his wife and associates in misfortune, for there were other five ministers condemned with him, viz., Mr Forbes, Mr Duncan, Mr Durie, Mr Sharp, and Mr Strachan.

On arriving in France Welch set about learning the French language most earnestly, and such was the facility with which he acquired it, he was soon able to preach. He was then called to the ministry of a Protestant congregation at Nerac (somewhere not very far from Bordeaux), and shortly afterwards to another congregation at St. Jean d'Angely, in Lower Charente, where he remained some years. While Welch was following his sacred calling at the latter place, war broke out between Louis treize and his Protestant subjects, and the town of St. Jean d'Angely was besieged by the king in person. On that occasion Welch not only entreated the inhabitants to make a bold stand, but actually ascended the ramparts and aided the artillerymen at the guns. But after a time a treaty was made, and the king being admitted he sent for Welch, who still continued to preach. At the time the king's messenger arrived in pursuit of the brave man and gallant soldier of the Cross, he was engaged with his pulpit ministrations. The messenger, who was the Duke d'Espernon, entered the church where Welch was preaching, and upon the minister recognising him, he bid his Grace sit down and hear the Word of God. The magic of Welch's voice was striking. The Marshal of France complied, and remained till divine service was over, expressing himself much gratified with what he had heard. On its conclusion Welch accompanied the duke to the presence of the king, who at first challenged him for preaching in France, it being contrary to law for a Reformer to preach there. "Sir," answered Welch, "if your majesty knew what I preached, you would not only come and hear it yourself, but make all France hear it. First, I preach that you must be saved by the merits of Jesus Christ, and not your own; and I am sure your conscience tells you that your own works will never merit heaven. Next, I preach that as you are king of France there is no man on earth above you; but those men whom you hear subject you to the Pope of Rome, which I will never do."

How bold, and yet how sagacious was Welch's rejoinder, and it so struck and delighted the king that his Majesty immediately exclaimed—" He bien ! vous serez mon ministre."

The king, therefore, not only considered him his spiritual father, but gave him ample proof of his friendship, for when St. Jean d'Angely was again besieged, he took every care of Welch and his family, by safely removing them to Rochelle.

After all Welch's trials and sufferings, it was no wonder that his health gave way. He was in 1622 seized with an illness the only human remedy for which seemed change of air and scene, and on the advice of his physicians he set out for Scotland, in order to try the effect of his native climate. His first destination was London, for he had there to apply for a passport before he could proceed on his journey north. But he did not find the King of England (though a Scotsman like himself) so friendly as Louis XIII., and unless he submitted to the Bishop, which a man like Welch was not likely to do, the king declined to give him permission to visit Scotland.*

---

* The following incident connected with the king's refusal is narrated by Dr M'Crie in his "Life of Knox":—Mrs Welch, by means of some of her mother's relations at court, obtained access to James VI., and petitioned him to grant this liberty to her husband. The following singular conversation took place on that occasion. His Majesty asked who was her father. She replied, "Mr Knox." "Knox and Welch," exclaimed he; "the devil never made such a match as that." "It's right true, Sir," said she, "for we never

His death occurred in May 1622, when he was in his fifty-second year.

> " Escap'd from persecution's cruel rod,
> The pious Welch in safety dwells with God ;
> No more in prayer he spends the lonely night,
> His voice is tun'd to praise in endless light.
>
> " As aged rock on stormy ocean's shore,
> Resists the beating wave's incessant roar ;
> So Welch's zeal, from what his heart approv'd,
> By frown or favour never could be mov'd."

THOMAS BOSTON comes next before us ; for though there were doubtless men between the two, such as CUNNINGHAM of Ettrick and RUTHERFORD of Yarrow, who may have lived respected and died lamented, they left no marks of distinction behind them that I can trace. I therefore proceed at once to take up the author of the "Fourfold State," who was minister of Ettrick, where he died, after an incumbency of about a quarter of a century, on the 20th May 1732. Thomas Boston was a man of the Merse, son of John Boston and Alison Trotter, having been born on the 17th March 1676, at Dunse.

He was first brought to a knowledge of the truth by the preaching of Henry Erskine of Cornhill, the father of Ralph

speir'd his advice." He asked how many children her father had left, and if they were lads or lasses. She said three, and they were all lasses. "God be thanked," said the king, lifting up both his hands, "for had they been three lads I had never bruiked my three kingdoms in peace." She again urged her request that he would give her husband his native air. "Give him his native air," replied the king ; "give him the devil !" a morsel which the king had often in his mouth. "Give that to your hungry courtiers," said she, offended at his profaneness. He told her at last that if she would persuade her husband to submit to the bishops he would allow him to return to Scotland. Mrs Welch, lifting up her apron, and holding it towards the king, replied in the true spirit of her father—" Please your Majesty, I'd rather kep his head there." He was debarred from preaching even in London till the king was assured that his end was near ; and then he was able to preach only once, for he expired within two hours of his leaving the church. In his last illness he was so filled and overcome with the sensible enjoyment of God that he was overheard to utter these words :—" O Lord, hold Thy hand, it is enough ; Thy servant is a clay vessel, and can hold no more."

and Ebenezer Erskine, and after studying for, and being called to, the ministry, was ordained to the parish of Simprin, afterwards united to Swinton, in his native county, some time about the close of the seventeenth century; and after a short ministry there, he was translated to Ettrick on the 1st May 1707, an important date, being the day the legislative union of England and Scotland, which he was rather opposed to, became law. Though Thomas Boston took the oath of allegiance to Queen Anne, he was nevertheless what may be termed a Presbyterian non-juror, for he declined to take the oath of abjuration, even after it was modified in 1719. There were a few others who, notwithstanding the modification of the oath, also persisted in finally rejecting it; and we know that in England, men of the same ardent piety and devotion to the glory of God, were also non-jurors, though on other grounds—for instance, Bishop Ken, the author of those beautiful morning and evening hymns, so dear to the people of England, and Isaac Watts, the author of the divine songs which, I may say, are dear to all Christian people, were both non-jurors.

Mr Boston's ministry, first at Simprin, and afterwards at Ettrick, was characterised by great zeal and faithfulness; and both by his writings and labours, he contributed much, as his monument at Ettrick states, to promote the advancement of vital Christianity.

Though his immediate predecessor, James Macmichan, translated to Hownam, was a painstaking and diligent pastor, as the records of the parish show, his removal from Ettrick, nearly four years before Boston was appointed, had deprived the people of a stated ministry, and no doubt scattered the flock; but he was not long in gathering a large congregation round him. I have seen it stated that on his first dispensing the Lord's Supper, there were only about sixty communicants, while at his last celebration of it there were upwards of seven hundred. One would suppose from this that the population in Boston's time was greater than it is now, but it ought to be taken into account that in former times sacramental services attracted great crowds. Some of us are old enough to remember those gatherings, even in later times, when tent-preaching was a concomitant of the services. But happily these occasions are less exciting now, though it may be a question whether they could not still be made even less so, and their frequency rather increased. For instance, the Fast days, too often made days of pleasure, might be done away with, and the sacrament administered four times at least in the year by the several ministers themselves, without calling in friends to assist. I have heard so much of the abuse of the Fast days, as they are called, since I came to reside permanently in Scotland, that I feel strongly on the point, and I fear, from what I can learn, they are too often, both in town and country, devoted to pleasure and dissipation. The Scotch get the credit of being not only a long-headed, but a well-educated and a religious people, but our consciences must tell many that, though we are a people of great religious professions, we are very far behind in genuine, practical, everyday religion—the religion of common life. Drinking, poaching, and impurity (this last vice makes us a bye-word among the nations) prevail to such a serious extent that if we do not take heed to our ways, our many mercies—and assuredly we have many—may be withdrawn.

Mr Boston wrote the "Fourfold State," and other books, one of the most popular being a small one called the "Crook in the Lot." But the book that brought him into the greatest prominence was the "Marrow of Modern Divinity," the twentieth edition of which he published in 1726, with copious notes. He had, however, long previously been acquainted with it, having first seen it at Simprin, in the house of a parishioner, whither it had been brought from England by a soldier during the Civil wars. It was a book written by Edward Fisher, a member of the University of Oxford, and the son of a man of rank, though to throw discredit upon it a report was circulated that it was the production of an illiterate barber. Mr Fisher was a man of good scholarship, and well acquainted with the Fathers—the earlier Christian writers of the second, third, and fourth centuries. He was also a man of great piety, as the work under review, with all its faults, undoubtedly testifies. It discusses both the Covenant of Works and of Grace, with their use and end, condemning the Legalists on the one hand, who assert the doctrine of human merit, and the Antinomians on the other, who deny human accountability, setting forth, as it states, " the middle path, which is Jesus Christ, received truly, and walked in answerably, as a means to bring them both unto him, and make them both one in him."

Another Scotch minister, who was a contemporary of Boston's, I mean Mr Hog, of Charnock, also greatly admired the book, and in 1717 published the tenth edition, with a recommendatory preface. This caused the General Assembly to criticise the work, which they censured, rebuking the adherents of it, consisting of twelve, who were familiarly called the Twelve Apostles, or Marrow Men, and of whom Mr Boston and Mr Henry Davidson, of Galashiels, belonged to Selkirkshire, though two other members of the Selkirk Presbytery, domiciled in Roxburghshire, were among the number, viz., Mr Hunter, of Lilliesleaf, and Mr Wilson, of Maxton. The Assembly finding there was a growing feeling in favour of the Marrow, thought it prudent not to do more than rebuke the parties, which, however, was not much heeded, for it was after that that Mr Boston published his new edition of the work; and though he continued, as long as health and strength were given him, to labour diligently, both in his parish and in the Church Courts, he was not satisfied with the result of the deliberations of those Judicatories, but having a great dread of separation, he was kept from seceding.

Mr Boston, whose death, as I have already mentioned, took place in 1732, never seems to have had robust health, and yet he seldom allowed himself to desist from preaching. It was his earnest desire to be found so employed when his death summons arrived, and for two or three Lord's Days, during his last illness, he preached from a window in the manse till that even was impossible, but he was only laid aside for two or three Sundays at the most, till called on Saturday the 20th May 1732, to celebrate the eternal Sabbath in that place where "The inhabitant shall not say any more, I am sick."

The celebrated Ralph Erskine thus apostrophises Boston's death :—

> "The great, the grave, judicious Boston's gone,
> Who once, like Athanasius bold, stood firm alone;
> Whose golden pen to future times will bear
> His fame, till in the clouds his Lord appear."

Such was his popularity that when his son published two volumes of his father's sermons, upwards of seven hundred individuals subscribed, some for a large number of copies, and one for two hundred, and in the list of subscribers are some well-known names.

Mr Boston married, before he left Berwickshire, Katherine Browne, daughter of Dr Robert Browne of Barhill, Culross, by whom he had ten children, four of whom only outlived him.

HENRY DAVIDSON of Galashiels was born at Eckford in 1687. Mr Davidson was an especial friend of the author of the "Fourfold State," and like him, was a warm supporter of the "Marrow," being one of the twelve.

Boston describes Mr Davidson as "a man of great gravity, piety, and tenderness, learned and judicious; well acquainted with books; a great preacher, delivering in a taking manner masterly thoughts in an unaffected, elevated style; endowed with a gift of prayer in heavenly oratory beyond any man that I ever knew; extremely modest and reserved in his temper, but a kind and affectionate friend."

Mr Davidson, though he continued incumbent of Galashiels till his death, cooled in his great zeal for Presbytery, which he once believed to be "juris divini," and became Independent or Congregational both in principle and practice. To his honour, however, be it stated that he offered to give up his living, but neither his flock nor his brethren in the Presbytery would hear of it, such was their admiration of his character. He died at Galashiels on the 24th October 1756, in the sixty-ninth year of his age and forty-second of his ministry, and was the last survivor of the twelve Marrow men. Another minister of Galashiels was

Dr ROBERT DOUGLAS, who succeeded in 1770 Alexander Glen (the immediate successor of Mr Davidson), who was translated to another parish. Long incumbent, Dr Douglas's increasing efforts were directed for the good of his parishioners. He was also one of the greatest benefactors to Galashiels, which was an insignificant place when he was first appointed minister, but which he lived to see greatly improved, and enriched. Since then, through the energy and public spirit of its manufacturers, of whom Richard Lees was one of the earliest, it has now become a most important manufacturing place, and bids fair to rival Leeds, the busy hive of Yorkshire.

Dr Douglas was also a warm friend to agriculture, and a great improver. He wrote the Statistical Account of Galashiels, and also a volume on the Agriculture of Roxburghshire and Selkirkshire, giving a general view thereof, and communicating many very interesting facts.

Dr Douglas was a friend of Sir Walter Scott, to whom he sold that part of Abbotsford on which the house is erected, the original name of the property being " Clarty Hole."

Dr ROBERT RUSSELL of Yarrow, previously of Ettrick—a Royal Chaplain—who wrote the first Statistical Account of both parishes,

THOMAS ROBERTSON, minister of Selkirk, who wrote the first Statistical Account of that parish ; and

JOHN CAMPBELL, his successor, who wrote the last, all deserve to be mentioned with respect.

Mr Campbell, whose demise has comparatively recently

occurred, must have been well known to many amongst us. Though of an old and perhaps not very strict school of divinity, he was an amiable man, possessing dignified manners and a good address. He moreover abounded with wit and humour, and had an excellent ear for music. Some of you may remember how well he sung that noble song of the talented author of the "Pleasures of Hope," his namesake, "Ye Mariners of England."

The last Established Kirk Minister connected with the county to be noticed is

Dr JOHN LEE, born at Torwoodlee Mains in 1779.

Dr Lee deserves a prominent place among the notables of Ettrick Forest, for he not only conferred high honour upon his profession, but added greatly to the literary reputation of Scotland. Indeed he was unquestionably one of the remarkable men of the day. After being licensed as a Preacher of the Gospel, he went abroad for a time, and then to London, where he commenced his ministerial life, in the Scotch Church, Swallow Street, but he did not remain long there, soon leaving for Peebles, of which parish he was appointed minister. After continuing there for a few years, he went to St Andrews as Professor of Church History, where he remained some time, holding with it, for one session, the Chair of Moral Philosophy, at Aberdeen. He, however, relinquished both Professorships for a church in Edinburgh which he obtained in 1822, being anxious again to devote himself to the work of the ministry, and feeling more deeply convinced, to use the words of the elegant and eloquent Robert Hall, that, "in carrying into effect the designs of the Gospel, we are communicating that pure element of good which, like the solar light, pervades every part of the universe, and forms, there is every reason to believe, the most essential ingredient in the felicity of all created beings."

In the transaction of all ecclesiastical business, Dr Lee stood unrivalled, and his researches connected with the history of the National Church of Scotland were most laboriious, such as to draw from the venerable Dr M'Crie a high eulogium.

Dr Lee, after about eighteen years of ministerial labour in Edinburgh, was appointed in 1840 to the honourable and important office of Principal of its University, which he held till his death in 1859, and he conjoined with the Principalship the Chair of Divinity, to which he was nominated in 1843.

Few men have held more numerous and important appointments, and his friend Dr Dickson of the West Kirk, with reference to the Doctor's many changes, it is said, jocosely remarked, that Lee, " if he was in heaven could not sit still, but would be wanting a change."

The worthy parents of Dr Lee were members of the Burgher Meeting at Stow, in which parish Torwoodlee Mains was situated, the home the Doctor was born in being now pulled down. Our hero's education was commenced at Caddonlee School, near Torwoodlee, where the celebrated John Leyden was assistant teacher, and from thence he went to Edinburgh, then to Selkirk, where he studied for a time under the venerable Lawson, Professor of Divinity for the Associate or Burgher Body, with a view of following the ecclesiastical views of his ancestors. But John Lee's bent towards the Established Church soon showed itself, and he accordingly returned to Edinburgh to complete his divinity studies and prepare for the ministry, though at the same time he studied medicine and graduated in that faculty before he took orders.

While John Lee was at Selkirk he had for a fellow-student the afterwards well known John Brown, and in their leisure hours hearty good humour seems to have prevailed among all the young men, one of whose amusements was epitaph writing, and I have heard one on John, by his friend John Brown, to the following effect :—

" Here lies John Lee who died laughin',
  Reader, this says to thee beware of *daffin*."

ANDREW MOIR, was the first minister of the Associate

congregation at Selkirk, having been ordained there in 1758. Mr Moir was a native of Perthshire, and studied at Glasgow, where he was licensed as a preacher. He did honour both to the place of his birth and education, being a man of very considerable attainments. His preaching also was very impressive, and he became a great favourite, attracting crowds to hear him. Even those who held sceptical opinions were drawn by his eloquence, considering, as they said scoffingly, that Moir " spoke his nonsense in a graceful way."

He published sermons and tracts which were not only highly spoken of, but gave evidence of the ability and power of Mr Moir, who in 1761 preached a sermon at the ordination of Alexander Shanks, first Associate and Burgher minister at Jedburgh, from the peculiar text, " What will this babbler say ? "

The successor of Mr Moir at Selkirk was his son-in-law GEORGE LAWSON, a native of Peeblesshire, and born 1749. From his earliest years Mr, afterwards Dr, Lawson, evinced a great desire to acquire knowledge, and after obtaining all the learning he could get at a rural school, he went to Edinburgh for the purpose of entering the University, which he did, and he became a diligent and successful student. After going through the usual college course, he determined upon commencing the study of divinity, and of doing so through the medium of the Burgher Associate Synod and under its professors. This he accomplished, and such were his attainments and qualifications, that he soon got ordination, and Selkirk had the good fortune to secure the services of George Lawson in the pastorate of the Associate congregation, to which he was accordingly appointed in 1771, at the early age of twenty-two, and he was not long of approving himself a faithful workman. Such were his abilities and his piety that when Mr Brown gave up the Professorship of Theology, Dr Lawson was unanimously elected in his room, and from 1787 down to his death in 1820—a period of thirty-three years—he discharged the important duties of the Professorial Chair in such a manner as to gain the admiration of the whole body. His successor was Dr John Dick, and his mantle could not have fallen upon one better calculated to uphold the character of the chair which had been filled by a succession of distinguished theologians.

To mark the high respect entertained for Dr Lawson, the University of Aberdeen conferred upon him the degree of Doctor of Divinity, but such was his modesty that it was some time ere he consented to accept the honour, which, however, he finally did in the following terms :—

"I never aspired to literary honours—I do not feel myself worthy of them, but since the partial esteem of my brethren have sought this honour for me, and obtained it, from the learned men of the north, I will accept it with gratitude and pleasure, and from the great love for my brethren, and the high esteem with which I regard learned men of a liberal spirit, I will do all in my power to be more deserving of their esteem and love, than I have ever yet been."

Lawson's attainments in Biblical literature were extensive. He was indeed mighty in the Scriptures, and could without difficulty quote any portion, either from the original or our own English version. Such was his acquaintance with the Hebrew and Greek texts, it has been said he could have reproduced them from memory without much change, had such been necessary.

His publications, though highly creditable, afford no criterion of the ability of the man; but a further insight into his character will be obtained from his memoirs.

The Doctor was much respected by his brethren, who no doubt looked up to him as a spiritual father and counsellor. A story is told of Alexander Shanks, already referred to—a man of much eloquence as a preacher, but of singular modesty and simplicity of character, going from Jedburgh to Selkirk to consult Dr Lawson on a point which was really so trivial as to cause the Doctor to smile at the innocence of Mr Shanks, who knew his friend too well to feel offended. But notwithstanding Mr Shanks' childlike simplicity, he was a highly gifted man.

Dr Lawson's two sons followed him in succession, and now a grandson fills the place of his sires, the family occupancy of the pastorate at Selkirk amounting in the aggregate to upwards of one hundred years.

LEGAL CELEBRITIES.

I come now to the legal celebrities of Selkirkshire, and I commence with those who rose to seats on the Bench of the Court of Session. The first in order of time was

SIR GIDEON MURRAY of Elibank, descended from the old family of Murray of Blackbarony, who became a Lord of Session in 1613, in succession to William Melville, Commendator of Tongland. He was originally designed for the Church, but having accidentally killed a companion, he was committed to prison, where he was confined a length of time, and the imprisonment, as well as the remembrance of the melancholy occurrence that led to it, had such an effect upon him, as to cause him to abandon his intention of taking Holy Orders. He then acted as Chamberlain to Sir Walter Scott of Buccleuch, the celebrated commander, who, for his valiant conduct and able services in the Netherlands, under the Prince of Orange, was raised to the Scottish Peerage in 1606, and Murray, whose mother was widow of one of the Buccleuchs, acted with great forethought and prudence in the affairs of his relative. Sir Gideon Murray was appointed Lord Treasurer in 1611, his nomination to the Bench taking place soon after, viz., in 1613, as already mentioned, the Court dispensing with an examination, " because of the certain knowledge they had of his qualifications." He appears to have held both offices, and to have been a most successful administrator of the public purse, for his management was so good that he not only restored and added to Holyrood House, the Castle of Edinburgh, and other public buildings, but was able to save as much as defrayed the expenses of King James and suite, "when His Majesty's salmon-like instinct induced him to visit Scotland in 1617."

Scotstarvet, I mean Sir John Scott, a Lord of Session, and an author of high repute and great veracity, states that the King had a great respect for Sir Gideon, and mentions an anecdote in verification of it. Murray happened to drop his chevron in the King's room, when James stooped and gave him his glove, adding, " Queen Elizabeth, my predecessor, thought she did a favour to any man who was speaking to her when she let her glove fall that he might take it up and give it to her, but sir, you may say a king lifted your glove."

Notwithstanding this, His Majesty sent this faithful servant to prison, in consequence of some charges being made against him, which, it was said, King James did not believe to be just, and such was the effect of this treatment that it brought Sir Gideon to his grave, for he took to his bed, and abstained from all sustenance, dying on the 28th June 1621.

Elibank, from which Sir Gideon took his judicial title, is in the parish of Yarrow, in Selkirkshire, for which county he served as a commissioner at one time. Elibank also gave a peerage title to his son, Sir Patrick Murray, who was created, in 1643, Baron Elibank of Ettrick Forest, his Lordship being one of the six peers who opposed the delivering up of King Charles I. to the English Parliament in 1647.

The next Lord of Session to be brought forward is

SIR ARCHIBALD NAPIER, first Baron Napier, son of the celebrated inventor of logarithms. Sir Archibald Napier was appointed to the Bench 23d November 1623. He had previously been attached to the Court of King James, was a Privy Councillor, and Treasurer-Depute. He held the office of Lord Justice-Clerk for a short time; but on the accession of Charles I., was removed from the bench altogether, on the ground of his being an officer of State. Being a favourite of King James, and having been recommended by him to his son, King Charles, the latter reappointed Sir Archibald to the Bench, by making him an Extraordinary Lord. He also made him a Baronet, and then a Peer, and moreover endowed him with a pension. Being the recipient of so many honours, a large amount of jealousy was excited against him, and having sided with Charles in his troubles, Napier was doomed to imprisonment, which he underwent both at Edinburgh and Linlithgow, but, after a time, was released, and died not long afterwards at Fincastle, in Athol, where he had retired after the defeat of Montrose at Philiphaugh, whom he had supported in that battle—the Marquis being his brother-in-law. An interesting autobiography of Lord Napier was published from the original manuscript in 1793, to which I refer you for further details respecting his life, and the persecutions he suffered; but he was graciously delivered out of them all. I may say of his Lordship, in the words of the Psalmist, "Mark the perfect man, and behold the upright, for the end of that man is peace."

Shortly afterwards, viz., in 1626, another member of the Napier family was appointed a Lord of Session, in the person of

SIR ALEXANDER NAPIER of Lauriston, uncle to the preceding, though not appointed till after his nephew. Sir Alexander was half-brother of the inventor of logarithms, and survived him more than twelve years; but he was not long on the Bench, his death occurring in less than four years after being appointed.

I now come to the Philiphaugh family, but before discussing them, I will say a few words about this old race. The Murrays of Philiphaugh have long been identified with Selkirkshire, having acquired their lands at several periods, but the greater part early in the sixteenth century. The original designation of the family was Falahill, which property they acquired about two centuries earlier; and you will perhaps remember that John Murray, the fourth of Falahill, was the celebrated chieftain called the "Outlaw Murray," whose song or ballad is coeval with the time of James IV., to whom the outlaw bid defiance; but though it may seem hardly possible that so excellent a king could have incurred such hostile feelings, still, as James was so fond of Ettrick Forest, and over which his Queen, Margaret, had her dowry, he may have touched upon Murray's supposed rights, and thereby laid a foundation for the song. However that may be, it is undeniable that the outlaw got a charter from the king, dated the 30th November 1509, of the heritable Sheriffship of Ettrick Forest, which was ratified in 1540 to his grandson, and was continued in the family till Parliament abolished these Judicatories about the middle of last century, when I observe, from a list of claims then put in, that £8000 was claimed by the then Mr Murray of Philiphaugh for the Sheriffdom.

But to take up the two members of the family who were Lords of Session, I have to state that they were both eminent legal functionaries, and what is more remarkable still, that they were brothers. The elder,

JAMES MURRAY was appointed to the bench as Lord Philiphaugh on the 1st November 1689. He had previously been in Parliament for the County of Selkirk, and was, of course, Sheriff, which was then hereditary in the family. While acting as Sheriff, Urquhart of Meldrum, a military commander, usurped his office. "This insolence," says that profound lawyer, Lauder of Fountainhall, "may give us a taste of what a military government would be." Murray was accused of showing too great leniency towards supporters of conventicles, and suffered imprisonment for a time. He was, however, afterwards released, his views becoming less favourable to the Covenanters, but then his change of opinion rather detracted from his fame, though the Government benefited by his services.

He got the appointment of Lord Register in 1702, in addition to the Judgeship, in succession to Lord Selkirk, and held the office, first for about two years, and afterwards, on its being again conferred on him, he retained it for other four years; in fact, till his death, which occurred at Inch on the 1st July 1708.

Lord Philiphaugh was a learned and able man, and notwithstanding his endeavours to save himself in the way he did, continued a great man and good servant of the Crown. His brother,

JOHN MURRAY, Lord Bowhill, became a Lord of Session in 1707, in succession to Sir David Home of Crossrig, a little more than a year before Lord Philiphaugh's death, having previously represented Selkirkshire in Parliament, both before and after the Union. Lord Bowhill was not long in getting another gown, for on the resignation of Lord Fountainhall in 1709, he was nominated to the Justiciary seat, and he held both till his death in 1714. From a book of Scottish Elegiac Verses, I take the following on the death of Lord Bowhill, viz. :—

"O! thou my muse, that's now bedew'd with tears,
Sob these dire sighs, pierce adamantine ears;
For darlings of the muses now do mourn;
Their sable weeds with tears they all adorn.
Why? pale-faced death, on his winged steed did fly
From the utter gate of Eternity!
And hath our senate-house bereav'd, of one
Who, for his virtue, might have filled a throne:
Judicious, great, and pious Lord Bowhill:
His empty seat, upon the Bench to fill
Scarce any of our wits he's left behind,
With such judicious, and a pious mind.
O! senators, who sable-weeds put on,
Bowhill has scaled the heavens to a throne;
And trumpets forth the Mediator's praise;
Where angels flee about, delight to gaze.
Who did pronounce pointed decreets 'mongst you,
With open face the Deity doth view,
Justice doth cry, while equity doth moan,
Of all my sons Bowhill's my only one,
Who through the fogs and mists rais'd at the Law,
The equal cause, in justice always saw;
And angel-like, who wisely cou'd repel
Quirks of the law, foam'd up in Bacchus-cell.
The sons of Levi cause the pulpits groan,
While for the loss of thee, Bowhill, they moan;
(No wonder; for he, amongst great and small,
Jure Divino Presbytery did call);
The Acts of Parliament, beyond the Pole
Did fill his heart, and his sublimer soul!

And so, he always liv'd to punish crimes,
In these profane, degenerating times.
He caus'd Hell's brats find stroak of Justice hand,
When they impanell'd for their crimes did stand.
The poor, whom he supported, now do mourn,
While friends prepare his body for its urn.

" Joys on nimble wings, have taken flight ;
O how Cimmerian darkness vails our night.
How can heroick virtue joys have ?
Now like him now ! tho' he must down to grave.
May Heaven fill his empty seat below,
Until Rome's cursed strength no pow'r can show.
Right reason in his civil orb did move !
Religion, waft him to a seat above !
And all who live within our hemisphere,
Ye may bedew your eyes, and drop a tear."

I ought to mention that the father of these two celebrated senators of the College of Justice—Lords Philiphaugh and Bowhill—was Sir John Murray of Philiphaugh, whom Parliament appointed one of the Judges of Roxburgh and Selkirkshires, for trying those who joined the standard of the gallant but ill-fated Montrose, who, after aiding the Covenanters, became a firm and decided Royalist, carrying everything before him, till Philiphaugh landed him in a signal defeat, being there—on the 12th September 1645—surprised, attacked, and routed by General David Leslie. Sir John Murray claimed upwards of £12,000 for damage done to his property on that occasion.

There are two other Judges connected with the County of Selkirk to be brought forward—one, JOHN PRINGLE, Lord Haining, and the other ANDREW PRINGLE, Lord Alemoor, but before reviewing them, I shall give you a brief sketch of the Pringle family generally, as they stand identified with Ettrick Forest. Their patronymic is supposed to have been derived from Pilgrim, one of their ancestors having made a pilgrimage to the Holy Land in the thirteenth century. Originally the name was Hop Pringle, but the syllable Hop, which I believe only meant son, was long ago dropt. The Pringles prevailed in the counties of Berwick, Roxburgh, and Selkirk. Th earliest principal stocks were those of Smailholm and Galashiels, and Torsonce and Stichill. From the former were derived the branches Whitebank, Torwoodlee, and Clifton, though the lineal representative is Major Scott of Gala, whose ancestor, Hugh Scott of Deuchar, third son of Sir William Scott of Harden, and of Mary Scott, the Flower of Yarrow, married Jane, the elder daughter of Sir James Pringle of Galashiels, and inherited that property (Smailholm having been previously sold) on the death, in 1650, of Sir James's son John, his ancestrix's brother. Then the male representation devolved upon Robert Pringle of Howlatson, who died without issue, when James Pringle of Whitebank, descended from David Pringle of Smailholm by a second wife, claimed to be made representative of the Galashiels Pringles, the Scotts of Gala being the heirs-of-line. This James Pringle of Whitebank departed this life in 1667, leaving an only son, Alexander, who died without any family, though married twice. I believe Yair was about this time acquired from George Pringle of Balmungo, Alexander's uncle, who no doubt bought it from the Kers, kinsmen of my own ancestors, both being descended from Ferniehirst. The simple and striking epitaph in Melrose Abbey—" Here lies the race of the House of Yair," has reference to the Kers of Yair, and has been much admired for its simplicity.

But to continue the Pringles. John, the grandson of George of Balmungo, and son of John, minister of Fogo, and Jane Shaw, daughter of the Rev. Patrick Shaw, minister of Selkirk, succeeded to Whitebank and Yair, who carried on the line of the family; but his son Alexander, who married a Rutherfurd of Edgerston, and had twelve children, was forced to sell Yair to provide for his numerous family. It was purchased by the noble House of Buccleuch, and on the return, in 1783, of the son of the seller, an Alexander also, from India, where he had acquired a fortune, Henry, the then Duke of Buccleuch, kindly and most considerately offered to restore the estate, which M

Pringle accordingly re-purchased, and afterwards built the present mansion-house, where he settled, becoming a useful country gentleman, as did his amiable and excellent son and successor, the late Alexander Pringle.

The Torwoodlee family are also descended from the Pringles of Smailholm and Galashiels, having apparently come off at an earlier date, their first ancestor, William, being the second son of James Pringle of Smailholm, and Isabella Murray of the Falahill, now Philiphaugh family. This William Pringle fell at Flodden, and the next laird of Torwoodlee deserving notice was George, who suffered greatly on account of his religion, being a staunch friend of the Covenant, but, in addition, he incurred great displeasure by refusing to take the oaths of allegiance and supremacy. His assisting the great Earl of Argyll to escape, was another cause of trouble to him, but fortunately he was able to get out of the way, though he lived to see the Revolution, and to serve his country in the Convention of Estates, called by the Prince of Orange. George Pringle had two sisters,

Janet, married to Walter Pringle of Greenknowe of the Stichill Pringles, the celebrated Covenanter whose memoirs are well-known; and Sophia, married to John Riddell of Haining, who will be noticed hereafter.

With respect to the Stichill Pringles, who represent Torsonce, as I have treated of them in my lecture upon the celebrities of Roxburghshire, to which county, as long domiciled at Stichill, they more particularly belong, I need say nothing respecting them here, except that some members of the family, of whom two were Lords of Session, were men of great worth, high character, and unbounded talent, shedding lustre upon the name; and I only regret they have lost Stichill, though they still possess Newhall, in Selkirkshire, from whence one of the two judges referred to took his judicial title.

I have now arrived at the Haining branch of Pringles. Lord Haining was second son of Andrew Pringle of Clifton, and was called to the bar in 1698. He was long member for

Selkirkshire, which honour he only relinquished on obtaining the higher and more honourable one of a seat on the bench, which he got on the 1st of July 1729. He continued a Lord of Session till his death, which happened on the 19th August 1754, when in his eightieth year, his public services extending over the lengthened period of about half-a-century. We have already had an instance of two brothers, in the persons of Lords Philiphaugh and Bowhill, obtaining the ermine, and now we have an instance of father and son reaching the bench, highly honourable to the parties, and very creditable to the county of Selkirk ; for the son of Lord Haining,

ANDREW PRINGLE, after being successively Sheriff of Wigton and Selkirk, and Solicitor-General, was raised to a judgeship as LORD ALEMOOR, in 1759, when he obtained a double gown, as it is called. Few men have conferred greater honour upon the bench than Lord Alemoor, which he adorned for upwards of sixteen years, when his death occurred, on the 14th January 1776, at Hawkhill, near Edinburgh.

Lord Alemoor possessed great legal abilities,* and the most spotless integrity, and long ought Selkirkshire to be proud of this eminent judge, the last and one of the best of her sons who attained the distinction of a Lord of Session. To corroborate what I have said of Lord Alemoor, I give an extract from a well-known periodical, which says :—" His abilities as a lawyer, and his integrity as a judge have been long admired. His decisions were the result of deliberate consideration, founded on law, tempered with equity ; and his opinions were delivered in such an easy flow of eloquence, and with such a dignity of expression, as captivated every hearer and commanded attention."

* Lord Alemoor excelled all the laymen of that period for genuine argument and eloquence ; and when on the bench he delivered his opinion with more dignity, clearness, and precision than any judge I ever heard either in Scotland or England. It was a great loss to this country that he did not live to fill the President's chair, and indeed had not health to go through the labour of it, otherwise it was believed that he would have set an example of elegance and dignity in our law proceedings that could not easily have been forgotten.—" Autobiography of Dr Carlyle," p. 252.

There are two other legal celebrities connected with Selkirkshire, who, though not senators of the College of Justice, were judges. The first was

ANDREW PLUMMER, son of Dr Andrew Plummer, who was Sheriff-Depute of the county for about seventeen years. Mr Plummer passed as an advocate in 1771, was appointed to the sheriffdom about 1782, and died on the 21st November 1799. He married a daughter of Pringle of Torwoodlee, by whom he had no family; and the male representation of the Plummers of Middlestead, of whom there were three generations, all being Andrew Plummers, has consequently been lost. Sheriff Plummer had a considerable literary and antiquarian reputation, and I have understood he was a good mechanician. He was highly eulogised by Sir Walter Scott, who succeeded him, and who is the remaining legal celebrity to be noticed.

SIR WALTER SCOTT was called to the Scotch bar in 1792, and was appointed to the Sheriff-Deputeship of Selkirkshire on the 16th December 1799. I hold in my hand an original letter from Sir Walter, then Mr Scott, to one of my ancestors, applying for his interest in his favour when a candidate for the office. Scott's talents had not then become generally known, or instead of his canvassing for the sheriffship, it would probably have been conferred upon him without the necessity of his making any effort to obtain it.

Having treated of Sir Walter among the Notables of Roxburghshire, which county claims him as a son, not by birth, for he was born in Edinburgh, but by ancestral ties and by long residence at Abbotsford, I have now to speak of him as a judge, which identified him with Selkirkshire. The county records and the statue in the town speak volumes as to his fame; and it would be presumptuous in me to add my testimony to what is so patent. His subsequent early appointment to the office of principal clerk of Session shows the reputation he bore and the estimation in which he was held. Before he was nominated to the principal clerkship, which required him to be more resident in the Metropolis, he lived much at

X

Ashiesteel, the seat of his cousin Sir James Russell, whose mother, like Sir Walter's, was a Rutherford, both ladies being daughters of the Rev. John Rutherford, minister of Yarrow, in which parish Ashiesteel is situated. Sir Walter's residence there arose from the lord-lieutenant of that period conceiving it necessary that the highest legal functionary in the county should, during the alarm then felt connected with the threatened invasion, live, at any rate for part of the year, within its bounds ; and this arrangement was a happy circumstance, for it enabled Sir Walter, not only to be on the spot to watch over and protect the interests of his county, but to follow up his literary and antiquarian researches, and to prepare his early works for the press. Sir Walter Scott was well assisted in his judicial functions by his popular substitutes ; first, Mr Charles Erskine of Melrose, and afterwards his cousin, the late William Scott of Raeburn, a man who was excelled by none in the history of Border families. Sir Walter, after an incumbency of nearly thirty-three years, closed his bright career on the 21st September 1832, aged sixty-one.

MEDICAL CELEBRITIES.

I come now to the Medical Celebrities of the County of Selkirk, and the first deserving of notice is

Dr JOHN RUTHERFORD, born 1695, son of the Rev. John Rutherford, Minister of Yarrow, and grandfather of Sir Walter Scott. He was one of the original founders of the Medical School of Edinburgh, which at first consisted of the celebrated Alexander Monro, sen. ; the humane Sinclair ; the learned Alston ; and the well known John Innes and Andrew Plummer. All of these gentlemen became Professors in the University of Edinburgh, Dr Rutherford, of whom I am treating, being appointed to the Chair of the Theory and Practice of Medicine on the 9th February 1726, holding it for a period of about forty years, say till 1765, when he retired in favour of Dr John Gregory, and during that long period he discharged the duties of his office most efficiently. He had a thorough knowledge of Latin, and possessing, it was said, greater command of that language than of his native tongue, he preferred delivering his lectures in Latin, which language was perhaps more current then than it is now, though to this day physicians in England write their prescriptions or directions in Latin, not always most intelligible, and no doubt sometimes most puzzling to apothecaries' youths, not well grounded in the ancient Roman language.

Dr Rutherford during his Professorship, introduced clinical lectures, which greatly improved the medical curriculum ; and on this subject I quote from the "Scots Magazine" of the time. "These three winters past, a course of Clinical Lectures has been given in the Royal Infirmary (that noble institution founded through the instrumentality of Provost Drummond and Dr Alexander Monro, sen.), on the cases of patients there by Dr John Rutherford, Professor of the Practice of Physic in the University of Edinburgh, which are attended by a great number of students."

As I have already stated, Dr Rutherford resigned in 1765 in favour of Dr John Gregory. When, however, his resignation became generally known, a feeling seems to have prevailed that Dr William Cullen, then Professor of Chemistry, should be appointed Dr Rutherford's successor, but the patrons adopted his recommendation by appointing Dr Gregory, who, though not so ingenious as his rival, was not only a distinguished physician, but descended from an illustrious ancestry. Gregory, however, lived but a short time, dying suddenly in 1793, in the forty-eighth year of his age and seventh of his Professorship in Edinburgh, and is thus apostrophised by Beattie :—

"Art thou, my Gregory, for ever fled !
And am I left to unavailing woe !
When fortune's storms assail this worthy head,
Where cares long since have shed untimely snow,
Ah, now, for comfort whither shall I go ?
No more thy soothing voice my anguish cheers,
Thy placid eyes with smiles no longer glow
My hopes to cherish, and allay my fears,
'Tis meet that I should mourn ; flow forth afresh my tears."

I should explain that Rutherford and his contemporaries were generally disciples of Bœrhaave, the illustrious Dutch physician, whose medical works were regarded as text books, as his sound religious advice should also be. This renowned man prescribed morning devotions as the best method of preserving the health; for, said he, "nothing can tend more to the health of the body than the tranquillity of the mind, and the due regulation of the passions; and nothing more effectually restrains the passions, and gives spirit and vigour through the business of the day, than early meditation and prayer."

The second medical star connected with Selkirkshire was

Dr ANDREW PLUMMER of Sunderland Hall, son of Andrew Plummer of Middlestead, who acquired the estate of Sunderland Hall, through his wife Miss Ker.

The Doctor was probably born about the beginning of last century, and after studying at Edinburgh, proceeded to Leyden, where he completed his medical education under the great Bœrhaave, and took his degree in 1722, after which he returned to Edinburgh and commenced practice in his profession, in which he attained a high degree of proficiency and success. As already mentioned, he was one of the founders of the medical school in Edinburgh, and became on the 9th of February 1726 (the date of Rutherford's appointment to the Chair of Medicine) Professor of Chemistry, which he held till 1755. Being in good worldly circumstances, Plummer had some time previously relinquished private practice, and it was supposed he had intended giving up his Professorship too. Cullen's friends were anxious that the Metropolitan University should have the benefit of his transcendent talents (the Doctor being then at Glasgow), and they accordingly interested themselves in the matter with the view of getting Plummer to retire in his favour, but while this, about which there were difficulties, was being attempted, Dr Plummer was disabled by a paralytic seizure. Then his friends arranged with Dr Black, an able chemist, to supply his place for a few months, which he did, but Plummer still continuing unable to fulfil his duties, the patrons appointed Dr Cullen Joint-Professor, reserving to Plummer all his former rights and privileges. Early in 1756 Cullen commenced his brilliant career in Edinburgh, not, however, without meeting with opposition in some quarters. Plummer's death, however, occurring in July of the same year, removed all difficulties, and left Cullen the sole Professor of Chemistry, which Professorship he held for about ten years, when he was appointed in succession to the lamented Gregory, sole Professor of Medicine, his Chemistry mantle falling upon Dr Black, Plummer's assistant, called by Lavoisier the illustrious Nestor of the Chemical revolution.

Black, like the lamented Gregory, died very suddenly, but he had attained the allotted term of man's existence; and during his career must have made a considerable fortune, for I have read that he actually divided his property into ten thousand shares.

But before closing my sketch of Dr Andrew Plummer, I must tell you more about him. He was celebrated for a Thesis called "de Phthisi Pulmonalia Cattarrhe erta," which he dedicated to the Duke of Roxburghe, and for an antimonial and mercurial preparation, by which he is known far and wide by every dispenser of medicine. The composition actually bearing his name, and having stood the test of a century and upwards, bids fair to go down to the end of time. As a lecturer his diffidence was much against him, but he was a good chemist, and most painstaking in communicating his knowledge. Though his extreme modesty and hesitation, even when perfectly acquainted with his subject, was a great bar to his success as a prælector, nevertheless such was Plummer's knowledge that even the great Maclaurin appealed to him as to a living library. I may add that he contributed greatly to the prosperity of Moffat, for in his analysis of the water there he was most laborious, and the result of his investigations no doubt stimulated people to resort thither to drink. Dr Plummer published other papers.

About the middle of last century

DR MERCER lived and practised at Selkirk, but I have no particulars to communicate touching his medical skill or the success he attained in his profession, to which he did not confine his attention, for I find he was much devoted to agriculture, like his co-practitioner at Melrose, Dr Rutherford, who I suppose flourished about the same time. Dr Mercer was the first *at Selkirk* who devoted his attention to agricultural improvements, though in the county there were others, and amongst the number Lord Alemoor, who was a very spirited and successful improver. George Chalmers says, "the late Dr Mercer was the first who began meliorations at Selkirk town. In 1759 his enclosures and culture were admirably skilful. The sowing, in rotation of turnip, barley, and grass seeds, was his favourite plan." But it has been said that owing to his crops having been destroyed one year by the weather, he became so disgusted that he sold off and gave up agriculture.

The next celebrity of the medical profession connected with Selkirkshire was

MUNGO PARK, but as he obtained greater laurels in the fields of history and science, and will fall to be brought before you hereafter, I will not dwell upon his professional acquirements, for though they were doubtless considerable, his heart was evidently not in his work, and as a proof of this, it is affirmed that before proceeding on his second and fatal journey to Africa, he wrote to a friend, "that a few inglorious winters of practice at Peebles was a risk as great, and would tend as effectually to shorten life, as the journey he was about to undertake."

I must, however, give you an anecdote respecting his brief medical career in this locality, which shows how highly he was prized. One dark night he had missed his way, and seeing a light in the distance, made for it, and finding a woman at that very house, where the light was that attracted him, requiring medical assistance, he accordingly rendered his services. On his departure, the husband of the woman chaperoned him to aid him in reaching the main road, but the worthy shepherd (presuming he was one), kept behind Park, instead of preceding him, upon which Park enquired the reason, when his guide replied, "My wife says you are an angel, and I wish to see you fly up," which, by keeping in the rear, he thought he was sure to do.

Mungo Park got his first knowledge of medicine from Dr Thomas Anderson of Selkirk to whom he was bound an apprentice, and whose eldest daughter he married, after his return from his first visit to Africa.

DR THOMAS ANDERSON was long a most respectable practitioner at Selkirk, and his business, which he derived from Dr Chisholm, was transmitted to his son, who bore the same name, and who like his father, long enjoyed the confidence of the neighbourhood, and it afterwards descended to Dr Henry Anderson, the present practitioner, who maintains the reputation which his sires so deservedly acquired.

Dr DANIEL RUTHERFORD, son of Dr John Rutherford and grandson of the minister of Yarrow, is the next in order. He was also uncle of Sir Walter Scott, and brother-in-law of Colonel Russell of Ashiesteel, so that though probably born in Edinburgh, he is amply identified with Selkirkshire.

Daniel Rutherford was born in 1749, and followed his father's profession, becoming like him, a professor in the Metropolitan University, his election to the Chair of Botany taking place in 1786, on the death of Dr John Hope, whose fame is well known, having done much to promote the cultivation of botany on the Linnæan system, which has so popularised it, as to make it one of the most attractive, as it is one of the oldest studies in the whole range of natural philosophy.

Dr Rutherford's thesis "De Ære Mephitico" on Matriculating, was a very remarkable production, and entitled him to a high place among modern chemical philosophers. It was dedicated to Lord Alemoor of Haining, who had been a warm friend and patron of Dr Rutherford and his father's family. After the attainment of his Doctorship in such an honourable manner, and at such an early age, much was expected from him in the future, and he did all that devoted diligence to his profession could secure. He repaired to the continent, both to France and Italy, in order to extend and improve his medical knowledge, and after a considerable absence he returned to Edinburgh, where he settled as a physician, thus following, as I have already said, his father's profession, and finally succeeding to the chief part of his extensive practice which, added to the Botanical Professorship, must have placed him in most independent circumstances.

Dr Rutherford who enjoyed a high reputation as a practitioner as well as the confidence and esteem of the faculty, died in 1819 suddenly, though for a time previously his health had not been good.

Next in order is

Dr EBENEZER CLARKSON of Selkirk, who was the friend and country medical adviser of Sir Walter Scott. Such was his reputation, he had been often recommended to exchange his Selkirkshire practice for an Edinburgh one. Sir Walter had a high opinion of his hard-riding, benevolent and sagacious old friend's professional skill and enthusiasm, his intelligence, humanity, courage, and science, and when the baronet returned to Abbotsford in July 1832 in a dying state, attended by Dr Thomas Watson of London, the illustrious patient was made over to the good old country surgeon of Selkirk.

I now come to the two last of the medical celebrities connected with the county of Selkirk in the persons of John and William Scott, father and son, than whom the county never produced abler men. The father,

Dr JOHN SCOTT of Singlee, Ettrick, where he was born on the 2d January 1795, was a distinguished Edinburgh physician, well known and deeply valued, and especially mourned over in the Forest and on Tweedside, his skill, time, and means being always ready for any of the suffering and destitute natives of those districts. His father, William Scott, was a well-known store farmer. John was the youngest of fifteen children by one mother, ten sons and five daughters, two of whom, girls of seventeen and eighteen, were drowned when bathing in the River Ettrick, a sad event still remembered in the Forest. Dr Scott was for two years at Yarrow school— then for some time at Jedburgh. Between fifteen and sixteen he went to Edinburgh College. He got a diploma in 1813, and soon after went to Ceylon as an assistant surgeon to the Rifles of that Island. He returned home in 1818, and took his degree of M.D. at Edinburgh in the following year, after which he went to Paris, where he studied under the famous Lœnna, finally returning to Edinburgh, where he settled, and practised for many years, dying on the 3d May 1853, in his fifty-eighth year. Dr Scott was singularly gifted as a discoverer and healer of disease. He seemed, by a sort of native instinct, to get at the essence of the mischief, and pointed to the cause as a pointer does to game. There it is ;—and more than this, he was both pointer and shot. He was a most sagacious and successful physician, and one of the tenderest-hearted and most disinterested of men, as many in this county doubtless know. His extreme modesty—what in Scotland may be called blateness—was the only thing in the way of his becoming the greatest physician of his time, and he was not merely a doctor, but a man of fine taste and true literary faculty. He wrote very pleasing verses when young. He was an enormous and retentive reader, and always alive to everything that could improve mankind, in mind, body, or estate. I must not forget to mention that John Scott was one of the most unselfish of men, carrying his disregard of money to an extent quite uncalled for, and in his absent moods he has been known to light his candle with a bank note ; but the most gifted have frequently some points of singularity in their character.

I now come to Dr John Scott's son, his only son,

WILLIAM HENRY SCOTT. This young man—and lamentable to say he did not live to become an old one, indeed, not even to reach full manhood—studied medicine, and took his degree of M.D. He was a prodigy of knowledge, quite equal at the same age to the precocious Leyden, and his memory was almost miraculous. Indeed, he used to say he *did not know how to forget*. But in addition to his vast general knowledge, he concentrated himself in numismatics, the science of coins and medals, and also in the study of history and of languages. In the department of memismatology, a very difficult department of knowledge, he held a high rank for so young a man, having made some primary discoveries. You will perhaps hardly believe it, but when a lad of eighteen, he was the habitual correspondent of the chief Savans of Europe in their own languages, and when this marvellous youth died, letters came from all quarters of the world full of amazement at his age. He had been thought at least a man of fifty from his accomplishments and immense stores of knowledge.

Dr William H. Scott died on the 4th October 1855, aged twenty-four, and was buried beside his father and uncle, Henry Scott, a well-known and much-respected tradesman of Edinburgh, and a great player at chess, in the Dean Cemetery, near to the grave of "George Combe, author of the Constitution of Man," who was a great friend of Dr John Scott's.

POETS.

I now come to the poets, giving precedence to a poetess, who, at any rate, is first in chronological order.

Mrs ALISON COCKBURN, daughter of Robert Rutherford of Fairnalie, a cadet of the old family of Rutherford of Hundalee in Roxburghshire, and wife of Patrick Cockburn, advocate, youngest son of Adam Cockburn, Lord Justice-Clerk, and brother of John Cockburn of Ormiston, one of the earliest, and certainly the most celebrated, of Scottish agriculturists at the time.

Mrs Cockburn was a good and clever writer. Indeed, she was an honour to her native county, and her memory ought to be fondly cherished. One of her best songs is called "The Flowers of the Forest," written in a turret of the old house of Fairnalie. A detached verse or two is all that exists of the old ballad bearing that designation, but Mrs Cockburn and Miss Jane Elliot, another good poetess and charming person, by their admirable elegies, make it less a matter of regret that the ancient ballad, which commemorated the fatal battle of Flodden, has, by the effluxion of time, been lost. Both ladies must have had the old dirge in view when they wrote their respective verses, for they have adopted from the fragmentary remains of it a striking line :

"The flowers of the forest are a' wede awa'."

I shall now read both Mrs Cockburn's and Miss Elliot's productions, commencing with that of the former lady, which I believe is the oldest :

"I've seen the smiling of fortune beguiling ;
I've tasted her favours, and felt her decay ;
Sweet is her blessing, and kind her caressing,
But soon it is fled— it is fled far away.

"I've seen the forest adorned of the foremost,
With flowers of the fairest, both pleasant and gay ;
Full sweet was their blooming, the scent the air perfuming,
But now they are withered, and a' wede away.

"I've seen the morning, with gold the hills adorning,
And the red storm roaring, before the parting day ;
I've seen Tweed's silver streams, glittering in the sunny beams,
Grow drumly and dark, as they roll'd on their way.

"O fickle fortune ! Why this cruel sporting ?
Why thus perplex us, poor sons of a day ?
Thy frowns cannot fear me, thy smiles cannot cheer me,
Since the flowers of the forest are a' wede away."

Now for Miss Jane Elliot's stanzas, which were first published anonymously, but afterwards acknowledged :

"I've heard them lilting at the ewe milking,
Lasses a' lilting before the dawn of day ;
But now they are moaning on ilka green-loaning ;
The flowers of the forest are a' wede away.

"At bughts in the morning, nae blythe lads are scorning,
Lasses are lonely and dowie and wae ;
Nae daffing, nae gabbing, but sighing and sabbing ;
Ilk ane lifts her leglin, and hies her away.

"In har'st at the shearing nae youths now are jeering ;
Bandsters are runkled, and lyart or gray ;
At fair, or at preaching, nae wooing, nae fleeching ;
The flowers of the forest are a' wede away.

"At e'en, in the gloaming, nae younkers are roaming
'Bout stacks, with the lasses at bogle to play ;
But ilk maid sits drearie, lamenting her dearie,—
The flowers of the forest are a' wede away.

"Dool and wae for the order that sent our lads to the Border ;
The English, for ance, by guile wan the day ;
The flowers of the forest that fought ay the foremost,
The prime of our land, are cauld in the clay.

"We'll hear nae mare lilting at the ewe-milking ;
Women and bairns are heartless and wae,
Sighing and moaning on ilka green-loaning,
The flowers of the forest are a' wede away."

Mrs Cockburn was a very talented, as well as a most fascinating person. Sir Walter Scott says of her :—"Even at an age, advanced beyond the usual bounds of humanity, she retained a play of imagination, and an activity of intellect, which must have been attractive and delightful in youth, but was almost preternatural at her period of life. Her active benevolence keeping pace with her genius, rendered her equally an object of love and admiration." Among her earlier friends were David Hume, John Home, Lord Monboddo—the latter that literary curiosity who thought that men were originally born with tails like monkeys,—and though she lived in a small house in Crichton Street, off George's Square, she frequently entertained those, as well as other distinguished characters there, her conversaziones being of a very recherché character, though her suppers were not of the most costly kind, being, as she used to say, quoting from Stella one of Swift's characters :

"A supper like her mighty self,
Four nothings on four plates of delf."

Mrs Cockburn died at Edinburgh on the 22d November 1794, being then upwards of eighty years of age, and one of her acting executors was Mark Pringle of Clifton and Haining. She had a niece, Elizabeth Rutherford of Cape Hope, married to Walter Scott of Wauchope, who was also remarkable for her talent, of which Burns the poet had a very high opinion.

JAMES HOGG, the Ettrick Shepherd, is next in order. Next to Robert Burns, who I suppose was nature's greatest poet, ranks James Hogg. Born, like the Ayrshire bard, on a 25th of January, though twenty-three years afterwards (viz., the 25th January 1782), of humble but respectable parents, their names being Robert Hogg and Margaret Laidlaw, he showed a precociousness of intellect as well as an ardent thirst after knowledge truly astonishing. In his sixth year he gave proof of his genius by writing "The Dialogue in a Country Churchyard," occasioned by the death of Mr Bryden of Crosslee (a descendant of the town-clerk of Selkirk, of Flodden fame), who was a kind friend and benefactor to Hogg's family. Unfortunately, however, an interruption was put to his schooling at the age of seven, a time of life when most children are only beginning their rudiments, by being sent to service as a cowherd. The circumstances of his family had rendered this necessary, but after a time he was again placed at school, though only for a few months, on the expiration of which he returned to his former occupation of herding cows, his promotion to the more honourable employment of tending sheep in due time taking place.

The office of a shepherd is a very suitable one for a lover of minstrelsy, and Hogg having the opportunity did not neglect to cultivate his genius. Music and poetry he was passionately fond of. Such was his devotion to the former science, that at the age of fourteen he had saved as much as enabled him to purchase a violin, on which he statedly played after his daily work was over. When in the service of Mr Scott of Singlee, his fondness for the fiddle seems to have been discovered, though his parents had long previously been aware of his invincible predeliction both for music and poetry, and had tried to check his enthusiastic ardour in their prosecution, fearing that he might be led into too much expense and be tempted to neglect his duties; but notwithstanding the restraints put upon his "practisings," he soon became an excellent performer. From Singlee he went to Elibank, and from thence to Willerslee, to act as shepherd to Mr Laidlaw, farmer there, with whom he served two years, by which time he had reached the age of seventeen. At this period he was beginning to make some progress in literary pursuits, and removed to Blackhouse, when yet in his eighteenth year, to serve with Mr James Laidlaw, its tenant, who had a good library, which he kindly allowed Hogg access to, and of which he made good use. Here he made the acquaintance of William Laidlaw, the son of his master, and the future companion of Sir Walter Scott, which ripened into a warm and stedfast friendship. And here also he commenced poetry in right earnest, at the age of twenty, which he attained in 1793, and the first verses of his manhood were entitled an address to Henry Duke of Buccleuch. Ballads and pastorals followed. Previously to 1799 his poetical effusions appeared in the "Edinburgh Magazine," but he soon published on his own account. One of his early pieces, called "Will and Kate," established his reputation, and classed him, as the then critics thought, not far behind Burns, or, at any rate, Robert Ferguson. The following are some detached verses of the "Pastoral":—

> "Nou my yellow hair I plaited,
> Gae my downy chin a shave,
> Thence my tales of love repeated,
> Fearing I should misbehave.

> "Where the burn wi' mony a turnie,
> Wimpled thro' the sandy plain;
> Willows louting, kiss'd the burnie—
> There I'm left to lie my lane.

"Oft, to every care unus'd,
When the daylight ceased to shine,
Oft on you I've gaz'd and mus'd,
Oft adored that Pow'r Divine,

"Who those fluid films that wheel'd
Loosely thro' primeval night,
By a breath to worlds concealed,
Masses of illuvid light.

This last stanza contains sentiments of grandeur and sublimity. About the beginning of the century Hogg withdrew from Mr J. Laidlaw's service at Blackhouse, and for a time joined his parents at Ettrick House Farm, which plan not succeeding, he started on a visit to the Highlands, for which he had a great partiality, and where he intended to settle, bidding farewell to the Forest, which he did in a well-known ballad, but this move was not attended with the advantages he expected, and he accordingly returned. To break the disappointment, however, he set out for England, where he remained a short time, afterwards returning to his native country, and having lost his money he put a bold face upon it and again took to the office of shepherd, hiring himself to Mr Harkness of Mitchelslacks, in Dumfriesshire, where he completed his "Mountain Bard," which he published in 1807, dedicating it to "Walter Scott, Sheriff of Ettrick Forest, and minstrel of the Scottish Border," with whom Hogg was on the most intimate and cordial terms. Sir Walter, then Mr Scott, introduced him to Constable, the great publisher then, who at first threw cold water upon Hogg's writings, doubting whether their publication would be a safe speculation. But the wary publisher gave them a trial, and to his surprise found the result satisfactory. To his honour he behaved liberally to the Ettrick Shepherd, who found himself possessed of about £300, on his getting which, he himself says, "he went perfectly mad." And so it seemed by the result, for he went extensively into farming, and lost every penny, and with his pecuniary embarrassments he ran the risk, by his random conduct, of losing the good opinion of his friends in Selkirkshire, whither he returned. He, however, bore the losses with fortitude and equanimity, making a bold push to retrieve himself, and accordingly, during 1810, with his "maud" on his shoulders, he again went to Edinburgh to try his fate in the literary market, anticipating another successful speculation through the agency of Mr Constable, but alas, with all his genius he could not get more than a bare subsistence, though he turned his attention to general authorship, as well as to ballad writing, which he continued to pursue for a few years. During this period he got from Charles Duke of Buccleuch, a lease for his life of Altrive Farm at a mere nominal rent; but again, anxious to go deeper into agriculture, he took the adjoining farm of Mount Benger, which he had soon to abandon, and to content himself with Altrive.

About this time the coronation of George IV. took place in London, when Sir Walter Scott, anxious, as he thought, to gratify Hogg, actually got him a ticket to the imposing ceremony, and asked him to be his companion thither, but to the great novelist's surprise, the Ettrick Shepherd declined the offer.

In the following year, however, when George IV. came to Scotland, Hogg made up for his previous apparent want of loyalty to his sovereign and courtesy to Scotland's immortal son, by attending His Majesty's court at Edinburgh, on which occasion he wrote a poem which procured him the king's thanks. After continuing for a time his literary labours, and finding himself at the age of sixty literally in poverty, he started for London, where he published his "Altrive Tales."

Shortly after this his health showed symptoms of giving way, but his pen did not stop till it was frozen by sickness and death, before which he had published his last work called the "Montrose Tales." Soon after the issue of these tales a rapid decline in the Shepherd's health became visible; and though he tried to enjoy the pleasures of the sun, he became hopelessly ill in October, and in a month afterwards he breathed his last, on the 21st November 1835, departing, as his friend William Laidlaw states, as calmly, and to appearance with as little pain, as if he had fallen asleep in his grey plaid on the side of the Moorland Rill.

The next celebrity to present to you, and one well worthy of following Hogg, is his friend

WILLIAM LAIDLAW, born at Blackhouse, in Yarrow, in November 1780, his parents being James Laidlaw and Catherine Ballantyne.

Laidlaw, being a native of Selkirkshire, is of course in his right place among the notables of Ettrick Forest; but having been the bosom friend and amanuensis of Sir Walter Scott, and as such long resident at Abbotsford or the neighbourhood, I have included him in my Literary history of Roxburghshire, with his illustrious friend and master, so that it is unnecessary to say much about him now. I have said he was fond of

> "The songs, to savage virtue dear,
> That won of yore the public ear,
> Ere polity, sedate and sage,
> Had quench'd the fires of feudal rage."

He supplied Sir Walter Scott with that fine ballad, "Auld Maitland," which, till it appeared in the "Minstrelsy," had never before been published.

HISTORIANS.

Selkirkshire claims two historians among her celebrities. The first is

ALEXANDER CUNNINGHAM, a writer of the eighteenth century. He was born at Ettrick in 1654, his father being then the incumbent. He was chiefly educated at Selkirk school, from which he went to Holland to finish his education. He did not, it appears, return to Scotland till the Revolution;

and having made the acquaintance of the British refugees, when resident at the Hague, he was honoured with the friendship of the leaders by whom that event was accomplished. After the final settlement of affairs he seems to have returned to the Continent as a travelling tutor; and such was his knowledge of foreign languages that he was selected for the British Envoyship at Venice, which appointment he held for a few years. After quitting that position he returned to London, where he lived in retirement, and died in 1732, aged eighty-two. Mr Cunningham was a good Latin scholar, and the British history for which he is celebrated was written in that language and translated by that most industrious compiler and writer, Dr William Thomson, in 1787. Though a work of merit and much historical interest, the prejudices of the author are rather strong and marked.

Many years ago there was a dispute with respect to two Alexander Cunninghams, viz., our present hero and the critic and editor of Horace. The two were confounded, but I think the controversy was settled satisfactorily in the pages of the "Scots Magazine," as far back as 1804, it being then proved that the critic, who was by birth an Ayrshire man, died in Holland in 1730; while the historian died in London, and was buried at St. Martins, in 1737. Both were successful authors, for the former had an estate in Ayrshire, and the latter was possessed of plenty of money, the bulk of which he bequeathed to friends in the west of Scotland, which I think proves, though born in Selkirkshire, his extraction must have been Ayrshire, the cradle of the Cunninghams, and one of whose three districts bears the name. In addition to the two Alexander Cunninghams just mentioned, there were two others in the same century, both distinguished men also, viz., Archibald Cunningham, Professor of Latin in Edinburgh College, and Alexander Cunningham, Professor of Law in the same university; and a century earlier there lived the great patriot and reformer, Alexander Cunningham, the Fifth Earl of Glencairn.

WILLIAM RUSSELL was author of the "History of Modern Europe, with an Account of the Decline and Fall of the Roman Empire, and a View of the Progress of Society from the Rise of the Modern Kingdoms to the Peace of Paris in 1763," a work of very considerable merit, and one which raised Mr Russell's fame and established his reputation, which his previous writings had not done. He was born at Windydoors, in 1741, his parents being Alexander Russell and Christian Ballantine, and after pursuing his studies, first at Innerleithen and afterwards at Edinburgh, he entered, say in 1757, the establishment of Messrs Martin and Wotherspoon, booksellers and printers in that city, in which he spent some years as an apprentice, and during that period he not only did not neglect the opportunity of increasing his knowledge, but sedulously stored his mind with all the information which he could acquire, as many in the same situation did before him, such as Ruddiman, Smellie, Richardson, and others, who became renowned in the annals of literature. When Russell's apprenticeship ceased, he made a small beginning as an author, by issuing some selections from modern poets, including the sublime Gray and the touching Shenstone ; and while engaged in a printer's establishment, he joined the Miscellaneous Society of Edinburgh, which brought him into contact with several literary characters. This proved rather a snare to him, for after relinquishing his legitimate business of printing, and proceeding to London—which so many think is paved with gold—he found he had over-estimated his powers as a literary man, for he could not obtain a living, and was obliged to take refuge again in the printing line.

Mr Strahan, the bible printer, gave him employment, and while occupied as corrector of the press for his new employer, he continued writing both prose and verse, though without adding to his fame or increasing his riches, till his last effort, which produced the "History of Modern Europe," gave him a niche in the Temple of Fame, with which he was apparently highly satisfied. Shortly after completing this work, which is in three volumes, and which occupied him about three years, he married Miss Scott, a lady of talent and accomplishments, and settled in Eskdale to spend his remaining years, which, however, were not destined to be of long duration, for he died suddenly, from a stroke of palsy, in 1793, leaving behind him a character for probity and fidelity not to be surpassed.

Before coming to the Miscellaneous Celebrities of the county, I have to notice the famous traveller

MUNGO PARK, born at Fowlshiels, parish of Yarrow, on the 10th September 1771, his father being then the tenant of that place, under Henry, Duke of Buccleugh. Mungo showed great application in youth both at home and at school, at Selkirk, where he uniformly took the lead, and his after career at Edinburgh University was marked by the same unwearied application and diligence.

I have already introduced Park to you as a medical man, and I therefore proceed with his history as a traveller. His first start was as assistant-surgeon on board an Indiaman, the "Worcester," in which he sailed for the East, and having landed at Bencoolen, in the Indian Archipelago, during the voyage he acquired much useful information in the science of botany and natural history, of which he was very fond, and on his return to London he was enabled to impart to the Linnean Society sundry important discoveries he had made in the finny tribe of the Indian Ocean. Ship board not affording sufficient scope for such an enthusiastic mind as Park's, he accepted an offer made to him by the African Society of London to take charge of an expedition that body was sending out for the purpose of exploring Central Africa, and more especially the River Niger. Having been duly equipped with every appliance necessary for such an important undertaking and journey, he accordingly sailed from Portsmouth in the "Endeavour," in May 1795, for the West Coast of Africa, arriving at Sillifreia, on the Gambia, on the 21st of the following month. I need not tell you what hardships this distinguished traveller endured, nor what difficulties he encountered in fulfilling his great mission, for both are patent to the world; and though he did not accomplish the great object he had in view, viz., that of tracing the "Niger" to its termination, he had the proud satisfaction of seeing the mighty stream, and determining its course to the eastward, thus settling a question which, since the days of Herodotus the Greek historian, called by Cicero the Father of History, there had been doubts and many conflicts about. It must have been a stunning sight to Park, when at Sego, the capital of Bambarra, on the 21st July 1796, more than a year after his arrival in Africa, he got a first view of " his long-sought-for majestic Niger, glittering to the morning sun as broad as the Thames at Westminster, and flowing slowly to the eastward." After tracing it as far as Silla, and finding himself without money or the means of transport, his horse having dropped down by the way, he thought prudence the best part of valour, and accordingly commenced his journey back, being obliged, to his deep mortification, to leave the problem of the termination of the Niger unsolved. He returned by its course for a considerable distance, and finally, but not till after great exposure to banditti, as well as the horrors of thirst, arrived at the British Factory, Pisania, where he met Dr Laidley one of its attachés, with whom he had parted eighteen months previously. From thence he proceeded to the coast, where he embarked, but though bound for England he had first to go to the West Indies, there being no vessel for Britain direct. Besides the geographical information this expedition enabled Mr Park to give to the world, his accounts of the Moor and Negro races are highly instructive; and the easy and frank manner in which he tells his tale, and the fine moral feeling with which it abounds, invest it with the deepest interest.

He arrived in England in December 1797, and after being lionized in London and attending to the publication of his travels, which no Forest or Teviotdale library should be without, he returned to Scotland, married the eldest daughter of his old master, Dr Thomas Anderson of Selkirk, and settled in 1801 at Peebles, as a surgeon or general practitioner, and there he made the acquaintance of those great philosophers, Adam Ferguson and Dugald Stewart, who resided in the neighbourhood of that town. But Park could not remain in such a circumscribed sphere. His love of travel knew no bounds, and he could not resist joining a second mission to Africa projected by the same body, but under government sanction. The command of the expedition was entrusted to him, and he was supplied with a liberal allowance of money and an efficient staff, so that he started under the most favourable circumstances and with the most sanguine expectations. He had the escort also of two friends from Scotland—one being his brother-in-law James Anderson of Selkirk. Departing from England on the 30th January 1806, a little more than ten years after he had started on his first mission, they reached the British factory of Pisania on the 28th April—in rather less than three months. There they made every preparation for the journey to the interior, and soon started, Park abounding with enthusiasm and confidence, but alas ere he sighted his beloved Niger " which was rolling its immense stream along the plain," the rainy season, always dangerous to Europeans in tropical climates, having set in, produced dysentery and all kinds of sickness. Park, however, with lieutenant Martyn, a valuable assistant, and Anderson, reached Sego, the limit of our hero's first journey, after much suffering and many difficulties, but *there* alas, his brother-in-law died, which added greatly to his distress. Despite, however, of his past calamities and future perils Park fitted out a sort of schooner and set sail in it down the Niger, accompanied by Martyn and two soldiers—all that were left out of a band of forty-four. And though all perished and no one was left to tell the tale, it is believed they sailed down to Boussa, within 300 miles of the termination of the Niger, there called by the natives " Quorra," when they were attacked, and in their endeavours to escape were drowned in the very river Park almost idolised.

Other Scotchmen have penetrated into the wilds of Africa. James Bruce of Kinnaird, a highly accomplished and wealthy man, went out as you all know to explore the other great African river the "Nile," and despite the sneers of some, performed his hazardous and perilous journey with honour and success, returning after a few years' absence to his native land in safety, dying, which he did from an accident, about one year before Park started on his first expedition in 1795. Bruce too was fond of natural history, and both Park and he must have often dwelt upon the 33d verse of the 4th chapter of the 1st book of Kings.

Later travellers in Egypt, for instance Salt, Pearce, and Dr Clark have all verified Bruce's statements.

After Bruce and Park arose Clapperton, the third great African traveller, who was anxious to follow up and enlarge the discoveries Park had made. Clapperton (who was accompanied by the spirited Major Dickson, and Dr Oudney, and by a confidential servant, Richard Lander), penetrated into the interior of Africa, going over a great part of Park's ground, proceeding even further. But in this expedition his companion Oudney died. This journey took place in the years 1822, 1823, and 1824. But in the following year Clapperton, with Captain Pearce, and Richard Lander made another start and completed a journey across the continent of Africa. They again tracked Mungo Park, and visited Boussa, where he was lost, and afterwards, upon visiting Sockatoo, with a view of proceeding to Timbuctoo, Clapperton was cut off by dysentery in 1827, Lander surviving, and afterwards on his return home, published a history of the expedition under Clapperton, which proved a valuable addition to the knowledge previously obtained respecting Central Africa.

Lander being determined to bring his conceptions respecting the Niger to a culminating point, again started for Africa, along with his brother, and having proceeded to Boussa, which Park reached, and where he met his death, they sailed down the Niger, called by the natives, as already mentioned, "Quorra," until they entered the Atlantic, which they did by one of its branches, thus discovering and settling its course. Overjoyed with their success they returned to England in June 1831, having started about eighteen months previously, and soon published a statement of their travels, for which they received a large sum of money. But alas! Richard Lander was not satisfied with the success that had attended him, and the fame he had consequently acquired, for we find him afterwards taking part in an adventure from Liverpool to the Niger, which not only proved disastrous as a speculation, but cost him his life, the party having been attacked by the natives, when Lander sustained a wound from the effects of which he soon died.

The other principal African travellers were Hermman, Burchardt, Belzoni, Bowdich, Peddie, Campbell, Tuchey, and Lyon, and in the present day there are other explorers, and one who is especially well-known to Scotchmen, I mean David Livingstone, a Renfrewshire man, who has not only been a large contributor to science, but what is far better, a great benefactor to the Negro race. In fact he is a man who, to adopt the language of Scripture, has hazarded his life for the Lord Jesus Christ.

MISCELLANEOUS NOTABLES.

JOHN RIDDELL of Haining, whom Satchells eulogizes, occupies the first place. He was the son of Andrew Riddell of Haining, and Jane Stuart of the Traquair family, and was Sheriff-Principal of and Member of Parliament for Selkirkshire, and also Provost of the Burgh, some little time after the middle of the seventeenth century. He married Sophia, third daughter of James Pringle of Torwoodlee, a woman of great worth, who, according to her brother-in-law, Walter

Pringle's memoirs, died on the 28th September 1663, with a full hope of immortality.

It may appear unimportant to notice that the grandmother of John Riddell of Haining, Violet Douglas of Pumpherston, who was the second daughter of Riddell of Riddell, and who seems to have brought up her grandson, owing no doubt to the early death of his father and the marriage of his mother, lived when a widow at Bowland, which at that time belonged to the Haining Riddells; and during her residence there she had a contest with James Pringle of Torwoodlee, about a seat in the Parish Church of Stow, which some of you may have seen by the records of that parish which have been published, was very warmly maintained. But the contest did not prevent the marriage of her grandson with the daughter of her antagonist.

John Riddell, however devoted to his wife, did not apparently sanction her covenanting tendencies, or the doings of the Covenanters, for he seems to have been one of the Commissioners for keeping that body in check, and he actually fined heavily both his brother-in-law, George Pringle of Torwoodlee, and Alexander Pringle of Caddonlee, for Church irregularities.

The estate of Haining, originally the property of one of the families of Scott, was acquired early in the seventeenth century by Andrew Riddell, Baron of Riddell, a man of great power as well as high character, who left it to Andrew Riddell of Windydoors, his eldest and favourite son by his second marriage with Violet Douglas. In consequence of the early death of this much loved son, who was a man of great promise, the grandson, John, about whom I have been speaking, inherited Haining, and his descendants held it till the beginning of the eighteenth century. Terminating in an heir female, who married David Erskine, Lord Dun, the property was sold, being purchased by John, second son of Andrew Pringle of Clifton, who became Lord Haining. It is singular that after the lapse of little more than another century the

Pringle proprietors of Haining also terminated in an heir female.

Since the union of the two kingdoms the County of Selkirk has been represented by six Pringles, of whom five have belonged to the Pringles of Haining, who finally got Clifton also, at the failure of the issue of the elder brother of Lord Haining, and one to that of Whytebank comparatively recently and within the recollection of many of us.

About the middle of last century there was a break in the Pringle representation, and the county was represented by

Sir GILBERT ELLIOT, the third Baronet of Minto.

The Burgh of Selkirk, which was associated with Linlithgow and others, was generally represented by strangers to the neighbourhood, among whom were the following—Ross, Dickson, Cockburn, Stopford, Moor, Grieve, Maxwell, and Monteith. There were three exceptions—

JOHN MURRAY of Philiphaugh.

JOHN PRINGLE of Clifton and Haining ; and

Sir JOHN B. RIDDELL of Riddell ;

all local gentry, who at various times represented the Burgh, the first at the time Sir Gilbert Elliot represented the County about the middle of last century, and the two last in the early part of this. Mr Pringle merely represented it for a short time after Sir John Riddell's death, in 1819, till the then Parliament was dissolved.

Sir John Riddell deserves special notice. He was a man of commanding person, and elegant though stiff manners, and as the representative of an old and long line of ancestry, he was doubly respected. His business habits were good, but in spite of this his affairs got into sad confusion, which caused his downfall. High farming and extensive improvements contributed to his difficulties, but in carrying out his gigantic schemes he was a great benefactor of the working classes, to whom he gave extensive employment, and the present proprietor is reaping the benefit of Sir John's immense outlay.

Alas that fine old place, which had been in the family nearly seven hundred years, and to which Sir John succeeded, quite unencumbered, soon passed away, and I do lament that at its sale the name of Riddell, which was given to it by the family after themselves—a very unusual thing in the history of proprietors—had not been changed, and a new name awarded, or even the old name of Wester Lilliesleaf restored.

There is a branch of the Philiphaugh family, viz. :

THE MURRAYS OF DEUCHAR, long since extinct. This Deuchar race flourished in the seventeenth century, the first being James Murray, younger son of Patrick Murray, ninth of Falahill and second of Philiphaugh. James Murray was a merchant in Edinburgh, and married Bethia Maule of the Panmure family. He was a man of singular good qualities, as the following quaint old epitaph testifies :—

> Stay passenger, and shed a tear,
> For good James Murray lieth here ;
> He was of Philiphaugh descended,
> And for his merchandise commended.
> He was a man of a good life,
> Marry'd Bethia Maule to's wife ;
> He may thank God that e're he got her,
> She bore him three sons and one daughter.
> The first he was a man of might,
> For which the king made him a knight ;
> The second was both wise and wylie,
> For which the town made him a baillie ;
> The third a factor of renown,
> Both in Camphire and in this town ;
> His daughter was both grave and wise,
> And she was married to James Elies.

James Murray of Deuchar died in 1640, aged sixty-eight. His three sons referred to in the epitaph became distinguished men, and all had the honour of knighthood conferred upon them, an honour which in olden time was conferred, as Dodd says, "with discrimination and judgment on men distinguished for religion, valour, and gallantry, for justice, honour, and princely bearing." Edmund Spenser, one of England's most illustrious early poets, thus versifies on the order—

> Nought is more honourable to a knight,
> No better doth become brave chivalry,
> Than to defend the feeble in their right,
> And wrong redress, in such as wend awry."

Sir Patrick, one of the three knights, succeeded to Deuchar, and his elder son, James, married my ancestrix, Anna, daughter of Sir Andrew Carre of Cavers, in 1681, is the last of the Deuchar family I have to mention. It afterwards became extinct, and is now represented by the Murrays of Philiphaugh.

I have found an epitaph on a

Mr INGLIS, who appears to have been Treasurer of Selkirk at one time, and though I possess no further information about him, it is enough to mark his reputation and character.

> Here lies a man without a lirk,
> Who was a friend to town and kirk;
> Whilst in this office he took great pleasure,
> To manage well the public treasure.

The last name I have to mention is

JOCK GRAY of Gilmanscleugh, who, though perhaps not a celebrity, was a character, and a very odd one too. Jock was well known in Selkirk and Roxburghshire as a mimic and singer. He used to travel, and lived chiefly upon alms. He was particularly noted for mimicking the Clergy, and with respect for some, did it to the life. He was asked on one occasion by the wife of a Selkirkshire minister to imitate her husband, which he said he would do, but as the divine read his sermons, once almost a crime in Scotland, Jock, before he could commence, called for "the papers," which, not being a popular request, terminated the interview.

John belonged to the Old Light Body of Dissenters, and I have heard he and his father at one time would walk to Edinburgh to attend a communion.

Jock, however, has been known to carry on his antics in

places of worship, and on one occasion he helped himself to a fellow-worshipper's hat to put into a broken pane of glass at a meeting-house he was attending.

But though Jock was an Old Light Seceder, he had a catholic spirit, and did not scruple to attend at times the Established Kirk, and on one occasion when at a parish church, Jock having arrived early, ascended the pulpit, where he was found when the minister entered the building, who immediately desired him to come down, but instead of obeying, Jock asked the reverend gentleman to walk up, giving as his reason that the congregation were a stiff-necked and rebellious people, and required them baith.

Jock has been known to ask his father this question, " Father, whether are you or I oldest ? " But though an absurd and perhaps derisive question, he could not have meant to ridicule his father, for he abounded with affection for his parent, and would, it has been said, sleep on his grave.

MISCELLANEOUS CELEBRITIES.

ON the 16th of December 1872, Mr Riddell Carre delivered in Hope Park United Presbyterian Church, Edinburgh, a lecture on "Border Memories," in which were included some of the sketches which had been introduced in other lectures, but some were either new or given with greater fulness, and these we have thought it right to subjoin. The lecture was well attended, and the chair was occupied by Lord Jerviswoode. The subject was divided so as to include in succession warriors, divines, lawyers, physicians, poets, historians, travellers, and miscellaneous celebrities. Passing over the naval and military heroes, in which there is nothing that has not been given under some other heading, we find among the legal men a brief account of

DAVID ROBERTSON, son of an Anti-Burgher minister of Jedburgh.* He practised as a Scotch solicitor in London, where he was a member of the Middle Temple. Mr Robertson was a man of good legal attainments, as well as a first-rate man of business. He published a book on the Rules of Law of Personal or Moveable Succession, which is one of the best works on the subject, and though written upwards of thirty years ago, has not been superseded by a better, and is still a text-book. Of course amendments have happily taken place in conformity with Mr Robertson's views, but there is

* The father of Mr Robertson was the Rev. John Robertson, minister of the Anti-Burgher congregation, Castle Street, Jedburgh, which afterwards joined the United Presbyterian Church, but is now extinct. It was a small congregation, and the stipend of the minister, whose pastorate lasted from August 1765 till April 1806 never exceeded £40 a-year.

still a cardinal one which he wished to see carried, but which has not yet been effected. I mean the anomalous law, which shuts out the relatives through the mother in moveable intestacies, and gives the succession wholly to the paternal side, to the entire exclusion of relatives through the mother, even though the property may have come through the mother, and when no paternal next of kin exist, the Crown comes in as *ultimus haeres.* This rule of law, which did not always exist, seems to have been taken from the Twelve Tables, but the sooner, in my humble opinion, these tables are overturned the better, on account of the slur cast upon and the injustice done to relatives through the mother. To them the law of England is much kinder and fairer, for it divides in such cases of intestacy personal property between the two sides, viz., the paternal and maternal next of kin.

Surely, in these days when women's *rights* are so vigorously upheld, this *wrong* done to relatives through the mother should be redressed.

Among the poets mentioned in the lecture is one in whom Mr Riddell Carre took much interest, and to whom he often referred both in conversation and in newspaper communications—

The Rev. HENRY FRANCIS LYTE. He was of ancient lineage, and was born at Ednam West Mains, in 1793. His father was Thomas Lyte, a gallant officer in the British Army, and latterly a lieutenant in the Roxburgh Cavalry Fencibles, commanded by Sir John Scott of Ancrum. Mr Lyte was a sacred poet of a very high order, and in most of the modern selections of hymns many of his beautiful compositions are introduced, and in no selections are there more than in the Lord Chancellor's excellent Book of Praise, and Mr Spurgeon's "Own Hymn-Book," very opposite works, but both entitled to commendation. Mr Lyte was originally intended for the medical profession, but, changing his mind, he became a clergyman, and took orders in the Episcopal Church, being ordained in Ireland, where he studied after leaving Scotland,

and at Trinity College, Dublin, he was a distinguished student. At first his religious views were by no means decided or satisfactory, but the peace of God having touched his heart, he became in a short time an earnest and devoted minister of God's word. Soon after being called to the ministry he went to England, and finally settled on the south coast of Devonshire, being appointed to the incumbency of Lower Brixham, in the diocese of Exeter, where, as an author states "he laboured for nearly a quarter of a century, among its rough seafaring population." His labours were signally blessed, though at length he sank under them. While in Devonshire many of his hymns were composed, and he published several poetical books, including the poems of Henry Vaughan, the Silurist, whose pious and striking poetry first saw light in the 17th century. Mr Lyte's tales in verse, illustrative of the Lord's Prayer, are thought to be his best works. But his hymns are better known, and some of them have a world-wide reputation. For instance—

> " Abide with me, fast falls the eventide ;
> The darkness deepens, Lord, with me abide :
> When other helpers fail, and comforts flee,
> Help of the helpless, O abide with me.
>
> " Swift to its close ebbs out life's little day ;
> Earth's joys grow dim, its glories pass away ;
> Change and decay in all around I see ;
> O thou, who changest not, abide with me.
>
> " Hold thou thy cross before my closing eyes ;
> Shine through the gloom, and point me to the skies ;
> Heaven's morning breaks, and earth's vain shadows flee ;
> In life, in death, O Lord abide with me."

This beautiful hymn, of which I have given only three verses, is founded on the words in the 29th verse of the 24th chapter of St. Luke—"Abide with us, for the day is far spent."

Another specimen of his poetry I will now give, founded on the text "My beloved is mine and I am his."

"Yes, He is mine! and nought of earthly things,
  Not all the charms of pleasure, wealth, or power;
The fame of heroes, or the pomp of kings,
  Could tempt me to forego His love an hour.
Go, worthless world, I cry, with all that's thine;
  Go, I my Saviour's am, and He is mine.
Whate'er may change, in Him no change is seen,
  A glorious sun that wanes not nor declines;
Above the clouds and storms He walks serene,
  And on His people's inward darkness shines."

When one of the Cabinet ministers was in Scotland last year, after the loss of H.M.S. "Captain," he referred in a public address to this calamity, and also to Mr Lyte's touching lines on the burial of a naval officer in the Atlantic, which was felt to be applicable to the sad occurrence alluded to. The lines were the following :—

"There is in the wide lone sea,
  A spot unmarked but holy;[1]
For there the gallant and the free
  In his ocean bed lies lowly.

"Down, down, within the deep
  That oft to triumph bore him,
He sleeps a sound and pleasant sleep
  With the salt waves washing o'er him.

"He sleeps serene, and safe
  From tempest or from billow,
Where the storms, that high above him chafe,
  Scarce rock his peaceful pillow.

"The sea and him in death
  They did not dare to sever;
It was his home while he had breath,
  'Tis now his rest for ever.

"Sleep on, thou mighty dead,
  A glorious tomb they've found thee—
The broad blue sky above thee spread,
  The boundless waters round thee!

"No vulgar foot treads here,
  No hand profane shall move thee;
But gallant fleets shall proudly steer
  And warriors shout above thee.

"And when the last trump shall sound,
And tombs are asunder riven,
Like the morning sun from the wave thou'lt bound,
To rise to live in heaven."

Mr Lyte was equally gifted as a preacher, and on one occasion when the great statesman, Mr Canning, heard him, from the words "Without God in the world," he was so struck with the force and power of the sermon that he sought an interview with the preacher. For a long time his health was delicate, which laid him aside from the active duties of his profession, and obliged him to seek change of climate, though without benefit, and when travelling in the year 1847 he was taken ill at Nice, where he died, on the 20th November, and was buried in the English Cemetery there. A marble cross is erected to mark the last resting-place of one whose highest honour and desire had been to exalt the cross— who meekly bore up through years of suffering, and who, trusting in the merits of his blessed Saviour's cross and passion, calmly resigned his life, in the sure and certain hope of a blessed immortality.

My miscellaneous group of celebrities includes a mention of JAMES WILSON of Hawick, a laborious and useful public servant, who died suddenly in India, while holding the important office of Chancellor of the Exchequer of our eastern Empire; and, says Mr Riddell Carre, "did my history include living celebrities, I might mention that eminent statesman and Minister of the Crown, and highly gifted man, Mr Gladstone, who can claim Border descent, through the old family of Gladstains, of that Ilk, an old Roxburghshire race."

The Politicians include several members of the Senate, the best known in our day being the Honourable John E. Elliot, who was a staunch supporter of his party, as well as a useful member of the House of Commons, in which he represented the County of Roxburgh for about sixteen years. In early life Mr Elliot went to India, where he held high and important situations, discharging his duties with honour and credit, and always making himself popular by the manifestation of a broad, rich, and genial nature.

Among the philosophers who are merely mentioned in the lecture are Sir David Brewster, who had died very shortly before, James Veitch of Inchbonny, and John Gibson, Kelso, both of whom were conspicuous for their attainments in Natural Philosophy and Mechanics.

The names mentioned in the Literary and Journalistic group are those of John Duke of Roxburghe, the Ballantynes, James Gray of the Edinburgh High School, James Douglas, Esq. of Cavers, James Simpson of Teviotbank, William Scott of the same place, Charles Elliot, and James Sibbald, Publishers; James H. Dawson, Journalist; and William Stenhouse, of musical fame.

JOHN, THIRD DUKE OF ROXBURGHE, was a great patron of literature, as well as a man of the most accomplished mind and polished manners. His collection of choice and rare books had world-wide fame; and the Roxburghe Club, founded by His Grace, to promote the object he had so much at heart, viz., the Collection of Books and Articles of Vertu, all connected with literature and the arts are well acquainted with.

His Grace died in 1804, after which his splendid library was sold, and did not, unfortunately, descend to his successors, first Lord Bellenden and then Sir James Innes, both distant kinsmen.

JAMES GRAY of the High School, Edinburgh, was born of respectable parents at Dunse. After his education was completed he became Rector of the Academy at Dumfries. For several years Mr Gray filled the situation of a Master of the old High School, but failing in getting the Rectorship in succession to Mr Pillans, he resigned his appointment, and became Rector of the Belfast Academy.

Mr Gray was a learned man, and a very eminent scholar, particularly excelling in Greek, in which language he had in his day but one equal in Scotland, viz., Professor George Dunbar, who was likewise a man of the Merse. Gray was also generally accomplished, and a very good poet. He was the author of "Cana," and a "Sabbath among the Mountains," and left in manuscript a poem entitled "India." He, moreover, edited the works of Robert Fergusson, which included a memoir of the poet. While at Dumfries he was the companion of Robert Burns, some of whose sons were Gray's pupils, and in after-life he was the friend of Thomas Campbell, John Wilson, and James Hogg, whose sister-in-law, Mary Philips, he married. The Ettrick Shepherd had a great opinion of Gray's genius, and of his kindness and large-heartedness, and introduced him in the "Queen's Wake" as the fifteenth bard who sung the ballad of "King Edward's Dream," in the following terms :—

> " The next was bred on southern shore,
> Beneath the mists of Lammermore,
> And long, by Nith and crystal Tweed,
> Had taught the Border youth to read.
> The strains of Greece, the bard of Troy,
> Were all his theme and all his joy ;
> Well-toned his voice of wars to sing ;
> His hair was dark as raven's wing,
> His eye an intellectual glance ;
> But every bard to him was dear,
> His heart was kind, his soul sincere."

But the most interesting part of his life has yet to be told. When in Ireland he became animated with a missionary spirit and great love for souls, and after being ordained to the holy ministry in the Episcopal Church, went out to India as a chaplain in the East India Company's service, and was afterwards appointed by the Government tutor to a young native King, indicating the high opinion which those in authority had of Mr Gray, who was thus honoured in being the first Christian tutor to a native prince.

Mr Gray, in writing home, with reference to his appointment, said, "I have no doubt I shall be able to make him one of the most learned kings that ever were in India, as he promises to be one of the most humane ; " and added, " Oh !

that I may be enabled in the course of his education to impart to his mind a portion of that wisdom that cometh down from above, and that alone maketh wise to salvation. These are the subjects that engross my thoughts, that are the theme of my evening and morning and midnight prayers. Join your prayers to mine, that my exertions may be blessed towards the cleansing of this land from its pollutions and abominations."

JAMES SIBBALD was the son of a farmer not far from Melrose. After trying his father's profession without success, he took to bookselling and bookmaking. He first joined Charles Elliot, a fellow Borderer, and an enterprising Edinburgh publisher, and after acquiring a competent knowledge of the trade, he started on his own account, purchasing the business of Mrs Yair, the possessor of Allan Ramsay's library, which, after Sibbald's death, was acquired by Alexander M'Kay.

James Sibbald carried on a large and successful business, with much spirit and enterprize. Sir Walter Scott and other eminent men were readers of his library, and seconded his literary efforts. In 1783 he started the "Edinburgh Magazine," which was well patronised, and in which, as editor and chief contributor, he showed rare talent and research, but such were his modesty and unostentation, his own productions were not known except by his friends, many of whom were among the first men of the day. Anxious, however, to participate in the literary society and enjoyments of London, he set out for the Metropolis, after making arrangements for carrying on his Edinburgh business in his absence, but his expectations of pleasure from the change were not realised, and he did not remain away very long. He was so much engrossed, however, with London, he forgot to write to his friends in Scotland, who were ignorant of his address; but on learning his whereabouts they lost no time in communicating with him, to enquire about his prosperity and the locality he had fixed upon for his residence, when he laconically replied—

" My lodging is in Soho,
And my business is So-so."

After a time he returned to Edinburgh, resumed his business, and commenced a new line of authorship, establishing and conducting a musical periodical. He also wrote a chronicle of Scotch Poetry, which alone will perpetuate James Sibbald's fame, being a work of taste and erudition, and a valuable accession to our national literature in a most difficult field of antiquities.

Mr Sibbald died in 1803, aged fifty-six, and such was his popularity that for several years after his death his friends kept his birthday by a social meeting. But though a man of much amiability of character, he was very eccentric.*

JAMES HOOPER DAWSON was editor of the *Kelso Chronicle*, the successor of the *British Chronicle*, established in 1783 by his grandfather, an eminent Border farmer.

Mr Dawson was a member of the English bar, but relinquished his profession and took to literary pursuits, for which he was well adapted, being a man of acquirements. At the time of his death, which happened suddenly at Dumfries in 1861, he was engaged on duty as examiner of registers for the southern districts of Scotland, an office for which he was well qualified, as his masterly reports from time to time testified. Mr Dawson was the author of an abridged statistical account of Scotland, which is a monument of his industry, as well as a proof of his ability, both as a writer and statistician.†

* Sir Walter Scott, in his autobiography, says, "I fastened also like a tiger upon every collection of old songs or romances which chance threw in my way, or which my scrutiny was able to discover on the dusty shelves of James Sibbald's circulating library in the Parliament Square. This collection, now dismantled and dispersed, contained at that time many rare and curious works, seldom found in such a collection. Mr Sibbald, himself a man of rough manners but of some taste and judgment, cultivated music and poetry, and in his shop I had a distant view of some literary characters, besides the privilege of ransacking the stores of old French and Italian books, which were in little demand among the bulk of his subscribers. Here I saw the unfortunate Andrew Macdonald, author of 'Vimonda,' and here, too, I saw at a distance the boast of Scotland, Robert Burns."

† He had previously written other works, the most valuable of which was "The Legitimate Consequences of Reform," showing the benefits which had accrued and would yet result from the passing of the Reform Bill. The book was dedicated to Earl Grey.

The Agricultural Improvers were an extensive class, and though, through the means of machinery and chemical appliances in the manure and feeding departments, immense strides have been made, which almost exalts farming into a science, our ancestors acted up to their knowledge, and wrought wonders in their day of comparative darkness, both in enclosing and cultivating their lands; and are entitled to our thanks for their exertions. This group includes many well known names, among whom are

HENRY, Duke of Buccleuch.
LORD SOMERVILLE, fifteenth Baron.
SIR JOHN RIDDELL of Riddell, who ruined himself by high farming and improvements, of which the present proprietor of Riddell is reaping the benefit.
Dr RUTHERFORD of Melrose.
Dr MERCER of Selkirk.
Mr DAWSON of Frogdean.
Mr CHURCH, Mr BLAIKIE, Mr HART, and others.

The Duke of Buccleuch, who was grandfather to the present amiable and excellent Duke of Buccleuch, was not only an early improver in agriculture, but a producer of good stock. With reference to his Grace's stock, I have seen it stated that in 1775, nearly ninety-seven years ago, a wager was determined at Fortune's Tavern, a noted one in former days, as to the quality of two bullocks—one fed by the Duke, and the other by a Berwickshire laird,—when his Grace's was pronounced the best. The cattle were not exhibited as at present, but a sirloin of each, which required two waiters to place on the table, were partaken of by a large company at Fortune's. The Duke and other notables were at the dinner, and all present were dressed in the manufactures of Scotland; for it should be noted that the Duke, while a devoted agriculturist, was a great encourager of manufactures, then in their infancy. Indeed, everything that tended to the good of the country was patronised by his Grace, who was intensely beloved and respected. He was a man also of the most simple habits and gentle manners. He was walking one day to the Castle of Edinburgh to join his regiment, when he was accosted by a country girl, who seeing his Grace in uniform, asked him if he could tell her where she would find her brother "Wull," who was also in the Fencibles. The Duke could not inform her, but allowed the young woman to accompany him to the parade-ground, and when passing two sentries they presented arms to his Grace, which she asked the meaning of, but the Duke did not tell her, only saying it was done "either to you or me." When they arrived at the parade-ground she discovered "Wull," who asked his sister if she knew who her companion was, when she replied, "I dinna ken wha he is, but he was a very civil lad ;" and on hearing it was the Duke of Buccleuch, she was amazed at her freedom with his Grace, as well as astonished, no doubt, at the Duke's condescension and humility. The Duke died on the 11th of January 1812, and Sir Walter Scott, who had experienced much kindness from him, refers to his funeral as follows, in a letter to Joanna Baillie :—" Yesterday, I had the melancholy task of attending the funeral of the good old Duke of Buccleuch. It was, by his own direction, very private; but scarce a dry eye among the assistants—a rare tribute to a person whose high rank and large possessions removed him far out of the social sphere of private friendship. But the Duke's mind was moulded upon the kindliest and most single-hearted model, and arrested the affections of all who had any connection with him. He is truly a great loss to Scotland, and will be long missed and lamented, though the successor to his rank is heir also to his generous spirit and affections. He was my kind friend."

A few words about the only other agriculturist I shall present to your notice—I mean James Hart of Wiltonburn, whose soubriquet was "Hart of Harts." He died in 1818, lamented by an extensive circle of farmers and friends. His physique was extraordinary, and to that I confine my observations. At the age of twenty-five he weighed thirty-three stones, and stood six feet three inches, being at that time considered the strongest man in Scotland since the days of Sir William Wallace.

The Merchants I next refer to, as agriculture and commerce ought always to be united. Many families connected with the Borders have had scions engaged in trade or mercantile pursuits ; several having reached distinction or obtained municipal honours. Some went to London. For instance, Sir John Pirie and Sir Peter Lawrie, both of whom were successful in their respective trades, as well as eminent members of the corporation of London, each attaining the dignity of Lord Mayor. Others were successful Edinburgh merchants, among whom I would name,

THOMAS DOUGLAS, descended from the Douglas of Otterburn fame, who became a bailie of Edinburgh, and who, it is said, " performed and discharged all the duties of a godly man and good citizen towards his lineage and relations, towards his city, and towards the poor."

Several tradesmen in Edinburgh came from the Border land, but I can only select two, viz., John Grieve and James M'Donald.

GRIEVE, who was in the firm of Grieve & Oliver, was long a most reputed citizen of Edinburgh. He was born at Ettrick, where his father was a Cameronian minister, and died in Edinburgh in 1836, deeply regretted by a large circle of friends, among whom were the chief literary men of the day. Mr Grieve not only possessed the most refined taste, but was a very good writer of verses. He was, moreover, the great friend and patron of poets, and to John Grieve, the Ettrick Shepherd was indebted for many kindnesses, particularly when he lived with him during a long visit to Edinburgh, on which occasion Hogg's purse only contained one guinea, which Grieve would not allow him to spend.

I believe the Ettrick Shepherd was also greatly indebted to John Grieve for considerable help rendered to him in the preparation of the "Queen's Wake," which the closing stanzas of that work fully bear out, for Hogg says—

> "Friend of the bard, peace to thy heart,
> Long hast thou acted a generous part;
> Long hast thou courteously, in pain,
> Attended to a feeble strain,
> While oft abashed has sunk thine eye—
> Thy task is done, the wake is bye.
> I saw thy fear, I knew it just,
> 'Twas not for minstrels long in dust,
> But for the fond and venturous swain
> Who dared to wake these notes again."

Grieve's chief production was "Lochiel's Farewell," a song characterised by much vigour of style, as I think you will admit on hearing it, or rather the closing verses, which I have only time for—

> "Shades of the mighty and the brave,
> Who faithful to your Stuart fell;
> No trophies mark your common grave,
> No dirges to your memory swell.
>
> "But generous hearts will weep your fate
> When far has rolled the tide of time;
> And bards unborn shall renovate
> Your fading fame in loftiest rhyme."

My last character among the traders is

JAMES M'DONALD of the Lawnmarket, clothier, who died some few years ago. He was born at Hawick, but his ancestors for some generations belonged to Bowden. Though a tailor is said to be only the ninth part of a man, my late friend James M'Donald—and I am proud to call him friend—was a full-grown man. Indeed he was an uncommon one. He was well up in family history and antiquities, and his stories of the olden time were often narrated to the great pleasure and profit of his auditors. But I must say something of his business relations, which were conducted with honour and success.

He invented a machine for measuring the human frame,

an account of which was published in 1856, under the "Physical Capabilities of Man," and the invention was much referred to in some periodicals of the day, and its value and utility were attested by some eminent tailors. At one time the Bank of England had a governor who was an army tailor, but I don't think he lived to see his brother professional's instrument, which I believe was much thought of, and might have been adopted, had it not interfered with the office having gains arising from the clothing of the army. Professor Ballingall of Edinburgh referred to it in his lectures in describing the formation of men likely to make good soldiers; and "Chambers' Journal" of June 1852, under an article headed the "Philosophy of the Shears," gives a description of the instrument.

I come now to the Mechanics, some of whom were natural philosophers as well as good mechanicians. The principal were—

Mr ROGERS, who invented an instrument for winnowing corn.

JOHN GIBSON of Kelso, a man possessed of considerable intellectual powers.

JAMES VEITCH, of Inchbonny, Jedburgh, well acquainted with the science of optics. His name ought to be doubly dear in this parish, of which his worthy son, Dr Veitch, has been for nearly thirty years the respected minister.

Sir PETER FAIRBAIRN of Leeds, born at Kelso, who was a great practical engineer, and also an extensive manufacturer of locomotives. Smiles says Sir Peter "is entitled to high merit, the work turned out by him being of firstrate excellence, embodying numerous inventions and improvements of of great value."

Sir Peter's brother, WILLIAM, also a Kelsonian, demands the acknowledgment of his countrymen for his great engineering improvements, if not inventions. If not the founder, he was one of the earliest members of the Association for the Advancement of Science.

KELSO, I may add, produced a good painter in the person of Robert Edmonstone, who left behind him some good pieces, and, having distinguished himself at the Naples Academy, he got two prizes.

Then ANCRUM, or Ashieburn, near it, gave birth to Archibald Elliot, a good architect, who went to Edinburgh as a common mason, and rose to eminence as an architect, several of the principal buildings being planned and erected by him, including the Jail, the County Hall, and St Paul's Episcopal Church, York Place.

I now close my lecture with a few characters from the miscellaneous class of worthies, which includes wits and humourous characters. The two first are father and son :—

Robert and Thomas Shortreed, the elder being sheriff-substitute and the latter procurator-fiscal for Roxburghshire. Both were honoured with the friendship and respect of Sir Walter Scott.

To ROBERT SHORTREED the great baronet was indebted for many of his rich Border stories. Sir Walter describes his friend as a cheerful companion, and a good singer and mimic, and moreover a man of worth and character. In one of their rides in quest of ballads and materials for the great minstrel's works, they visited Willie Elliot of Millburnholm, the original of Dandie Dinmont, to whom Sir Walter was introduced. Willie received the then "great unknown" with ceremony, and insisted on Sir Walter's dismounting, that he might lead his horse to the stable. Shortreed followed the host, and after Willie had peeped at Sir Walter, then Mr Scott, out by the edge of the door-cheek, whispered to Shortreed, "Weel, Robin, I am no a bit feared for him noo. He's jist a chiel like ourselves." *

---

* It was in the autumn of 1792 that Walter Scott was introduced to Mr Robert Shortreed by an old companion, Charles Kerr of Abbotrule, and a raid into Liddesdale was forthwith arranged. They started from Abbotrule, and entered the wilds of Liddesdale, where there were neither roads nor

THOMAS SHORTREED, the son of Robert, whom I well knew, and whose funeral I attended at Camberwell in Surrey, where he died many years ago, was the assiduous assistant of the great minstrel in Border history and heraldry, and was without a rival in the way he gave the "Douglas Tragedy" and the "Twa Corbies."

In "Scott's Life," by Lockhart, there is a note describing Thomas Shortreed as "a young gentleman of elegant taste and attainments, devotedly attached to Sir Walter, and much beloved in return. A ring found in a grave at Jedburgh Abbey was given to Sir Walter by Robert Shortreed in

inns, but Shortreed, as sheriff-substitute, knew the people and the country well. The first farm-house they reached was Milburnholm, near Hermitage Castle; and when Willie Elliot, the tenant, was informed that Scott was an advocate from Edinburgh, he felt somewhat awed, till he saw his visitor on friendly terms with the dogs which had gathered round him. Then he whispered to Shortreed—"Weel, Robin, I say, de'il hae me if I'se be a bit feared for him now: he's just a chield like ourselves, I think." It was Shortreed's opinion that Willie Elliot was "the great original of Dandie Dinmont." When recording this opinion in his "Life of Scott," Lockhart adds: "As he seems to have been the first of those upland sheep-farmers that Scott ever visited, there can be little doubt that he sat for some parts of that inimitable portraiture. And it is certain that the James Davidson, who carried the name of Dandie to his grave with him, and whose thoroughbred death-bed scene is told in the Notes to 'Guy Mannering,' was first pointed out to Scott by Mr Shortreed himself, several years after the novel had established the man's celebrity all over the Border, some accidental report about his terriers and their odd names having alone been turned to account in the original composition of the tale." The farm-house of Milburn, where Scott and Shortreed visited Willie Elliot, does not now exist, but it might have been seen twelve years since in somewhat of its original form. It stood facing the road from Hawick to Newcastleton, fifteen miles from Hawick, and six from the chief village of Liddesdale. It was a thatched house, with a stone and turf erection against the wall, between the door and the window, which was called the "loupin'-on-stane," and which was a necessary adjunct of every farm-house in the days when the only mode of travel was on horseback or on foot. It was customary for the husband to ride in the saddle and the wife on what was called a pad behind him, and to aid the ladies in transferring themselves to the pad on the back of the horse the "loupin'-on-stane" was needed. The house at Milburn had two "ends," one of which was the kitchen, and the other was the parlour, but through it was another little room called the "spence." The upper flat consisted only of very low-roofed attics, and such out-houses as were required for a hill-farm were immediately adjoining the house.

memory of his son, which Sir Walter says he would preserve with especial care. His diary, dated next day, states that he waked after a restless night, in which he dreamed of poor Tom Shortreed.*

PECULIAR CELEBRITIES.

ARCHIE ARMSTRONG was a Liddesdale man and a dexterous sheep stealer, and, moreover, a great wit.† Archie ingratiated himself into favour with King James, who on account of his wit and powers of repartee appointed him his jester. Both James and Charles, his son and successor on the throne, had jesters or merry-andrews attached to their court, but after Charles' reign the office was abolished, though many noblemen kept jesters down to a comparatively late period. Owing, however, to the length they carried their jokes, they frequently made their places too hot for themselves. For instance, a jester in a Scotch nobleman's establishment paid his addresses to one of the young ladies, and not only offered her marriage, but published the banns *nolens volens*.

Archie, who accompanied James to London on his ascending the English throne, got into disgrace by the unlimited freedom of his wit, but continued court jester down to 1637, when he was dismissed for his impudence, of which the following is a specimen. One day when Archbishop Laud was about to say grace at dinner, at court, Archie begged of his royal master

* This was in the autumn of 1826, when Sir Walter was at the circuit court at Jedburgh. As usual he was the guest of Mr Shortreed. He says : "went to poor Mr Shortreed's, and regretted bitterly the distress of the family, though they endeavoured to bear it bravely, and to make my reception as comfortable and cheerful as possible. My old friend R. S. gave me a ring found in a grave at the Abbey, to be kept in memory of his son. I will certainly preserve it with especial care."

† Archie did not belong to Liddesdale, but to Eskdale, and lived at Stubholm near Langholm.

permission to perform the duty, which was granted, when he impiously said :—

> "All praise to God
> And little Laud to the deil."

This impudence resulted in Archie's dismission.*

There were other Armstrongs, freebooters, some being wits as well, and I will summarily give their names and peculiarities.

JOHN OF GILNOCKIE was one of the chiefs of the clan, and the subject of the spirited ballad of "Johnie Armstrong," who with his troopers were executed at Carlenrig, or, as the ballad says :—

> "John murdered was at Carlenrig,
> And all his gallant companie ;
> But Scotland's heart was ne'er sae wae,
> To see sae many brave men die
> Because they saved their countrey deir
> Frae Englishmen ! Nane were sae bauld
> While Johnie lived on the border syde,
> Nane of them durst cam near his hauld."

---

* The history of Archie Armstrong is worthy of being told at greater length. He was a native of Eskdale, and lived at Stubholm, immediately below the junction of the Esk and the Wauchope. A portrait of him may be seen in the first volume of Chambers' "Book of Days." Like all the Armstrongs he was addicted to the habit of "lifting" what did not properly pertain unto him ; and on one occasion he had lifted a sheep, but being closely pursued by the shepherd, was seen to enter a particular house. Into this domicile the shepherd followed, but saw nothing save a lad with a vacant-looking face rocking a cradle. He was charged with the theft, but is reported to have said in reply :—

> "If e'er I did sae fause a feat
> As thin my neibours' faulds,
> May I be doom'd the flesh to eat,
> This very cradle haulds."

But a search disclosed the fact that inside the cradle was the body of a sheep and not a human baby, and the simple-faced lad, who was no other than Archie Armstrong, was brought to Jedburgh where King James VI. had arrived to hold a court of justice. The proof was positive and Archie was condemned to die ; but pleaded that he was a poor ignorant lad who had just heard of the Bible and wished to read it through for the benefit of his soul, if it would please the king to grant him a respite so long. The prayer was granted, when Archie rejoined with a sly look, "'Then deil tak

KINMONT WILLIE, whose name adorns one of the finest ballads in all the literature of the Border, was likewise an Armstrong, and the friend of the bold Buccleuch who performed the ever memorable feat of releasing him from Carlisle Castle. As the ballad says :—

> " We crept on knees and held our breath
> Till we placed the ladders against the wa' ;
> And sae ready was Buccleuch himsell
> To mount the first before us a'.
> He has taen the watchman by the throat
> He flung him doun upon the lead.
> Had there not been peace between our land,
> Upon the other side thou hadst gaed.
> Wi' coulters and wi' forehammers
> We garr'd the bars bang merrilie,
> Until we cam to the inner prison
> Whar Willie o' Kinmont he did lie.
> Then shoulder high, with shout and cry,
> We bore him down the ladder lang ;
> At every stride Red Rowan made
> I wit the Kinmont's airns play'd clang.
> Buccleuch has turned to Eden water,
> Even where it flowed fra bank to brim,
> And he has plunged in wi' Willie and a' his band,
> And safely swam them through without a rafter ;
> He then turned him on the other side,
> And at Lord Scroope his glove flung he—
> If ye like na my visit in Merry England
> In fair Scotland come and visit me."

---

me if I ever read a word o't as lang as my e'en are open." The king saw that there was humour in the man, and had him brought to court, where he was at first employed as a sort of gentleman groom of the chambers to the king, preceding him when travelling, and looking after the Royal quarters. While acting in this capacity he was made a free citizen of Aberdeen. From the king he had a patent for the manufacture of tobacco pipes, and he gained not a little from bribes administered to him for presenting petitions to the king. His position at court is exemplified by the fact that when appointed to accompany Prince Charles to Spain, he claimed to have the service of an attendant, the same as gentlemen of the royal suite, but as this was objected to by the gentlemen, it was not allowed. He was dismissed from court about the year 1637.

Then "JOCK O' THE SYDE," the hero of another ballad, of whom Maitland wrote :—

> " He is well kenned, Jock o' the Syde,
> A greater thief ne'er did ride ;
> He never tires
> To break Byers
> On muirs or myers,"

And CHRISTIE'S WILL were also both members of the Armstrong Clan. There is a story told of Christie's Will, that when confined in Jedburgh Jail, the Earl Traquair, who knew him well, got him released, in order to send him to Edinburgh, to aid his Lordship in terminating a law plea, which he proposed doing by getting the Counsel opposed to him out of the way. Christie's Will undertook to do this. He said he liked to do a "pawky trick," and engaged to remove the opposing lawyer, whom he accordingly inveigled away on the promise of giving him some " flowing fees," and when he succeeded in getting the advocate into his own freebooting domain, he incarcerated him in a tower till Traquair gained his suit. This Earl was perhaps Charles I.'s friend, who fought with his son at Preston on behalf of his Sovereign, and fell into the hands of the rebels, when they were committed to Warwick, and imprisoned like the counsel, though for a much longer period, their captivity extending to four years, and after the Earl's release and return he suffered extreme poverty.

Towards the middle of last century there was a character named Armstrong, who went by the soubriquet of "Sorbie," the name of his place. He was a friend of Lord Justice-Clerk Elliot of Minto, and when that Judge went to the Circuit at Dumfries, he usually called on Sorbie, who lived close to the road, who was always pleased to see the Justice-Clerk, and invariably produced his whiskey bottle.

Sorbie was a noted toper, and lamented in his latter days the degeneracy of the times, when men drank out of glasses instead of direct from the bottle, adding that it was a better world when there were more bottles and fewer glasses.

My last character is
JOCK GRAY of Gilmanscleugh, well known to, and illustrated by, Sir Walter Scott. At his birth the old women of the faculty pronounced that he had a want, which was proved as he grew up, and more especially by his inability for mental or bodily labour, though it often happened that his idiocy was an excuse for neglecting duty. Jock, however, had talent as a mimic and singer. Like David Gellatley in "Waverley," Jock had just as much wit as saved him from the imputation of insanity; but though half crazed, he possessed warm affections, a wonderful memory, and a good ear for music. He was constantly singing scraps of ballads or songs. He acted, as it were, strolling player to the Ettrick Shepherd, for he committed many of his songs to memory, which he sang to the people. But Jock tried his hand at composing too. He added a chorus to the ballad of the "Ewe buchts Marion."

"Come round about the merry knowes, my Marion,
Come round about the merry knowes wi' me,
Come round about the merry knowes, my Marion,
For Whiteslaid is lying lea."

But Jock's powers as a poet were not to be compared with his talents as a mimic; and well did he imitate some of the Border ministers, being most successful with those who read their sermons, which habit he disliked as much as a celebrated doctor who has reiterated what a well-known professor once said, "Have nothing to do with the paper;" or as an old minister used to say, "Have nothing to do with the white horse, but walk on your own feet." Had Jock acted like another fastidious individual, and removed his seat, "an had nae the minister sae far atween his een," he would just hae thocht him as good as threshing Willie himself.

But Jock had been known to ascend the pulpit at Ettrick, going by times and forestalling the minister, who, on entering the church, desired Jock to come down, which he did with reluctance, insisting that the folk were such wicked and rebellious sinners they needed them baith.

www.ingramcontent.com/pod-product-compliance
Lightning Source LLC
Chambersburg PA
CBHW032021220426
43664CB00006B/317